A **FALCON** GUIDE®

Mountain Biking
Moab

A Guide to Moab's Greatest
Off-Road Bicycle Rides

Second Edition

by Lee Bridgers

FALCON®

GUILFORD, CONNECTICUT
HELENA, MONTANA

AN IMPRINT OF THE GLOBE PEQUOT PRESS

A FALCON GUIDE ®

All photographs by Lee Bridgers unless otherwise noted

Maps and elevation profiles designed and produced by
Beachway Press

Map for Bar M Loop created by XNR Productions Inc.
© The Globe Pequot Press

ISBN 0-7627-2800-0

Manufactured in the United States of America
Second Edition/First Printing

Contents

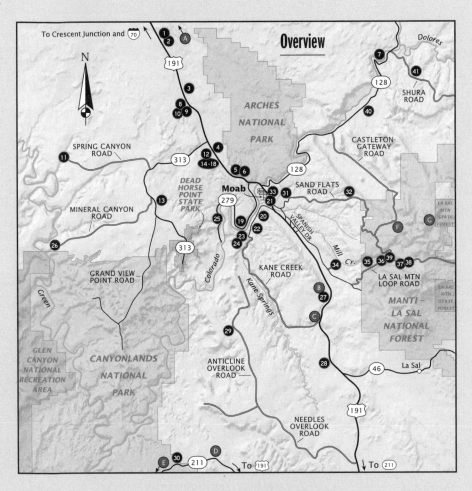

Moab West and Southwest 181

Moab East and Southeast 275

Preface

"Moab, Utah is a mean little town filled with mean little people."—Edward Abbey

Moab History in a Nutshell

I live in the middle of nowhere.

I drive 100 miles just to buy a pair of shoes, but a singletrack 100 yards from my front door leads to the backside of the Moab Slickrock Trail, the most famous mountain bike trail on planet Earth.

Millions of years ago this place was on the edge of a vast sea covering much of the Midwest. Now it's a maze of twisted canyons and towering mountains. Once it was flat as a pancake, home to a thick tropical jungle and massive dinosaurs of the Jurassic and Cretaceous eras. Now it's an undulating, nearly vertical mountain bike ride with dino tracks leading the way. These behemoths were schlepping through the mud at the edge of the sea . . . then, one day, it stopped raining for 1,000 years. Then a million years later the sea came back, and evaporated, and came back, and evaporated again, and again, and again. Then the Moab Fault gave way and the sedimentary layers tilted 3,700 feet in one huge flop.

Lots of stuff happened here, lots of times. The evidence is everywhere.

I once met a group of Seventh Day Adventists from Castle Valley who claimed to have found a series of dino tracks with human footprints walking alongside. Led by a couple of Bible-toting, middle-age women in weird granny dresses and blue hair, I joined a small caravan of schoolkids in cars and trucks for a morning trek to a place off Castleton Gateway Road where the smooth black bedrock was embossed with perfect dinosaur feet, some so pristine that you could see scales and toenails. The tracks led to a cliff and disappeared over the edge.

I was staring into the chasm below when Eric, a spacy blond schoolboy, came up behind me and said, "Look, them dinosaurs walked right off this here cliff. That was one of the ways they was killed. Seven thousand years ago man created the dinosaurs and they got outta hand, just like in that movie, *Jurassic Park,* so they had to get rid of them, and this here place is where they ran a bunch of 'em off a cliff."

I let his words go in one ear.

"Where are the people tracks?" I asked.

The coy women shoved blond-headed Bob forward to do the talking. "They're up this-a-way," Bob answered. Bob was eighteen, another dirty-blond boy dressed in greasy camouflage fatigues and cowboy boots, carrying a Bible.

We walked for another quarter of a mile. The tracks began to disappear. Pretty soon we were walking across typically rain-pocked Entrada sandstone.

"Here it is!" Bob said, clutching his Bible tightly as he stared at the ground into a depression about 30 inches long. It looked like the impression of a giant cowboy boot.

The old women stood behind Bob with thin, proud smiles, as he placed his own stylishly uncomfortable boot into the depression and recited in a thick drawl, "Looks like 'bout a size 30."

The Mormons and the Seventh Day Adventists were not the first primitive humans to inhabit Canyonlands.

The first humans in the fossil record are a couple of green skeletons that Moab old-timer Lin Ottinger found in a copper mine a few years ago. He calls them "Malachite Man" and swears the skeletons predate stone tools and petroglyphs, and that they are white people! Take everything Lin says with a barrel of salt, but visit his rock shop. He'll show you a couple of green bones. Check 'em out. Believe what you want.

Petroglyphs and pictographs, the ancient art pecked or painted on stone, are labeled as Archaic, Anasazi, or Fremont culture by scientists and researchers, the Park Service, and people like that. Frankly, I think they're making things up. One thing is for sure: The wiry little supermen left expressions of their ways, thoughts, and feelings on the rock, and if you want to get to know them, check out the rock art. Some of the petroglyphs (carved into rock) and pictographs (painted on rock) read like party napkins or novelty cards from your crazy uncle. Some of them are Stone Age Rembrandts, Picassos, and Matisses. Canyonlands is an open-air museum with thousands of art objects left to us by these ancient peoples.

The ancients pecked and painted on the rock for a number of understandable reasons. Doodling, certainly. Some glyphs are calendars, maps, or diaries; some exist for ritual or prayer; and some were left as messages for someone like us—someone not there at the time. With a bit of common sense, trust, and understanding in the likeness of all men, these messages become decipherable: People with different head-dresses holding hands in a line must signify some kind of big party or maybe a peace treaty, right? Little Kokopelli dancing across the blackened sandstone with a flute, a huge erection, and a feather in his hair must be a celebration of life, wouldn't you think? Like the god Pan dancing about with his flute and his goat legs? The warriors with swollen chests must mean, "You have filled my heart with gratitude." Am I wrong?

What we can be certain of is that sometime between 500 and 1,000 years ago, these early residents began to get the hell out of Dodge. Where did they go?

Let's ask a local.

Lin Ottinger says: "Many years ago some white guy found the rock art and ruins and asked some Navajo guy, 'Who were the people who made these things?'

"The Navajo replied, 'Moki Anasazi.'

"So the whites called these people either 'Moki' or 'Anasazi.' White men are like that. They ask an Indian what something is called and the Indian says 'I don't understand' in Navajo and the white man calls that place 'I don't understand,' or 'I don't know,' or 'ask the chief,' or 'boy, are you ugly,' or 'go away, you're frightening the antelope.'

"The word *moki* in the Navajo tongue means, 'dead.' The word *anasazi* means roughly 'ancient enemy.' It is actually more derogatory, more like, 'ancient assholes we used to kill.' For 100 years the 'white eyes' have been calling these people 'dead' and 'ancient enemy.' Just what do you think happened to them?"

Lin stands, staring you right in the eye, and says just like W. C. Fields: "That's right, you stupid idiot; they're *Dead!*"

There is another opinion. The Hopi tell us that the Anasazi are still here. The Ancient Ones were the Hopi's ancestors. They say that after the Navajo and white men hassled and molested them away from Canyonlands, they simply settled into the lands their descendants currently occupy in Arizona. They call their most recent home the promised land.

The Hopi not only possess an uncanny understanding of the past, but know the future as well. The Hopi prophesy the end of the world and say that the Hopi lands will be the only place on earth to be saved from utter destruction.

Everybody to Hopi land! Bring your bike.

I believe the Hopi. Why not? Besides, in Moab I can believe any damn thing I want to, even if I am stone-cold wrong. You see? That's Moab.

The beautiful chert shards and thin flakes of semiprecious stone found on trails around Moab were produced during the process of making stone tools and weapons. These can be Ute camp middens, or they can be much older, belonging to more ancient residents, like the Fremont or the Anasazi or those really old dudes, the Archaic People.

If you ever need proof of human devolution, check out the rock art. The more ancient the work, the more expressive and beautiful. The most ancient are meticulously done dancing figures, aliens from another planet, and the natural gods. The most recent are quickly scratched obscene words, names and dates, figures with dangling penises, breasts, and ugly faces.

The Utes are the most recent of Moab's "truly Native peoples" and have inhabited the area for quite some time, clashing sometimes with the more powerful Navajo to the south, sometimes with the whites. But really, that's a simplification. Suffice to say, the Utes were certainly between a rock and a hard place in Moab during the late nineteenth century. It hasn't changed much. Today, most nice white Moab residents will tell you: "There ain't no more Indians around here. They were run off a long time ago. Ain't it sad?"

Well, they're lying!

Look into the trailer parks. The Utes and Navajo are still here!

It was the Utes who were dominant in Canyonlands when the Mormon government in Salt Lake City sent an all-male party of settlers to colonize the Moab Valley in 1855.

Nowhere is the history of cultural clashes between aboriginal tribes and white settlers more poetic and demonstrative than in the story of the ill-fated Elk Mountain Mission. Cover-up and omission cloud Mormon accounts of the failed mission,

Lee Bridgers on rare desert singletrack, which, by nature, generally doesn't last long due to mismanaged use and erosion.

but a breath of truth can be found between the lines of written history. Despite the moaning of their detractors, Mormon settlers, as a matter of policy, had very good intentions when it came to working and sharing the land with the aboriginal tribes, whom Brigham Young called the Lamanites, peoples referred to in the Book of Mormon as sons of Israel. The policy was to feed the Natives rather than fight them. Brigham Young even went so far as to say that it was better for a white man to be killed by an Indian than an Indian by a white man, because the white man knew better and the Indian was merely an ignorant savage. Brigham mistakenly saw the Indians as unintelligent, but he also viewed them as potential converts and allies against Utah's colonization by the United States.

The historical record maintained by the Church of Latter Day Saints omits the fact that the missionaries who started the Elk Mountain Mission were armed to the teeth. But the shot, powder, and guns were not meant to defend the colony from the Natives, but rather from the U.S. government. Hell, it was 1855. It was all right to kill Indians, but being at war with the United States of America was a good reason to keep their weapons secret.

The flaws of humankind come to the surface in the frontier where culture meets culture. At the newly founded Elk Mountain Mission, temptations, conflicts of morality, and cultural differences caused the mission to self-destruct. The Mormon record omits a statement of the relevant deeds, but admits that a certain allied Ute chief called attention to childish behavior by some of the men that required "rededication and repentance." It turns out that the devout settlers rebuffed an offer of Ute women—or at least rebuffed it after some of the missionaries sampled the goods (hence the rededication and repentance). This angered their only allies. A formerly "friendly" Ute the Mormons called St. John (because they couldn't pronounce his real name) shot a settler in the back and stole his horses. The Utes killed two missionaries who were returning from a hunting trip into the La Sal Mountains. Things were pretty bad up until this point, but the mission fell apart rapidly after these killings.

What ensued was a confusing situation that saw some Indians "allied" with the whites, some very angry, and some downright hostile. The angry Utes gathered outside the fort and berated the missionaries with insults in Navajo, Ute, and broken English. The friendly Utes informed the white men that the Navajo were pressuring them to attack, destroy the fort, and kill the missionaries. The "friendly" Utes offered to assist the whites in a retreat to Salt Lake City. It was good cop, bad cop, Indian style, and it worked like a charm.

One group of Ute "renegades" stole most of the settlement's cattle, and a band of "friendly Utes" offered to retrieve them in exchange for half. When they got the cattle back, half were wounded and had to be slaughtered on the spot. So the "friendly" Utes offered to slaughter them in exchange for half the meat. This method guaranteed that the Utes ended up with over three-quarters of the Mormon cattle. The Utes played the Mormons like a harp and saw them out the back door with grace and, probably, a lot of side-of-the-mouth giggling.

The failed mission assured that Moab would forever be retarded in its Mormonization, opening the floodgates to sinful uncircumcised gun toters, Indian lovers, outlaws, and cattle rustlers, who had come to plunder the new West's expanding economy, sell liquor and guns, steal cattle from the local cattle barons, and rob the train line to the north. Moab soon became known as "Robber's Roost" and "the toughest town in the West," where the worst of the worst drank, fought, and caroused. Moab was outlaws, cowboys, whores, whiskey, and shoot-'em-ups.

The infamous Butch Cassidy robbed trains from Moab by placing a scout on top of a huge butte just north of Seven Mile Canyon. From here he was able to spy trains 75 miles away. From this distance he spotted payroll trains and any ensuing posse trains, which generally ran a few miles back. This bit of ingenuity made Butch and his friend, the Sundance Kid, a fortune.

Great names, huh?

Butch Cassidy holds a special place in American folklore, sort of the Robin Hood of the Old West, but Syd Swasey was perhaps the most interesting Moab outlaw of all. Since Syd was kind of a dirtbag, the movies have ripped him off for everything he ever did, avoiding his unromantic persona while stealing his deeds and attributing them to more attractive, romantic folks.

He deserves fame for being the pattern of the outlaw in deeds, even if he wasn't the pattern of the outlaw in looks, success, or ambition. Butch Cassidy stole a million-dollar payroll. Syd stole a cow. Butch Cassidy eluded capture by moving to Bolivia. Syd just whined and cried until the sheriff let him go. Butch was a lady's man. Syd was more interested in cows.

In the time since Syd and Butch, the pervasive Mormon culture eventually seeped back into Moab, but Moab remains an outlaw town at heart. The national parks, condos, disappearing orchards, stinking cattle, cow flies, old mines, mountain bikes, and uranium tailings are just a complex disguise. Under that bandanna is one tough hombre. The kind of guy who asks: "What are you looking at?"

Up until the early twentieth century, Moab remained a desert oasis with huge cottonwoods sheltering soft pale yellow sand in cool, deep shadow. As more and more white people moved into the valley, the cool shade was gradually replaced by hot black asphalt roads wide enough to turn a twenty-mule-team wagon around in.

And then came a wagon of a different ilk. In 1949 John Ford came to Moab to make *Wagonmaster*. The movie starred John Wayne, a fresh, handsome young actor destined for fame. The movie was a hit. Ford was so impressed by the money he made off the movie that he came back time and again to make more Westerns, until in the early 1960s the public's desire for Westerns dried up.

Then came the Cold War.

A destitute miner named Charley Steen, living off a $200 loan in a beat-up, borrowed trailer, his dirty kids playing in the desert with no shoes, struck a rich vein of uranium ore just south of town. Overnight Moab became the uranium-mining capital of the world, and Charley made $25 million in one day.

Frankly, we can bemoan the toxic mine tailings north of town and demonize Charley Steen till our throats are sore and our hair falls out, but without the uranium boom of the 1950s and 1960s mountain bikers wouldn't have any trails to ride. Ninety-nine percent of the classic Moab trails were built by miners in search of uranium. So, if you love to ride this place, you may as well thank God for the bomb.

In the late 1950s and 1960s, a new appreciation of nature emerged, and with it a newfound love for the desolation of canyon country. Edward Abbey wrote books about this place and tourists began to tell their friends about the beautiful Shangri-la in Utah's Canyonlands.

Soon legislation created what are now Arches and Canyonlands National Parks from former cattle land. Karl Tangren, a former Moab horseback tour guide and singing cowboy who once ran cattle along the White Rim, says, "They run me off just like they run off the Indians."

People used to think Lin Ottinger was crazy to take tours out onto the desolate White Rim. Today the White Rim draws thousands of people in jeeps and on motorcycles and bicycles, turning the trail into the primitive road to nowhere with regular vehicular accidents and traffic jams.

It was inevitable that the individual spirit of the Old West would clash with the new legislated appreciation of the scenery in Canyonlands. The Sagebrush Rebellion was born as a reaction to the marching intrusion of the federal government into southeastern Utah. The grassroots revolt bore all the trademarks of the true Moab outlaw style. Strong resistance to the idea of preserving nature for nature's sake still hides out in city and county governments. These insiders build roads to nowhere with our tax dollars to block annexations of wilderness, trashing the most pristine canyons to preserve them for commercial use sometime in the future. These folks are some of the goodest, good ole boys in the country. When you have the good ole boys of local government against the good ole boys in federal government, you got bad guys on both sides. No white hats anywhere.

There is no middle ground in Moab. It's us or them. "There ain't enough room in this town for the both of us." It's high noon, the streets are empty, and both parties are waiting in the shadows to shoot the other guy in the back as soon as he shows himself.

The movies came and went, and the uranium mining industry went bust. Moab's property values sank like a rock and the population dropped. Then, somewhere around 1985, we happened—us mountain bikers, the cheapest tourists anywhere. We steal the forks, knives, and toilet paper, and leave humiliating tips, but we are bigger than the movies, the Mormons, the four-wheelers, and the sight-seers. We are serious! We are truly religious! We flock in droves to mecca to pay homage to what many consider the North Shore, the Mount Everest, the Vatican, the Taj Mahal, the Empire State Building, the Marilyn Monroe of mountain biking, Moab, Utah.

Moab is not for everybody. Nowhere is the terrain more challenging and dangerous. Nowhere are the standards any higher or the difficulty ratings more absurd. Nowhere is the penalty stiffer for screwing up, but if you don't ride Moab you will forever dream of what could have been. Believe me, Moab is absolutely the best mountain bike destination on earth. No question. No controversy. No ifs, ands, or buts. It gets under your skin. If you come here once, you'll come again and again.

Like many of the people living in Moab, I came to escape the drudgery and stress of a respected profession, turning my back on the real world to cash in on my knobby hobby. Now I guide mountain bike and hiking tours, hold photography workshops, scout for film companies, and write tour guides. Every day I ride, hike, or four-wheel into the deserts, mountains, and canyons, and deduct it from my taxes. Over the past few years, I have gotten to know Moab better than most by making movies in and about the place, by scouting from the sky in helicopters and airplanes, and by befriending many of the Moab old-timers, but nowhere have I learned more about this place than from the saddle of a mountain bike, and when I've seen the whole damn place I'm leaving. I expect to depart sometime in the mid-twenty-third century.

In the pages of this book, I am sharing the flesh of the goose that laid the golden egg, giving away my prize possessions and some of my sweetest secrets. Please use *all* of the information in this book to find your way, but call a touring company if you need a guide. Understand that with an educated, skilled professional guide you will avoid the pitfalls, learn how to treat the desert, see much more than you would without, and have a better time.

Moab *is* mountain bike mecca, but there is much more to this place than mountain biking. Though I make fun of it, the town is pretty special. I wouldn't live here if it weren't. Actually I wouldn't live anywhere else. I love this place with all my heart.

I hope you will treat this incredible place with the respect necessary to preserve and expand mountain bike access to the best trails on earth into the distant future. Please heed the old cliché: "Leave only footprints. Take only pictures." On second thought, don't leave any footprints, either.

Four-wheel-drive Ken Moody ▶

Acknowledgments

The author would like to acknowledge the following individuals and institutions for their invaluable contributions to the spirit and letter of this guidebook.

Thanks to the vandals who continuously deface the sign that welcomes folks from Colorado to Utah on Interstate 70. It was supposed to say, UTAH: THE RIGHT PLACE TO BE. When they corrected it, it said, UTAH: THE RIGHT *WING* PLACE TO BE.

Thanks to the Utes who ran the first Mormons outta here in 1855, making way for the outlaws who finally made the place their own.

Thanks to Butch Cassidy and the Sundance Kid, our most famous outlaw locals, who stole millions from fat jerks who raped the West, then gave the dough to modest settlers right here in town. Butch and Sundance attended their own hanging more than once, and Butch actually had his picture taken with a sheriff who had just hung two innocent young men he swore were Butch and Sundance. To this sheriff and others, the reward and the glory seemed worth being loose with the law. Butch's smile in that picture says it all. When the law is evil and mean spirited and intolerant, being an outlaw is a virtue.

By the way, Butch and Sundance did not die in Bolivia, as in the movie. They lived long and prosperous lives in Washington State after stealing the identities of two unfortunates who were also mistaken for Butch and Sundance, killed by Bolivian

Tim Knouff

police, and then buried to hide the dirty deed. Indians led Butch and Sundance to the graves, where they dug up the passports and then reentered the States.

Butch and Sundance stole millions back when millions were billions. Syd Swasey, on the other hand, was a petty thief who never stole anything worth more than five bucks. A 15-foot span over a 700-foot-deep canyon in the vast barren lands between Moab and the San Rafael Swell is now called Swasey's Leap because Syd jumped it on his horse to get away from a local posse. Once that posse finally regained his tracks and rode into the swell, Syd had created a fake camp. He placed his hat and a frying pan next to a smoldering campfire and led his horse back and forth on the bank of a poisonous spring. When the posse arrived, seeing the makeshift camp and tracks, they let their horses drink until the poor animals went crazy and keeled over dead. The sheriff's men were sick for weeks.

Syd once stole a cow, and when caught red handed by the local sheriff, he cried like a baby, pleading: "I found this cow, sick and stranded in the desert when it was just a skinny little calf. I raised it from when it was just a baby and just cannot bear to see it slaughtered because I love it so. Sob. Sob. Sniffle. Sniffle." The sheriff was so moved that he let Syd go. If Syd were alive today he would be on a freeride bike for sure.

Nate Toone

Moab old-timers Lin Ottinger, Rusty Musselman, Karl Tangrene, Verle Green, Tex McClatchy, Millie McClatchy, Bette Stanton, Irwin Sheets, George White, Fran Barnes, Pete Plastow, and Stewart Summerville deserve sincere thanks for revealing the heart and soul of Moab in story, poem, song, film, paintings, and through the example of their own lives. These folks made me fall in love with something beyond the surreal beauty of canyon country—the spirit of its people.

In that same vein, thank God for Nic Hougen who, despite harassment by local police and the destruction of all that is sacred to him in the Moab Valley, retains the privilege of living the true-to-the-West desert rogue lifestyle out there somewhere past Sand Flats with his dog and his horses. Nic wins the award for the best quote: "I am not mature enough to live in Moab."

Irene Knouff and her children and in-laws, Tim, Becky, Jason, Kate, Donna, Jack, and Terry, have supported the emotional well-being of my family over the past ten years as we made the transition from big-city artsy-fartsy to small-town funk. Tim Knouff's Hotel Off Center has been a base of operations for me since my first visits to Moab as a filmmaker in the early 1990s.

Mystery Johnson deserves special mention. I first knew Mystery in San Francisco where he was a Haight Street fixture and psychedelic relic. By a twist of fate, I crossed his path on the streets of Moab many years later and ended up meeting all the folks I have mentioned here because of him. I have been privileged to witness

Jerry Daniels

Mystery's long, strange trip from the Haight Ashbury to the Mexico City Earthquake to the jungles of Guatemala to being the only black man in Moab, Utah. Currently he resides in the Utah State Prison. Mystery is the answer to the question, "What does a Rastafarian do in Utah?"

Jerry Daniels, Nathan Toone, and Ken Moody rode with me on the most difficult and dangerous trails while I evaluated, performed mileage counts, and took photographs. Nathan deserves special credit for most of the stunt photos in this guidebook and for winning four Utah State Downhill Championships while sponsored by Dreamride. Jerry, too, deserves special credit. He has been building trails in nearby Fruita, Colorado, and is an avid advocate and protector of the desert wildlife in Moab.

Lorraine Guild, the Dan O'Laurie Museum, and the Moab Library were sources for information on Moab history, characters, and other documentation.

Thanks also to Jose Knighton for being the only bookstore owner in Moab to stand behind this book's first edition.

The biggest thanks goes to my son, Vincent, for letting me drag him all over the country in search of a place to settle down, and to my wife, Miki, for holding down the fort while I explored, for calling for help when I went missing, for helping with research into the natural history of canyon country, and especially for putting up with male chauvinist pig Lin Ottinger long enough to absorb a ton of information and learn to love him despite his flaws.

And last, but not least: Thanks to Ryan Croxton and David Singleton, editors of the first and second editions, for appreciating and fighting to preserve the literary style of this guidebook, for keeping the pages clean and the language "colorful," and for picking my verbal boogers.

Read This!

The rule "help others in need" (see Trail Etiquette in the Introduction) is especially important in canyon country. Sure, it could put a dent in your fun, but the sacrifice of placing the safety of others above personal comfort and fleeting vacation fun makes us human. If you come across someone who needs your help, maybe someone who has fallen or is acting strange or irrational, or even if you find an abandoned bike, stop for a while to evaluate the situation. If the person is in shock, dehydrated, or has taken a blow to the head, they are usually not in any condition to give you a rational or accurate answer to the question, "How are you?" Ignore the answer if they say, "I'm okay." Stop long enough to know the true answer to that question yourself. Evaluate their physical and mental state by asking questions, listening to the answers, and watching their movements. If they start talking about the purple giraffe or mention that they can't remember where they are, then you know something is off.

If, in the middle of a trail, someone asks if they can ride with you and you really don't mind, go ahead, be nice, but if you would rather ride alone, or feel they would be a burden, ask them first: "Are you lost? Do you have enough food and water?" Carrying more food and water than you need could save a life, and if you insist they not ride with you, the gesture of offering route-finding advice, food, and water will soften the rejection. If you have ever been in the position where you received help from someone, you know the drill. If you haven't, just be human. Help.

Introduction

Welcome to the new generation of bicycling! Indeed, the sport has evolved dramatically from the thin-tired, featherweight-frame days of old. The sleek geometry and lightweight frames of racing bicycles, still the heart and soul of bicycling worldwide, have lost much ground in recent years, unpaving the way for the mountain bike, which now accounts for the majority of all bicycle sales in the United States. And with this change comes a new breed of cyclist, less concerned with smooth roads and long rides, who thrives in places once inaccessible to the mortal road bike.

The mountain bike, with its knobby tread and reinforced frame, takes cyclists to places once unheard of—down rugged mountain trails, through streams of rushing water, across the frozen Alaskan tundra, and even to work in the city. There seem to be few limits on what this fat-tired beast can do and where it can take us. Few obstacles stand in its way, few boundaries slow its progress. Except for one—its own success. If trail closure means little to you now, read on and discover how a trail can be here today and gone tomorrow. With so many new off-road cyclists taking to the trails each year, it's no wonder trail access rests precariously between universal acceptance and complete termination. But a little work on your part can go a long way toward preserving trail access for future use. Nothing is more crucial to the survival of mountain biking itself than to read the examples set forth in the following pages and practice their message. Then turn to the maps, pick out your favorite ride, and hit the dirt!

What This Book Is About

Within these pages you will find everything you need to know about off-road bicycling in Moab, Utah. This guidebook begins by exploring the fascinating history of the mountain bike itself, then goes on to discuss everything from the health benefits of off-road cycling to tips and techniques for bicycling over logs and up hills. Also included are the types of clothing to keep you comfortable and in style, essential equipment ideas to keep your rides smooth and trouble-free, and descriptions of off-road terrain to prepare you for the kinds of bumps and bounces you can expect to encounter. The major provisions of this book, though, are its unique perspectives on each ride, its detailed maps, and its relentless dedication to trail preservation.

Without open trails, the maps in this book are virtually useless. Cyclists must learn to be responsible for the trails they use and to share these trails with others. This guidebook addresses such issues as why trail use has become so controversial, what can be done to improve the image of mountain biking, how to have fun and ride responsibly, on-the-spot trail repair techniques, trail maintenance hot lines for each trail, and the worldwide-standard Rules of the Trail.

Each of the forty-one rides is complete with maps, photos, trail descriptions and directions, local history, and a quick-reference ride information guide including such items as trail contact information, park schedules, fees/permits, and alternative map resources. Also included at the end of each regional section is an "Honorable Mentions" list of alternative off-road rides (forty-nine rides total). An appendix details local bike stores, dining, lodging, entertainment, and more.

It's important to note that mountain bike rides tend to take longer than road rides because the average speed is often much slower. Average speeds can vary from a climbing pace of 3 to 4 miles per hour to 12 to 13 miles per hour on flatter roads and trails. Keep this in mind when planning your trip.

A Personal Hystery of Mountain Biking

I got some of this stuff from the *Christian Science Monitor*'s Web site. Turn your kids onto it. Save money on an encyclopedia.

1817. Baron von Drais puts a board between two wooden wheels for Germans to career out of control on wagon roads, through horse shit and mud on the farm, and in the city.

1839. A Scottish blacksmith connects a crank to the rear wheel with articulated rods. Hey, it's self-propelled.

1870. Englishman James Starley invents the high wheeler, or penny farthing, also known as the "ordinary" bicycle, with the huge front wheel and the guy with the mustache, introducing serious upper body injury to a population with no concept of helmet use outside of warfare.

1884. Englishman H. J. Larson's "Safety Bicycle" has same-sized wheels, a chain and gears, workable brakes, and good handling characteristics. Larson, however, soon fades penny farthingless into a footnote.

1885. Nephew of the penny farthing guy steals Larson's idea, calls it the "Rover" safety bike. Cashes in.

1887. Former slaves enlisted in the all–Black United States Army 25th Infantry Bicycle Corps, ride single speed Spalding safety bikes from Missoula, Montana to St. Louis, falling into the trend where descendents of slaves do more–than–equal things just for the *chance* to be considered equal.

1900. A cult of the bicycle is created by enthusiasts known as "wheelmen," who race safety bikes, market cereals, hats, fashion, and tobacco products using bicycles. They sell bicycles, invent suspension and brake designs (later borrowed by hoity-toity high-tech companies), and steal each other's ideas to make them better. All this is possible because, if you wanted to get from point A to point B, you'd better have a horse, a good pair of shoes, or a bike.

1906. My grandfather has his picture taken as an eight-year-old standing beside a stripped down, muddy Spalding safety bike. Every part not for "whoa" or "go" has been removed for light weight.

This is what mountain bikers looked like in the early twentieth century.

1913. Henry Ford invents the auto assembly line relegating workers to one action and one thought for the rest of their lives. Model Ts become available to the general public, beginning the downward slide of the bicycle in America and spawning a nation of suburban environmentally-destructive motorheads.

1940. Japanese mountain bikers invade and conquer Burma, running out Limey troops and command staff.

1945. Nuclear bombs fall on Hiroshima and Nagasaki killing more bicyclists than military troops.

1955. Cars rule. The process is complete. The bicycle becomes a "low-status" symbol. The only grown man on a bike in Goldsboro, North Carolina is a fifty-year-old dirtbag living in a cardboard box in the lumber yard, who rides around town on a brown bike with two buckets, drunk, cussing, smelling of cheap liquor, and with no awareness of any concept of "anger management."

1957. I strip a 1948 Schwinn "step-through" cruiser with 24-inch wheels, clothespin cards to the seatstays, and fart noisily through the neighborhood dirt roads, along the borders of tobacco and corn fields, through the forest behind our house in rural North Carolina. I call it "riding a bike in the woods." I must be the father of mountain biking. My grandfather must be the great grandfather of mountain biking.

1975. I move into Haight Ashbury of San Francisco, a low-rent district in transition from heroin and hippies to queers and yuppies. I cannot afford a car. A naked guy at my front door holding a three-speed English Dunelt road frame with full Campy drivetrain grafted onto it, says "Twenty bucks." I buy it.

1978. Repack Race is on TV. Longhaired wildmen in jeans and flannel blast and slide down a narrow fire road on cruisers, tossing rooster tails sideways. The next day I take the weird hybrid Dunelt onto a Golden Gate Park singletrack, roll the front tire off the rim trying to be like those guys and bash my nuts into the stem, thereby rediscovering the most basic and elementary feature of any good off-road bike—a low top tube. Columbia and Schwinn Excelsior frames jump in price to more than $300. Joe Breeze begins producing his Breezer bicycles, the first truly homemade off-road bicycle frame based on the old Schwinns. I find a 1947 Schwinn "step-in" (used to be called a "girl's bike") reminiscent of my childhood bike, in a dumpster. I trade a trick skateboard for an early Redline BMX racing bike and put a six speed drivetrain on it for my daughter Bubble. Dago (the naked guy), Tosh Alcala (a early pro skateboarder), my wife Miki, and I begin a long-standing tradition of riding Golden Gate Park and Lands End nearly every day.

1979. Gary Fisher and Charlie Kelly open a shop selling things called Mountainbikes built by steel-brazing whiz-kid, Tom Ritchey. Ritchey borrows Breeze's design ideas that were borrowed from Schwinn. Kelly publishes *The Fat Tire Flyer.* Yuppie upstart Fisher claims to be the father of mountain biking and gets away with it for years.

1981. Specialized releases the Stumpjumper, a good mass-produced bike that almost anyone can afford. The Marin handmade bike thing is practically snuffed out.

1982. Charlie Cunningham makes bikes from aluminum hang-glider tubes. They go fast uphill *and* downhill. Cunningham "Balooners" and "Indians" are the first off-road bikes weighing less than 20 pounds. He sells them for $4000 apiece to trust-funders, rock stars, and unhip brokers fed like bloated pigs on Bay Area real estate speculation. His wife, Jacquie, wins the first mountain bike races easily.

1983. Unable to afford a dreamy Cunningham, I buy a Diamond Back Ridge Runner, the best of the first Japanese imports.

1984. I buy a used Ritchey Commando from a really stupid guy. Still great riding in Marin, but the hikers and horse lovers are getting upset with the crazy guys on bikes on the singletrack of Mount Tamalpais. Tosh Alcala's son, Chivo, after a day of "freeriding" on the greens of the Lands End golf course, smashes his bike into an old lady hobbling down the path with a "walker." The walker flies ten feet into the air, and before it even lands, Chivo turns and hollers at the group following, "Man, did you see that old lady? She ran right out in front of me."

1986. Kestrel displays a carbon fiber full-suspension prototype, the product of collaboration between NASA carbon fiber wizards, motorcycle mechanic Paul Turner (founder of Rock Shox), and Keith Bontranger of Santa Cruz. The cat is out of the bag.

1988. Sherwood Gibson of Ventana connects the act of sex with the craft of tig welding aluminum tubing and manages to weld as many as fifty aluminum frames a day. Sherwood is the first real engineer to build high end, handmade aluminum bicycle frames and offer them at a somewhat reasonable price.

1989. Lots of trail closures in Marin and Sonoma. Riders have to drive to the South Bay to ride singletrack, or face the law. I move to Colorado to teach film where the singletrack is way better and the mountains way bigger.

1990. Kent Ericson invents the softail, puts his childhood chi-chi alligator friend on the headtube and calls it Mr. Moots. The Moots YBB (Why Be Beat?) uses flexing chainstays and a tiny damper as an effective way to make the bike climb better and the saddle a more comfortable place to be. Cutie-pie-wonder-boy John Tomac races on Doug Bradbury's elastomer-damped-Manitou-Springs-garage-built forks. Heads turn. Ned Overend and Greg Herbold win World Championships on Rock Shox suspension forks. Rigid bikes become a novelty item in a matter of months.

1993. I buy a McPherson strut full suspension Mantis Pro-Floater and spare no expense. Within the first one hundred yards on a hill next to my home, I reach over 50 miles per hour. Unable to stop, I land in a bush under a neighbor's living room window. Two weeks of riding later, the rear shock pops like a .22 pistol on every bump. I sell the Mantis, settle in on a titanium Fat Chance, and wait for the industry to pump out a reliable suspension design, to invent brakes that will stop it, and build shocks that will work for more than five or six rides.

1996. I move to Moab, Utah after spending years on a documentary about local residents. I move in with a subject of the film, Lin Ottinger, and start a mountain bike fantasy business called Dreamride, striving to give guests the best technical riding possible, bikes, food, and the most comfortable places to stay in town. Our motto is "ride hard, rest easy." One of my guides, Nate Toone, *defines* freeriding on the slickrock formations of Moab before "freeriding" has a name.

1999. Mountain biking is mainstream. "Love the ride" is now "Look at me, Mommy." Profit-hungry companies create and take advantage of diehard consumers of high-tech, high-dollar, boing-boing shit soon to be obsolete. I end up riding a bike that weighs 35 pounds, just like my 1948 Schwinn, and think it's the greatest thing ever. Fat race promoters who don't ride and whose races destroy the environment have joined with bicycle advocacy groups to form organized cycling religions that seek to conquer and subdue the world, and get the boring sport of mountain bike racing on TV.

2000. The market, flooded with bike design choices good and bad, is fed by lies and sleazy marketing tactics. The best stuff is made in America by small companies run by pot-smoking, beer-drinking garage engineers. The worst is made in Taiwan, supported by huge marketing budgets and magazine bribery. The first edition of this book is published as *Mountain Bike America: Moab.* It causes an uproar after a local "wag" thumbs through it, misquotes it repeatedly in the local paper "as a joke." The controversy garners a few death threats, but sells books and gets me on the radio and front page of the *Salt Lake Tribune.* The book is well received by the literate, however. I am compared to Edward Abbey, but cannot seem to drink enough to warrant realistic comparison.

2003. Sherwood Gibson muses, "Somebody called me to say that I was nominated for the Mountain Biking Hall of Fame, but said that he had never heard of me. I told him that if he didn't know who the ★@!# I was, then maybe I shouldn't be in any kind of hall of fame."

2004. The best Moab mountain bike guidebook is stripped of its colorful Moab tourist service reviews to be able to get the damn thing in local bike shops.

The Ecosystem

"If you can't use it, what good is it?"

This is Chuck's take on the whole damn land deal. Chuck nurses a helicopter for a local Moab film service, stands around, and smokes cigarettes next to the fuel truck. He does this stuff a lot. He's a pro. He puts all the Hollywood crap in perspective, because he's "worked for a lot of them Hollywood types."

Though I disagree with almost everything Chuck says, I see a lot of common ground out there somewhere. I like Chuck. Everybody likes Chuck. Chuck has the right to be stone-cold wrong. He makes perfect sense.

"Crypto. Schmypto. Them damn environmentalists think the cryptobiotic soil crusts are damaged by the cattle. Hell, imagine what a few million buffalo used to do to it. The stuff is still out there, ain't it? This place ain't fragile and weak; it's tough as hell. It's this damn generation raised by Walt Disney on that Walden Pond shit. They think they have to save the whole goddamn planet from *people.* What a bunch of crap!"

Chuck is right. The desert will be here long after we are gone. The flaw in his cowboy logic is that the desert takes a long time to heal itself and, and since we only live seventy-five years or so, we will not be around long enough to see our tracks erode away or revegetate. The stuff takes 225 years to recover. Every time I take a group of bikers out on a ride into the desert, I am reminded over and over again of the timelessness of this environment as we pass the same spot over and over again, and I see that same perfectly preserved Ritchey Z-Max tread cutting across that same bed of cryptobiotic crust that took 1,000 years to grow. A bicycle track is not like a footprint. A footprint catches water, holds it, and allows it to seep into the ground. A bike track is a straight line, funneling water down its course, gaining momentum, and carrying the soil with it. A bike track will be a canyon someday. I'll be seventy years old and those annoying tracks will still be there, turning into ditches, eating away at the precious soil that nurtures the beautiful desert flora.

Cryptobiotic Soil Crusts

Cryptobiotic soil crusts, formerly known as cryptogamic or microbiotic soil, make up the topsoil in canyon country. "Crypto" consists of colonies of delicate lichens, algae, and mosses that form in and on rain-pocked sand, and in potholes and cracks in the rock. The predominant organism is cyanobacteria, a life-form that is neither plant nor animal. It builds the foundation of the colony like a microscopic vine, reaching out and grabbing grains of sand with threadlike fibers. This stabilizes the surface sands, binding them together to form a hard crust. Mosses and lichens build onto this living netting and begin to photosynthesize and break down minerals in the soil. You can think of the cryptobiotic crusts' relationship to the deserts as you would plankton's role in the propagation of ocean life. The

soil crusts form the very bottom of the food chain, photosynthesizing valuable nutrients for the grasses, bushes, and trees, as well as holding the moisture necessary for seeds to germinate. In rare areas where the crypto has been protected from cattle, it has grown over many, many centuries into spires of dark, weathered sandcastles. In the midst of these clumps are many plant species.

In order to truly understand the value of the cryptobiotic soil crusts, you need only examine the desert. In areas where drift sand dominates, there is little opportunity for seeds to take hold so there is only sand, but in areas where cryptobiotic crusts dominate, grasses grow and bushes and small trees thrive. This in turn allows animals to thrive on the plant life and predators to thrive on the plant eaters. Destroy the crypto and all you have is drift sand, and what fun is riding that stuff?

Note the bike tracks through the cryptobiotic soil crust. These tracks form a watercourse—it will be a canyon someday.

Soil-filled and blackened potholes you find in the rock contain fragile desert shrimp, snails, and toad eggs. Some of these tiny ecosystems are lushly bordered by thick cryptobiotic crust that harbors nutrients necessary for the flowers, bushes, and herbs to take hold. These places become mazes of gardens in the cracks and pits of the Moab Entrada Slickrock Tongue, and home to thousands of living organisms. It is completely boneheaded to ride through this stuff when it is surrounded by slickrock, the most fantastic surface for mountain biking anywhere. But the slickrock is not a free-kill zone, either. Anchored on its surface are fragile lichens and mosses that stabilize the rock the way the crypto stabilizes the soil. On designated trails across slickrock, you'll notice that bicycle tires have completely decimated the lichen and moss and killed all life in the potholes. Some are eroding away at a measurable rate. Staying on these trails keeps damage to a minimum elsewhere and ensures that we will have something to look at while we ride.

I see a converted bus at trailheads sometimes. It has a Web site on the side, something like funbus.com. They park the bus on state land to avoid having to deal with the Bureau of Land Management (BLM)—which would kick them off in a hurry. They take people out to the trails but provide no guides, so they don't have to have a commercial permit. Leaning against the bumper of the bus is an old shovel with a roll of toilet paper impaled on the handle.

The desert is dry. A banana, orange peel, apple core, or turd will mummify in a matter of hours and be part of the scenery for longer than you and I will be alive. Simple solution. Whatever you bring into the desert, pack it out. This means that if you are going to defecate in the desert, bring a Ziploc bag and carry that baby back with you. We carry diseases that kill or weaken wildlife, so it is not only unsightly but downright dangerous for the bees, birds, coyotes, and raccoons. Plastic and paper products are known to clog the digestive systems of native animals. Burying that turd doesn't help much, but at least it is better than just crapping in the parking area like funbus.com.

Water in the desert is a precious commodity. Potholes are for wildlife. Do not take a dip in any standing water. Oils on our skin, along with sunblock and soaps, kill the fragile plants and animals that cling to life in these rare desert pools. These creatures, in turn, support other fragile lives farther up the food chain. I have seen once vibrant pools alive with shrimp turn into puddles of lifeless muddy water with an oil slick on top because someone thought that it would be nice to take a bath in the pool and/or let their dog run amok.

On that note: Leave Fido at home. Dogs do not belong in the wild desert. A very few trails around Moab (like Hurrah Pass and Sand Flats Road—see Dogs Are Family chapter) are okay for your pet, but most are not. I have a dog. I love my dog. But there are places he does not belong. Even if a coyote doesn't love me the way my dog does, it is the coyote's desert. Besides, if you love your dog, you won't run him across fifteen-grit sandpaper. If you are running a dog on slickrock, at least give him some shoes.

Speaking of dog lovers, here is the king.

Want to see wildlife? Shut up. Animals hear you and just go away. Noise interrupts the breeding patterns of desert wildlife like desert bighorn sheep and birds of prey. How would you feel if you were tucked in and making love and all of the sudden some jerk ran into your bedroom and screamed, *"Yahoo!"*

Surviving Your First Moab Rides

Education

Take it from a guide, you need me. You may not want, or think you need or can afford a guide, but if you are in Moab for the first time, you certainly should have one. A friend who has a lot of experience riding these trails would be the perfect companion. If you are riding with this book alone as your guide, remember that *no* guidebook, no matter how thorough, can eliminate the possibility that shit might happen. The mileage counts in this book were done on a mountain bike, which means they are approximations. Variances in tire circumference, air pressure, and tire wear all have bearing on the readings. Cairns and signs disappear overnight. Give yourself a chance to learn the desert riding facts of life and get a feel for Moab terrain under your wheels by traveling with a guide for your first three rides in the

Moab area. Not only is a guide your lifeline to a more relaxed, sane, safe, and fun trip, but a really good guide offers the opportunity to learn. Nowhere is knowing about the wildlife more important than in the Moab desert, where life is fragile in the extreme.

Shop for your guide as you would any other professional. As always, you get what you pay for. Lower fees usually mean the guide is illegal, the group is going to be huge, or the trail is going to be really easy. Commercial guides usually don't offer the good information unsolicited, but will gladly give it up for a tip. Ask questions constantly. Get your money's worth. Ask about side spurs to interesting features, water sources, and ancient artifacts. How do you build a fire in a driving rain? Your guide should be aware and enthusiastic about educating you about bike etiquette and the environment.

Be careful who you ask for information. Even the best Moab bike shops, and bike shops in general, are notorious for occasionally hiring, with the best of intentions, young, inexperienced, transient, even stoned-out mountain bikers who come to Moab and try to get by on an attitude and a pipe. There are many things that kill tourists in canyon country. Bad advice is one.

Flash floods

The most popular way to die is "too much water." Flash floods are just that: In a flash there is a flood. Staying aware of where you are, the current weather forecast (actually an educated weather guess), as well as the clouds in the sky and the water in the wash, are the best ways to avoid being ripped to shreds and flushed into the Colorado River. If a clear stream suddenly runs muddy, get up the wall of the canyon, fast. If a dry wash suddenly develops a stream, get the hell outta there. Things happen fast. In a canyon you may not even see the clouds that dumped the water. When you hear the water, it is usually too late. The weather in canyon country is very localized. One area can get as much as 12 inches of rain in half an hour (no kidding, this has happened here), while a mile away there is not a hint of moisture.

Water and hydration

The second most popular way to die in canyon country is "not enough water." The physiology of dehydration is not at all pleasant. Imagine your blood turning the consistency of mustard and you'll have an idea of just how hard it might be for it to travel through your veins and arteries. Water evaporates at an alarming rate out here. Since your body is mostly water, you, too, will evaporate, if you are not careful. In order to keep the chances of this happening to an absolute minimum, carry more water than you need, drink constantly, and do not travel during the midday sun in summer. Take a backpack hydration system capable of carrying one hundred ounces or more, and two large water bottles, as a minimum on three-hour rides in summer weather. Double up on the bladders in the water pack and take a couple of water bottles minimum for rides from four to six hours. Remember, these are approximate

Sandstone cross-bedding—remnants of ▶
layered sea bottom sediments in the
Entrada geological layer at Bartlett Wash

minimums! In midsummer it is physically impossible to carry enough water to ride all day, and judging how much water you may use personally is a guessing game at best. Every person's water needs differ from day to day. Having just enough water to do the ride may be a recipe for disaster, if you have a mechanical problem in the middle of nowhere, or flip over the bars and break the bladder.

The most dangerous aspect of dehydration, especially in a situation where you are alone out in the desert, is that when your blood thickens, it cannot carry oxygen to supply your brain with the power to *think*. You get dizzy, then you get really stupid and make bad decisions. After a while you begin to see clowns on cows riding across oceans of Jell-O, then you lose consciousness and eventually die. Even if you are rescued, your saviors can kill you. Never give a dehydrated person cold water to drink. Warm water only, and slowly! Cold water will shock the body into total shutdown. Shock kills far quicker than dehydration.

Drink water before you get thirsty and snack before you get hungry. If you follow this simple rule, you will hydrate effectively and maintain strength throughout your ride. Never eat a bunch of food in the middle of a ride. All the blood goes to your stomach. Your legs will feel like rubber. Snack all day, but do not sit down for "lunch." Drink all day, but do not gulp.

A word about coffee, tea, and alcoholic beverages. They are diuretic. This means they make you pee. If you drink a lot of coffee or black tea before a ride, you will need an extra water bottle or two.

Fitness

An important element for surviving your trip to Moab is fitness, because the third most popular way to die here is "existing health problems." If you are diabetic, you will have to exercise extreme caution. If you have a heart condition, are overweight, or have been enjoying a sedentary lifestyle, it is best not to ride here. Take a car tour of Arches or Canyonlands National Parks, or take a sight-seeing flight via helicopter or fixed-wing craft, but avoid the mountain bike and hiking trails. It cannot be said enough: Mountain biking in Moab is not for everyone. The riding here is very strenuous and technically challenging. If you are not up to the test, the results could be unpleasant and painful at best, deadly at worst. Toes-up in a box is not the way to fly home.

Route finding and map reading

Always ride with a map, compass, and bike computer. Learn how to use them. Never rely upon cairns, signs, mileage counts, or directions alone. Signs disappear. Cairns are not permanent trail markers and are sometimes placed there by persons who are lost.

Mileage counts in this guide are prey to variances in computer calibration. Bike computers, when set by a calibration log supplied with the unit, or calibrated using personal measurement of wheel circumference, will never be 100 percent accurate. Differences in tire air pressure, surface, and speed will cause these units to be off by as much as 20 percent. Whenever you use this guide, carry other methods of route finding for comparison. This trail guide is just a supplement, and in no way replaces a compass, a good map, or a guide. Local maps are not updated to include changes in the trail such as rockslides, new trails, closed spurs, cairns, degradation, or improvements. Even the compass is not a sure deal.

A compass should never be read while on the bike. Magnetic materials will cause the unit to give a false reading. Whenever you read the compass, get off the bike and walk at least 20 feet away. Compasses will also give a false reading if you are wearing magnetic material or are near machinery or even a concentrated iron deposit in the ground below or next to you. Landmarks, when correctly identified, will help you navigate more effectively with the compass.

Contained in some of the routes in this book are longitude and latitude readings (waypoints) taken from a Global Positioning System (GPS) unit. GPS systems require the location of three satellites to get a read, so if you're in a canyon or otherwise blocked from the sky, you won't get a read. And keep in mind, cold weather can freeze the LCD screens and render the unit useless. In other words, do not bet your life on a GPS unit or the waypoints I offer.

I have specifically chosen not to use GPS waypoints as guiding mechanisms for the guidebook, mostly for safety reasons. Since GPS units operate by pointing the direction to the next or last recorded point, the convoluted nature of many of the trails in canyon country can cause troubling confusion. Suppose your next waypoint is ninety degrees to your right and you are at a point where the trail takes a left, eventually winding around a feature to connect with that accurate waypoint. Sometimes a deep gorge separates you from a waypoint. If you are feeling lost and a bit panicked about getting back to a trailhead before you run out of water or it gets dark, this kind of conflicting information can cause stress that can push a solo rider into making a bad decision. Bottom line: A good map and compass, and the ability to read them correctly, are the best tools for navigation.

Even if you are a fit rider, beware of the lure of slickrock expanses and unmarked trail spurs. It is very easy to get lost in canyon country, even if you can see where you are going. What good is being able to see your destination if there is a 200-foot-deep, 10-mile-long canyon between you and it?

Again, never rely upon a single device, map, or guidebook for route finding. Please plan, prepare for the worst, and expect to spend the night in the desert.

Bike-handling skills

Clint Eastwood once said in one of those horrible *Dirty Harry* movies, "A man's got to know his limitations." On the remote trails around Moab, truer words were never spoken. Do not attempt distances or maneuvers you are not certain you can accomplish. If you go over the bars and break your leg, who knows where you are? Walk all sections of trail that are beyond your skill level, and remember, if you are pushing a mountain bike, you are still mountain biking. Live to ride tomorrow.

Rock is good.

Extreme weather changes

Hypothermia is a serious threat to mountain bikers riding in mountains and deserts at any time of year. You may not think that a 105-degree day can turn into a chilling experience, but at any time a thunderstorm can dump bone-chilling hail that will stick to you like little wet snowballs and suck every bit of warmth from your body in a matter of seconds. In a desert thunderstorm the temperature can drop into the forties or fifties faster than you can say, "Ididasport." In some areas where the trail crosses shale sedimentary layers, rain and hail turn the trail into soupy clay that sticks to everything, turning your bike into a seventy-five-pound deadweight. The combination of hail and shale is really unpleasant. Always carry a rain shell, even if it doesn't look like it is going to rain and the weatherman swears it ain't gonna. The fact is that the weather in the desert does whatever it wants to do, so be prepared.

Your bike

Okay, you're fit, you've read all the literature, you have a guide, you're watching for flash floods, you're tiptoeing around the endangered dirt, and you're carrying enough food, water, and clothing. What about your bike? Is it as fit as you are? Do you have tools? Guess what the most popular way to get injured in Moab is. That's right, "equipment failure." Moab exacts a huge toll on equipment. A crummy set of brakes can be fatal here. A cracked frame can ruin your life. A broken chain, compounded by not carrying a chain tool or enough water to be able to walk out, is the perfect formula for a hell of a survival tale to tell your buddies upon your return—if you are lucky.

Check your bike before and during every ride and carry the tools necessary to fix any problem that might arise. Ride within the limits of your equipment. Steep slickrock is a great workout and a serious challenge to your fitness, but you can snap a chain on a steep climb and eat it big. And by the way, full suspension is highly recommended in Moab. This means there are more parts to break, but it also means that you ride smoother and safer.

Wildlife

If you hear a bee in a bush in Moab, it ain't a bee. It is a pygmy rattler. A pygmy rattler's rattles are so small that they do not "rattle," they "buzz." These particular rattlesnakes are beautiful, shy beings. It takes an appointment to get bitten, but if you manage to sit on a little rattler or stick your hand into a bush where one is hiding, you could be in trouble. An adult rattler will usually "dry bite" in self-defense, saving the venom for its predatory pursuits, but a baby rattler just lets go of all its venom at once.

Dealing with a rattlesnake bite is best done by immobilization and quick transport to a hospital, but on a bike this is usually impossible. Riding alone can be fatal if a rattler bites you. The best "we have no antivenin" solution for the hemotoxin of a pygmy rattler is a Sawyer extractor, a little device you can purchase at most sporting goods shops. It gets mixed reviews by doctors and medical technicians, but it is probably effective if used immediately after the bite. It is a spring-loaded device that sucks, literally. The old cut-and-suck method is not recommended, unless you are "playing" snakebite. The best solution for sidewinder (found in the Mojave Desert) neurotoxin is a compression wrap. Never compression-wrap a hemotoxin wound, however. You will lose the limb.

Scorpions come in a couple of varieties in canyon country. The tiny yellow or translucent fellow is called a bark scorpion and is capable of killing a human, especially a child. The larger varieties are not as toxic. Scorpions, like rattlers, are very easy to avoid. They generally are found under organic debris, tree bark, or dead tree stumps and limbs. Using a tent when camping can take you out of the statistical window. If you put your helmet down in the desert, be sure to check it thoroughly before putting it back on. I have heard of tiny scorpions hiding out in helmets and crawling in an ear. Doesn't sound good, does it? Imagine the control it will take not to piss it off.

Centipedes are nastier than large scorpions and can be found in the same places. Digging in the dirt under rock outcroppings where the soil is moist is the best way to come across one. Don't dig with your hands!

Yellow jackets and wasps can also be a problem if you happen to disturb a nest, so pay attention to what you're doing and who you're doing it to. These nasty guys nest in the ground and in constructed shelters. Rumors are afoot that we now have Africanized "end of the world" bees. Desert ants are cousins to the wasp and if you

Coyote, bike, cyclist tracks

happen to kill one, it releases a scent that draws its pissed-off friends over to the spot. After a while you have a lot of very mad ants who are packing heat.

Mosquitoes can be a problem in the mountains in washes at the break of day, but usually they're not a serious threat in the desert. Cow flies, on the other hand, can be epic and biblical. Some bug spray may be necessary during early summer in some locations around Moab.

Bears are prevalent in the La Sals and especially the Abajo Mountains south of Moab. The old advice to climb a tree may be a ticket to being mauled or killed if you come across a mother and her cubs. Maternal bears are startled easily, so your best defense is to remain still and calm. Let the bear make the move. If she threatens you, move away slowly. As a last resort, play dead. Don't make any sudden movements! If a male bear threatens you, scream at it. Do what you can to get away, but don't turn your back to it. A .44 pistol bullet and a solid slug shell in a 12-gauge shotgun are the only projectile weapons available to us that will stop a bear. The noise alone will drive away most bears, but if a bear is focused on hurting you, you had better be a good shot.

Mountain lions also populate the high desert and mountains and are especially prevalent in the Abajos and out in the deserts around Moab. If you see one or you see tracks, count yourself as one of the blessed. It is not a good idea to make eye contact with a big cat, but generally they have a lot of game to prey upon and have no interest in eating you. If they are interested in your flesh, you just won't see it coming. I paint eyes on the back of my helmet with nail polish, just in case.

For your information, the mountain lions and bears of the Abajos are in far more danger from us than we are from them. If you love these creatures enough to make a commitment to their preservation, I suggest you go to the Forest Service office in Moab or Monticello and purchase a hunting permit for a bear or lion. There is a finite number of lion- and bear-hunting permits. If you purchase a permit and don't exercise that permit, then one more lion or bear goes free. Just don't tell the Forest Service that you have no intent to hunt. Keep your lion-loving motives to yourself. Make yourself look like a bloodthirsty trophy hunter and they'll think you are normal.

The animal kingdom is not the only living threat to your survival in canyon country. Yucca (better known as bayonet yucca) can kill you if you fall on it. Cactus can attack and poison ivy can really mess up your vacation. Poison ivy turns red in the fall. It is so pretty some kids have been known to pick it and carry it around. Fishhook cactus has barbs that look like, well, fishhooks. You can imagine what happens if you sit or fall on one. Just don't get up. There are quite a few variety of cacti out there, and each one has its own charm.

Being Prepared

A basic rule to follow when it comes to survival in the desert or mountains is to always be prepared to spend the night out there. Always carry matches, extra clothing, food, and water. I am a conservationist to the core, but when it comes to survival I will burn down the Vatican before I will let myself get stressed from cold.

Here is a list of things to carry on every ride in Canyonlands.

Equipment

- Helmet.
- Riding gloves.
- Two spare tubes, a patch kit, a tire boot (a plastic library card works great), and a pump.
- Small tool kit that will enable you to perform all minor repairs on your bike.
- Zip ties and a bit of duct tape.
- Three large full water bottles (five if you have no water pack).
- Water pack with a one-hundred-ounce bladder.
- Riding shorts are recommended.
- Bike, hiking, or cross-training shoes.
- Rain jacket, tights, and an extra top layer.
- Sunscreen and lip block.
- Two energy bars for every three hours of riding (jerky is a great survival food).
- Matches and/or a lighter.
- Map and compass (and a cell phone).
- Space blanket.
- A friend with a brain.

CPR and first aid

Personally, I recommend that everyone take a first aid and CPR class with their local Red Cross or fire department. The life you save could be your child's or your spouse's. Knowledge is power, and ignorance is regrettable. That said, most accidents on a mountain bike in Moab require blood-loss control or "last aid." Maybe learning "last rites" would be a good idea. The only time I have ever ridden all-out in the desert was to save a life, so bike-handling skills are a real survival tool when shit happens.

Trail Etiquette

If you're a mountain biker with enough skill to attempt Moab terrain, you already know how to behave on the trail, but if you need a refresher, here are the basic rules of trail etiquette that every mountain biker must know and exercise in order to maintain access, assure safety, and generate trust and acceptance for our sport in the general public. Say them with me:

- Stay on the trail.
- Share the trail—be courteous to other trail users.
- Slow your speed for hikers. Give them plenty of warning as you approach. Dismount if the trail is narrow.
- Dismount for horses as they approach and, if you approach from behind, talk to the riders (and the horses—they like to hear you coming) if you wish to pass.
- Don't leave bikes in the middle of the trail if you are stopping for any reason.
- Beware of blind turns and severe ledges and drop-offs.
- *Help others in need* (see Read This! before the Introduction).
- Take pictures. Leave absolutely nothing.
- Respect, do not molest, the native creatures.
- Whenever possible, perform simple trail maintenance.

Getting around Moab

Area codes

The area code **435** serves the Moab area. The area code **801** serves the Salt Lake City area. The area code for the Grand Junction area is **970.**

By air

Salt Lake City Airport (SLC). A pit stop for most major airlines, Salt Lake City Airport is your best bet in terms of price and convenience. From Salt Lake City it's a four-hour drive to Moab. To book reservations to Salt Lake City on-line, check out your favorite airline's Web site or search one of the following travel sites for the best price: www.cheaptickets.com, www.expedia.com, www.previewtravel.com, www.priceline.com, travel.yahoo.com, www.travelocity.com, www.trip.com—just to name a few. **Grand Junction Airport** (GJT). Flights into Grand Junction, Colorado, are quite a bit more expensive, but it is certainly closer and will allow you to drive into Moab on scenic Utah Route 128. It's a two-hour drive. United has a subcontractor flying shuttles from Denver to Grand Junction, but these can be unreliable. **Canyonlands Field** (CNY). Located twenty minutes north of Moab on U.S. Route 191, Canyonlands Field is our local airport. Great Lakes Aviation (435–259–0566) operates flights daily to and from Moab and Denver or Phoenix utilizing turboprop aircraft seating twenty people; expect your luggage to get lost. If you are traveling with bikes, you should arrange to have them shipped to a local bike shop or to your hotel. The Hotel Off Center is the most bike friendly and accommodating in this regard. Redtail Aviation operates a shuttle service with Skywagon aircraft, flying a maximum group of three to and from Salt Lake City for $575 each way. Bikes can also be a problem for Redtail, though they are flexible. Weight is the concern here. For Redtail call (435) 259–7421. To reserve a shuttle for you and your equipment from Canyonlands Field, call Roadrunner Shuttle Service at (435) 259–9402. Check www.dreamride.com/travelservices.html for updated Moab travel logistics.

By train

Amtrak travels from Oakland, California, through Reno and points west; and from Chicago, Illinois, and points east to Green River, Utah, and Grand Junction, Colorado. There is no shuttle service from Green River and no rental car office, so it is wise to book through to Grand Junction. The train ride is *awesome* from either direction. Call (800) 872-7245 or visit www.amtrak.com for more information. Grand Junction has checked baggage service, and it's $12 to carry a bike.

By bus

There is no bus service to Moab at all. **Greyhound** goes to Green River, but no shuttle or car rentals are available there. Greyhound will carry boxed bikes for $15, and boxes are available at most major terminals for $10. Call Greyhound at (800) 231–2222 or visit www.greyhound.com for more information.

By van shuttle

Bighorn Express operates daily van shuttles to and from Salt Lake City for $49 one-way. Contact them at (888) 655–RIDE or visit www.bighornexpress.com.

Rental cars

Thrifty or **Budget** rental cars, both of which have an office in Moab, no longer allow you to drop a rental car from Salt Lake City off in Moab without a fee. The drive from Salt Lake City to Moab takes four to five hours. The drive from Grand Junction takes two hours. Rental cars from Grand Junction can be dropped off, but you will have to fight with the office to get them to agree.

Taxi services

None. If you're flying into Canyonlands Field, don't expect to see one waiting at the curb. You'll need to arrange a shuttle pickup. Call Roadrunner Shuttle Service at (435) 259–9402.

Bike shipping

For information on bike shipping, cases, and such, visit www.dreamride.com/travelservices.html#bike.

Visitor information

The Moab Information Center at the corner of Main and Center is the place to call for general information on local services. The phone number is (435) 259–8825. For travel and tour cancellation insurance, contact your credit card provider or a travel agent. For general tourist information on the Internet, visit any of these local Web sites: www.mountainbiketours.com, www.moab-utah.com, and www.moab.net.

How to Use This Book

Unlike many mountain biking guides, which do an adequate job of describing the trails and what you need to know to go riding in a certain area, *Mountain Biking Moab* is written in a very literary way. The book features forty-one mapped and cued rides and ten honorable mentions. But there is something more included in this book. Interspersed between the rides are stories about famous local Moab characters such as Lin Ottinger, Rusty Musselman, and Nic Hougen. There are stories about my experience riding around Moab, what I've seen, and what I disagree with. In general the placement of these stories relates to the ride descriptions that follow.

Mountain Biking Moab is divided into five different sections, representing the most distinct riding areas near town. Each chapter is then subsequently divided into a variety of components. The ride specs are fairly self-explanatory. Here you'll find the quick, nitty-gritty details of the ride: where the trailhead is located, ride length, approximate riding time, the difficulty, type of trail surface, the lay of the land, and the total climbing. You'll also find information on who manages the land, other trail users you may encounter, and what season is the best for the ride. There are two very important sections in this preliminary information: Environmental concerns gives you an idea about what needs to be protected to keep the desert from being trashed, and the Warning! section alerts you to hazards both for your safety and convenience. The Getting there section gives you directions from town right down to where you'll want to park.

The ride description is the meat of the chapter. It's my impression of the trail from guiding and riding the trails everyday. In the Miles and Directions section I provide mileage cues to identify all the turns and trail name changes, as well as points of interest. Between this and the route map, you should have enough information to keep from getting lost. The Ride Information section contains more useful information including: Trail Contacts, Schedules (when the best time is to ride the trail), Permits and Fees, and what Maps you will need.

The Honorable Mentions sections detail additional rides in each region that will inspire you to get out and explore.

How to Use These Maps

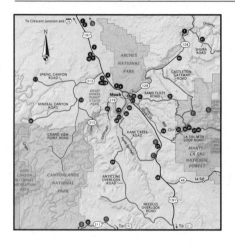

Regional location map

This map helps you find your way to the start of each ride from the nearest sizable town or city. Coupled with the detailed directions at the beginning of the cue, this map should visually lead you to where you need to be for each ride.

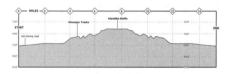

Elevation profile

This helpful profile gives you a cross-sectional look at the ride's ups and downs. Elevation is labeled on the left; mileage is indicated on the top. Road and trail names are shown along the route, with towns and points of interest labeled in bold.

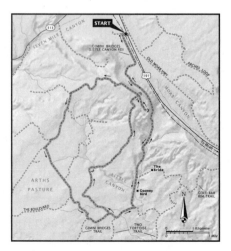

Route map

This is your primary guide to each ride. It shows all the accessible roads and trails, points of interest, water, towns, landmarks, and geographical features. It also distinguishes trails from roads, and paved roads from unpaved roads. The selected route is highlighted, and directional arrows point the way. Shaded topographic relief in the background gives you an accurate representation of the terrain and landscape in the ride area.

The Maps

For your own purposes, you may wish to copy the directions for the course onto a small sheet to help you while riding, or photocopy the map and cue sheet to take with you. These pages can be folded into a bike bag or stuffed into a jersey pocket. Just remember to stop when you want to read the map.

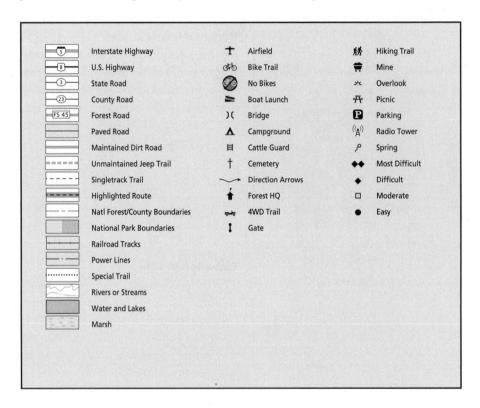

Interstate Highway		Airfield		Hiking Trail	
U.S. Highway		Bike Trail		Mine	
State Road		No Bikes		Overlook	
County Road		Boat Launch		Picnic	
Forest Road		Bridge		Parking	
Paved Road		Campground		Radio Tower	
Maintained Dirt Road		Cattle Guard		Spring	
Unmaintained Jeep Trail		Cemetery		Most Difficult	
Singletrack Trail		Direction Arrows		Difficult	
Highlighted Route		Forest HQ		Moderate	
Natl Forest/County Boundaries		4WD Trail		Easy	
National Park Boundaries		Gate			
Railroad Tracks					
Power Lines					
Special Trail					
Rivers or Streams					
Water and Lakes					
Marsh					

Moab North and Northeast

Defined by the land north of Utah Route 128 and east of U.S. Route 191, this region encompasses all of Arches National Park, the Moab Entrada Slickrock Tongue geological formation, Courthouse Wash and its maze of canyons, Willow Springs, and the Yellow Cat Mining District to the far north. The trails in this area are almost always impassable when wet. Most of the rides documented here can be ridden from the highway. This means very strong riders without fossil-fuel vehicles can gain access to most of these trails from Moab via US 191, the Old Moab Highway, Old Arches Road, and the fresh gas pipeline service road that runs parallel to and east of US 191.

The rides in this area are incredibly scenic, mostly moderate in technical challenge (for Moab), and extremely educational. These lands are among the most environmentally sensitive in the Moab area due to sparse rainfall, fragile vegetation, and the virgin condition of much of the countryside. An interpretive mountain bike tour in this specific area is a great way to gain desert survival knowledge, learn environmental mountain bike etiquette, and see the old mines and scattered deposits of rare fossils and minerals. Students of the stone book of geology will find this place to be a religious experience. Kids will love the dinosaur tracks and bone quarries, and the chance to brag about riding slickrock in Moab.

This area is particularly interesting to photograph. Nature photographers will certainly notice the inexcusable mountain bike tracks across the fragile desert soil crusts in the Klondike Bluffs area specifically. Local bike shops have been sending folks out on the Klondike Bluffs Trail without so much as a whisper of warning about the sensitive nature of this beautiful area. I have heard a few locals say, "Well, some areas have to be sacrificed." This logic eludes me. As mountain bikers we had better learn to coexist with nature or else we'll lose the privilege to enjoy it from the saddle. In this area it is extremely important that you keep your bike on the trail at all times. When walking off-trail, stay on bare rock not encrusted with lichens or mosses, or in sand wash bottoms and watercourses. If you are exploring the old mining areas, be especially careful. I have personally found old blasting caps lying on the slickrock and have seen the mouth of one mine collapse.

Some of the most notable attractions include views of, and trails into, Arches National Park, the vast expanse of the Courthouse Wash area, and the psychedelic

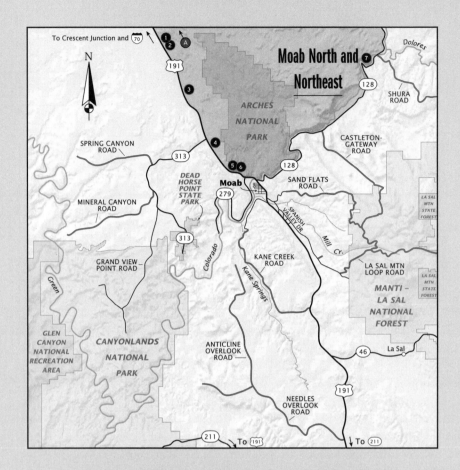

rock formations of the Entrada and Morrison geological layers. Slickrock in this area welcomes novices and is extremely compatible with intermediate skills.

There is abundant wildlife in this area, and if you're early and quiet you'll most likely get a chance to view the most impressive examples. Mountain lion, coyote, antelope, bobcat, and deer live and thrive here in a climate that at first glance seems brutal and sparse. For sure you will see darkling beetles, ravens, and an assortment of lizards, hawks, eagles, falcons, ground squirrels, rabbits, and other small desert critters. Grotesque weathered junipers and piñon pines squeeze from narrow cracks in the rock into twisted shapes.

Arches National Park, despite the harsh sand and even harsher restrictions, should be seen if you are in Moab. Set aside a day or an evening early in your trip for a car tour and hike to Delicate Arch or into the Devil's Garden. A guided tour of the Fiery Furnace is among the highlights of a visit to the park. These attractions are simply required viewing. If you don't want to drive in, ride your bike into the park on the Arches Loop ride in this guide or ride in on the Arches Road. A 50-mile out-and-back road ride to the Devil's Garden is a real treat in fall, winter, and early spring. The Winnebagos vacate around the end of November and return in late April.

Cow Pies, Dead Guys, and Verle Green

The cattle approached, noisy, nervous, and timid, faltering at the end of the bridge over the Colorado River just north of Moab. A single cowhand out ahead of the herd began screaming at the top of his lungs over the maws of hesitant cows: "Get it off the goddamn road! Get it out of the way! Get that damn truck out of the middle of the road! . . . *Hey, buddy, get that goddamn hunk of crap off the road!*"

A truck was parked on the shoulder, right smack in the middle of the "cow lane." It took a couple of wide-eyed, confused cows bashing into his fender to convince the driver to move his truck before it was stampeded into scrap metal. He backed the truck off the highway as the forwardmost of the cows stood trembling, slowly being shoved forward by the force of the phalanx of cows behind.

A group of bikers pedaled up from Utah Route 128, impatiently coasting into the middle of the intersection in front of the herd. It wasn't going to be pretty.

I settled back to watch the impending disaster when I spotted Verle Green galloping across the bridge with a whip in his hand, charging to the rescue.

I screamed, "Verle!"

Verle is over seventy years old, hard as nails, and tough as leather. So are his eardrums.

"*Verle!*"

Nothing.

He rode right past me on the other side

of the road, cracking his whip at the balking cattle standing confused and scared when confronted by the group of dumbfounded and impatient bicyclists. Verle yelled: "Heeee . . . yaaaa! Get on there!"

I dodged cows to get to Verle. I hadn't seen him in a few months and relished the opportunity to photograph him in his natural environment.

"*Verle! Hey, Verrrlllle!*"

He saw me and immediately broke into a harelipped smile.

Verle is one tough-looking cowpoke. His pronounced harelip, scary sunken eyes, and leathery face give him a timeless cowboy aura that says: "There ain't room enough in this here town for the both of us." Verle is so thin that you wonder how he balances the cowboy hat on his head. His wiry frame and hard looks make people think he is about to draw a gun and shoot, or say angrily, "What you lookin' at?," but this impression greatly contrasts his personality. Verle is the quintessential western gentleman: soft spoken, extremely polite, kind, very warm, and friendly—even if he does carry a concealed weapon like every unbalanced redneck in Utah. Verle's harelip is as much a source of humor for him as it is a hindrance to conversation. When you speak to him at length, you begin to pick up the slur yourself, and Verle says: "It's catching, ain't it?"

Verle used to be the deputy sheriff of San Juan County during the 1960s and early 1970s. At the time, Rusty Musselman was sheriff of San Juan County, and for many years, after the dust settled on the 1960s, Rusty shared stories of Verle with anyone who would listen. There still is a beautiful pen-and-ink drawing of Verle's uniquely western, wrinkled, and worn face beside the front door of Rusty's Monticello home. When Rusty mentioned Verle Green—someone he admired and considered a best friend—he glowed like a bug light. Their love and respect for one another was something epic and mythological.

Rusty's eyes shone and he chuckled as he spoke of Verle. "Verle was a great deputy, reliable and very faithful. He worked ninety hours a week and was very dedicated. Verle was especially good with dead people.

"One time we got a call that an Indian had died in the hospital and nobody came forward to collect the body. They didn't know what to do with him. A doctor in Tuba City said he had a big refrigerator up there, so, well, we didn't think no more about it. I sent Verle up there with the body and pretty soon he called saying: 'These guys don't want this fella up here.' I told him to leave the guy right there on the doctor's porch and get back down here. He did just that."

Rusty continued: "Another time I had Verle put this dead guy under a tarp in the back of my pickup and take him all the way to Salt Lake City for an autopsy. He stopped for gas somewhere around Price, and this kid was filling up the tank. Verle told him he was going to go have a coffee and asked the kid to park the truck in the shade after he filled it up because there was a dead guy in the back and he didn't want to leave him out in the sun cause he might start to stink. The kid didn't believe him. Verle watched the kid park the truck in the shade, peek under the tarp, and take off running. Yup, Verle was great at taking care of dead people.

"He had a heck of a good memory, too. He can still tell you the license plate numbers of cars he pulled over thirty years ago. He was a hell of a deputy, except for the time he went to the Ute Reservation to investigate a shooting and left the truck open with about forty guns in it." Rusty chuckled and took a swig of Roughlock whiskey.

Verle sat on his horse on the side of the highway, whip in hand, as if a hundred years of history had suddenly been erased. He smiled widely and, noticing I was carrying a camera, posed instinctively. This is the kind of moment that hooked me on Moab. This is the kind of moment that put a hurt in my heart every time it crawled into my memory while I was working like an educated dog in some godawful community college back east. This is the kind of moment that cemented my soul to the place and made me sacrifice a good salary, pension, and health care plan to live in a place that can be 130 degrees in the summer and 35 below in the winter.

Scared cows were everywhere, but before long Verle had them under control with whip and harelipped verbal discipline. After Verle poked the cows off the road

Verle Green

and up the trail on the backside of Moab, I returned to the truck, started the engine, and proceeded to drive north, leading about a hundred vehicles into the horrible smell at the other side of the Colorado River Bridge. Here we found the result of cow panic—about a ton of fresh cow dung generously sloshed about the highway. A bridge must be a frightful thing for a cow because every one of the herd had evacuated its bowels in this single spot.

When at last I arrived at the trailhead, the cow crap inside the wheel wells and on my fenders drew every cow fly within a 100 miles. As both hands were busy removing the bikes from the bed of the truck, I did the ritual cow fly dance in vain. I must have lost a quart of blood before my tires hit the trail.

1 Book Cliffs Overlook

Start: From just off U.S. Route 191 at the Y intersection, past the sign to the dinosaur tracks.

Length: 5.8-mile out-and-back.

Approximate riding time: 1 to 2 hours, but you'll want to hike around and hang out on the cliff to take in the view.

Difficulty: Technically difficult, but easily traversed by novices who dismount for obstacles. Physically easy to moderate due to its short length.

Trail surface: Loose rock and soft sediments, shale, slickrock, and hardpack on a 4WD doubletrack.

Lay of the land: The Moab Entrada Slickrock Tongue emerges like a huge tilted tabletop from the Dakota and Manchos shale layers. This slickrock slab is not flat at all, but rather like mounds of kneaded dough divided by deep cracks filled with fragile vegetation. To get to the slickrock, you will be riding through the Morrison layer up a hill of loose rock and pebbly hardpack.

Total climbing: 605 feet.

Land status: Bureau of Land Management (BLM) and Utah State Trust lands.

Other trail users: Hikers, rockhounds, and off-road vehicles (ORV).

Best seasons: Spring and fall.

Environmental concerns: Extremely fragile! Cryptobiotic soil crusts and rare desert mosses abound on and between the slickrock. Since this is not traditionally a mountain bike area, make sure that you leave no tracks through any virgin vegetation, or through any areas of virgin soil. The soils in this area are not "dirt"; they are living soil crusts. Do not ride off the trail. While on the rock, do not ride over patches of moss or lichen.

Warning! This area is impassable when wet.

Getting there: From Moab: Drive 20.4 miles north of Moab on US 191, past mile marker 148. There is a road on your right that crosses the railroad tracks. Just over the tracks is a sign that reads DINOSAUR TRACKS—TWO MILES. One tenth of a mile in from the highway is a Y in the road. Park in the Y and ride northeast on the left-hand spur.

The Ride

This trail is not maintained or marked and is frequented only by ORV-supported rockhounds. Either of the book's first two routes can be done as a quickie, or combined for more variety and mileage. These are trails for the nature lover that beg you to dismount, examine mineral deposits and vegetation, and take photographs of little things at your feet, like coyote and bobcat tracks or tiny flowers. Please try to stay on rock or in sandy washes to avoid crushing fragile desert vegetation under foot or wheel. A simple rule is: If it's unmarked by vehicle tracks or there is any chance that it's alive, don't step on it or ride through it. And though taking stones is not immoral, it is illegal on public lands.

Not many people know about this place, and now that you do, please be nice to it. This area is like an open-air natural history museum, so taking a desert wildlife

The Morrison formation's green and red bands emerge from the desert fire.

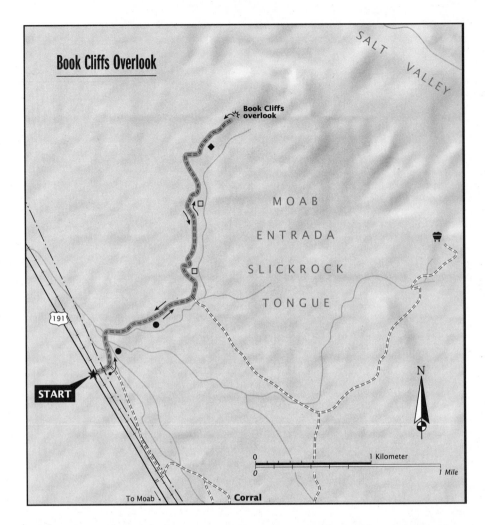

Book Cliffs Overlook

Book Cliffs
overlook

SALT VALLEY

MOAB

ENTRADA

SLICKROCK

TONGUE

191

START

N

0   1 Kilometer
0   1 Mile

To Moab   **Corral**

and/or geology handbook is recommended. (See the list of naturalist guides in Ride Information for suggestions.) This ride, and the ride that follows, is truly for amateur photographers, geologists, desert lovers, and naturalists who just happen to ride a mountain bike—folks who consider the mountain bike a hiking accessory. If you are more interested in the places you go than the act of riding itself, then rides like the first two in this book are for you. Riders intent on pure mountain biking will find much better trails in this book to satisfy the testosterone knobby urge.

A steep climb at the start on a loose, rugged, and varied track takes you to an exposed section of the Morrison formation. As you climb a bit more, you gain access to the Moab Entrada Slickrock Tongue—one of the geological formations that make Moab such a wonderful place to mountain bike. This particular section of the Entrada is too fragile and convoluted to offer any kind of satisfying "bike surfing."

BOOK CLIFFS

The Book Cliffs hold the distinction of being the longest continuous escarpment in the world. Shaped by millions of years of erosion, the Book Cliffs run over 100 miles from Palisades, Colorado, to Green River, Utah, then hang a right and go northward to Price, Utah. Interstate 70 follows the cliffs from the foot of the Rocky Mountains to where they veer north at the eastern end of the San Rafael Swell.

Exposed strata in the Book Cliffs include the Manchos shale and the Mesaverde Group's marine sands, coal, and sandstone. These seabeds, eroded away and missing in much of Canyonlands, record the advances and retreats of the late Cretaceous shorelines when sea level was in a state of flux.

The plateau above the Book Cliffs contains some of the most remote and pristine wilderness in the continental United States, though some areas have been overgrazed.

The Book Cliffs seen from the Yellow Jacket Canyon section of the Kokopelli Trail.

After achieving the Entrada layer, you'll climb a bit more to a cliff edge that over-looks Salt Valley and the Book Cliffs—the longest continuous escarpment in the world and the only mountain range in the Western Hemisphere that runs east to west. Needless to say, the ride back downhill gets steep enough to require advanced skills, though walking the bike is not a problem due to the short distances involved. Actually, this trail is offered to those who use the bike as a hiking accessory. Feel free to get off the bike and hike, avoiding the fragile soil crusts, of course.

The slickrock out to the viewpoint is covered with patches of moss and color-ful lichens, so do not bust the crusts. This stuff takes hundreds, even thousands, of years to form and can be destroyed in a heartbeat. These features are the prime attraction of this ride. The cryptobiotic gardens are not only fragile and extremely rare, but also incredibly haunting and beautiful. Take your camera to gain full advan-tage of the pristine natural state of this short ride. Animal wildlife abounds, especially at night and in the soft light of early morning.

Like any ride in this area, the roads and trails are impassable when wet because the surface is composed mostly of the Manchos shale layer. Locals call the resulting gluelike clay "gumbo." Don't underestimate this stuff. It is horrible when wet. If you get stuck and have to leave your vehicle, it will be encased in cement when you return to try to drive it out. This is no joke!

Miles and Directions

0.0 **START** by heading out on the left-hand spur of the Y to the northeast.

0.8 Go left at the T.

1.0 Take the spur left into a gully.

1.2 At the base of the hill, go past the spur left and head straight up. The loose rock on this hill will require a bit of concentration to negotiate.

2.4 Continue on the 4WD track up to the rim in the distance.

2.9 Enjoy the view of the Book Cliffs and Salt Valley below. Be careful if you're walking across any loose rocks near the cliff edge. This is your turnaround point.

5.8 Arrive at your vehicle.

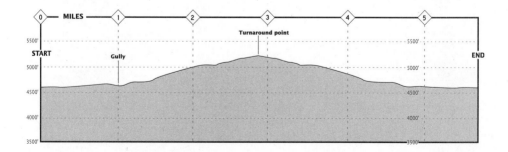

Ride Information

Trail Contacts

Bureau of Land Management
82 E. Dogwood
Moab, UT 84532
(435) 259-2196

Utah State School and Institutional Trust Lands Administration
1165 South US 191, Ste. 5
Moab, UT 84532
(435) 259-3760

Schedule

Trail is open year-round but is best during spring and fall.

Other Resources

Desert Wildflowers of North America
by Ronald J. Taylor

The Desert Year
by Joseph Wood Krutch

Canyon Country Wildflowers
by Damian Fagan

Flowers of the Canyon Country
by Stanley L. Welsh
with photos by Bill Ratcliff

The Colorado Plateau: A Geological History
by Donald L. Baars

Canyon Country Geology
by F. H. Barnes

Maps

USGS maps: Valley City, Klondike Bluffs

2 Brontosaur Copper Mine

Start: From just off U.S. Route 191 at the Y intersection, past the sign to the dinosaur tracks.
Length: 7-mile out-and-back.
Approximate riding time: 1 to 2 hours; more if you are into geology or paleontology.
Difficulty: Technically moderate to somewhat difficult. Physically easy to moderate.
Trail surface: Hardpack, loose sedimentary soils, and bedrock on old 4WD mining road.

Lay of the land: Traverse the Moab Entrada Slickrock Tongue, a huge tilted stone shelf overlooking Salt Valley.
Total climbing: 874 feet.
Land status: Bureau of Land Management (BLM) and Utah State Trust lands.
Other trail users: Hikers and off-road vehicles (ORV).
Best seasons: Spring and fall.

Environmental concerns: Though hammered by mining, the area is recovering nicely. Avoid side spurs or any faint tracks veering from the main trail. Cryptobiotic soil crusts and rare desert mosses abound just off the trail.

Warning! This area is impassable when wet. Also, the mine shafts contain radon. Mining sites left in this condition have old caches of explosives. Blasting caps may be scattered anywhere. Be extremely cautious. If you find anything that appears suspicious, don't touch it. Report it to the BLM. The shafts can collapse without warning, so venturing even into the mouth of the shaft can be extremely dangerous.

Getting there: From Moab: Drive 20.4 miles north of Moab on US 191, past mile marker 148. There is a road on your right that crosses the railroad tracks. Just over the tracks is a sign that reads DINOSAUR TRACKS—TWO MILES. One tenth of a mile in from the highway is a Y in the road. Park in the Y and ride northeast on the left-hand spur.

The Ride

This short out-and-back ride, past a dinosaur tracking site and an old copper mine, is particularly educational and a treat for anyone interested in paleontology, geology, and mining history. Though the trail is not maintained or marked, and is very difficult in sections, it's not particularly difficult to follow. The trail is a bit technical on the way up, so it's probably not a great place to have the kids on bikes—though as a family *hike*, it is prime. Add this to the Book Cliffs ride to extend the mileage.

Just past the head of the rugged 4WD trail at mile 1.8 is a well-marked dinosaur tracking area. The largest trackway reveals the movements of a sauropod turning right. There is also an allosaur trackway a few feet up the hill to the east that records the creature's limp.

The mining area above the dinosaur tracks was abandoned and never reclaimed—there was no effort to return the environment to its original state. Old

An ore crusher is just inside the opening of this mine shaft.

sluice lines that once carried ore to containers in which the copper was separated are scattered everywhere, along with abandoned vehicles, machinery, and piles of mine tailings. In these tailings you'll notice green sands flecked and small blue stones. These are forms of malachite and azurite that are ores of copper formed by oxidation and crystallization. You can be assured that there are many other minerals lying about on the surface. Of interest to mineral sifters: Copper ores are usually found among deposits of uranium, so chances are the place is radioactive. At the top of the trail is the boarded-up shaft of the old copper mine with an ore crusher in the opening. There is evidence of explosives here, and so there's cause for caution. Blasting caps can still be found in the debris. The caps are small and metallic and can look like a pencil. If they're old, they can be very volatile due to the degradation of gunpowder into nitro. Don't pick one up!

Some may consider this huge mess a disaster, while others see the garbage as historic relics. Beauty is in the eye of the beholder. Personally, I consider the place extremely interesting.

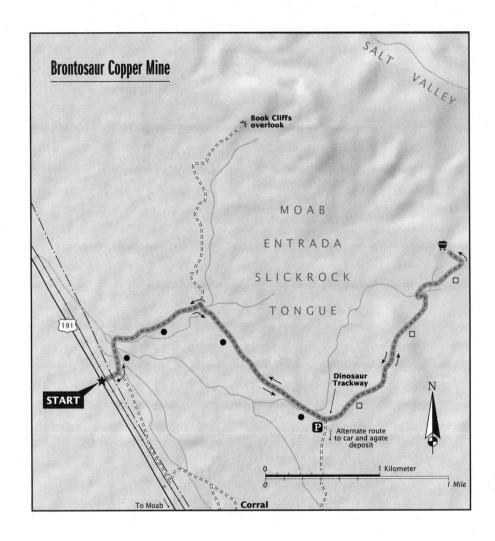

Brontosaur Copper Mine

SALT VALLEY

Book Cliffs overlook

M O A B

E N T R A D A

S L I C K R O C K

T O N G U E

191

Dinosaur Trackway

START

P

Alternate route to car and agate deposit

N

0   1 Kilometer

0   1 Mile

To Moab

Corral

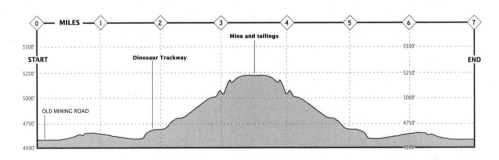

| 0 | MILES | 1 | 2 | 3 | 4 | 5 | 6 | 7 |

Mine and tailings

5500'

START

Dinosaur Trackway

END

5250'

5000'

OLD MINING ROAD

4750'

4500'

5500'

5250'

5000'

4750'

4500'

Salt Valley

Miles and Directions

0.0   **START** by taking the right-hand spur at the Y.

0.1   Take a left at the Y.

0.8   Take a right at the Y. (The signed right-hand turn to the dinosaur tracks goes to the same place, but the left is a tad more challenging.)

1.4   A seeping spring in the road causes a mud puddle that remains most of the year.

1.7   This is the parking area for the dinosaur tracks. Go up the hill toward the tracks.

1.8   You are now at the dinosaur trackway.

2.4   There's an optional slickrock play area to the right that affords a chance to get in some bunny-hopping and ledge practice.

2.7   Take the right-hand spur past the old Chevy truck remnants that lie off the trail to your right.

2.9   Take the left spur up the hill.

3.0   The mining PVC sluice is on your left.

3.3   Take a left to the mine at the top of the hill. Straight ahead is a view of Salt Valley, which warrants a visit if you are carrying a camera.

3.5   Reach the mine and tailings. After enjoying the mining area, turn around and ride back the way you came in.

7.0   Arrive back at your vehicle.

Ride Information

Trail Contacts
Bureau of Land Management
82 E. Dogwood
Moab, UT 84532
(435) 259-2196
Utah State School and Institutional
Trust Lands Administration
1165 South US 191, Ste. 5

Moab, UT 84532
(435) 259-3760

Schedule
Trail is open year-round but is best during spring and fall.

Maps
USGS maps: Valley City, Klondike Bluffs

DINOSAUR TRACKWAY SITE
The Jurassic beings of 150 million years ago left their marks along the trail. Among dinosaurs tracks found in this layer are the stegosaurus, sauropods like the brontosaurs (apatosaurus) and diplodocus, and theropods like the allosaurus (T. rex's uncle). In 1989 the site below the old copper mine across from the Moab airport became the first brontosaur trackway to be discovered in Utah. It is unique in that the tracks record the animal making a hard turn to the right. Above the sauropod tracks are a series of large theropod tracks, most likely allosaurus. The alternating long and short steps of this large animal reveal an irregular gait, perhaps the result of a limp. Visible during hours of low sun angle, there are a series of smaller theropod tracks just to the right of the sauropod tracks facing up the hill.

Note for photographers:

If you are here to take photographs, you will want to arrive early in the morning or late in the afternoon when the sun is low enough to provide shadows enabling you to recognize the more subtle dinosaur tracks barely visible at other times of day.

Note for rockhounds:

Heading down from the mine to the dinosaur track parking area, there is an opportunity to visit a particularly interesting deposit of agate if you go left instead right back to your vehicle. After taking the alternate left, in about 0.5 mile there will be a small hill on the left past a shallow gully. Keep an eye out for increased evidence of shards of agate. On top of the hill you'll find a fantastic agate deposit with stones of every size and color imaginable. Many of the Native American middens found on the Klondike Bluffs ride (Ride 3) were quarried from this very spot. It is illegal to take these stones from public lands.

Bad Mud at Klondike

The group moved in under the low sandstone overhang locals call "Fred Flintstone's house." I warned them of the little land mines that Mother Nature has set out for us in the Klondike Bluffs area. "The rattlesnakes are only a problem if you sit on one. I would worry more about scorpions in this rubble and in the bark of that juniper. Make sure you check your helmet when you pick it up."

"Scorpions?" Janice's eyes popped out.

The group was East Coast hodgepodge, as diverse as could be imagined, with a common bond established by the belief that nature was unnatural and frightening. While their skills were novice, their senses of humor were advanced. Thank God.

Out in Wilma's garden it began to hail pellets the size of Ping-Pong balls. The temperature dropped thirty degrees in a matter of seconds and lightning was striking in every direction. The thunder was deafening.

Judy, my sweep rider, patted me on the back, "Good call by the guide. Whew."

"What about the scorpions?" Janice insisted.

"Scorpions like to crawl into your helmet. There are two kinds. The big ones have a painful sting, but bark scorpions, the little translucent or yellow ones, are really deadly. Last year I heard about a woman on a river trip who left her helmet outside all night, and when she put it on a scorpion crawled in her ear."

"Oh my God!" Janice picked up her helmet, shook it out, and put it back on her head.

It will take hours to clean your bike after a ride like this.

"Did you know that scorpions are very intelligent? They actually make very good pets." I waited for the skeptics to raise their attentive little heads.

"Whaaat?" Peter sneered.

"Aw, come oan, pull tha otha one," Mary added.

"No, really, scorpions make good pets."

"Is he serious?" Peter asked.

"Usually," Judy answered.

I continued, "Last season I worked for Lin Ottinger, the fellow who owns the Moab Rock Shop. At one point someone gave him a huge scorpion. He put it in a small fish tank on his desk and spent an hour every morning hunting for spiders and crickets to feed it. Every day for the next few weeks he paraded the thing around on his hand and on his shoulder for tourists who came into his rock shop. He talked to it like a dog and let little children handle it as their parents cringed, cowered, and turned away.

"One morning Lin left the shop to guide a tour, leaving me to mind the shop and the scorpion. As soon as he split, the scorpion went limp in the corner of the tank. It looked dead. It just lay there loose and crumpled with a spider standing on its head.

"After a while I got worried. I shook the tank.

"Nothing.

"Every now and then during the day I looked in on the scorpion and it hadn't moved. I knew it was dead and that I was in for a cussing out when Lin came back.

"At 5:30 Lin returned from his tour. Before I could break the news to him that the scorpion was dead, he walked through the door and shouted, 'Daddy's home!'

"The scorpion hopped up and ran around the tank in circles like a dog in a pen.

"Lin walked up to the tank and stood over it.

"The scorpion tried to crawl up the side of the tank toward him.

"Lin put his hand into the tank and the scorpion ran up his arm onto his shoulder, as perky as you please.

"Lin said, 'That-a-boy.'"

There was a silent moment, then . . .

"Bullshit!" said Peter.

"No, he's telling the truth," insisted Judy. "If you knew Lin Ottinger you'd believe him for sure. Lin is the kind of person who hates people, but gets along with rattlesnakes and scorpions just fine."

The group huddled under the ledge for another thirty minutes as the cold front passed and I told another true tall tale. When the hail and lightning eased up, we mounted our bikes and headed toward the trailhead in a heavy drizzle.

I dreaded the next 5 miles and silently thanked myself for parking near the road. The van would probably be stranded in deep "gumbo" had I parked farther in.

I briefly dropped back to ride beside Judy. She was a godsend today, taking care of the folks at the back of the pack and filling the gaps in my botanical knowledge.

"Judy, I'm going to ride ahead and get the van ready. If the mud isn't too bad I'm going to drive in to pick up Tammy. Make sure she doesn't ride alone."

"Sure. She's really beat," Judy replied.

"I know."

Tammy had fallen just before the storm started. I approached her as she lay motionless on the slickrock, fearing she was unconscious.

"Tammy? Are you all right?" I asked, half expecting to have to drive in to scrape her up.

"Oh, I'm fine. I'm just enjoying lying down here. I'm really tired."

Alone, I rode off through the wet sand toward the van, hoping the rain had been localized toward the bluffs. Reaching the dirt road, I pedaled hard down the long stutter-bump straightaway, then climbed and crested the last hill. The mud was not bad up until that point, but when I picked up speed on the descent and took the gentle left turn at the bottom, my wheels suddenly slid sideways as if I were on ice. At 20 miles an hour, I was wallowing in and out of huge slimy ruts, constantly on the verge of disaster, scaring myself with the speed necessary to maintain momentum and not be bogged down.

The brakes froze up, and the chain began to skip across the rear cogs. I knew if I stopped I would have to walk all the way to the van in ankle-deep slime . . .

My worst fears had been realized. The shale sediments of the road were as messy as mud gets anywhere. Within seconds my bike picked up fifty pounds of the gray stuff. The brakes froze up, and the chain began to skip across the rear cogs. I knew if I stopped I would have to walk all the way to the van in ankle-deep slime, so I pedaled gingerly, coaxing as much speed as I could out of the stuttering drivetrain.

I prayed for my suspension pivots.

The tires were flinging chunks of gumbo goo into my face as I looked down and underneath to see the top of the fork, and seatstay links were now masses of clinging mud. I was amazed that I was still moving as I pedaled the clogged bike miraculously to the trailhead.

Three young women had just passed through the gate and were heading out on the trail.

"Don't do it! Look at my bike. Don't even think you can ride here today."

They looked at me like I was crazy and pedaled onward into the slime. Some people have no faith in their fellow man.

"You're gonna regret it," I called after them.

I got off my bike, opened the gate, and skated through the muck to the waiting van. Two kids playing in the mud at the trailhead helped me lift my seventy-five-pound mount onto the roof rack. I climbed back down, got into the driver's seat, and started the engine. For a few minutes I tried to maneuver the van through the parking area in the hope that I could coax it through the mud out onto the trail, but the wheels spun hopelessly and the van pitched sideways every time I hit the accelerator.

In front of me I saw the three women who had refused to listen to my pleas, returning to the trailhead, their bikes horribly clogged with mud. I didn't say, "I told you so," but I should have. In a while I saw Peter adeptly riding one of our precious full-suspension rental bikes through the mud. He had ridden the entire way, verifying the bike's mudworthiness and his own tenacity. Shortly thereafter Janice and Mary approached, walking their bikes. I could tell that this was the last mountain bike ride for them. It was back to shopping carts and BMWs. In a few more minutes Don walked up. His brand-new Rocky Mountain full-suspension bike was a horrible mess. The muddy drivetrain dangled from the bike, dragging through the mud like a mangled limb. He confessed, "When the mud began to make my chain skip, I shifted hard into a lower gear, and the derailleur sucked into the rear wheel and ripped off the bike." His rear dropout was bent inward at a ninety-degree angle. "You know, when I bought the bike I thought to myself, 'Why would such an expensive bike not have a replaceable derailleur hanger?'"

"Time for a new swingarm. At least with the full suspension you won't have to replace the whole frame." I tried in vain to encourage.

After another twenty minutes Tammy, Vernon, and Judy slid up to the trailhead.

Vernon said: "I was doing fine, but when I came down that slippery hill I knew I had to turn around to warn Tammy. Once I stopped I couldn't get started again."

I lifted the bikes onto the roof rack as the group made themselves comfortable inside the van. When I pulled onto the highway, the mud-laden bikes on the roof made the van so top-heavy that it felt as if it would topple over. I kept the speed to 45 miles an hour all the way back to Moab. It must have been a sight—a muddy van with mud-coated bikes on the roof, drooling clumps of gray gumbo syrup onto the cars behind.

For some reason I had thoroughly cleaned and vacuumed the company van the night before. What a mistake! Back at the shop it took two hours to hose the mud off the bikes and another two to clean the van. There is now more shale than gravel in my driveway, a constant reminder of that day on the Klondike Bluffs Trail when Fred Flintstone's house saved us from certain death, and the road turned into snot of the gods.

3 Klondike Bluffs

Start: From the Klondike Bluffs Trailhead.
Length: 15.4-mile out-and-back.
Approximate riding time: 2 to 4 hours, depending on your fitness level and interests.
Difficulty: Technically easy to moderate. Deep sand and a few ledges and slickrock transitions offer challenges for novice to intermediate riders. Physically easy to moderate. The route is a piece of cake for intermediates, but the steady climb can be trying for kids and novices.
Trail surface: A 2WD dirt road, a 4WD mining road, and a short singletrack. Slickrock, sand, bedrock, shale, and loose sediments.

Lay of the land: Subdesert expanse leading to the Moab Entrada Slickrock Tongue. Cottonwoods are seen in wash bottoms, and piñon and juniper trees spring from cracks in the slickrock.
Total climbing: 1,313 feet.
Land status: Bureau of Land Management (BLM) and Utah State Trust lands.
Other trail users: Equestrians, hikers, and off-road vehicles (ORV)—but this is predominantly a mountain bike trail.
Best seasons: Spring and fall.

Environmental concerns: Extremely fragile! Cryptobiotic soil crusts and rare desert mosses abound on and between the slickrock. Stay on the trail at all times. If it is alive or it looks like dirt and it is off the trail, don't ride or step on it. You're in the desert. Things revegetate very slowly out here. Just look at the mountain bike tracks out here and you'll get the picture. If you leave a track, it's gonna be here for 200 years or more.

Warning! This area is impassable when wet. The bluffs can be a very dangerous place in the event of a thunderstorm. The top of the trail is especially exposed to lightning strikes.

Getting there: From Moab: Drive north 16.6 miles on U.S. Route 191. At a point 0.4 mile past mile marker 142, turn into the unmarked, impacted area to the right and park your vehicle. Mount up and go through the gate to the east, closing the gate behind you. Beyond the cattle gate, adjacent to the parking area, is a BLM trail marker. Just follow the road.

The Ride

This trail is fairly well marked and maintained. Other routes in this area utilizing the old mining road network that weaves through the gullies and hills are best explored with the assistance of a guide—one who can offer you skills lessons, geology workshops, and dinosaur hunts. The consequences of getting lost can be dire at Klondike Bluffs, especially in the heat of summer, so stay on the main route if you are not riding with a legally qualified guide.

At many points in time, as the Cretaceous seas repeatedly intruded and retreated, this area was part of the shoreline. Evidence remains in the form of layers upon layers of petrified mudflats and tidal washes, locally referred to as "ripple rock." Here sauropod and allosaur roamed, foraged, and hunted, leaving tracks in the soft mud. Despite the rich deposits of dinosaur bone at the top of the Morrison formation to

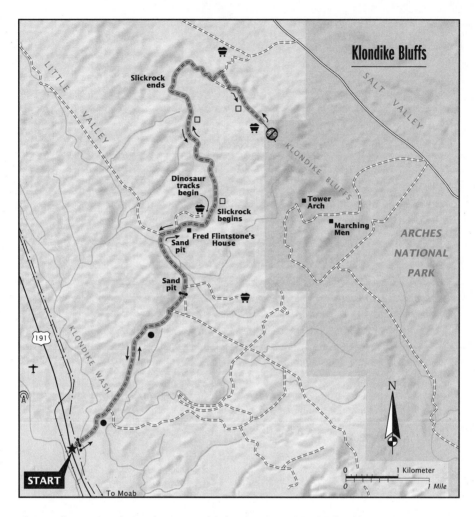

Klondike Bluffs

LITTLE VALLEY

SALT VALLEY

Slickrock ends

KLONDIKE BLUFFS

Dinosaur tracks begin

Slickrock begins

Tower Arch

Marching Men

Fred Flintstone's House

Sand pit

Sand pit

ARCHES

NATIONAL

PARK

191

KLONDIKE WASH

N

0   1 Kilometer

0   1 Mile

START

To Moab

the north, many paleontologists avoid the site due to its high radioactivity.

Yes, like most Moab rides, Klondike Bluffs is set upon a uranium-mining and exploration route. Huge tractors carrying core-sample drilling rigs crunched across the slickrock and cryptobiotic soil crusts, poking holes into the surface whenever the Geiger counter gave a high reading. Along the first few miles of the trail, at the base of the eroded hill to the left, tractor-tread marks and core-sample drilling holes remain alongside dinosaur tracks.

The out-and-back to Klondike Bluffs is a perfect introduction to Moab terrain, a Whitman's Sampler of southeastern Utah's mountain bike challenges and canyon country geology. This area's easy-to-moderate slickrock and ledges are perfect preparation before you step up to the bigger surf.

A note of caution. The slickrock to the south may be tempting, but stay against the hill to the north until you reach the huge cairn and painted dotted white line marking the slickrock traverse. Stay on the cairned and marked trail. The slickrock to the south is a maze of deep washes, small canyons, and is mostly inside Arches National Park, where off-road vehicles (including mountain bikes) are forbidden by law. The Park Service strictly enforces this. Remember, the side canyons below and above Klondike Bluffs Trail are hauntingly similar in appearance to the small canyon-gully that carries the main trail out to the slickrock. If you get lost, you may travel miles without realizing you are in the wrong gully, until you notice it is a dead end. Whoops.

Wildlife attractions at Klondike Bluffs include raptors, snakes, lizards, frogs, deer, rabbits, jackrabbits, bobcats, coyotes, mountain lions, and antelope squirrels. The jackrabbits can be so large that you may mistake them for deer, but they generally travel during the early morning, before most humans stir. Antelope squirrels (or picas) are small ground creatures with erect white tails like a white-tailed deer. Antelope squirrels do not drink water and possess a body temperature and metabolism unique to their species.

When visiting Klondike Bluffs keep in mind that it is unlawful to collect any antiquities or dinosaur bone. Very steep fines and long jail terms are levied against transgressors. As leader of many tours into this area, I extend a sincere and personal plea to treat this area with extreme respect—though there is certainly a lot of evidence of disrespect.

Miles and Directions

0.0 **START:** Take your bike through the gate and pedal northeast on the dirt road.

2.6 After a short descent that curves to the right, take the marked trail spur that bears left at the Y in the road. Just ahead is a funky cattle gate that gets trashed beyond function at times. Close it once you are through.

3.6 The green and red banded cliffs of the Morrison formation are on your left.

3.9 Just past the sandy wash under the cottonwood tree, take the spur right at the T.

4.2 The overhang to your right is called Fred Flintstone's House.

4.5 Dropping down a small hill, you end up on the slickrock shelf. On your left, just before the hill begins to ascend the slickrock, are a few fine examples of dinosaur tracks. Examining these will get you in tune to recognizing tracks farther up the hill. Keep an eye on the base of the hill on your left as you ride ahead. There are a lot more tracks to find on

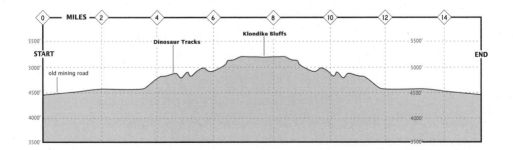

the sandstone surface, where they become visible as the hill erodes away. As they become exposed, they begin to erode into the potholes—which you'll be dodging as you climb the slickrock. Avoid stepping or riding in the tracks!

5.7 At this point you'll see a large cairn (pile of rocks) on the hill to your left. I personally have been laying cairns in front of the best dinosaur tracking area here, so if you are moved by their rarity and beauty, please help me in building this wall of stone to keep jeeps from riding over them. The trail crosses the G-out crack to your right and heads around the hill. After rounding the hill, do not follow the 4WD track against the hill to your left (it should be blocked off); rather, follow the cairns and the painted white lines right onto the slickrock. The Moab Tongue of the Entrada slickrock generally erodes into parallel rows. Follow this particular finger up along the cairns and painted markers. Please, stay off the cryptobiotic soils and avoid the water-catching potholes. Look to your left and right to see the damage bikes have done to the cryptobiotic crusts. If you're a nature lover and wonder what this place looked like before mountain bikes, ride the first trail in this book, but please try to keep what has happened at Klondike Bluffs from happening there. *Stay on the trail. Don't cross the moss. No bikin' on the lichen. Tiptoe through the crypto.*

CONCRETIONS IN SANDSTONE AND ROCK VARNISH
The orange to dark red rocks, ridges, elevated brown chunks, and vivid stains in the slickrock at the bluffs are sandstone concretions. These are formed whenever sand sediments cover an organic compound. The organic material can be anything from leaves to algae to pollen to dino pee. Over eons sedimentary sand hardens into sandstone, and trapped organic matter breaks down into simple compounds that leach heavy metals and minerals from rainwaters seeping through the rock. This causes the area of organic material to become far more dense than the surrounding rock. Over millions of years the sandstone erodes away and the dense "concretions" fall out onto the ground. At Klondike Bluffs some concretions may appear as rings of a growing tree or like huge flowers preserved in the rock; as calcite marbles or randomly shaped brown bumps. Some concretions in other areas are so perfectly round that the original settlers thought them to be marbles for a game played by the ancient peoples who once lived here. They were given the name "Moki Marbles." Moki was the name originally given to these early peoples by white settlers. It is another Navajo word that is not a suitable name for these remarkable ancients. It translates simply as "dead." (See the preface for more information on the "Moki.")

The baked brown, flat, and sometimes shiny surface on the rocks of the bluffs is often called "rock varnish," the result of oxygen, sunlight, and water interacting with iron and manganese in the rock.

6.5 As you reach the base of the hill, a brown trail marker directs you onto the spur to the right along the base of the eroded hill to your left.

7.4 Near the end of the trail—below the singletrack that snakes up the hill into Arches and about 100 yards to your right—you can see an old uranium mine with a large wooden sluice container and cinder-block collection pond where water-soluble uranium was separated from rock collected from the cliff to the southwest.

7.7 At the top of this singletrack, you'll have to dismount and hike into the park. But before you do, examine the crest of the copper mine tailings to your right (south). Be careful! The tailings are very loose rock and the mineshaft behind and in these tailings is vertical, supported by a low-tech system of posts and ties. If you walk around to the right just under the juniper tree against the hill, you'll have a good vantage point from which to see the shaft—while you safely hold on to a limb of the tree. Leave your bike at the top of the climb and hike into Arches National Park on the obvious trail behind the signs. Take a left when you reach the slickrock and follow the cairns along the eastern edge that overlooks Salt Valley. In the park at the top to the trail, you'll notice Stone Age middens sparkling in the sand on the way to the bluffs. These chips and chunks are chert, a form of volcanic stone that ancient peoples who inhabited this area used to shape tools, knives, and arrowheads. Large chunks of broken chert signal areas where men hunted, foraged, and camped. Small chips signal where they lived with their families and worked the raw pieces into fine tools. This particular spot was a base camp for the entire family. Examine the middens, but please, do not walk across them or put them in your pocket. Up ahead are the bluffs. The view is spectacular, and if you have forgotten your camera, this is where you'll be kicking yourself. The bright crimson rocks lying on top of the sandstone and the strange elevated shapes to your left, at the point before you reach the bluffs, are sandstone concretions. The scenic area here is great for hiking, but cleats can be dangerous on the exposed cliffs, so exercise caution if you choose to venture out onto the bluffs. Turn around and return via the same route.

15.4 Arrive at your vehicle.

Ride Information

Trail Contacts

Moab Bike Patrol
c/o Bureau of Land Management
82 E. Dogwood
Moab, UT 84532
(435) 259-2196

Utah State School and Institutional Trust Lands Administration
1165 South US 191, Ste. 5
Moab, UT 84532
(435) 259-3760

Schedule

Trail is open year-round but is best during spring and fall.

Maps

USGS maps: Merrimac Butte, Klondike Bluffs
Moab East Trail Map by Latitude 40° Inc.
Moab Recreation Map by F. H. Barnes

In Addition

Stone Age Middens

Middens are essentially ancient garbage, the trash of Stone Age cultures; however, they amount to an invaluable archaeological record of just where and how ancient peoples lived and survived. In the Moab area these artifacts are mostly pottery shards, corncobs, and the scraps of stone weapon- and tool-making. Most evidence of use in this area by human residents—aside from the Europeans, who have made an unmistakable impact through mining—reflects the Archaic, Anasazi, Fremont, and Ute Native peoples who hunted below the buttes and camped atop the Entrada Slickrock Tongue and in various places across the rock expanse. Though I use the names *Fremont* and *Anasazi,* for lack of better terms, the actual people to whom they refer would probably take offense at the names. The Navajo word *anasazi,* for instance, loosely translates to "ancient enemies."

The middens on top of Klondike Bluffs are evidence of a settlement, not just an encampment. The small stone chippings scattered about under the junipers and piñons were left by artisans working on the smallest details of agate and chert tools and arrowheads. There are a few other sites along the slickrock below Klondike Bluffs; many more are scattered about in almost every area mentioned in this book. Sometimes trails travel across these ancient homes or campsites, and the middens are sadly being pulverized by the tires of off-road vehicles (ORV) and mountain bikes—as well as the feet of horses, cows, and people. I have been picking up middens over the past few years and tossing them in the sand above any track. I try to block off these sections of trail wherever possible in order to preserve what remains of the integrity of these sites. If you come across a spot like this, please toss any chips off the trail onto the sand beyond the track.

Chunky "hunting camp" middens at Klondike Bluffs are found to the north of the trail on top of and at the base of the eroded hill. Here the chert was broken into pieces small enough to carry back to the main camp.

The use of vibrant-colored chert and agate is evidence of artisans who were concerned with beauty *and* functionality. In some cases the color of a specific instrument had a symbolic meaning. I have seen arrowheads and tools made out of very interesting pieces of agate, where colors collide to form beautiful rainbows of stone. Arrowheads of pure white chert that end in a point of bright red most likely represented the drawing of blood. Tools created by master craftsmen required dedication and hard work beyond simple toolmaking. The brightly colored chert and agate found in the middens along the Klondike Bluffs Trail come from the area to the north. The pinkish and blue hues come from across the highway to the west in the area of the Monitor and Merrimac Trail.

Fragments in a Native American midden.

Please do not disturb the middens and do not remove stone tools or arrowheads from the sites. If you find a particularly beautiful example in the trail, the Bureau of Land Management (BLM) requests that you place it out of harm's way. If you're carrying a camera, take a picture of it and bring the photo and a description of where the object is to the BLM office just south of town at 82 East Dogwood Avenue.

If you wish to view examples of pristine stone tools or arrowheads, visit the Dan O'Laurie Museum next to the Grand County Library, across from the courthouse on Center Street. Lin Ottinger's Moab Rock Shop will have originals and even finer replicas for sale. Replicas worked by local artisans like Donny Dale are especially desirable and make wonderful gifts for anyone interested in Native American stonework. The work of many local artisans who specialize in creating stone tool and weapon replicas for museums and educational displays appreciates in value over time.

Dalton Wells Fourth of July Celebration

O n July 4, 1997, I spent the morning hours scouting north of Moab. It is ironic that I visited this particular historic marker on Independence Day. At home, my twelve-year-old son was beside himself with excitement in anticipation of sparklers, firecrackers, and the fireworks show at Spanish Valley Arena scheduled for the evening hours. Driving out of town I remembered when I was twelve and John Kennedy was assassinated. I thought of my own personal patriotic leaders and a lump grew in my throat. Bobby Kennedy was the only politician I ever got excited about voting for. I haven't registered and voted since he was killed. When Martin Luther King was killed I was in college not to get an education, but to avoid the draft. Watching a couple of dear friends come back from Vietnam in boxes cemented the bitterness I have harbored since I was twelve and things went south for the United States of America. When Richard Nixon was elected president, that was enough for me to leave the country and take up residence in Holland. It just seems that since I was twelve years old it has rained puss on my Fourth of July parade year after year. I can't help it if this date reminds me of the worst aspects of being an American. It just does. I've still got cultural shell shock, and firecrackers in celebration of war give me a headache and a form of post-traumatic stress that only us "hippies" understand. I wasn't looking forward to taking my boy out to Spanish Valley to watch the

fireworks, but at least riding through this hauntingly beautiful place managed to elicit a love of country separate from nationalism and my sour government grapes.

As I pulled into the parking area to read the historic marker at Dalton Wells Road, fittingly, in the distance, I saw a family gathered at the trailhead, standing together, in one another's arms, staring solemnly at the plaque. At first I thought they were Japanese tourists, but as I grew closer I could see and hear they were obviously

Americans, Japanese Americans, representing four generations. After a few minutes the group moved away from the marker, tears streaming down their faces. Without a word they got into a van and drove away. It was then that I read the marker for the first time. I knew what it referred to, so I'd never felt the need to read it, but reading the words on this steel plaque brought back that horrible clarity that seems to keep me from celebrating the Fourth of July.

The small marker just off the highway is a reminder of two great tragedies in American history and the ironies that surround them. Beyond the marker, at the base of the cliffs of the Morrison formation, next to the small grove of cottonwoods, stood the Dalton Wells Civilian Corps Camp, one of many built nationwide during the Great Depression. From 1933 to 1942 the camp housed 200 young men who assisted with public works projects, earning a small wage to send back to starving families in the dust bowl. In 1943 the facility was converted into a concentration camp for male Japanese American citizens during the Second World War. Men sent here were considered "troublemakers" in other camps. These men and their families had been charged with no crime, but because they were racially different they were rounded up and shipped off, like the Jews in Germany. Men who stepped out of line, complained, or protested this unfair treatment were separated from family and friends and brought here to Dalton Wells. After a train ride to the small town of Thompson to the north, the men were driven to this bleak and lonely location in buses with windows painted black. Here they were kept until, after a couple of nasty incidents that resulted in the beating of an informer and the killing of inmates by camp guards, they were separated and shipped off to other camps. The Dalton Wells camp was burned shortly thereafter, along with all records of the event in the National Archives. The only remaining testament is in the office of the *Times Independent*, the local Moab newspaper.

After a few minutes the group moved away from the marker, tears streaming down their faces. Without a word they got into a van and drove away.

Today all that remains of the camp is the tiny stand of cottonwood trees planted by the men of the Civilian Corps, and the marker placed here by the state, a bold reminder of just how awful Americans can treat Americans. I stood in front of this tiny monument and remembered intolerance, racism, and bigotry, and, frankly, I felt like crap. Well, at least the author of the plaque tried to right a bit of the wrong done here by being blunt and honest.

4 Bar M Loop

Start: From the Gemini Bridges parking area just off of U.S. Route 191 west of the highway.
Length: 7.5 miles, if done on its own. Can be added to Old Moab Highway route.
Approximate riding time: Half an hour to 2 hours, if done on its own.
Difficulty: Physically easy. Technically easy to moderate at times.
Trail surface: Hardpack, sand, rock, and packed loam on 4WD track.
Lay of the land: This ride travels along a flat road, then over rolling hills, affording views of Arches National Park. There is barely any available shade on the route. Due to its proximity and use of the Old Moab Highway, it is a perfect extension for anyone who wants a technically easy ride with a bit more mileage.
Total climbing: 200 feet.
Land status: Bureau of Land Management (BLM) and Utah State Trust lands.
Other trail users: 4WDs, ATVs, motorcycles.
Best seasons: Spring and fall.

Environmental concerns: Do not venture off trail. This ride skirts the border of Arches National Park and restricted BLM lands where off-road vehicles, including bicycles, are prohibited. The fine for riding on restricted lands is $500.

Getting there: From Moab drive north on US 191 to the Gemini Bridges Trailhead on the west side of the road. Turn into the parking area, grab your gear and bikes. Be careful of traffic as you cross the highway eastward to the Old Moab Highway above the Bar-M Chuckwagon restaurant.

The Ride

This route is fine for novices, even families with children. There are many small climbs and a couple of spots where the trail gets a tad technical, but this is indeed a ride for anyone scared shitless by other trails in this book. It is short, near the highway, and easy to navigate. The scattered stone you see on the trail is chert, a form of agate used by Native Americans to produce tools and weapons.

Miles and Directions

0.0 Cross US 191 to the Bar-M Chuckwagon (a funky restaurant with a covered wagon out front). You cannot see the restaurant until you are close to it.

0.1 Go right on the track marked as the Bar M Loop.

0.55 Stay straight, avoiding the spur to the right.

1.36 Go right just before Seven Mile Canyon wash passes under the highway. As you travel away from the highway, you come in contact with the gas pipline right-of-way. The trail will offer you a few fast rollercoaster hills. Be careful to control your speed, if you are a novice.

1.73 Go left away from the gas pipeline and into the sandy wash bottom.

The beginning of the loop

2.87 Stay straight. Avoid the spur to the right.

3.89 Bear right around the small hill.

4.2 Stay straight. Avoid the spur to the right.

4.7 Go right at the T heading west to the Old Moab Highway. This little section of trail is a bit more technical than the rest of the ride, so be sure to watch your speed on the downhill and be ready for some large rocks after you twist through an area of confusing spurs in both directions. Stay on the main trail. **Option:** If you want more mileage, more scenery, and a chance to get off the bike and hike into a rarely visited portion of Arches National Park, here is your chance. Go left at mile 4.7 to continue along the eroded hill you have kept on your right for the past few miles. At one point prior to the park fence there is a view of a beautiful box canyon to your left. Be careful if you walk out to the viewpoint over the canyon to step only on rock, avoiding mosses and cryptobiotic soil crusts. If you must travel over sand, make sure it is in a watercourse. Do not leave footprints—they last a long time, as you will see. Continuing on past the overlook you will come to a fence at the park boundary. From here you must leave your bike and walk. Stay on existing trail, avoiding the fragile soil crusts and mosses. On your return, turn left along the hill following the pur at mile 4.7. There is a black stain from an old garbage heap that signals your left-hand turn.

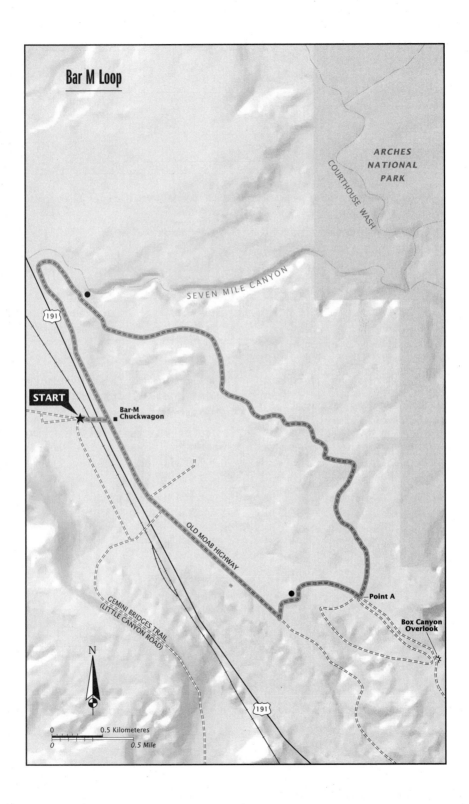

Bar M Loop

ARCHES
NATIONAL
PARK

COURTHOUSE WASH

SEVEN MILE CANYON

191

START

Bar-M
Chuckwagon

OLD MOAB HIGHWAY

GEMINI BRIDGES TRAIL
(LITTLE CANYON ROAD)

Point A

Box Canyon
Overlook

191

N

0   0.5 Kilometeres

0   0.5 Mile

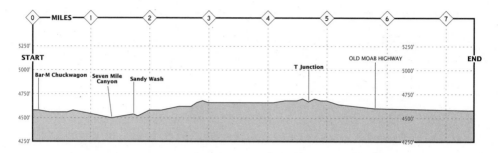

5.8 Go right onto the Old Moab Highway. This is a long straightaway that takes you directly to the Bar-M parking lot.

7.4 Go left at the Bar-M. Cross US 191 to your waiting vehicle.

7.5 Trailhead.

Ride Information

Trail Contacts

Moab Bike Patrol
c/o Bureau of Land Management
82 E. Dogwood
Moab, UT 84532
(435) 259–2196

Utah State School and Institutional Trust Lands Administration
1165 South US 191, Ste. 5
Moab, UT 84532
(435) 259–3760

Schedule

Trail is open year-round but is best during spring and fall.

Maps

USGS maps: Gold Bar Canyon, Merrimac Butte
Moab East Trail Map by Latitude 40° Inc.
Moab Recreation Map by F. H. Barnes

Dogs Are Family

I was the only puppy Sheba ever had. She slept in my room for ten years, in my bed when it was cold, next to the window when it was hot. From kindergarten to high school, Sheba taught me more about life than both parents, the public school system, and ten years of higher education ending in two undergraduate and one "terminal" degree.

Sheba was a collie, like that TV icon Lassie; the perfect companion for a young boy, the perfect bike buddy. Sheba followed on tight singletrack through briers and spiderwebs, panting and trotting in rhythm to my pedaling, her nose inches from the back tire of my Schwinn cruiser. She always knew the way home, and her purpose in life was making sure I got there.

Sheba's one vice was chasing cars on the dirt road in front of our house. As the town of Goldsboro, North Carolina, grew toward us, enveloping woodlands and fields, turning rural countryside into sparse suburbs, roads were paved, traffic increased, and Sheba eventually lost her game of automobile roulette.

I never kept pictures of girlfriends. I don't even have a picture of my deceased first wife, but I have a picture of Sheba. I take one look at her and remember what unconditional love really is.

One morning more than thirty years after Sheba went to dog heaven, I had a dream of resting my head on her heaving furry chest. The hypnotic sound and motion of her breathing, the soft sweetness of her scent were the very essence of peace, love, and tranquility. When I awoke, the smell of Sheba's fur remained in my nostrils.

I needed a dog. I needed a bike dog.

I went through the classifieds in the *Boulder Camera* over breakfast, found a woman named Darla with Australian shepherd puppies for sale, and drove 50 miles to Berthoud, Colorado, following the smell of that dream of Sheba.

When I walked into Darla's backyard, a ball of fluffy puppy galloped sideways over to me, yapping, snipping at my feet, nipping at my ankles, and tugging on my shoelaces. I picked it up . . . and it literally smiled at me, then sniffed and snapped at my nose playfully again, then smiled again and barked. Every color I had ever seen on a mammal was splashed across this puppy's face—Jackson Pollock's idea of a raccoon. Its eyes were honest brown with a tiny blue supernova exploding across the iris of the right eye.

I smelled its fur.

It was Sheba.

Some folks say that dogs are like us. People who love them know that dogs *are* us. The only thing we have over dogs is that we can balance a checkbook and dial a cell phone. The thing your dog understands best is you. Screw the checkbook. Your dog knows the checkbook is irrelevant. Dogs don't need a cell phone because they can read your mind. They know what you are feeling, when you are leaving, when you are coming back, when you are sick, when you need forgiveness, and when you need to be bitten. Even if *Homo sapiens* are too arrogant to consider themselves anything other than "masters," dogs are in control in just about every way—unless, of course, you do not love your dog. Dogs need to be loved, just like us. The only reason dogs don't live as long as we do is because they know that if we die, they are toast.

I had great expectations for the puppy I called Mookie, thinking, "This dog is going to be the best mountain bike companion imaginable. He's fast. He loves to run. He will protect . . . and obey."

Wrong.

From the first day I took him on a bike ride in the Rockies, Mookie began every ride like he was shot out of a cannon, nipping uncontrollably at ankles and heels, jumping well above handlebars to snap at noses, barking so loud that ears were ringing for the first ten minutes of the ride. It was not hard to understand what Mookie was saying with every muscle in his body: "Come on! Get your ass in gear, now! Let's go, damnit! Dee dee mow!"

Mookie barked louder than any dog, but once we were under way, he shut up. This silence signaled his second mode of operation: Tear off everywhere through the woods to test the distance he could safely track me and/or the group and still be able to pee on stuff. You wouldn't see him for minutes at a time, then he would burst from the woods right in front of your bike and begin to gather riders in "his" group to "protect" us from other riders and hikers on the trail. In other words, he scared the crap out of everyone on the trail, including me. There is something about an animal that looks like a psychedelic badger with a raccoon face coming at you, barking like crazy, teeth glaring in a smile (that just looks like a snarl to anyone but an Aussie owner). Mookie did this until he was totally exhausted. Then, and only then, would he settle down and allow me to control him . . . but if he rested, he went right back into aggressive-protective-containment mode, and once again we were all sheep to corral.

Mookie was, after all, an alpha male of the Australian shepherd breed, bred to work hard. His mom and dad were both working cattle dogs. Mookie was a Frisbee dog, not a bike dog; a friendly guard dog, not a cuddly whore. Give him a job and he literally grinned ear to ear. To him, existence meant the honor of doing a job right. He had every tool to fetch, herd, and protect. I have never met a more fair judge of the moment. To Mookie, the one attacked was always the one to defend, no matter the circumstances.

This is what Mookie, and Sheba, taught me.

I tend to put just about everything I do nowadays into a mountain bike context. Mookie never fit into that part of my life, but he guarded my family while I was out

Mookie

on the bike, guarded my wife on her hikes alone into wilderness, guarded my bikes in the shop when I was on the toilet. After he died I saw everything that he protected still standing in my life. He guarded my heart from a kind of loneliness that only a dog can soothe, and gave me a kind of understanding that gives me reason to believe, to know, that dogs are our equals, if not our superiors. Never once did I make a move that Mookie did not completely understand. If I hit him, he forgave me, because he understood my reasons, my flaws, my mistakes, my anger, my futility.

So out of love of man's best friend, the dog, out of respect for the environment, and the memory of Mookie and Sheba, I am offering the Old Moab Highway ride as a perfect trek for you and your dog. Other trails listed in this book that are fine and dandy for a dog to run are Sand Flats Road, Hurrah Pass, Gemini Bridges, and Flat Iron Mesa.

Dogs don't belong on environmentally sensitive rides, but they do deserve to have trails chosen especially for them. Sometimes you just cannot leave them at home.

5 Old Moab Highway

Start: From the turnout for the Old Moab Highway on U.S. Route 191 just north of the Arches National Park entrance.
Length: 8-mile out-and-back.
Approximate riding time: 1 hour for beginners and kids.
Difficulty: Technically very easy. This used to be a highway. It is wide and smooth. Physically easy. A bit of climbing, but nothing too steep. If you are taking kids, be sure to keep their speed under control on the way back. It is tempting to let it rip. There are a couple of sharp turns at speed.

Trail surface: Old highway and dirt road. Broken pavement, hard-packed dirt, and gravel.
Lay of the land: Tilted layers due to geological displacement of the Moab Fault. You will be climbing alongside a deep canyon, then across a flat area.
Total climbing: 331 feet.
Land status: Bureau of Land Management (BLM) and Utah State Trust lands.
Other trail users: Hikers, joggers, dog walkers, and motorists.
Best seasons: Late spring and early fall. Best avoided during the heat of midday during summer months.

Environmental concerns: Cryptobiotic soil crusts exist just off established trails.

Getting there: From Moab: Take US 191 north. Cross the bridge spanning the Colorado River. Continue past Potash Road and the entrance to Arches National Park. About 0.5 mile past the Arches National Park entrance and 6 miles from Moab, there is a large gravel parking area on the right side of the road. Park here and ride, following the deteriorating paved road that heads north and parallels US 191 along the edge of a colorful wash.

The Ride

Hey, beginners and families with little kids, welcome to the easiest ride in Moab. For others this bit of abandoned highway is a great way to shuttle Moab to or from Gemini Bridges Trail, the Eagle's Perch, Gold Bar Rim, Bull Canyon, Two Tortoise Rock, and Day Canyon Overlook, if you are without a motor vehicle. You can have a local shuttle service like Road Runner or Coyote take you to the top of Gemini Bridges and then ride all the way back to Moab via this route. The route described here is an out-and-back on the dirt road and deteriorating old two-lane highway that runs parallel to US 191.

As described here, the route is uphill from the parking area (just north of the present entrance to Arches National Park) and downhill going back south toward Moab from the Gemini Bridges Trailhead on US 191. Very hot in summer, it is still nice for early-morning rides and possibly in the late evening. If you choose to ride to or from Moab on your bike, be very careful of the Colorado River Bridge and the windy cruise along the highway between the bridge and Arches National Park entrance. Big trucks roll along this corridor, and the bridge has no shoulder. It can be deadly. Time your crossing well.

Eagle's Perch viewed from Old Arches Road

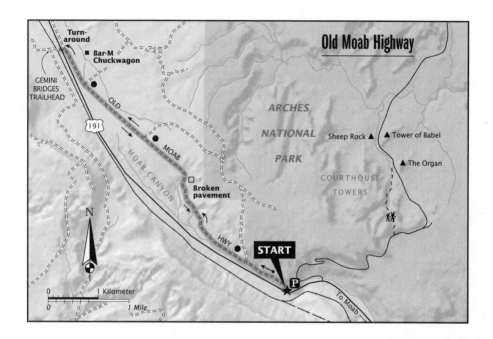

The ride takes you along the Moab Fault, a place where the unstable salt layers below collapsed millions of years ago. Going north from Moab, as you round the turn just past the Arches entrance, notice the geological layers slanting downward on your right and the sheer walls of the rim on your left. This is the point of greatest displacement. The geological layers to the west are as much as 3,700 feet above corresponding layers below you. This ride goes up on worn, degraded pavement, then flattens and turns to dirt as you ride out to the Bar-M Chuckwagon and the spur left to Gemini Bridges Trailhead. It may be considered boring, but for beginners and kids it may be just the ticket. If you are using this ride for a return to Moab from the Gemini Bridges Trail or zooming back down for the return trip to your vehicle, don't let gravity divert you from the really interesting erosion to the west. Below you is beautiful pink, purple, red, orange, green, and beige slickrock in small canyons at the southern end of the ride just before you reach the parking area adjacent to US 191.

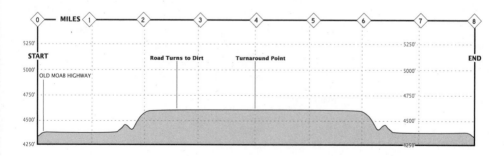

Miles and Directions

0.0   **START** from the parking lot and head north.

2.6   The road turns to dirt, then levels out.

4.0   After the flat area you come to a western tourist diversion called the Bar-M Chuckwagon. Some of the buildings are supposed to resemble an old western town, including a corral, a flagpole, and a restaurant. If you want to turn this into a destination, the place opens at 5:00 P.M. Across the highway and to the west of the Bar-M Chuckwagon is the Gemini Bridges Trailhead. Turn around for a downhill back to your vehicle, or cross the highway to join the Gemini Bridges Trail.

8.0   Arrive back at the parking area and your vehicle.

Ride Information

Trail Contacts

Bureau of Land Management
82 E. Dogwood
Moab, UT 84532
(435) 259–2196
Utah State School and Institutional Trust Lands Administration
1165 South US 191, Ste. 5
Moab, UT 84532
(435) 259–3760

Schedule

Trail is open year-round but is best during spring and fall.

Maps

USGS maps: Moab, Gold Bar Canyon, Merrimac Butte
Moab East Trail Map by Latitude 40° Inc.
Moab Recreation Map by F. H. Barnes

6 Arches Loop

Start: From the Old Moab Highway parking area just north of the Arches National Park entrance on U.S. Route 191.
Length: 26.1-mile loop.
Approximate riding time: 4 to 8 hours, depending on your fitness level and interests.
Difficulty: Technically easy to moderately difficult. The ride starts out easy enough as you skirt the edge of the Moab Entrada Slickrock Tongue. On the pipeline service road section, there are a few rollies that will require momentum to negotiate, but just before you reach the pumping station and Willow Springs Road (the old road into Arches National Park) you are presented with some very technical riding in sand and loose rock. Walk it. The rest of the ride is a piece of cake. Physically moderate to difficult. This is a long ride with some sandy

stretches, so you will be expending quite a bit of energy, especially on the road out of the park at the end of the ride.
Trail surface: Broken pavement, gravel, loose rock, sand, hardpack, and slickrock.
Lay of the land: The Moab Entrada Slickrock Tongue is the primary feature, with Courthouse Wash cutting a deep canyon through the middle. Arches National Park is simply indescribable. The Entrada and Navajo formations have eroded into some pretty strange features.
Total climbing: 2,148 feet.
Land status: Bureau of Land Management (BLM), Utah State Trust, and national park lands.
Other trail users: Hikers and off-road vehicles (ORV).
Best seasons: Spring and fall.

Environmental concerns: The route takes you through some fragile slickrock surfaces and areas where fragile soil crusts are just off the trail. If you stay on the route, there's no problem.

Getting there: From Moab: Take US 191 north. Cross the bridge spanning the Colorado River. Continue past Potash Road and the entrance to Arches National Park. About 0.5 mile past the Arches National Park entrance and 6 miles from Moab, there is a large gravel parking area on the right side of the road. Park here and ride following the deteriorating paved road that heads north and parallels US 191 along the edge of a colorful wash.

The Ride

This ride is a great way to experience Arches National Park on a mountain bike—a great ride for strong novices and intermediates, with only a bit of easily avoided technical challenge and plenty of mileage. It is perhaps the perfect first mountain bike ride for a strong road rider wishing to make the transition, but expect a lot of sand.

You may have to pay to exit the park at the present Arches National Park entrance. Currently the fee is $10.00 for a car and $5.00 for a bicycle. At any point, if you encounter a ranger, you may be asked to provide proof of payment or you'll have to pay on the spot.

The beginning of the ride takes place on the old highway into Moab, then the newly replaced natural gas pipeline service road. The final dirt portion of the ride takes on Willow Springs Road, the original entrance road into Arches National

Balanced Rock and friends

Park. Once you crest the first hill after leaving the Old Moab Highway, a series of interconnecting 4WD spurs can be confusing, but they afford a bit of scenic exploration if you want to deviate from the described route. The mileage here describes the most direct route. Mileage counts can become skewed if you twist around and explore, so pay attention to time spent and your mileage count.

Rolling terrain and Moab Entrada Slickrock Tongue expanses soon give way to sand as you join the pipeline service road and then Willow Springs Road. This ride enables you to visit many overlooks both on public lands outside the park and from the pavement in the park. The paved Arches Road can be crowded with cars, Winnebagos, and tour buses in peak season. That said, if you have never visited Arches National Park, the pavement section of the ride can be very rewarding. Be sure to take a camera.

Miles and Directions

0.0 **START** from the parking lot and head north on the decrepit asphalt road.

2.6 Just after the road turns to dirt, grab the first opportunity to turn right. Go uphill, avoiding spurs off the main route. I have documented all these spurs below to avoid confusion. This route can be confusing the first time you read it, though it is fairly straightforward when you ride it.

2.8 Go right.

2.9 Go right.

3.0 Continue straight.

3.2 Go left at the Y.

3.3 Go left at the Y. **Option.** Going right at the pile of garbage (nice, huh?) will take you on a 5-mile out-and-back detour that will end with a fence delineating the park boundary.

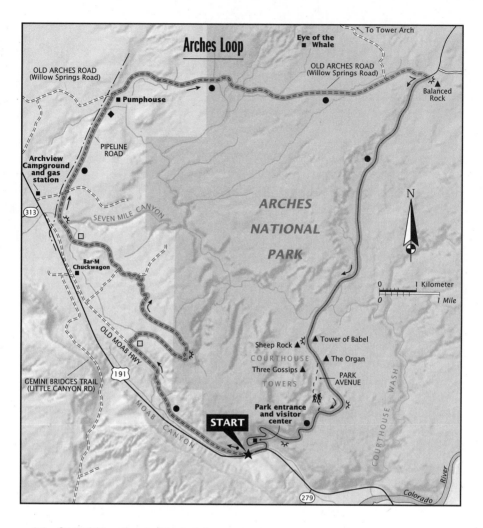

3.6 Go straight up the small bedrock face.

3.9 Go straight. (Left escapes to the pipeline service road.)

4.0 Bear right. (Left escapes to the pipeline service road.)

4.3 Take the sharp left around the hill. The downhill spur simply takes you onto a slickrock area that you may want to play on. Remember your mileage count and be careful not to cross any fragile soil crusts if you choose to freeform on the slickrock.

5.1 Veer left and west around the hill. Do not go right. Stay against the eroded hill to your left and you will have no problems.

5.4 Don't travel into the gully at the back of this cut. Bear north and downhill.

5.7 Go straight through the intersection on the dominant spur to the northwest.

5.9 Continue straight.

6.0 Continue to wrap around the hill, avoiding the downhill spur to the east.

6.9 Go left and west in the sand wash at the bottom of the hill.

7.1 Welcome to the pipeline service road. Follow it to the right. Going left will take you along the pipeline to the Bar-M Chuckwagon off the Old Moab Highway. If you wish to shorten the ride, this is a good place to do it.

7.3 Just prior to the pipeline, at marker 612, is a suitable place to walk down the narrow wash (do not cross the soil crusts—always walk in watercourses in the desert) to view Courthouse Wash. There is a singletrack along the edge that is tempting, but if you are sucked in by this singletrack, you should know that it is dangerously exposed on the edge of Courthouse Wash and could get you twisted around if you are not familiar with the area.

7.5 Go through the fence and straight ahead across the wash bottom, and then go uphill to reconnect with the pipeline road.

7.9 Go left at the Y.

8.1 Go straight through this intersection, avoiding spurs left and right. Follow the pipeline, avoiding the dominant road. If you want an emergency exit, you can go left to US 191. The Archview Campground and gas station are visible to the northwest.

9.5 Follow the pipeline markers downhill to the pumphouse in the distance. The pumphouse has a gasoline engine in it, so you will probably be able to hear it in the distance.

10.0 Enter the wash and ride about 100 feet to the right, where you can exit the wash bottom at the small concrete culvert or just beyond to regain the trail to the pumphouse.

10.4 Go right onto Willow Springs Road just past the pumphouse. Stay on the main road, avoiding the following spurs to the left, including the continuation of the pipeline road.

11.0 Stay right.

11.6 Stay right.

11.8 Go left, avoiding the steep uphill.

12.3 You are now in Arches National Park. Do you have a park pass? If you complete the loop back to US 191, you will eventually have to pay the entrance fee. Fees are always going up. Currently, they are $10.00 per motor vehicle and $5.00 per bike.

15.6 The sandy track to your left heads out to the Eye of the Whale and to Tower Arch below Klondike Bluffs. Stay straight on the main track toward Balanced Rock.

16.4 You made it to the Arches Road. Behind you is a picnic area with a toilet; in front is Balanced Rock. Go right on the pavement for a road tour of the park. As you continue down Arches Road, you will see Brigham's Unit on your right (a giant stone penis).

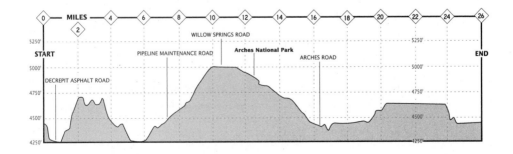

Delicate Arch is not on the route, but it's worth the hike—1.5 miles out and 1.5 miles back.

21.5 Courthouse Wash and some of the more famous (and mentionable) rock formations of the park, including the Tower of Babel, Three Gossips, the Organ, Nefertiti, and Park Avenue. All features except Brigham are well marked and have pull-outs.

25.5 The park entrance. Pay and head up to US 191 (if you time your return after 7:00 P.M., you will not have to pay). Turn right when you emerge onto the highway and head north.

26.1 Arrive at your vehicle.

Ride Information

Trail Contacts

Arches National Park
Visitor Center, US 191
Moab, UT 84532
(435) 719-2100
Moab Bike Patrol
c/o Bureau of Land Management
82 E. Dogwood
Moab, UT 84532
(435) 259-2196
Utah State School and Institutional Trust Lands Administration
1165 South US 191, Ste. 5
Moab, UT 84532
(435) 259-3760

Schedule

Trail is open year-round but is best during spring and fall.

Fees and Permits

Arches National Park: Fees are always going up. Currently, they are $10.00 per motor vehicle and $5.00 per bike.

Maps

USGS maps: Moab, Gold Bar, Merrimac Butte, Windows Section
Moab East Trail Map by Latitude 40° Inc.
Moab Recreation Map by F. H. Barnes

7 Yellow Jacket Canyon

Start: From the boat ramp parking area just west of the Dewey Bridge.

Length: 14.4-mile loop.

Approximate riding time: 2 to 4 hours.

Difficulty: Technically moderate. The ride has a few ledges at the start and some wheel-sucking sand. Loose, rocky climbs are sparse, but happen. Physically moderate to difficult, depending on sand conditions. During seasons when we receive a healthy dose of rain, the sand will be packed. If we haven't seen rain or snow in quite a while, the sand becomes very deep. This is the kind of sand people are talking about when they say: "Sand sucks!"

Trail surface: A 4WD track and a paved road with sand, hardpack, bedrock, a small amount of slickrock, gravel, and loose rock.

Lay of the land: Hilly and rolling high desert. Rolling piñon and juniper arid lands with varied surface.

Total climbing: 886 feet.

Land status: Bureau of Land Management (BLM) land.

Other trail users: Equestrians and off-road vehicles (ORV).

Best seasons: Spring and fall.

Environmental concerns: As with all desert and subdesert rides, do not venture off the trail, out of respect for the fragile soil crusts and mosses and lichens that inhabit virgin surfaces.

Getting there: From Moab: Drive north on U.S. Route 191 and take a right onto Utah Route 128. Reset your mileage counter. Parking for the trailhead is 29 miles—just before the Dewey Bridge on the left-hand side of the road. Park at the boat launch and ride across the highway bridge to the trailhead 0.4 mile away. If you wish, you can ride across on the Dewey Bridge, but beware. The cacti and goatheads will flatten your tires if you are not careful—not a great way to start your ride.

The Ride

This ride has sandy sections and transitions and enough rough trail challenges, climbs and descents, and scenic beauty to make it a standout section of the Kokopelli Trail system (which travels 150 miles from Loma, Colorado, to Moab). The entire trip is overrated, but undeniably scenic. Some of the trail system is fine mountain biking for strong intermediate riders who want to be challenged by distance rather than surface, but only a few short sections of the system can be considered truly technically challenging. Awful sand and boring gravel roads dominate the bulk of the Kokopelli system, overshadowing sparse sections of rock and classic rough trail considered by locals to be difficult and dangerous—the sort of stuff some of us crave.

This is a section of the Kokopelli about forty minutes east of town toward Cisco on the river road. Starting at the historic Dewey Bridge, the trail offers a bit of technical and physical challenge, as well as geological areas of interest. But the real reason to ride this trail is for sweeping vistas of the Colorado River, Fisher Towers, and the La Sal Mountains.

Yellow Jacket presents beautiful views of the La Sal Mountains.

I ride this trail early in the morning in summer and never see other riders, but since it is part of a well-publicized trail system, the Bureau of Land Management has done a fine job of marking the route. All turns and spurs listed here were indicated by markers the last time I was on the trail. The markers have been known to disappear, so trust the mileage counts and use the markers to boost your confidence.

The ride starts with a climb over worn and angular bedrock, loose rock, hardpack, and sand. It then drops you into a sand straightaway. Once you're back on the rock, the trail gets really interesting and a bit more challenging until it crosses into the Morrison formation into the backside of the Yellow Cat District and becomes more open and desolate. Be sure to stop on top of the hills for the incredible views off to the southwest. Like most rides in Moab, there is no shade on the trail, so be sure to take more water. Portions of this trail are impassable when wet.

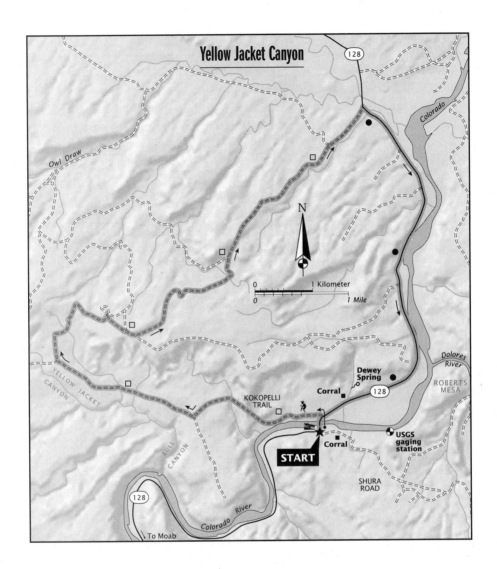

Yellow Jacket Canyon

128

Colorado

Owl Draw

N

0   1 Kilometer
0   1 Mile

YELLOW JACKET
CANYON

Dolores River

ROBERTS MESA

Dewey Spring

Corral

128

KOKOPELLI TRAIL

Corral

START

USGS gaging station

BULL CANYON

SHURA ROAD

128

Colorado River

To Moab

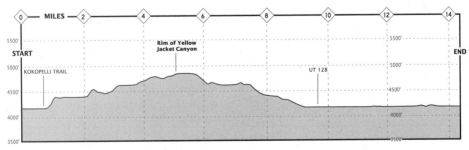

| 0 | MILES | 2 | 4 | 6 | 8 | 10 | 12 | 14 |

START   END

KOKOPELLI TRAIL

Rim of Yellow Jacket Canyon

UT 128

5500'
5000'
4500'
4000'
3500'

Miles and Directions

0.0 **START** from the boat ramp parking area and ride across the bridge.

0.4 The BLM marker just on your left past the bridge leads you onto the Kokopelli Trail.

0.8 At the gate go right and down over the ledges.

1.4 At the top of the saddle, there's a particularly good view of Dewey Bridge and the Colorado River below.

1.6 Here you'll encounter a series of rollies.

3.0 Go straight here on the predominant spur.

4.1 Go right.

4.7 At the top of the hill, be sure to stop to enjoy the view of Fisher Towers to the south.

4.8 Go right at the T and the marker. This is the slickrock rim of Yellow Jacket Canyon. Pueblan middens dot the area. Please leave any stone middens as you found them and avoid cryptobiotic soil crusts if you choose to take an excursion on the slickrock. The rim of Yellow Jacket Canyon is *exposed*, very dangerous, and not advised.

5.2 Go right at the T and the marker at the top of the hill.

5.4 The 360-degree view from the top of this hill is worth a short photo break. To the south are the La Sal Mountains. To the north are the Book Cliffs. To the east is Westwater.

5.6 Go left at the Y.

6.0 Go right at the Y.

6.1 Here is a slickrock wash bottom. Cross it by traveling to your left for a few feet and take the spur out of the wash bottom to your right. Ahead are a short hill and a series of rollies.

6.3 Take a hard left at the Y.

6.5 Take a right at the Y.

7.5 After crossing a more barren area, you reach an old gate. At this point there are a lot of minerals and fossils scattered on the ground, eroded out from the Chinle layer. Go through the gate and up the hill.

9.1 Continue straight through this intersection.

9.7 After descending the hill you intersect UT 128 at the river. Go right here to head back to the trailhead on the pavement.

14.0 Reach the trailhead.

14.4 Go left over the bridge and arrive at your vehicle.

Ride Information

Trail Contacts

Bureau of Land Management
82 E. Dogwood
Moab, UT 84532
(435) 259-2196

Schedule

Trail is open year-round but is best during spring and fall.

Maps

USGS maps: Dewey
Moab East Trail Map by Latitude 40° Inc.

MATRIMONY SPRING
Just a few yards east of the intersection of US 191 and UT 128 on the latter is Matrimony Spring, a great place to fill your water bottles. Legend has it that if you drink from the spring, you will certainly return to Moab. The waters of the spring have also been tested and are known to contain radioactive isotopes and bacteria. Drink up.

If you look closely at the sandstone slab the spring emerges onto, you'll see a series of small dinosaur tracks. More tracks are visible on the slab as it rises above the road and the parking area.

Honorable Mention

Northeast Moab

Noted below is one of the great rides in the northeast region that didn't make the A-list this time around but deserves recognition nonetheless. Check it out and let me know what you think. You may decide that it deserves higher status in future editions, or you may have a ride of your own that merits some attention.

A Yellow Cat Mining District

"We are glowing to the Yellow Cat District?" asked JD.

"Yup. Glowing into the historic uranium-mining area. Glowing to ride our bikes," I replied.

JD offered one last riddle as we turned off of the freeway past a road crew: "What is big and orange and sleeps four?"

He rapidly offered the answer: "A Utah Department of Transportation truck!"

The lands north and east of Arches National Park are otherworldly. Not only is the place a trip to see, but there are mine shafts, vents, and core-sample holes everywhere. Some cliffs are completely undercut by mazes of tunnels. There are metal droppings, machinery, shacks, trucks, rail lines, stuff, garbage of all kinds from Rastaman hats to 1933 Chevy trucks. Most of the really cool stuff was carted away by locals to put in their front yard as a radioactive monument to Moab's place in the Cold War, but there is certainly enough garbage left over for the rest of us to enjoy. If you like junk, beauty, distance riding, solitude, and geology, this is a great place to ride.

Vast. Desolate. Remote. Really remote. It's like a 1950s horror movie set with real teeth. Very impressive and very frightening. Old broken things are everywhere amid the vivid banded colors of spectacular sandstone and shale formations. Surrounding the sun-bleached remnants of human folly is a nature that just eats *everything,* very slowly. Even the most vile ecological insults turn to rust, dry out, and blend in with the dinosaur bone and petrified wood of the Morrison geological layers. There's poison in there somewhere, but it just blends in. It's a reminder that things can be tough, and that geology tells a story so big that it makes God run to the bathroom.

If it rains out there, you are screwed for sure. The Morrison and Dakota shales turn to really nasty slimy mud, and roads are totally impassable, even in the most macho of SUVs. If you ride at the wrong time or don't carry three times as much water as you think you'll need, you may die out here and just blend in with all the

Don't go in, boys! It's dangerous in there. It can cave in, and radon gas is abundant.

other junk. Only strong, prepared, smart people who dig solitude, distance, and natural weirdness need apply. This is not for people who refuse to notice any surroundings not necessary for controlling the bike. It's for explorers on mountain bikes, really. The Yellow Cat District is the final refuge for crusty locals who go back again and again to try to see it all before they die.

The riding is on doubletrack trails that range from nicely maintained to extremely rugged. Sand happens, yes, but so does bedrock, slickrock, rubble, and ledges. Staying on the main roads will present you with a few challenges, so your 4WD support vehicle should be stout and have high clearance. Exploring the fingers of roads that stretch toward Arches National Park can present you with some really interesting riding. The opportunities are endless.

Get yourself some good USGS maps of the area if you want to play with the Yellow Cat. Latitude 40° doesn't cover the area on their maps very well. Fran Barnes's maps, like the *Moab Recreation Map,* can help. You can get Fran's maps from Canyon Country Publications at P.O. Box 963, Moab, UT 84532. Gather information on the area from the Moab Information Center and Back of Beyond Books at 83 North Main Street. Talk to four-wheel guides in town. Four-wheelers frequent this area during events and in groups, so those guys know it as well as anyone.

You can get into the area around Owl Draw from the Yellow Jacket Canyon ride (see Ride 7) in this guide, or you can drive north from Center and Main in Moab on U.S. Route 191 for 26.5 miles. On the right-hand side of the highway, there's a road that goes over the railroad tracks. There is a stop sign here. This is the way to get directly into the Yellow Cat District via the Old Moab Highway.

My personal favorite way to ride the Yellow Cat is to park in the middle and ride out. To do this, take the ranch exit off Interstate 70. Here's how: Go 31.7 miles north of Center and Main in Moab on US 191 to the intersection with I–70. Go right onto the freeway, past the Thompson exit to the Yellow Cat exit (190) at mile 42.2 from Moab. Go right onto this very long, straight road. At mile 47.8, you'll see Skyline Arch on the horizon to your right. This landmark will help you navigate. Skyline Arch is a matter of feet from the main Arches Road, which runs along that high bumpy ridge to the west. There is a canyon between you and the park, so don't think hiking out is a piece of cake. At mile 48.7 go past the spur on your right. At mile 49.2 go over the cattle guard. Go right at the Y at mile 50.3. Stop at the intersection when you reach mile 51.1. I ride from here; you can design your own route. Loops and out-and-back rides will be mingled with browsing through the garbage. There are so many spurs out here that it takes a lifetime to know this place, so having the 4WD follow you around is the best way to deal. You can perform any number of shuttle routes out here, but the distances are great and you are a long, long way from help. Hire a 4WD guide or driver in town. A 4WD sagwagon is a stress reliever.

Moab Northwest

RAINBOW ROCKS

T his region falls north of Utah Route 313 and west of U.S. Route 191. Within its borders are expanses of sand and shale sediments, huge smooth slickrock formations of Entrada and Navajo sandstone, colorful mesas, and impressive spires and buttes of solid rock.

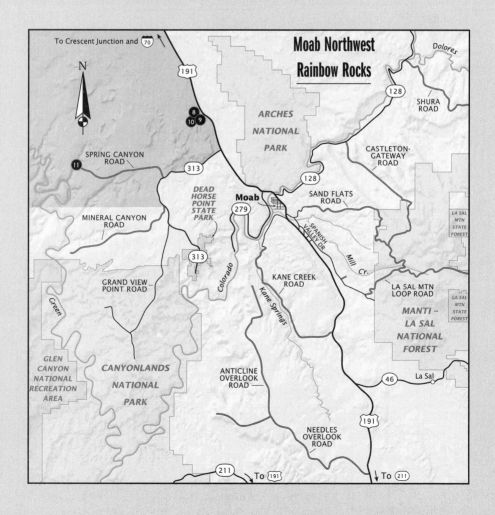

To Crescent Junction and (70)

N

191

Moab Northwest

Rainbow Rocks

Dolores

128

SHURA ROAD

8
10 9

ARCHES
NATIONAL
PARK

CASTLETON-
GATEWAY
ROAD

SPRING CANYON
ROAD

11

313

DEAD
HORSE
POINT
STATE
PARK

Moab

279

128

SAND FLATS
ROAD

LA SAL
MTN
STATE
FOREST

MINERAL CANYON
ROAD

313

Colorado

SPANISH
VALLEY DR.

Mill Cr.

GRAND VIEW
POINT ROAD

Green

KANE CREEK
ROAD

Kane Springs

LA SAL MTN
LOOP ROAD

LA SAL
MTN
STATE
FOREST

MANTI –
LA SAL
NATIONAL
FOREST

GLEN
CANYON
NATIONAL
RECREATION
AREA

CANYONLANDS
NATIONAL
PARK

ANTICLINE
OVERLOOK
ROAD

46 La Sal

NEEDLES
OVERLOOK
ROAD

191

211 To (191)

↓ To (211)

Given its name due to the colorful ribbons of layered sandstone sediments of the Entrada formations, Rainbow Rocks is a mountain biking photographer's heaven. The riding is most unusual due to surfaces that range from the exotic to extreme and dangerous. It is so cool to ride and take pictures out here that I feel uncool writing about it. I worry about this area's immediate future. It is so cool to roll around out here that mountain biking, ATV, 4WD, and motocross aficionados have begun to make a serious negative impact on the environment, and the BLM is responding with fences, signs, and ticketing.

Just so I feel good about pointing out the good cookies to a bunch of strangers, please read the environmental write-up in the introduction of this guide. Ride *in* this world, not *on* this world. Coexist with the desert by respecting its creatures and its stone. Know what and where those creatures are. Don't be an ecopath. Don't leave anything, including skid marks, on the slickrock. Skid marks are made by the unskilled and unwashed. And they ruin scenic mountain biking photographs.

All trails featured here can be ridden from the road, but roads in this area are absolutely impassable when wet. And remember, anywhere there is great sandstone to ride, there is brutal sand to deter wimpy visitors. If you are a sand snake, then you have the keys to mountain bike paradise. If you hate riding in deep sand, then sorry, this is not the place for you.

Lord of the Cowflies

hane was on his feet, insisting he was all right.

"Your elbow is a mess, Shane. Can you move it?" I asked, in a pitiful attempt to exercise a bit of tour-guide first aid.

"It's okay, but look, you can see the bone."

"Don't worry, that's just the white layer of skin underneath," Kevin stated with the force of vast experience. I think every spot on Kevin's body has revealed its underlayer at one time or another.

We paused for a few minutes to inventory Shane's wounds. His elbow was hamburger, both thighs were bloody and bruised, his hip was abraded and bruised, his hand was scraped and bleeding, his shoulder was black and blue.

Shane turned his attention to his bike.

"Oh, man, my brake lever is bent."

"That's not all that's bent. Look at your bar end," chided Adam.

"And your handlebar," I added.

"And your wheel," Kevin added.

"Aw, man, and I've ruined both my gloves."

It was a litany of war wounds and damage that went on for five minutes.

"Well, this will give me an excuse to upgrade. Dad did tell me not to do anything stupid until the last day. I guess it's the last day."

We washed Shane's wounds, put his tire back on the rim, and headed back toward the wash. Shane and Adam went ahead, spending a few minutes playing on the undulating surface as Kevin and I followed. Kevin rode in front of me, guiding his second bike beside him with one hand on each handlebar and brake. Kevin always takes two bikes out to Bartlett, one for jumps, one for bumpy chutes and fast stuff.

Shane picked up a nearly healthy fly and tore off its wings. "You little bastard."

When we came to a particularly steep sidehill, Kevin continued on. I released the high-side foot from my clipless pedal for more security as I watched Kevin effortlessly traverse the slope. When we came to a section of deep sand, Kevin maneuvered and manhandled both bikes up and down over the dune. I realized that if Kevin rode two bikes, I could keep up with him. Got to remember to make him take two on our next ride.

The closer we got to the wash bottom, the more cowflies gathered, until at last we found ourselves in a dense swarm. I watched the little buggers, ten to twenty at a time, hitching a ride on Kevin's butt. I cringed. I thought: "My butt is a bigger target and must have fifty on it right now."

The torture had just begun.

I blasted down the slickrock, leaving Kevin to portage with two bikes. I dangerously lifted my hands from the bars to spank my rear end and swat my thighs and arms as I went.

I wisely let Shane and Adam beat me to the wash. Cowflies flocked and attached themselves to the first rider, then swarmed the second, but it was not long before I was attracting more and more as we shot the wash and up to the camping area where I had parked the truck. It was here that all hell broke loose. I have never seen so many flies in my life. Each one of us was surrounded by his own private swarm. They were everywhere. When I dismounted the bike I saw twenty or thirty on my legs alone. One swat and I killed three at a time.

Shane and Adam went into a frenzy. Eyes wide with fear and panic, they threw down their bikes and danced around the locked truck like Indians at a 100-mile-per-hour powwow.

"Jesus!"

"This is *crazy!*"

I jumped from my bike and dug the keys out of my pack. "Into the truck, *quick!*" I shouted.

We scooted into the seats, slamming doors behind us. We had taken at least twenty flies into the cab and proceeded to take revenge on the determined little bastards.

"Where's Kevin?" Adam asked.

"He's back there bringing two bikes down the slickrock," I replied. "He's going to be eaten alive. This is like *Cujo* or something."

"Listen, I'll put my bike on the rack right here. Wait inside and when Kevin gets here, you guys jump out, get on your bikes, and ride like hell up the hill with him. The flies won't be so bad once you get out of the wash."

I jumped from the truck and began to remove the front wheel from my bike. In seconds the cloud of flies drove me back into the cab.

"How the hell am I ever going to get my bike on the rack?" I asked.

"This is *bad*," Shane said solemnly with the kind of desperation that young men display when surrounded by the enemy in some third-world hellhole.

I stepped out a second time and managed to get the wheel off, then jumped back into the truck in a panic. Outside, the flies swarmed against the window like a pestilence in some Hollywood B-movie.

I jumped out again and persisted this time, finally managing to get the bike into the bed of the truck and partially on the rack. The flies extracted a fee in blood for every move, every fumble. They eventually kept me from completing the chore when the skewer in the fork mount refused to tighten. I ran back to the cab and dove in, slamming the door behind me.

"Damn!"

Flies covered my legs. I could feel them on my butt, squished against the seat, like I was sitting on a pincushion.

One more trip out into the swarm and I tightened the skewer and fumbled with the rear wheel mount that was twisted in on itself. I gritted my teeth and tried to ignore the stinging bites and itches. When I got back into the truck, flies thumped against the inside and outside of the windows as Adam and Shane killed one after another. Eventually the inside was clear of unmaimed flies. The floorboard was covered with the dead and dying. Shane picked up a nearly healthy fly and tore off its wings. "You little bastard."

Behind us, rolling up the wash, Kevin approached amid a multitude of the winged gray monsters.

"Oh, my God, he's covered!" moaned Adam.

It was as if every fly that surrounded the truck saw Kevin and instantly headed for him. Within seconds he was overwhelmed.

"Man, he's got at least a fifty on each butt cheek," Shane commented.

"While they're busy with Kevin, get out and ride hard! I'm going to back this truck out of here and follow you up the road. We'll put your bikes in the back at the top of the hill. Get Kevin moving!" I almost had to pry them out of the vehicle.

Once Shane and Adam were out of the truck, they began to do the insane pow-wow dance as the flies instantly swarmed. The boys lifted their bikes from the sand, hopped on, and spanked themselves up the road out of the wash. I have never seen two people ride mountain bikes so fast, or at least *appear* to ride so fast. They were whipping their buttocks like kids pretending to be cowboys on a horse, furiously pedaling with all their might. Kevin followed them, almost calmly, riding up the hill with no hands on the handlebars of the bike he was sitting on. One hand controlled the bike to his right hand while he used the other to swat the flies off his ass.

I followed up the hill. Ahead, at the top, Shane and Adam turned around to use downhill momentum to outrun the flies. The only thing wrong with this tactic was that they were heading back down into the wash where the flies were gathering in vast numbers, waiting for more fresh blood.

Ahead, Kevin pushed onward and upward, crested the hill, and vanished from sight.

I jumped from the cab to help Shane and Adam, who were now off their bikes, running back and forth up and down the hill, eyes wide, arms and legs flailing. It was funny, scary, and pitiful.

"Get in the truck!" I shouted at the poor boys as I backed down to rescue them. Once they were in the cab, I gritted my teeth, ignored my primal fear, jumped out once again into the swarm, removed the front wheels from their bikes, and managed to get them mounted inside the bed in a blur.

Back in the double cab, Shane queried: "Where the hell is Kevin?"

I answered: "He's up the road trying to outrun the flies."

When we crested the hill, Kevin was still nowhere to be seen.

"Jesus, that guy can ride two bikes faster than most people can ride one," Adam admitted.

I drove onward into the desert. Soon I could see Kevin far ahead, kicking up dust, plummeting down another sandy slope *on two bikes.* Within a few minutes we caught up with him just as the flies thinned enough to allow him to slow down and stop.

As we loaded Kevin's bikes into the bed of the pickup, he said: "You know, it wasn't so bad as long as I could swat them. I could swat my right arm with my left hand, but I couldn't let go of the bike, so I had to just let them chomp away on my left arm."

"I hear that if you let them bite, the wounds don't itch. When you swat them they leave the saliva in the wound. It's the saliva that causes the itching."

Kevin said, "You know? You're right. The bites on my left arm don't itch at all."

Kevin removed his bike gloves.

Shane asked: "How did you lose that fingernail?"

"I've been working on a house and I hit my finger with the hammer. Hell, I hit this finger, too," Kevin said as he held up his battered hands for everyone to examine. One nail was hanging by a thin shred of skin. The other was black and curling backward. If you studied Kevin Dwyer's body, you could find a lot of things like this. And you could be asking him these kinds of questions all day long.

8 Bartlett Wash

Start: From the Mill Canyon parking area just off U.S. Route 191.

Length: 13.4-mile out-and-back, with opportunities to add miles freeforming.

Approximate riding time: 1 to 2 hours, with no freeform riding. Otherwise, all you can handle.

Difficulty: Technically easy to extremely difficult and very dangerous. The freeform nature of this slickrock area affords use by riders of just about any skill level, but not paying attention and choosing the wrong spots to ride can be fatal. Physically easy to difficult. You can spend as much time as you want out here and expend as much energy as you like. It can just be a sight-seeing trip or a real workout. It's up to you.

Trail surface: Dirt road to freeform slickrock area. A sand, gravel, shale, and loose-rock 4WD road that crosses a couple of wash bottoms. You end up on Entrada slickrock with lots of rollies, berms, chutes, bowls, jumps, and drop-offs.

Lay of the land: The area is sort of like a huge hot fudge sundae. The Entrada slickrock formations are perfect for surfing waves of rock on a mountain bike.

Total climbing: 654 feet.

Land status: Bureau of Land Management (BLM) land.

Other trail users: Hiking and off-road vehicles (ORV).

Best seasons: Spring and fall. Good in winter also. Avoid June and early July. Read the story at the head of this chapter! This is the worst place in the Moab area for insects.

Environmental concerns: The slickrock is somewhat environmentally sound. Mountain bikers have already destroyed the cryptobiotic pits on the rock. This is not a license to do more damage, however, so ride the rock and let the pits come back. Do not venture down into the washes, unless you plan to ride the extremely sandy watercourse. Deep sand should be enough of a deterrent. Motorcyclists do the most damage out here. You can see long tracks through the "crypto" from the mesa. Mountain bikers and motocrossers, lusting for more slickrock, leave the mesa and head across the fragile soil crusts. Their errant tracks usually go up or down a hill. The resulting linear track creates a watercourse and eventually a canyon. At this rate the beautiful cryptobiotic crusts and plant life in the washes will be reduced to drift sand in short order.

Please avoid skidding on the slickrock. Practice even braking. See the Slickrock Riding Skills In Addition after Ride 31 for help with this. Let's try to keep this beautiful place from becoming a constant big, black skid mark. Photographers who come out shortly after your visit will thank you for not dragging your rear tire.

Warning! The road in is impassable when wet. Flash floods can lock you in for a while.

Getting there: From Moab: Follow US 191 north from the intersection of Main and Center Streets for 15.4 miles (just beyond mile marker 141). On your left there will be a dirt road that immediately crosses the railroad tracks paralleling the highway. Turn here and bump over the tracks. Folks parking here to ride ATVs on the Monitor and Merrimac Jeep Trail have devastated this piece of state land. The damage is recent. This spot used to be shady with a lot of cottonwoods and expansive soil crusts. Now it is just plain screwed up. Park in a suitable place, which

Nate Toone, four-time Utah state downhill champ

by the time you read this may be anywhere beyond the tracks. If you would like to drive in a little farther, you can park at the intersection of Mill Canyon and Tusher Canyon Roads at mile 0.6. Driving farther than the marked spur to Tusher Canyon will require a high-clearance 4WD vehicle most of the year. If you have 4WD, or tires with good flotation and lots of ground clearance, you can drive all the way to the Bartlett Wash camping area.

The Ride

Just how do you describe Bartlett Wash slickrock? Ice cream sundae. Really big one, about the size of a small town. Lots of whipped cream and sprinkles and chocolate drops. Yeah, this place is God's Tastee Freeze. The sandstone globs out into the sand from a couple of hundred feet up and is melting constantly into formations that

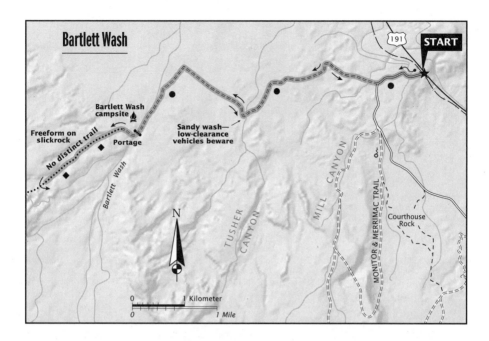

Bartlett Wash

resemble bulbous toes or breasts. Huge cleavage. The ride out can be on the vanilla or the hot fudge or you can hop around on the chocolate drops. It can be rough and it can be smooth and it can be sweet and it can be scary as hell. There are formations out here called Dolly Parton and Jayne Mansfield, Valley Grand, God's Bike Path, the Mushroom Drop, and the Breadloaf. Riding these spots is only for the most experienced and prepared freeride specialists. Be safe.

The first time you attempt to ride in this area, it is advisable to already have a good dose of slickrock riding under your belt. Knowing which spots are suitable for learning and which areas are deadly can be tricky for the uninitiated. Always ride with a friend out here—a friend who knows the area well. Kevin Dwyer, the fellow featured in the flies story, broke his femur out here and spent a horrifying day lying on a sandstone shelf below the mesa, waiting for someone to find him. I don't think you want this to happen to you.

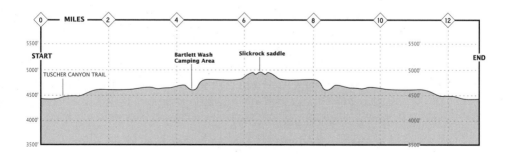

SOLUTION POCKETS
While you are out at Bartlett Wash, you'll be presented with some of the most beautiful sandstone in the Moab area. The Entrada has eroded into smooth forms, colorful layers, and cross bedding, all to create a mountain bike playground and a place where you can get those cliché photos that now represent Moab to millions of dreamers around the world.

One of the geological features that make photography here so interesting and mountain biking a bit more difficult are the solution pockets—eroded holes in the smooth sandstone faces of the Entrada. These are most likely caused by porous layers of stone where water is channeled across more dense layers and then out through the face of the rock. These pockets are also certainly caused by concretions—hardened sandstone formations resulting from buried organic compounds. Organic compounds attract minerals and form nodules that erode out of the softer layers to leave pockets where they once resided.

The Bartlett Wash slickrock area offers an infinite assortment of freeform slickrock areas and challenges. You don't have to endanger yourself if you choose to simply ride out-and-back on the ledges to enjoy the scenery—which is spectacular in the extreme, but be warned that slickrock chutes and bowls are enticing. Ease of access gives you every opportunity to do something stupid. The Entrada sandstone comes in a variety of textures and colors. You will find the deep red layers to be very tacky and substantial. The greener, grayer layers are less stable and generally erode out faster than the red. This means that loose sand particles are always on the surface

Dropping into "Dolly Parton"

as the wind, rain, temperature, and bike tires erode the rock. These particles can be like tiny ball bearings. If you are sidehilling across red and come to trust it, you may be surprised by the green. Watch your inside pedals. Hitting a pedal can be fatal.

This is my favorite listed riding area due to its overwhelming scenery and freeform possibilities. Bartlett presents photographers with fantastic opportunities and is second only to the Slickrock Trail as a destination for commercial mountain bike photography. Try not to leave marks.

South of the slickrock, down in the canyon, is the true Bartlett Wash, a strange slot canyon with red walls and a deep sand bottom. If you want a bit of weird and sandy mountain biking, then head out in the wash at the base of the slickrock. Only try this if you are a sand snake and want to get your camera gritty. There are spires and sculpted bedrock in the wash, and it is a thoroughfare for wildlife, but don't venture up any slot canyon if there is a chance of a rain. A flash flood in a slot wash could really ruin your day.

Miles and Directions

0.0 **START** from the parking area and ride your bike west toward Mill Canyon.

0.6 Take the spur right marked for Tusher Canyon. The track parallels the power lines for a ways.

2.5 When you reach the marked intersection with the Monitor and Merrimac Jeep Trail, continue across the sandy wash, dodge the rocks, and swing around to your right and up the hill to the north.

3.6 Turn left onto the spur just before the abrupt downhill to a very sandy wash bottom. If you find yourself crossing this second sandy wash, you have gone too far.

4.5 Ride through the Bartlett Wash camping area, across the stream, and through the cattle gate.

4.7 Just a few yards past the cattle fence and on your right is a sometimes overgrown sandy singletrack that takes you to a shelf allowing access to the slickrock above. Carry your bike up onto the ledge and head west (to your left). You will have to keep edging upward on the slickrock ledges, at one point crossing and ascending a sand bridge onto the next level. Try to favor the red layers above, saving the greenish layers below for your return route. I once saw a rattler just where you ascend the slickrock, so beware.

6.7 You've reached the flat and wide slickrock saddle above Bartlett Wash. Head due west or south to ride the massive bowls and fingers of Bartlett Wash's canyon rim, or turn right to head north to ride the huge slickrock bowl and the long *exposed* ledges of the northern rim. There is no defined trail. This ride is freeform from the moment you leave the sand of Bartlett Wash. Because it is freeform, *beware* of deceptive drop-offs. When accessing the saddle area, please ride the rock only. Get off and walk if it means you save a plant or two. When you have had your fill, return the same way you came in. Freeforming will add mileage to the ride.

13.4 Arrive at your car. (This mileage doesn't account for any freeform miles.)

Ride Information

Trail Contacts

Bureau of Land Management
82 E. Dogwood
Moab, UT 84532
(435) 259-2196

Schedule

Trail is open year-round but is best during spring and fall.

Maps

USGS maps: Jug Rock
Moab West Trail Map by Latitude 40° Inc.
Moab Recreation Map by F. H. Barnes

SLICKROCK FORMATIONS

There are many geological rock layers in the Moab area that offer up a slickrock surface to mountain bikers. The best known is the Navajo formation, which is comprised of the Moab Slickrock Trail and the freeform knobs at the end of the Poison Spider Mesa Trail. Another slickrock layer is the Rico, a deep red, highly abrasive stone that can be ridden at Fossil Bottom and in Jackson Hole. Another is the Kayenta that caps the Wingate Cliffs and supports the smooth Navajo formation. It is very ledgy and offers rhythmic vertical ridges like those on the Porcupine Rim Trail.

My personal favorite is the Entrada formation, of which the best example is Bartlett Wash. Unlike the Navajo and Rico, which are mostly uniform in color and consistency, the Entrada is made up of many colorful layers ranging from mint green to orange-red, with surfaces ranging from bumpy ridges and pocked ledges to frozen waves of ultrasmooth and sexy sandstone. Bartlett Wash affords access to these many layers as you travel up and down the rounded and multitextured mounds, across and between the fingers of rock that protrude out into the wash bottom.

Entrada slickrock

The layers of the Entrada have varying ride qualities. The tackiest of the layers is the deep red sandstone. It is reasonably stable and offers perhaps the best traction of any surface in the Moab area. The gray layers are a bit less tacky, and the quickly eroding green layers can be downright dangerous after you become used to the redder layer's grip. Be careful as you traverse the various layers while taking a downward gravity trip on Bartlett Wash slickrock.

Other dangerous factors at work on the frozen rock waves of Bartlett Wash are optical illusions created by light and geology and extreme vertical exposure that happens at the edges of the rock above the wash. At some times of day, the light on this surface can be very deceiving. The rhythmic rolling of the slickrock, combined with a lack of shadow definition, can be life threatening. You may find yourself diving off a nearly invisible drop-off if you're not careful. *Always preride the area before you "rock out."*

In Addition

Dreamride Mountain Bike Tours and Film Services

"The guys at Dreamride are fanatics who offer vacations for hardcore riders demanding the best. Unlike other tour companies that offer hundreds of vacations or corral thirty riders per trip, Dreamride offers highly personalized vacations for groups of five, and that includes the guide!"

—*Mountain Bike Action*

In 1996, I founded Dreamride after years of slaving away in university film departments for people whose idea of exercise was watching films on a flatbed or walking to the Jeep Cherokee in the morning holding a cup of coffee and a sweet roll. During my years as a college teacher and administrator I called in sick so I could ride or ski. I would give twisted assignments to my classes so that we could ride together or go on ski trips as part of the class. I repaired every faculty member's funky bike, desperately trying to get anyone on two wheels and into the woods. I was criticized for paying more attention to building trails around the school than to running the film program. I scouted and memorized every trail within hundreds of miles of jobs in three states, only to have to move away when my contract ran out. I felt like some poor schmuck in the armed forces who got new orders every couple of years and had to uproot his family just to survive in the "corps." I never picked a job because the department was chock full of snotty artists and famous filmmakers or had a great reputation for pumping out good workers. I picked teaching jobs based on the quality of the mountain biking.

I eventually gave up the charade, threw all that crap away, and moved to Moab where I started my own mountain biking business. I had been coming to Moab for years to ride and work on a personal documentary project about old timers in the area. I dragged my family here every chance I got and we ended up with many friends and acquaintances in canyon country. It was the only place that my entire family agreed was worthy of settling for.

Once we were settled in Moab, Dreamride started as a mountain bike day-tour company and extreme mountain biking film service located in Lin Ottinger's Moab Rock Shop. Over the next four years it grew into a high-quality mountain bike fantasy provider for couples, corporates, and very small groups of nature lovers and hardcore cyclists. For me, the idea of starting a mountain bike tour company grew out of a personal desire to do it right. So I designed the company around what I,

Nate Toone

personally, wanted from a guide and a tour company. I had joined commercial tours before, finding them boring, socially uncomfortable, and more focused on camping than real mountain biking. The food was always a letdown, even unhealthy. The guides were half my age, totally unprepared, and had no clue how to make the trip intellectually stimulating, let alone physically challenging. The groups were large and the costs exaggerated for the quality of services rendered. Because I was not interested in the single mingle thing, I was an outcast trying desperately to milk the most challenge out of every wimpy tourist mile. I am of the opinion that mountain biking should be mountain biking, and camping should only be done when you get terribly lost.

Dreamride's goal has always been to offer *real mountain biking*, on the very best trails on earth and in the most surreal landscapes in the solar system, while preserving and even deifying the environment. We do this with quality services and outrageously expensive, state-of-the-art bikes—we spend more on our rental fleet than other companies spend on their trucks. Dreamride's business is built around very small groups because, through vast experience (yes, age has its rewards), I know that a group of more than four is totally unmanageable. We stay in hotels and bed-and-breakfasts because when you ride hard, you get tired and hungry. Our motto is "ride hard, rest easy." Instead of a meal of tortillas and beans on a rock in the desert, clients are given the opportunity to eat something that they actually prefer, in a comfortable setting under a roof, followed by a glass of beer or wine, and maybe even a movie or a play. We give our clients a chance to recover in a Jacuzzi and a bed, not in a sleeping bag.

All routes offered by Dreamride are custom designed for a range of skill levels and guaranteed to challenge clients physically and mentally. Ask anyone who has ridden with us about our routes and they'll tell you that seeing other mountain bikers is a rare occurrence. Riding with us for more than three days demonstrates that the trails in this guidebook are just the tip of the iceberg. Repeat customers really get the goods dumped on them. If someone turns out to be a macho jerk, refuses to wear a helmet, or treats others in the group with disrespect, we send them packing—unless it is a private tour. You can be a jerk on a private ride.

The icing on any Dreamride vacation cake is the opportunity to learn about the natural world from our guides, who are an eclectic bunch of overeducated outcasts like myself. Our guides are the absolute best because we pay them well just to *ride*. With us they do not have to wipe snot or clean out chemical toilets. Our guides have lives aside from our business and are not the typical transients you find working for other tour outfitters. They would never consider guiding as a job, but they guide for us because we provide real mountain biking in surreal locations. Working for us is usually better than riding alone. These folks make Dreamride trips very special indeed.

If you are ever in the market for a Moab mountain bike vacation that can include: slickrock surfing, mountain singletrack, and rugged and technical desert riding; skills instruction; landscape, nature, and action photography; combinations of hiking, skiing, and biking; and rare natural science interpretation in the fields of anthropology, archeology, geology, and paleontology; *and* purchase of a custom exotic mountain bike, then get in touch with Dreamride.

Dreamride's mountain bike stunts, aerials, skills clinics, nightrides, photography, and production coordination services were featured in the IMAX film *Everest,* in multiple mountain bike video projects, on ABC's *Good Morning America,* and in feature articles in *Sunset, Mountain Bike Action, Max* and many other magazines worldwide.

As author of this guidebook, I personally invite you to ride with us and explore beyond the boundaries of this publication. I have shared a lot of my favorite rides here, but the very best will always be secret.

Big Rain in Canyon Country

Rain in canyon country is a phenomenon. It can come down in buckets or refuse to fall for months, even years, at a time. "Ghost rain," as the Navajo call it, can dangle above you like dainty white fingers from misty, sparse clouds or fall like sheets of smeared gray paint from huge thunderheads, and yet never reach the ground. The sky can be completely black and threatening, the wind ripping up dirt and gravel, but not a drop will fall, something we call "politician weather." The sky can be blue, without a cloud, and it'll rain on you anyway. An old fellow in Colorado once told me that if this happens to you three times, you die. Well, in Moab it's happened to me twice, so I'm sure enough watching out for it now.

Old-timers who have been here long enough to know the reality of rain in the desert around Moab can tell you about 10-foot-high boulders washed down across the highway north of town where Denny's is now located. Rain is so localized that it will wash out a section of railroad track on Potash Road while 100 yards away not so much as a drop will fall.

Most of the year the weather service is the biggest joke around. They will forecast a front of thunderstorms or a week of drooling rain for the entire Southwest and it just won't happen here. While the rest of Utah, New Mexico, and Arizona gets pummeled, there will be nary a cloud over the Moab canyon country. I have looked at weather satellite photographs taken only minutes before, testifying to cloud cover over the entire Southwest, but I look outside and maybe there will be a handful of puffy clouds. It's downright weird. Anyone who has lived here for a while forecasts the weather with the toss of the coin and speaks of Weather as if it were a being with a great sense of humor.

> Lin's clients began to panic as the rain tapered off enough to reveal the wide canyon ahead, completely awash in an encroaching muddy flow.

A few years ago Lin Ottinger was coming back from leading a 4WD tour of Canyonlands, shuttling his victims down the long meandering gully on Utah Route 313 called Seven Mile Canyon. The sky was clear and blue when the group left Moab that morning bound for the Walking Rocks and the huge capped rock spires called the Mushrooms that tower over the Colorado River canyon along the eastern tip of the White Rim Trail. As they sat in a tiny grotto enjoying lunch and Lin's dirt-funny tall tales, they noticed clouds forming over the La Sal and Abajo Mountains in the distance and heard distant thunder, but the storms were many many miles away. The sun continued to shine on the White Rim and showed no sign of giving up its hot hold.

From Hidden Valley the La Sal Mountains are obscured by an isolated shower.

When at last Lin drove back from the Island in the Sky toward the Knoll, the highest point in Canyonlands, his stories, homespun poems, and downright lies about cowboys, longhorn sheep, and Indians were drowned out by rattling thunder. As the red Suburban began to descend into Seven Mile Canyon, darkness dropped down the canyon walls like a curtain. A sudden blinding rain made it so difficult to drive that Lin had to stop the Suburban dead in the road.

Outside, the rain grew so heavy that the canyon wall only feet away to their left vanished behind sheets of water. Lin, ever the homespun scientist, rolled down his driver's-side window just enough to hold out a Styrofoam cup to measure the accumulation. As the torrent continued unabated for almost half an hour, the cup in Lin's hand was repeatedly filled to the brim. Each time he emptied it, he called out: "That's 3 inches," "That's 6 inches." As the rain began to abate, he finished with: "That's almost 12 inches of rain in less than half an hour." Lin's clients began to panic as the rain tapered off enough to reveal the wide canyon ahead, completely awash in an encroaching muddy flow. The ripping red floodwater tugged at the wheels of the Suburban as it rushed around the truck and leaked through the bottoms of the doors.

When Lin told me this story he was driving down this same canyon, returning from the same tour route. He pointed at a watermark along the roadside about 15 feet up the canyon wall. The highway is at least another 25 feet above the wash bottom of the Seven Mile Canyon, and the canyon itself is well over 100 yards wide at this point. The thought of all that water rushing down this wide canyon sent a chill up my spine.

9 Mill Canyon Mesa and Joe Camel Loop

Start: From Mill Canyon Road just off U.S. Route 191.

Length: 7.7-mile loop.

Approximate riding time: 1 to 2 hours.

Difficulty: Technically easy to moderate, with a few surprises. Deep sand is the most challenging here, with a very few ledges and sand to rock transitions thrown in. The wash bottoms on the way in and on the way out of the ride are always changing, so expect these to be the most difficult areas in the ride. Physically moderate. The sand and the moderate climb can take it out of you.

Trail surface: A 4WD doubletrack across slickrock expanse. Loose rock, stream-worn rocks up to the size of babyheads, deep sand, slickrock, hard-packed to loose sedimentary soils, and bedrock ledges on a classic technical 4WD track.

Lay of the land: Huge mesas made up of Entrada sandstone stand above the drainage of Courthouse Pasture. You will be going in through one creekbed and returning via a second.

Total climbing: 682 feet.

Land status: Bureau of Land Management (BLM) and Utah State Trust lands.

Other trail users: Hikers and off-road vehicles (ORV).

Best seasons: Spring and fall are best, but winter can also be a hoot out here if the sun is shining and snow is not covering the trail.

Note to the reader: The Moab Bike Patrol and the BLM refer to this trail as the Monitor and Merrimac Bike Trail, though it doesn't go near Monitor and Merrimac Buttes. Since I have included the original Monitor and Merrimac Trail in this book, I must call this route by another name. I have named the butte in the middle of Courthouse Pasture Joe Camel, because it has humps and a distinct camel formation visible during morning light as seen from across US 191—and there are a lot of cigarette ads shot in this area.

Environmental concerns: Fragile! Avoid cryptobiotic soil crusts and rare desert mosses on the rock. Stay on the main trail. Never ride through standing water on rock or darkened pits that once held water. The bottoms of these pits are covered with eggs and dormant water creatures.

Warning! Not advisable when area is wet due to potentially dangerous and gooey Machos shale ("gumbo") sediments on the road in. Flash floods out here can be really impressive and keep you from getting out for a while. You cross the main course of the Courthouse Wash, on the way in. Water drained from Mill Canyon and the canyon below Courthouse Butte come together to create a treacherous arroyo that drains into Courthouse Wash, where the flow becomes quite spectacular. It doesn't happen often, but if it rains and the wash is rushing with floodwaters, do not attempt to cross it. You will just have to wait it out.

Getting there: From Moab: Follow US 191 north from the intersection of Main and Center Streets for 15.4 miles (just beyond mile marker 141). On your left will be a dirt road that immediately crosses the railroad tracks paralleling the highway. There is a NO TRESPASSING sign on the far side of the tracks and a small sign, MILL CANYON ROAD. Turn in here and park just off the highway. Or bump over the tracks, and in 50 yards there's parking available under the cottonwood trees to

Standing water below Joe Camel Butte

your right or along the road anywhere there is a barren spot. It is getting more and more barren due to poor management, and I expect the cottonwoods will be gone in a few short years.

The Ride

The Rainbow Rocks area, 15 miles northwest of Moab, gets its name from the multicolored Entrada sandstone layers that have eroded into myriad scenic buttes, mounds, gullies, canyons, and spires. The area includes the Bartlett Wash and the Monitor and Merrimac rides in this book, as well as the routes that meander about Courthouse Pasture around a series of buttes between Seven Mile Canyon to the west and US 191 to the east.

Rides in this area are on clay, hardpack, bedrock, and loose rock, but the dominant surfaces here are sand and slickrock—heaven and hell. Routes in Rainbow

Rocks can be linked for increased mileage and challenge, if you are bent on the hardcore. Extended routes in this area are best accomplished with a guide the first time you ride out here. Chances are you will be all right if you are strong and bring enough water to allow for getting lost, but the environment will not fare as well if you have to walk across the crypto to find a way back. Please be kind to this area. It is one of the very best.

The route is marked with painted white lines and markers. Maintained by the Moab Bike Patrol and misnamed the Monitor and Merrimac Bike Trail, the route is easy to follow, but can be a sand headache to those who are not distracted by the beauty of the place. Once through the canyon, between Mill Canyon Mesa and Courthouse Butte, you'll emerge onto a slickrock expanse above Courthouse Pasture, a cattle grazing area during fall and winter. The trail then goes around Joe Camel, a majestic butte in the middle of Courthouse Pasture. Once around the backside of the butte, just follow the white lines down to and across the wash and through the sand into Mill Canyon—an area that was once home to a copper mill, hence the name. Remnants of the old mill can be seen above

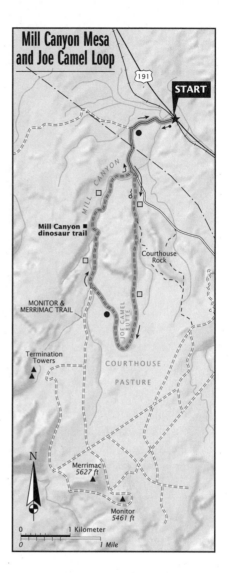

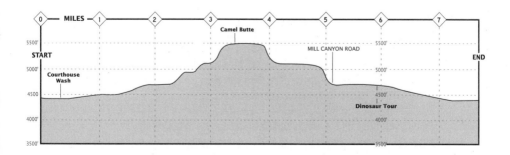

Dinosaur bone fragments on "ripple rock"

the trail on the right as you exit the canyon at the end of the ride. The stonework and old railway tracks are just across from the Mill Canyon Dinosaur Trail. Don't miss the self-guided dinosaur bone tour. Take a brochure from the box and hike the quarter mile to view the fossils. When you're done, place the brochure back into the box for others to enjoy.

Miles and Directions

0.0 START: Park and ride your bike west toward Mill Canyon.

0.6 Bypass the spur to Tusher Canyon.

1.1 Bear left and continue straight past the spur marked MILL CANYON on the road marked STAGECOACH HALFWAY STATION. After 100 yards or so, cross the wash and continue on the dominant spur.

1.4 A visit to the remnants of the stagecoach post is recommended. This pile of stones was a halfway stop between Moab and the railroad in Thompson to the north around the turn of the twentieth century. Continue south into the gap between Mill Canyon Mesa to the west and Courthouse Butte to the east. Here was once a large Ute settlement. This canyon used to be alive with huge cottonwoods and tepees. You'll encounter a rocky wash bottom and then deep sand. The trail is obvious and well marked with signs and painted lines. Keep an eye out for middens that sparkle in the sands just before you achieve the slickrock shelf that skirts the base of the mesa and carries you out to a slickrock saddle area. Don't take the middens, but do check them out. The chert stone here is especially beautiful.

2.6 At the southern end of Mill Canyon Mesa, look for the painted line markers that lead you out across the slickrock away from the mesa to Joe Camel Butte directly ahead. Joe Camel Butte looks like it has humps and a royal turban on it.

3.0 Veer left around the butte, keeping the cliff face to your right. The white lines and carson-ite markers with the sign M&M make this easy route finding. **Side trip.** If you want a diversion or a place to escape the heat, there is a small canyon cut into the butte's northern end. This is a great place to stop, enjoy the shade, have a snack, and explore. Be careful to avoid vegetation, and try not to leave too many footprints. From here you'll be encircling Joe Camel Butte clockwise by skirting its left side and continuing around its western edge, staying next to it until you reach the downhill run on a huge slickrock shelf. As you travel around the east side of the butte, be careful to ride on slickrock free of mosses and crypto by strictly following the dotted white line. The fragile vegetation aside, it can be dangerous for the novice if you venture off the trail.

5.1 (Note. This cue coincides with mile 2.6 of the Monitor and Merrimac Trail description.) The painted white lines have dropped you into a sandy wash. Cross it and turn right at the T in the road. **Option.** Take a left, instead of the right, and this is the connecting point for the "real" Monitor and Merrimac route. If you are a strong rider and love challenging sand stretches and big slickrock, then you should consider it. Otherwise head east (right). Follow this sandy track across the wash into Mill Canyon Gap ahead. The canyon gap can be a bit technical due to flash flooding and can also be home to some nasty insects. There is quicksand in the streambed at times, so riding down the wash through the water can be a real western experience. After negotiating the sand and the stream crossings, you'll emerge onto Mill Canyon Road.

5.9 Emerging from the canyon on your left, you'll find the Mill Canyon self-guided dinosaur tour. A box at the head of the 0.25-mile hike should contain pamphlets describing the fossilized remains of dinosaur and plant life. The hike is especially educational and well worth checking out. Across the road from the dino bones are remnants of mining.

6.6 Take a left and head back to the trailhead.

7.7 Reach the trailhead.

Ride Information

Trail Contacts
Bureau of Land Management
82 E. Dogwood
Moab, UT 84532
(435) 259–2196
Utah State School and Institutional Trust Lands Administration
1165 South US 191, Ste. 5, Moab, UT 84532
(435) 259–3760

Schedule
Trail is open year-round but is best during spring and fall.

Maps
USGS maps: Monitor and Merrimac, Jug Rock
Moab West Trail Map by Latitude 40° Inc.
Moab Recreation Map by F. H. Barnes

Eggbeater Exploits

At the end of the day, John Ruhl, the helicopter pilot hired to hump the gear, returned from the hangar to pick up the stunt team. As production and stunt coordinator, I got to ride in the cockpit and communicate with John through the intercom, because I hired him and he tried to repay me in any way he could. John was the best thing about working on this production, so I quickly buckled up and donned the radio headset, looking forward to another awesome glass-bubble sight-seeing trip back to town. Since I was the only one with a headset, John's interpretive narration of the ride was only for me, and over the previous two weeks of the shoot I had come to appreciate him more and more as someone who not only knew how to fly a copter like Sterling Moss knew how to drive a car, but knew canyon country in ways only a copter pilot with his years of experience possibly could.

John Ruhl buzzes the crew in his Jet Ranger. A few years later he ran out of fuel over his own helipad on the south side of town. May this helicopter rest in peace. Insurance paid for John's new rig.

Before this gig I knew John only by his reputation with Moab Search and Rescue, where he is touted for being a copter cowboy and an angel of sorts. John's years as a pilot in Vietnam not only gave him incredible skills but also instilled a dedication for getting people out of trouble, to the point that he will put himself in mortal danger without even a hint of hesitation if it means a chance at saving a life. John is noted for flying into terrain and weather conditions where Life Flight helicopter pilots simply refuse to go. I was told he once rescued a fellow from a cliff face in a 50-mph wind.

The seat belt tugged hard at my waist as I stared straight ahead at the sandy desert floor growing closer and closer. Somewhere between the edge of the cliff and the floor of the canyon I got religion.

For most of the stunt team, the shooting of Everest was their first experience with helicopters, and this was their first ride with John, who, compared to the Hollywood pilots who flew the camera ships, was somewhat of a . . . uh . . . cowboy. Where other pilots would lift off and fly away, John would just fly away. He omitted the liftoff. Watching John handle the controls is like watching Picasso paint. I had ridden with him when he landed his Jet Ranger among a collection of copters and fuel tanks and trucks, where his rotors had less than a foot of clearance in either direction. In short, the man can *really* fly an eggbeater.

As the stunt riders settled into the passenger compartment behind me, I noticed a sly smile spreading across John's face. I had never seen that smile. I was used to the stoic John Ruhl, the dry-humored and frank fellow who got up early and did his job. That smile was strangely disturbing, especially considering I was belted in the seat of this fellow's helicopter and he had a bunch of adrenaline junkies in the back. I knew it was too tempting a situation for John to pass up.

John shouted to the team in the back, *"Are we buckled up and ready to go?"*

"Yeah!"

"You bet."

"I'm ready. Let's rock."

I looked over at John. The smile widened to an evil grin.

"I've got to have some kinda fun with this damn job," John said as he winked at me and tore the helicopter off the cliff in one swift motion of incredibly coordinated stick and throttle, then put the copter into a "past vertical" dive straight down the sandstone face of Tusher Mesa.

"Aaaiiiiiieeeee!"

As the copter fell like a stone and my stomach rose into my throat, I spoke into the intercom, "John, the Spacecam dude told me, 'Helicopters don't dive, they crash.' What's the deal with that?"

"Bullshit! If helicopters didn't dive, I'd be dead a long time ago."

My head bumped the top of the cockpit. The seat belt tugged hard at my waist as I stared straight ahead at the sandy desert floor growing closer and closer. Somewhere between the edge of the cliff and the floor of the canyon I got religion.

"Yahooo!"

The testosterone was flowing freely.

John pulled up at the last possible moment. The ground rushed by less than 10 feet below my feet as John pulled out of the dive and we were faced with the beauty of Tusher Canyon and Termination Towers. Crash yelled from behind me: "He's going to go through *that*? Oh, shit, he's going to go through *that!* Hey guys, he's going to go through *that!*"

John was heading for the Towers, three sandstone spires 250 feet high, no more than 50 feet apart. He tipped the copter on its side, passed through the center gap, dropped to the slickrock and sand beyond, and skimmed across the surface of Courthouse Pasture as if we were on wheels.

In the backseats the stunt team wailed like drunk rednecks on a roller-coaster ride at the county fair as we barreled toward Monitor Butte, veering up abruptly only at the very last moment to clear the colossal sandstone monolith, then John simply let the beast fall down the other side.

John leveled out to cross Utah Route 313. We wouldn't want anyone to see what kind of fun we were having. Meanwhile I was beginning to realize that I *really* liked this helicopter thing, and that if I had known

John Ruhl

how much fun they were I may have had a different take on the Vietnam War. The possibility of learning how to fly one of these things could turn a pacifist into a drooling copter fiend. I was beginning to understand what Bego Gerhart, the legendary camera rigger, meant when he said that he wanted to be reincarnated as a helicopter.

Just past the fins of Upper Bull and Long Canyon, John threw both sticks forward and dived into the Day Canyon chasm—better known in the helicopter-tour business as "Star Wars Canyon." The copter dropped like a bowling ball in a vacuum, picking up breathtaking speed. John pulled out of the dive and began to bank the copter hard through the tight S curves of the canyon at maximum speed. The walls rushed by at either rotor tip. I glanced over at John, quick, sure, and unflinching at the controls, grinning from ear to ear. All the while he personally narrated each brush with death.

"I usually take the S turns out to the river from here, but this will be a little more interesting." He flew the copter directly at the cliff in front of us, a vertical wall of Wingate sandstone at least 500 feet high, and at the last moment, with the rotors merely inches from the wall, he stopped the copter dead in the air and forced it into a slow vertical climb, like we were in an elevator.

"Going up. Third floor. Lingerie. Fourth floor. Household goods. Fifth floor. Menswear." As the copter crested the wall, John inched it skillfully forward. The rocks at the top of the cliff passed a mere foot below the skids under my feet.

"I like making people crap their pants," John bragged.

Back at the hangar I thanked John profusely, gushing with that same bonded feeling hostages experience with their captors. "I would have paid $1,000 for that ride, John. Thanks for the ride of a lifetime. Next time you are flying the camera ship!"

Because of this little helicopter ride, anytime I come close to an amusement park I spend all the money I have on roller coasters. I never miss the chance to ride in a helicopter, and I send every tourist I can to John for a joyride. The last time I had a film production job, I hired John to fly the camera. He surprised me by mounting the camera on the "wrong" side of the copter so he could fly it backward to get the shot. It was awesome and can be seen in the opening segment of *Outer Extremities,* the extreme mountain bike video distributed by Qranc.

John Ruhl wears a leather jacket and tacky airman sunglasses, smokes nasty cigarettes, and is as slippery as a snake, but if I ever need to get Humpty Dumpty down from the wall, I'm hiring John Ruhl to fly the eggbeater.

John Ruhl owns Arches-Classic Helicopter. For a tour call (435) 259–4637. Don't expect the kind of ride documented here.

10 Monitor and Merrimac Buttes and Termination Towers

Start: From the Mill Canyon parking area just off U.S. Route 191.

Length: 14.2-mile circuit.

Approximate riding time: 2 to 6 hours. Freeforming on the slickrock may tempt you to hang around a bit. If you are a sand slug, it could take you quite a while (as much as 2 hours) just to get out and back across the sand section.

Difficulty: Technically moderate to difficult. Deep, deep sand for nearly 1 mile stops most folks and has caused the BLM to route the currently marked Monitor and Merrimac Bike Trail away from the actual Monitor and Merrimac Buttes. Once out at the buttes, the technical challenge is very big slickrock with exposure on three sides. Physically moderate to difficult. The sand will take the wind right out of you if you choose to ride it. Courthouse Pasture is rolling terrain, and some of that "roll" is deep, deep sand.

Trail surface: A 4WD doubletrack, slickrock, and sparse singletrack. Shale maintained county road, 4WD track through a wash bottom over sand, loose rock, hardpack, bedrock, and more deep sand. Flashes of singletrack, then Entrada and Navajo formation slickrock.

Lay of the land: Courthouse Pasture is a huge expanse where impressive Entrada sandstone buttes rise from cattle grazing lands. Rolling sand dunes are vegetated, giving the impression that there is soil out here, but under the plants and cryptobiotic crusts is sand and rock and not much else.

Total climbing: 1,558 feet.

Land status: Bureau of Land Management (BLM) and Utah State Trust lands.

Other trail users: Hikers and off-road vehicles (ORV).

Best seasons: Great in spring and fall and sometimes great in winter. Summer and sand only go together at the beach.

Note to the reader: This is the "real" Monitor and Merrimac Trail, utilizing a section of the infamous jeep route. The trail marked as the Monitor and Merrimac Trail by the BLM's Moab Bike Patrol is listed in this guide as Mill Canyon Mesa and Joe Camel Loop; see Ride 9.

Environmental concerns: Fragile! Avoid exploration into Courthouse Pasture, as it will surely mean trampling on cryptobiotic soil crusts and rare desert mosses in order to get back to a ridable trail. Deep sand is everywhere that slickrock or bedrock isn't. Out on the slickrock beyond Monitor and Merrimac Buttes, be aware of—and avoid at all costs—mosses, lichens, and blackened pits in the rock. The blackened pits are home to rare desert shrimp species. This area was saved from being destroyed by a big-budget movie project by some very protective souls, so please enjoy! Be an advocate for its breathtaking scenery should any other threats to its beauty and solitude arise.

Warning! This ride is not advisable when the Rainbow Rocks area is wet, due to the sticky Machos shale sediments (known as "gumbo") on roads into the area. The possibility of flash floods is also very high when storms create strong downpours or rain persists. These events can keep you out here for a day or two. Hypothermia can be a real problem, and carrying a good rain jacket and space blanket has saved my butt out here a couple of times. The upside is that,

Termination Towers

if it has rained recently, the sand will be packed and ridable. Don't ride immediately after a rain, though. Wait a day or so.

Also, mountain lions frequent this area at night!

Getting there: From Moab: Follow US 191 north from the intersection of Main Street and Center Street for 15.4 miles (just beyond mile marker 141). On your left will be a dirt road that immediately crosses the railroad tracks paralleling the highway. There is a NO TRESPASS-ING sign on the far side of the tracks and a small sign marking the road as MILL CANYON. The NO TRESPASSING sign refers to the railroad right-of-way and only restricts parking within 100 feet of the tracks. Park just off the highway or bump over the tracks, and in 50 yards there is parking available under the cottonwood trees to your right. There has been a lot of damage done here, so the place is turning into an open parking lot. Try not to make it bigger.

The Ride

Courthouse Pasture drains into two canyons, Mill and Courthouse. This ride begins in sand, drops into the sometimes torn-up Mill Canyon slot, and then rolls over hills of sand and ledgy bedrock. Monitor and Merrimac Buttes stand at the far edge of Courthouse Pasture in the west. Your approach to the buttes is through deep sand in the form of rolling

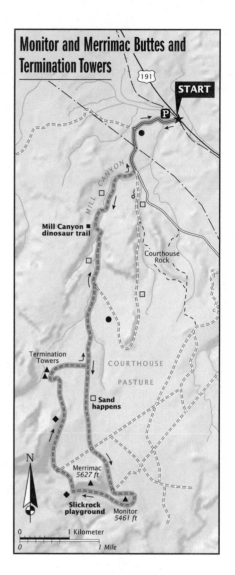

Monitor and Merrimac Buttes and Termination Towers

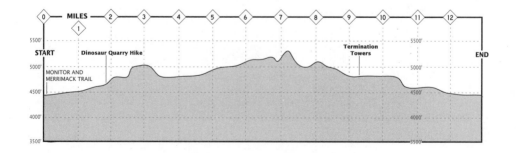

Two riders receive a broken thumb, a cracked rib, and a dose of rock rash within a mile of the trailhead and ride all day anyway.

hills—effectively, they are dunes. On the other side of the buttes is steep, exciting slickrock. I recommend that you ride with a guide the first time you ride in the Monitor and Merrimac and Courthouse Pasture area due to fragile desert flora and some particularly interesting, exposed, and dangerous freeform slickrock areas that are far more interesting and safe with someone who knows the area. It is a long way from any kind of help should something happen out here. This is most likely the reason the Bureau of Land Management and the Moab Bike Patrol have chosen to create a loop around Joe Camel Butte and call it the Monitor and Merrimac Bike Trail. As a result, not many bikers venture across the brutal beach sand to the slickrock on the other side of the buttes, where the original Monitor and Merrimac Trail carries you into danger and incredible scenery.

The deep sand that arrives midride can be especially difficult during late-summer months or in times of little rain, but it leads to easily ridable slickrock at the base of the buttes once you have paid your "sand dues." The white stones with the colorful interior on the slickrock at the bottom of the buttes are called chert, a volcanic rock that is eroding out of a couple of minor geological layers at their base where the Entrada gives way to the Navajo sandstone. This rock was used by the Anasazi, Fremont, and Ute tribes to fashion stone tools and can be found scattered as middens in various areas around Moab.

For more distance and challenge, combine this ride with Ride 9, Mill Canyon Mesa and Joe Camel Loop. It's best to start with the Mill Canyon/Joe Camel description, entering this ride from mile 2.6 of the directions here.

Miles and Directions

0.0   **START** from the parking area and ride your bike west toward Mill Canyon.

0.6   Bypass the spur to Tusher Canyon and continue on the marked Monitor and Merrimac Bike Trail.

1.1   Go right on the spur marked for Mill Canyon.

1.8   On your right is the Mill Canyon dinosaur quarry self-guided hike. It's worth the effort to take this 0.25-mile tour. Grab a brochure from the metal box. Past the dinosaur quarry, you will skirt along and across a stream. It can be technical here, depending on season and flash flooding, and presents you with some deep beach sand. Once out of the streambed, you will negotiate a couple of rolling dips into wash bottoms, then head straight out across the pasture's rolling hills and beach sand toward Merrimac Butte in the distance.

2.6   Continue straight ahead. The spur to your left connects the Mill Canyon Mesa loop with the Monitor and Merrimac Buttes and Termination Towers ride. (Note. If you are coming from mile 5.1 of the Mill Canyon Mesa and Joe Camel ride, turn left here to travel out to Monitor and Merrimac. Follow the mileage counts below.)

5.0   At the star-shaped intersection, take the second spur on the left that heads for the slickrock shelf. Once you leave the sand, go onto the shelf below the butte and go left around the base, between the big rocks, skirting the butte.

5.8 Once you reach the slickrock saddle between the buttes, go left on the rock and around Monitor Butte, keeping the smaller Monitor Butte to your right. Be careful to stay in the existing track and not tread on the vegetation. Stay against the butte and keep your eyes peeled for the singletrack on your left where the slickrock peters out into trees at the back of the slickrock shelf. Follow the singletrack as it widens and takes a right under a piñon pine and across its roots. It follows the base of the butte then gets bumpy just before you come to the point at the end of the butte. Go around the tip and hug the base of the butte for some great fun following the established trail. You will come out onto the slickrock saddle again once you have rounded the Monitor. Now head around behind the Merrimac, keeping it on your right. The basic route takes you along the steep slickrock shelf. There is some really great slickrock out here. Did you bring your camera? If not, kick yourself now. **Freeform.** (Off the mileage count.) On the back of the Merrimac is a slickrock playground, but it is covered with beautiful mosses and lichens, so you must take extra care to avoid the vegetation, rock mosses, and pits with cryptobiotic soil crusts. Once you have your fill of slickrock, go up the slickrock to the base of the Merrimac, then around to the left of the Merrimac. Once you have cleared the off-camber slickrock hill below the spires at the northwestern end of the Merrimac, ride down the bumpy bedrock and sand to the main 4WD spur that parallels the red cliff ahead, then go right on the sandy road below the cliff face. Behind you now is Wipeout Hill. If you pass the sign, you are going the wrong way.

9.3 After a lot of rolling and bumping over smooth slickrock ledges and bedrock nobs, you hit some downhill sand, then a spur. Go left on the spur and around the base of Termination Towers to the left. You have no doubt seen these spires in commercials. Once you round the towers, head across the rubble and scattered chert rock and find the 4WD track (usually marked by a cairn) that heads left down to a sandy 4WD spur.

9.8 Drop down to the sandy trail at the northern end of the towers and take a right.

10.2 Go left. You are now backtracking to the trailhead.

14.2 Return to your vehicle.

Ride Information

Trail Contacts

Bureau of Land Management
82 E. Dogwood
Moab, UT 84532
(435) 259-2196

Utah State School and Institutional Trust Lands Administration
1165 South US 191, Ste. 5
Moab, UT 84532
(435) 259-3760

Schedule

Trail is open year-round but is best during spring and fall.

Maps

USGS maps: Monitor and Merrimac, Jug Rock
Moab West Trail Map by Latitude 40° Inc.
Moab Recreation Map by F. H. Barnes

In Addition

Sand Riding Skills

Speed is the best tool for sand. Most short sand stretches can be negotiated with speed and good balance. Tires are your most important equipment edge in sand, but bikes with long top tubes, slack angles, and slightly longer chainstays have an advantage. Riser bars and short stems also help by shifting weight off the front end. As for the tires, it depends on the depth of the sand as to whether or not a narrow tire will work at all. If the sand is shallow, the narrow tire is an advantage. It will cut through to the hardpack below, but in deep sand wide tires with stout side knobs are best. *The fatter, the better* is the mantra as you chug through to the rewards on the other side of the dune. Believe it or not, a full-suspension bike will be an advantage also. It will smooth out the power to the ground as you chug. It will be a bit more of a chore to get rolling, but once you gain speed it will rip by the hardtails.

Before you attempt a relentless sand slog, deflate your tires to around twenty-five pounds. It's best to build speed on a fast section as you approach, but if you are coming down from a ledge or making a transition from slickrock, try to maintain momentum in a midrange gear, not too high and not too low. Just before you hit the sand, slide back on the saddle a few inches—feel the back edge of your saddle between your thighs. Almost lock your elbows and loosen your grip on the bars a bit. Now *go fast*. Search for ruts made by other bikers and put your wheel in the deepest, straightest one. Don't steer out of it. Let the bike follow the rut and adjust with hips and shoulders to maintain your line. To expedite a turn in sand, you must learn to steer with weight shifts of your hips and shoulders—back and forward with your hips and side to side with the shoulders. Steering with the front wheel is an advanced sand skill and recommended only to those who have already gotten the feel of riding in deep sand. If you get bogged, stand on your pedals and mash the bike down into the sand, sort of like you are on a pogo stick, shoving the rear wheel in for grip. In deep sand you must be able to do something I call the "Moab Track Stand," where you are clipped in and upright, but stationary. Now jump up and down, and as you come down hard, put power to the rear wheel so that it digs into the sand to the firmer surface below. Once you get rolling, smooth out your pedal stroke to an even spin and get back on the saddle as soon as you can. Maintain speed and float. It ain't easy.

Climbing in sand is a real chore. You must attack the sand with a ton of momentum. Going downhill is like skiing in powder and can be a load of fun. Keep your weight back, arms extended, and fly like Superman. Extreme sand on extreme downhill slopes requires that you get way behind the saddle and cantilever the front of the bike over the sand by pulling back on the bars with arms outstretched. This feels like you are grasping a handrail and leaning back.

Camping with Tony

"**H**ey, Tony, get your ass in gear and off that damn computer. Let's hit the road. It's getting late."

It was past 2:30 P.M. This is Tony Ellsworth's mode of operation: Leave late, get lost, and make sure something really bad happens so that you can do some male bonding and tell the story later. As if Tony weren't late enough, on the way out I accidentally drove past the unmarked turnoff to the trailhead, taking my passengers on an unexpected tour of Canyonlands National Park. When we finally mounted the bikes at the top of Spring Canyon, it was around 4:00 P.M.

"Aw come on, Lee, we can do a 35-mile ride in three hours," Tony whined. I had my doubts, but since I am always prepared for the worst and I had never ridden the Hey Joe loop, off we went into the fading afternoon.

The first part of the ride dropped us down into Spring Canyon on a very technical 4WD road. It had not been maintained in years and presented us with some extreme loose rock and ledges on the edge of a scary vertical cliff. By the time we made it to the bottom of the canyon, I was the only rider who had not taken a trip over the bars, not because I am more skilled, but because I am, frankly, a very cautious rider. It is my job not to be the one who breaks his face.

In the canyon Tony's half brother Mike Mulder had a flat, sucking up another twenty minutes, but the ensuing ride through Spring Canyon to the Green River was really sweet. We joyously ripped to the river's edge, where the ride immediately became sandy as hell. I searched for the old mining road along the river that I had been told about and seen in pictures, but it just wasn't there. I figured it must be farther on, so we pedaled through ankle-deep sand scanning the river's edge to our left. After 5 miles I came to the conclusion that the road had completely eroded away, leaving only a sandy ATV track to Hey Joe Canyon. Sand, as my tour clients will tell you, is my two-wheeled element, so I was able to stay out front for much of the ride along the river, sensing the group's frustration behind me. Only Bob Weissberg, who was the strongest rider among us, grew to appreciate its challenge and raced with me all the way to Hey Joe.

At the mouth of the canyon is an abandoned bulldozer. I took a couple of photos of Bob on the dozer while Mike dealt with a broken brake pad, then we ventured into the old mining area. From inside the canyon we took our first look at the portage above the mine shaft. No one can imagine how intimidating it is. We would have to suffer this nasty and nearly vertical 500-foot climb before we could mount up and ride.

> **"Aw come on, Lee, we can do a 35-mile ride in three hours," Tony whined.**

Tony Ellsworth

Tony and Mike decided to close the window on the day by exploring the old mine shaft for half an hour. When they emerged with enough radiation in their lungs to give the next four generations of their bloodline chromosomes that resemble spaghetti, Bob and I were already partially up the hill, discovering that the portage was even nastier than it looked. As we struggled up the cliff, I was glad I was with three other very fit riders. Hiking farther and farther toward the canyon rim, the portage became more and more difficult, finally requiring all energy just to get a body up the rock. Cleats compounded the problem. We formed a fire line up multiple rock ledges, handing the bikes up one at a time until we finally reached a spot where we could hike, then ride out and up onto the mesa above the canyon rim. The portage took over an hour to complete. It was already getting dark and we had over 20 miles to go.

We stood at the top for ten minutes trying to decipher the horrible guidebook I was operating from until we unanimously decided that we would finish the ride, find the author, and lynch the son of a bitch from a tree. I opted for relying on my memory of maps imprinted in my brain from writing permits for my tour company and the film industry. I knew how to get back, but if I took the route I was familiar with, this was going to be a lot longer ride than I had first imagined. I knew that if we headed out to the left, we would eventually end up at Dubinky Well Road just past Tombstone Rock; then we could take a right and head back toward the highway and grab the road we came in on. I knew it was going to be long, long, long, boring, boring, boring, and sandy, sandy, sandy.

We rode out as fast as we could through deep sand washes, over dunes and loose rock, across woefully short, but restful, stretches of hardpack that just dumped us into more and more deep, soft sand, until at last we reached Tombstone Rock. It was almost dark when I made the call to stop next to this appropriately named rock to make a fire, call it a camp, and pray to God that it did not rain or snow. It was early November, and the forecast was for the temperature to fall to twenty-eight degrees overnight. All Mike and Tony had for clothing were bike shorts and short-sleeved jerseys. Neither had more than half a bottle of water left—and almost no food. Bob had brought tights and a bike light. Tony had some precious sticks of jerky. Mike had a Walkman. Yay! I had two lighters, a couple of energy bars, rain gear, and too much water, as usual. Among us, we were going to be fine for the evening, though I was worried about the possibility of riding out at sunrise during the bitter-cold hours of dawn, back to the truck through the 20-plus miles of deep sand that I knew was ahead of us.

We tore up half the desert next to Tombstone Rock gathering creosote-soaked wood from a cattle fence. We picked up as many cow patties as we could rustle and heaped stacks of mangy sagebrush next to our camp. When at last the fire roared into the night sky, we settled in for some serious male bonding and our woefully inadequate dinner of jerky and energy bars, as the temperature fell to below freezing in a matter of minutes. It was like being on the moon. Body parts that faced the fire cooked like bacon on a grill. Body parts that were away from the fire froze. We kept our helmets on and soon discovered that they melted to our heads like heatshrink tubing. Mike and Tony, both unprepared in the clothing department, managed to snore loudly while entwined like Romeo and Juliet just inches from the fire. I expected them to ignite before too long.

I found out that if you cook a rock next to the fire it holds the heat for quite a while, making for a great warm pillow, but I could never sleep in a situation like this. As Mike, Tony, and Bob snoozed, I noticed a small yellow scorpion standing on my thigh appreciating the warmth of the fire. It sizzled and cracked when I tossed it into the flames with a twist of my hips. I watched shooting star after shooting star burn lines across the sky as I lay fully awake, scanning the horizon for the lights of the

Bob Weissberg

inevitable search and rescue vehicle. You see, I had left a note for my wife on our refrigerator that simply said, "Hey Joe with Ellsworth." We have a policy that if I am not back by midnight, it's time to call for help. This was Moab B.C.—that is, Moab Before Cell phones.

It was about 3:00 A.M. when I chucked the last cow chip on the fire and saw the lights of the search and rescue vehicle bouncing across the desert in the distance. Those folks are angels—even if Tony says that they ruined our camping trip. So you want to ride Hey Joe Canyon? My advice? Buy a cell phone, donate some money to Moab Search and Rescue, and don't ride Hey Joe Canyon as a loop.

11 Spring Canyon to Hey Joe Canyon

Start: From the top of Spring Canyon.
Length: 23.6-mile out-and-back. (The loop described in Camping with Tony is not detailed here and is not advised.)
Approximate riding time: 4 to 5 hours, depending on your fitness level and interests.
Difficulty: Technically difficult to extreme. If the dangerous and rocky descent into Spring Canyon doesn't challenge you, then the sand slog to Hey Joe certainly will. Physically difficult to extreme. Sand really takes it out of you. The climb back out is a real grunt.
Trail surface: Rugged 4WD and ATV track. Technical ledges, loose rock, sand, sand, and

more sand on the banks of the Green River. The descent into Spring Canyon is difficult. The road in may be dangerous and washed out in places, depending on maintenance or lack thereof.
Lay of the land: You will be leaving a desert plateau to descend into the depths of Spring Canyon and the Green River Gorge.
Total climbing: 3,141 feet.
Land status: Bureau of Land Management (BLM) land.
Other trail users: Hikers, equestrians, and off-road vehicles (ORV).
Best seasons: Spring and fall.

Environmental concerns: Cryptobiotic soil crusts are always just off the trail, but this ride is mostly sand. The sand will make you appreciate the crypto, because it's the crypto that stabilizes deep sand and turns it into fertile soil.

Warning! The roads in this area are completely impassable when wet! Watch the weather report the night before your ride, start early, and avoid the mine shafts in Hey Joe Canyon. Old mine shafts are everywhere around Moab. They always contain dangerous levels of radiation and sometimes house discarded explosives, which are extremely volatile when left to deteriorate. I found a blasting cap the very day I finished this chapter. It was lying on the edge of a watercourse just inches from my tire within a few yards of the Arches National Park boundary at Dalton Wells, so they are a lot easier to come by than I had ever realized. Do not touch anything that looks suspicious, especially anything that looks like a metal pencil; it could be a blasting cap. If there is any doubt as to what it is, don't pick it up! There are also old vertical mine and ventilation shafts in areas around mining activity. Careful where you step.

Getting there: From Moab: Follow U.S. Route 191 north for 12.5 miles. Go left on Utah Route 313 toward Dead Horse Point State Park and Canyonlands National Park. Travel 8.5 miles and turn right onto Dubinky Well Road, which may or may not be marked. Don't expect a sign. It was not there as of this writing. Drive for 6.5 miles in on this main road (the main road becomes Spring Canyon Road), avoiding all spurs off the dominant road, including the marked spur right to Dubinky Well. When the road begins to descend and the land ahead drops away into a deep canyon, park in a previously impacted spot off the road. Mount up and continue on your bikes, following the road down into Spring Canyon.

Hey Joe mine

The Ride

This ride features a dangerous descent, 9 miles of beach sand, and a chance to alter your genetic code with a visit into a radioactive mining area.

Okay, if you still want to ride to Hey Joe Canyon, here are necessary pointers. First, carry a lot more water than you would ever think you need. This means *two* bladders in your pack, or a hundred-ounce bladder and two large water bottles. Second, start your ride *really early!* Last, forget doing the loop that's documented in a couple of other guidebooks. The loop ride takes you up the side of Hey Joe Canyon on the sick portage described previously. Do this ride as an out-and-back from the top of Spring Canyon. Forget the loop! You'll like the out-and-back better anyway.

If you choose to do the loop, proceed at your own risk, but study the USGS quads and the Latitude 40° *Moab West* map carefully and thoroughly because *you can't*

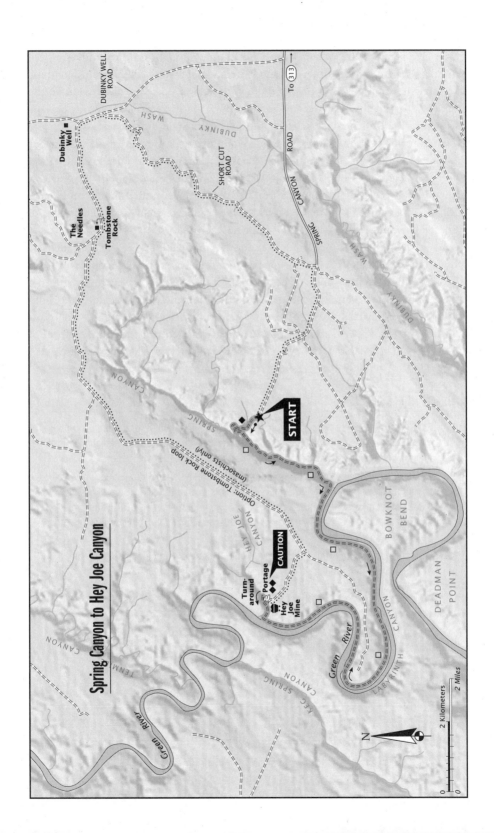

Spring Canyon to Hey Joe Canyon

To 313

DUBINKY WELL ROAD

DUBINKY WASH

Dubinky Well ■

The Needles ■

Tombstone Rock ■

SHORT CUT ROAD

SPRING CANYON ROAD

DUBINKY WASH

SPRING CANYON

START

Option: Tombstone Rock loop (masochists only)

HEY JOE CANYON

TENMILE CANYON

CAUTION

Turn-around

Portage

Hey Joe Mine

Green River

KEG SPRING CANYON

SPRING CANYON

Green River

LABYRINTH CANYON

BOWKNOT BEND

DEADMAN POINT

N

2 Kilometers

2 Miles

0

0

rely on descriptions in other guidebooks! It is a simple enough route to find using the Latitude 40° map, but the distance, sand, boredom, and wordy descriptions combine to create confusion that is not really there. If you do not take my advice and do the loop anyway, remember that once you are above the extremely dangerous portage out of Hey Joe Canyon, take a left. It just gets sandier, and this plateau section is a lot more boring than the sand grunt ride along the river. Far out on the loop, your most important landmark is Tombstone Rock. You can see it for quite some distance. The massive redrock butte looks like a huge apartment building. Just beyond it is Dubinky Well Road. It is here that you'll take a right. Another almost immediate right will take you back to the main road, where another right-hand turn will take you back to your vehicle at the top of Spring Canyon.

Again, the route documented here is not the horrible loop described in the preceding story, but rather a very challenging out-and-back. You'll encounter a steep and dangerous descent, 9 miles of deep sand along the Green River, and a visit to a uranium mine. The reverse trip has that same sand stuff and then a *very* difficult climb out. In summer Spring Canyon offers the opportunity for swimming in some great waterholes in the upper reaches of the canyon, if you detour right at the bottom of the Spring Canyon descent. Believe it or not, the return trip is like a completely different ride.

Miles and Directions

0.0 START from the rim of Spring Canyon. As you descend, watch out for the *big drop* and those nasty ledges that seem to happen right next to the cliff. Beware of sections of trail that may be totally washed out. The last time I rode this trail, it was a mess.

1.5 The descent ends and the 4WD road parallels the wash heading downstream to the river to your left. It is really pretty down here. When you reach the bottom, stop to take it in. **Side trip.** If the weather is hot, you can go right and up the canyon to visit some really fine swimming holes. These will require a bit of scrambling, depending on how far into Spring Canyon you travel.

3.1 When the trail hits the Green River, take a right and head upstream, staying on the dirt ATV track. It will probably be sandy as hell, but if you're lucky rain and ORV traffic will

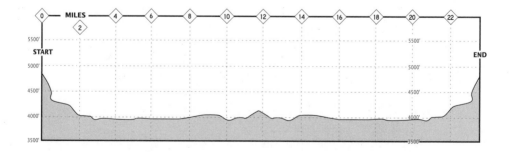

Spring Canyon rim

have packed it down a bit. The trip along the river remains sandy as it travels through groves of tamarisk trees and high grasses. It will present you with a few technical challenges, but mostly the sand is your biggest chore until you reach Hey Joe Canyon.

11.3 The big yellow bulldozer on the hill marks the entrance to Hey Joe Canyon and the old mining area. Go right here and ride into Hey Joe Canyon.

11.8 The old mine shaft is the destination. Once you have explored the area and taken your pictures, head back the way you came in. **Option:** The optional loop portage is a short distance past the shaft on the right-hand wall of the canyon and travels above the mouth of the mine, zigzagging its way up the rock face. I do not advise the portage or the ensuing loop on the plateau above, but if you must put yourself through this torture, be very careful on this portage. Take your time and carefully pick your way up the rock wall. Never attempt this ride alone!

Ride Information

Trail Contacts

Bureau of Land Management
82 E. Dogwood
Moab, UT 84532
(435) 259-2196

Schedule

Trail is open year-round but is best during spring and fall.

Maps

USGS maps: Dubinky, Bow Knot, Tenmile Point
Moab West Trail Map by Latitude 40° Inc.
Moab Recreation Map by F. H. Barnes

Moab Northwest

GEMINI BRIDGES AND
GOLD BAR RIM

North of the Colorado River, south of Utah Route 313, and west of U.S. Route 191 is where you'll find these rides. Many of the trails featured here can be ridden from Moab—by very fit, skilled, and prepared riders—by riding out the Old Moab Highway to the Gemini Bridges Trailhead on US 191.

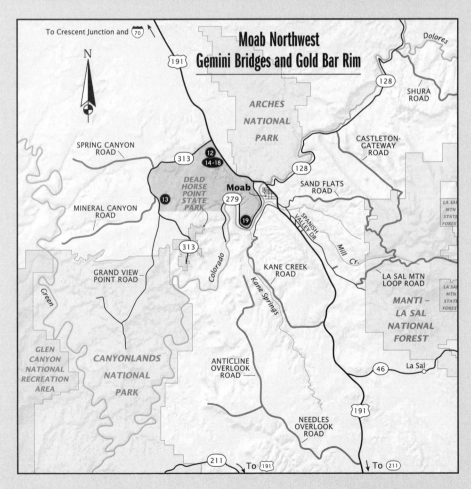

Myriad prospecting trails in the lands surrounding the twin rock span called Gemini Bridges have given birth to a network of recreational 4WD, motocross, ATV, and mountain bike trails. These trails provide a range of challenge from the most extreme technically and physically demanding to those easy enough for novices. Sadly, the Gemini Bridges area is seeing use that will require much more management regulation in coming years. We can only hope that there will be provisions made for our human-powered hiking accessory, the mountain bike.

The geology of this area varies greatly from the Rainbow Rocks and Klondike Bluffs area, where Entrada sandstone formations are supported by the Navajo sandstone underneath. The strata of the Gemini Bridges area is capped by the Kayenta and Navajo layers. The layers below the Navajo record ancient times before dinosaurs roamed the earth, while the seas were alive with bizarre monsters. This area was once swampland and tropical rain forest, home to beasts that resembled crocodiles on steroids. The Chinle layers exposed in the Gemini Bridges area contain fossilized remains of these animals and the huge trees of the forest.

The Chinle is also the layer where most of the uranium deposits were mined, hence the maze of trails through the canyons. Thank God for the bomb.

12 Eagle's Perch via Little Canyon Rim

Start: From the Gemini Bridges Trailhead on U.S. Route 191.

Length: 26.1-mile circuit.

Approximate riding time: 4 to 6 hours.

Difficulty: This ride offers moderate to very difficult technical challenges. The initial trek up from the trailhead is technically easy, but once you've exited the Gemini Bridges Trail the ride becomes more and more difficult due to repeated ledges, loose rock, and sand. Eventually a mix of slickrock and ever-challenging twists, turns, and climbs over and through loose rocks and ledged bedrock delivers you to the edge of the earth. The ride is physically difficult due to accumulated climbing and technical challenges that demand attention and strength to negotiate. Be especially cautious on your descent from the Eagle's Perch. Very difficult rock gardens appear suddenly around blind turns.

Trail surface: First on dirt road, then on a very technical 4WD track. Hardpack, loose rock, bedrock, slickrock, and sand on 4WD tracks. Lots of climbing. Dangerous downhill run on loose rock that surprises you with gnarly bedrock formations.

Lay of the land: You will be negotiating lovely redrock canyons to start with, then a long trek up to the very top of the rim above the highway takes you through a midget forest of piñon, juniper, and black bush. The rim is the highest point on the edge of the Moab Fault. The land surface behind the Eagle's Perch rolls, eroded into small canyons that widen as they retreat down and away from the edge of the Moab Fault—which means that during your ride you will gain and lose elevation repeatedly.

Total climbing: 2,100 feet.

Land status: Bureau of Land Management (BLM) and Utah State Trust lands.

Other trail users: Equestrians and off-road vehicles (ORV).

Best seasons: Spring and fall.

Environmental concerns: Cryptobiotic soil crusts and rare desert mosses abound. Please be especially careful as you approach the rim over the Moab Fault where the trail becomes less defined. Avoid mosses, lichens, and darkened pits, and stay off any soils that are not previously impacted and part of the marked trail.

Warning! Beware of standing too close to the cliff edges due to loose rocks, unpredictable bursts of wind, and thin rock overhangs (called "witch's tongue") that look like flat ground from above but are wafer-thin underneath.

Getting there: There are two ways to get to the trailhead: From Moab: Follow US 191 north from the intersection of Main and Center Streets for 11 miles to the Gemini Bridges Trailhead that is visible from the highway. If you come to Utah Route 313, you have gone too far. Turn left onto the access road, cross a cattle guard, and continue into the cleared gravel parking area bordered by a barbed-wire fence. A trail marker is on the left. Park and ride out on the Gemini Bridge Trail just ahead.

From Moab via bike: Ride north on US 191. Cross the Colorado River Bridge and pass the Arches National Park entrance. In less than 0.5 mile, after the looping right-hand bend in the road, you'll come to the Old Moab Highway pullout on the right. Pull into the parking area and

Little Canyon and the Gooney Bird

ride on the Old Moab Highway, avoiding any adjacent spurs, until you reach the Bar-M Chuckwagon. At the Bar-M Chuckwagon there's a spur left that will take you across US 191 to the Gemini Bridges Trailhead parking area.

The Ride

Famous as a very challenging 4WD route (called "Metal Masher"), this area is rarely visited by mountain bikers. Containing just over 2,100 feet of accumulative climbing, occasional technical ledgework, and a few exposed sections of trail, this ride is recommended only to strong riders with good skills. The trail is sometimes vague and this area is delicate, so be careful as you traverse the slickrock areas. I have included three GPS waypoints to assist you in finding your way, but as always, they are best used if you get hurt and need a helicopter. Take a cell phone with you on this one. If you can see the La Sal Mountains, the cell phone will work.

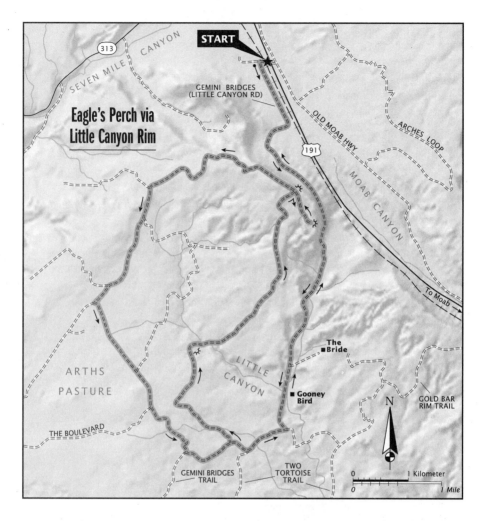

You will be climbing over the Moencopi formation on the Gemini Bridges Trail at the start of the ride, and then down and through Little Canyon, past a side canyon (where a spire famous to hardcore rock climbers called The Bride resides), under the Gooney Bird, across a wash, and then past the intersection with the Gold Bar Rim Trail, up a hill, and onto the edge of the expanse called Arths Pasture. When you finally depart the Gemini Bridges Trail, the ride becomes more and more technical until at last you reach the cliff face overlooking Arches National Park. From here the ride descends along the cliff edge, looping back to the west above Seven Mile Canyon, then across Arths Pasture and back to the Gemini Bridges Trail.

I have included the out-and-back to Gemini Bridges in the directions here. It is worth the bit of extra effort to put this stem on the lollipop, but if you are feeling a bit fatigued after your loop, you can go left at mile 16.5 and head directly back to the trailhead.

Miles and Directions

0.0   **START** from the Gemini Bridges Trailhead.

4.7   Intersect with Gold Bar Rim Trail. Head right and up the hill.

5.3   Go right on the marked Gemini Bridges Trail. The spur left is to Bull Canyon.

5.5   Take the obscure, sometimes partially blocked spur right.

7.5   Visit viewpoint on right over this scenic small canyon.

8.4   Go past the spur on your right.

8.5   Go past a spur on your left.

9.2   Go to the far side of the slickrock and take the defined road. Look for cairns.

9.8   There's a viewpoint on the right. Be careful: Wind and slippery rock can send you to meet your maker. (GPS Waypoint: N 38° 37.590' W 109° 40.460'.)

10.4   Carry your bike up the very ridiculous and almost impossible oil-and-rubber-coated 4WD spur right. The trail wraps around to your left with a challenging rock climb immediately ahead. Cairns are sometimes a help here, but just try to stay on the main track. If you get diverted, don't worry too much. All spurs here eventually reconnect.

10.6   Bear left. **Side trip.** The spur to the right heads to Eagle's Nest and a spectacular viewpoint. Go check it out.

10.9   Pull off to right below the large cairn on the cliff. The spot is perfect for photography. Careful on the edge. Remember that there are undercut surfaces ("witch's tongues") on the edge of the cliff. (GPS Waypoint: N 38° 38.235' W 109° 40.393'. Altitude: 5,814 feet.)

12.0   Take the spur left.

12.6   These power lines are a great help in getting you the hell outta here. You will be riding parallel to them.

13.0   Take the left spur at the Y across Arths Pasture.

14.4   Stay left at the Y. Ignore all spurs off this main road.

15.7   Stay left at the Y.

16.5   Reach a sign. Go right toward Gemini Bridges.

17.2   The Crack House is just off the trail only a few feet to your right. This is a famous climbing spot where folks practice traversing overhanging ledges with cracks in the bottom.

17.4   Go right at the Y.

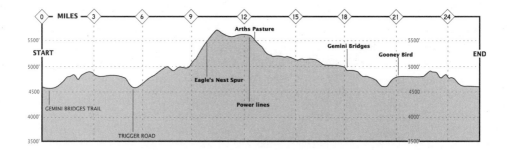

View from Little Canyon Rim. The bike on the right belongs to Terry Jackson, Bruce Willis's stunt double.

17.8   Go left to Gemini Bridges. This is a side spur to the bridges, not the main trail. It is currently well marked. The main trail to the right takes you up to the Gemini Bridges Trailhead on UT 313.

18.3   You are now at the area above Bull Canyon where the Gemini Bridges are located. (GPS Waypoint: N 38° 35.099' W 109° 42.556'. Altitude: 4,800 feet.) Return via same route you came in on and stay on the Gemini Bridges Trail all the way back to US 191. (For more information on Gemini Bridges, see the next five rides.)

19.2 Do not miss this left turn at the Y.

22.1 The formation above you is called the Gooney Bird.

26.3 Arrive back at the trailhead.

Ride Information

Trail Contacts

Bureau of Land Management
82 E. Dogwood
Moab, UT 84532
(435) 259-2196
Utah State School and Institutional Trust Lands Administration
1165 South US 191, Ste. 5, Moab, UT
(435) 259-3760

Schedule

Trail is open year-round but is best during spring and fall.

Maps

USGS maps: Merrimac, Gold Bar
Moab West Trail Map by Latitude 40° Inc.
Moab Recreation Map by F. H. Barnes

Rocks are hard, Girls are soft, Coyotes run off with your bones

When I first settled in Moab, I took a job with Lin Ottinger's land tours leading four-wheel-drive interpretive trips along the White Rim. I took this job even though every soul in Moab warned me about Lin's frightening temper and sleazy redneck ways. After spending time with Lin, I just couldn't help but love him for his accomplishments and his unparalleled knowledge of canyon country. I think it is because I had a difficult father that I can put up with Lin's "mess" more than most folks. Most of it just rolls off my back and, frankly, I came to Moab because of folks like Lin.

Lin Ottinger started Utah's first land tour business with a modified Volkswagen bus that he used to cart tree huggers out into the scary wilderness in every direction. Within a few short years, Lin's reputation grew to mythic proportions, based on his dramatic landscape photography, rare dinosaur finds, homespun common sense geological knowledge, furious anger, and legendary nightly slide shows held at his rock shop after each day tour. These slide shows are still talked about by Moab locals old enough to remember. In a room in the back of the rock shop he would display a shockingly beautiful and eclectic collection of slide images as he narrated each in his Tennessee hillbilly drawl, lambasting the Park Service, skewering educated scientists with

Let's have Lin Ottinger stuffed and mounted before he hurts someone.

pointed verbal barbs, and ridiculing organized Christian religion with obscene stories and comic heresy.

Lin's blunt wit, "flowery" language, and fiery and extremely effective temper have made him larger than life. He was and is loved, respected, hated, despised, ignored, and avoided. You name it. Lin was, and is, very high profile. I have so many stories about Lin Ottinger that I could fill this book with some of the funniest, scariest stuff imaginable. So here is a little story of a trip that should give you a taste for the life and times of the nearly mummified tour guide that is Lin Ottinger. There are other tiny tales of Lin in this book, but this little one is my favorite.

It was thirty-two degrees, midnight in the desert just outside Price, Utah. I was pushing Lin Ottinger's beat-up GMC diesel pickup 3 miles along a lonely highway to a mythical all-night garage. Lin was in the front seat eking out the engine's last gasps. It was burning just enough fuel to fill my bursting lungs and freeze my sinuses with smelly, intoxicating fumes.

He was and is loved, respected, hated, despised, ignored, and avoided.

Lin had nursed the sputtering monster across 100 miles of desert, temporarily mending symptoms of a dying fuel pump with spit, air, tape, and hillbilly ingenuity. The truck's top speed, however, slowly decreased to zero.

He stopped at a filling station to Mickey Mouse the problem.

I stood by and watched as he cussed and tinkered. You don't tell Lin Ottinger how to do anything. I tried not to get too close.

He blew into the line.

"Listen to the tank," he bluntly ordered.

I bent over and cocked an ear toward the filler.

"What are you doing? Did you hear what I said? *Are you stupid?*" He ran over, yanked off the filler cap, and pointed. "Right *here!*"

I was in this predicament for the sake of geodes. You know, hollow rocks, volcanic bombs. But more specifically, for Dugway geodes, found a stone's throw from the air force chemical weapons facilities at Dugway Proving Grounds. The air force was bulldozing a road into the Dugway test area and was exposing thousands of geodes for the taking. When I passed the rumor and a map to Lin, he simply couldn't resist.

They were waiting for us, the midnight mechanic, a fat, oily man with pants slung way low, and his two Mexican assistants, shy brothers who could not speak a word of English.

Mr. Pants Slung Low opened the hood of the truck and took a long look.

"Not getting enough fuel, huh?"

Lin pointed to the fuel pump. "Something is rattling around in there like a preacher's #@!★ in a calf's #@!."

The fat mechanic put gut to grill. He bent into the engine compartment, legs in the air, and called for a tool in Spanish. One of the brothers scurried to retrieve the tool, then scooted back to a bulbous kerosene heater roaring and fuming away like a jet engine on the greasy concrete floor.

The fat mechanic's butt glistened fully exposed under the hood, oily, hairy, and steaming.

I must have been grinning ear to ear when Lin walked by, screwed up his face, and said out of the corner of his mouth: "I don't think these guys know what they are doing."

I replied: "I'm amazed we found anyone. It's midnight, for Pete's sake. Check out that moon! It's worth pushing the truck 3 miles in the cold and dark for that butt shot."

Lin cocked his head and walked away. Lin can spot a desert bighorn sheep or an Indian paintbrush in bloom at 1,000 yards, but he didn't see that big flabby, shiny rear end? I began to worry about his eyesight, his sense of humor. I figured this was normal to Lin. He must deal with a lot of low-pants people.

I entertained the thought of running out into the road and flagging down a car. It seemed as if I was the only one present who could actually sense the comic purity of that moment. I wanted so much to share it with someone.

The butt-mechanic revved the engine in roaring spasms, blasting thick blue smoke into the shop for a full ten minutes. I was having a very hard time containing my laughter. Intoxicating diesel vapors rose from the floor like dry ice at a Doobie Brothers concert. The fat man's pale ass shown through the fog like tropical fruit.

Light headed from the fumes and the constant suppression of uncontrollable belly laughing, I weaved and stumbled up to Lin and said, "I don't think these guys know what they are doing."

"These idiots are going to blow my engine," he snarled in that unique twisted old-man Tennessee drawl of his.

I worried about his temper. I didn't want to witness a legendary Lin Ottinger explosion, 12.5 on the Richter scale.

Lin walked to the front of the truck and the sight of the fat mechanic's ass finally registered on his face. He winced comically, looked at me, looked at the glowing butt, looked back at me, looked back at the butt. He paused for a moment, then screamed above the whine of the engine: "The comet! *Have you guys seen the comet? Hey, I said, have you guys seen the comet?*"

The brothers stood warming themselves next to the thundering heater, eyes glazed.

"Que?"

Under the hood of the sputtering diesel truck, the mechanic peeked around his huge glowing ass.

Lin pointed up. "The comet."

"Ahhh, la commetta?" Smiles emerged from the blackened faces of the Mexican brothers.

Lin continued to point skyward. "Si. La commetta. In the sky. Right now. Come outside and see it."

Lin beckoned and roused the oily, nocturnal mechanics into the cold night air, under the stars.

I followed.

Standing in frozen mud, among the junked cars, Lin raised his arm over his head and pointed a crooked finger at an apparition above. "See it?"

As my eyes became accustomed to the darkness, the gargantuan comet revealed itself through the bare limbs of a giant cottonwood tree, the milky tongue of Aphrodite, covering a third of the night sky like a veil of delicate lace across a sparkling bed of frosted lights.

"Ahhhh, La cometta est grande."

"Si. Si."

"Gracias. Gracias."

Lin smiled and pointed, ever the tour guide, "Beautiful, si?" He spoke very slowly, waiting for a nod of feigned understanding after each phrase or word. "That long tail? . . . As . . . the comet . . . moves . . . through the galaxy . . . it points . . . away from . . . the sun." His arm still over his head, waving a crooked finger at the sky, Lin was the consummate interpretive guide, even in the desert on the edge of nowhere with three greasy incompetent mechanics, two of whom could not understand a word he was saying. Despite his age and the years he has spent observing the universe with only a sixth-grade education to show the way, Lin cannot avoid sharing the wonders of the natural world with anyone who will listen or simply nod a numb brain while it goes in one ear and out the other. With a sigh he lowered his arm and continued to stare skyward. His withered old face glowed with a timeless, innocent wonder as he said very softly, "It's made of ice."

This was Lin's way of softening the blow of failure for the midnight mechanics, and once the cold set in, we parted ways—the mechanics to their fumes and grease, Lin and I to the highway. I had to push the damn truck 3 miles back into Price with my tongue hanging out like that great big comet. I swear it was uphill both ways. I gave up on the geodes. I got what I came for though, a real Lin Ottinger experience.

I gave up on the venture after a day in Price hunting down parts for the truck, but Lin will do anything to get his rocks. After driving me back to Moab he turned around and headed for Dugway. Three days later he returned to town with a few tons of the nerve gas geodes in the back of his smelly, rattling GMC truck.

It was Lin Ottinger who first discovered and named Gemini Bridges, what may be the only side-by-side twin natural bridges in the world. Actually he found them twice. Sometime in the late 1950s, while prospecting for uranium in the area bordering Arths Pasture, he came across the bridges. He soon forgot where they were, though. While you are out here, imagine this area with no roads at all, and maybe you can sense why it was not until 1962 that Lin once again found these rare natural bridges. It was Lin who cut the first roads into this area and named all the features—the Gooney Bird, the Bride, the Eagle's Perch, and so on. Lin is now over seventy years old, a relic and still a Moab attraction, kinda like the Gemini Bridges themselves, though Lin is certainly more abrasive than any rock you will be riding on, and a lot more . . . temporary. I just hope that when he finally passes away, we can get a good taxidermist to stuff him. I would like to see him placed next to the bridges with his crooked finger pointing into Bull Canyon and one of those push-button recorded messages that you could listen to. It would be in Lin's southern drawl and would go something like this: "These are the Gemini Bridges, the only twin natural bridges in the entire world. A bridge is not an arch. An arch is formed from a single geological layer. HEY, get your ass away from the edge, *you stupid ★@!#ing idiot!*"

Lin Ottinger's rock shop

When in Moab, visit Lin's Moab Rock Shop. You can't miss it. It is just off Main Street at the northern entrance to town. Look for the big yellow sign and the radioactive uranium mining carts. Lin's reputation as the "dinosaur man" is well earned. Iguanodon's last name is "*ottingeri,*" by the way, so he is also acknowledged by the educational community as a valuable resource and discoverer of many fossilized species of plants and animals. The Moab Rock Shop is more of a museum than a place to buy rocks, and while you are there, ask Lin about the oldest human skeletons found in North America. He came across them in a copper mine south of Moab and still has a green fossil copper tibia in a glass case in his shop—the rest he gave to Brigham Young University. Lin claims that the skeletons are white people, which would effectively turn written anthropological history on its ear. "If those scientific plagiarists were to acknowledge these fossilized human bones, they would have to refigure the whole damn mess," says Lin. He goes on: "This phony archaeologist woman came in my shop. I told her about these bones and she said, 'I certainly hope you are wrong.' I asked her why and she said, 'Because it would ruin my career.' I said, 'Yer car-rear? Well, your career ain't crap. Do you think that the truth gives one rotten damn about your stupid ★@!#ing car-rear?' I had her crying in no time."

13 Gemini Bridges

Start: From the Gemini Bridges Trailhead on Utah Route 313.

Length: 13.1-mile point-to-point (or a 26.2-mile out-and-back).

Approximate riding time: 2 to 3 hours, depending on your fitness level and interests.

Difficulty: Technically easy. Physically easy. Since the route is mostly downhill, the only real workout you're in for is the final climb up to the top of the Moencopi formation just before the drop to the trail tail.

Trail surface: Dirt road. Downhill most of the way if done as a point-to-point.

Lay of the land: You'll be dropping down from the plateau of the Island in the Sky through wide-open cattle lands of Arths Pasture, then down into canyon country.

Total climbing: 1,924 feet.

Land status: BLM and Utah State Trust lands.

Other trail users: Motorists and off-road vehicles (ORV).

Best seasons: Spring and fall.

Environmental concerns: There is some pretty bad news about the Gemini Bridges Trail and other rides in this area: Arths Pasture, the upper reaches of the Gemini Bridges Trail, Dry Fork, and Bull Canyon have recently been raped by oil exploration. Huge thumper trucks weighing twenty-five tons with 8-foot wheels created a grid across the lands below Dead Horse Point, across Arths Pasture, as they performed seismic tests to milk Utah of its measly oil reserves, estimated to meet national consumption needs for two days. And in a move to secure the lands adjacent to the Gemini Bridges Trail for development in the future, the BLM and Grand County graded the Gemini Bridges Trail. What used to be one of the best mountain bike rides in all of southern Utah is now home to hordes of quad runners, motorcycles, and four-wheel-drive vehicles. Heck, you don't even need an off-road vehicle to drive to the bridges anymore. Any family sedan will do.

Getting there: From Moab: Follow U.S. Route 191 north from the intersection of Main Street and Center Street for 12.5 miles. Turn left onto UT 313 toward the Island in the Sky and Dead Horse Point. Continue heading west on UT 313 for another 12.8 miles. The signed Gemini Bridges Trail is located about a mile past the signed road to Horsethief Point and Mineral Canyon, and between mile markers 10 and 9 on UT 313. Pull into one of the cleared parking spots and mount your bikes.

Shuttle Point From Moab: Follow US 191 north from the intersection of Main Street and Center Street for 11 miles. There is a dirt road left that leads into a large dirt parking area, which is easily spotted from the highway. This is the posted trailhead that accesses the Gemini Bridges Trail. This is where you will leave your shuttle vehicle. If you like a good climb at the start of your ride, park and head up the trail from here.

Gemini Bridges

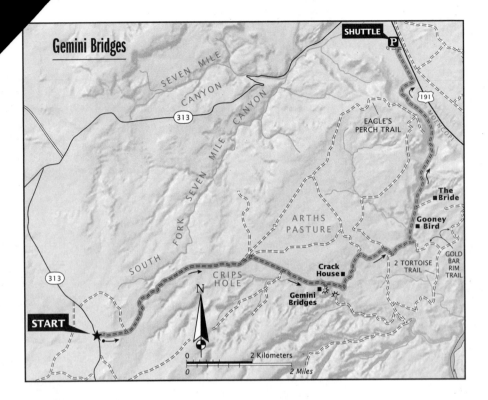

Gemini Bridges

SHUTTLE

SEVEN MILE CANYON

313

SOUTH FORK SEVEN MILE CANYON

MOENKOPI

191

EAGLE'S PERCH TRAIL

The Bride

Gooney Bird

ARTHS PASTURE

GOLD BAR RIM TRAIL

2 TORTOISE TRAIL

313

CRIPS HOLE

Crack House

Gemini Bridges

START

N

0   2 Kilometers

0   2 Miles

The Ride

This trail is well marked by the Moab Bike Patrol and the BLM and can be enjoyed as a point-to-point, mostly downhill trip with the use of a shuttle. (I say "well marked" knowing well that these trail markers are prized souvenirs. They can and do disappear on occasion.) The shuttled ride begins at the trailhead on UT 313. The out-and-back ride begins from the trailhead on US 191. The out-and-back is also possible by bike from Moab with a ride out US 191 past the entrance to Arches National Park and onto the Old Arches Road to a point across from the trailhead on US 191. You can also bike up UT 313 to the trailhead and do the ride as a huge loop.

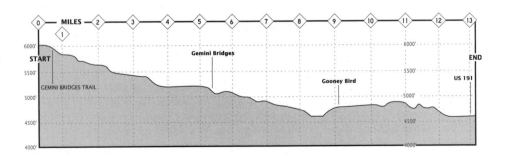

MILES 0 1 2 3 4 5 6 7 8 9 10 11 12 13

6000'   Gemini Bridges   6000'

START   END

5500'   5500'

GEMINI BRIDGES TRAIL   Gooney Bird   US 191

5000'   5000'

4500'   4500'

4000'   4000'

The Gemini Bridges area is host to many unique rock formations and fossil records. Little Canyon, the Gooney Bird, the Bride, the Crack House, Crips Hole, Four Arch Canyon, and Arths Pasture are all sights along this trail. The Gemini Bridges Trail is also the main artery to rides like Gold Bar Rim, Day Canyon Overlook, Bull Canyon, Dry Fork, and others. Though the trail is well marked, it can be confusing at the Bridges where the trail spurs down to the Bridges themselves. Remember, this is just a spur. In order to continue on your journey, you must climb back up to where this spur departed the main trail.

Miles and Directions

0.0 **START:** The trail here is also called the Boulevard, as it's wide and fast. Take the trail east through the top of Arths Pasture.

3.0 There is a sign marking the right-hand spur to Gemini Bridges.

4.6 Bear left next to the right-hand spur marked for Crips Hole and Four Arches Trail. **Option:** The Crips Hole spur right is worthy of a visit and holds many attractions, including a couple of 4WD spurs into tight canyons to the south and, as the sign says, if you travel to the east, four arches. It is, however, a sand trap. So if you don't like sand, don't venture here.

5.5 Go right at the Y. Immediately afterward, go straight on the spur to the Gemini Bridges. The spur is marked by white dotted lines to the Bridges. Enjoy the Gemini Bridges area by riding across the twin bridges, then scrambling across the rocks opposite the formation to get a good look. There is also a very beautiful view of Bull Canyon up a short spur to the right of the Bridges. Lots of exposure out here, so be careful. The bridges themselves are deceptive, and you don't really know the danger you are in until you see them from across Bull Canyon or from the undercut section next to the bridges themselves.

6.2 On the way out from the bridges, go right at the top of the short ledgy climb back to the trail and follow the trail markers to the right that read HIGHWAY 191.

6.5 Stay on the main spur, avoiding all spurs left or right.

6.8 Go left. Don't get sucked into the spur straight ahead.

7.8 Continue straight.

9.1 This is the intersection with the Gold Bar Rim Trail. Go left at the bottom of the hill. **Option:** There is an arch (I call it Cowgirl Arch) immediately up the short spur that branches left within a few yards, if you're interested. Directly ahead on the Gemini Bridges Trail is the Gooney Bird, a goofy-looking rock formation that dominates the entrance to the tightest point of Little Canyon. The Bride, a well-known climbing destination, is up a side canyon to your right just past the Gooney Bird. Both of these formations, like Gemini Bridges, were discovered and named by old-timer and human dinosaur Lin Ottinger. Stay on the main trail and you'll be presented with a short, steep climb that will take you over the top of the Moencopi formation and to beautiful views of the Moab Valley, the Moab Fault, the La Sal Mountains, and the US 191 corridor below. The remaining trail is downhill to your shuttle at the trailhead below on US 191.

13.1 The trail ends at the parking lot on US 191.

Ride Information

Trail Contacts

Moab Bike Patrol
c/o Bureau of Land Management
82 E. Dogwood
Moab, UT 84532
(435) 259-2196

**Utah State School and Institutional Trust
Lands Administration**
1165 South US 191, Ste. 5, Moab, UT 84532
(435) 259-3760

Schedule

Trail is open year-round but is best during spring and fall.

Maps

USGS maps: Merrimac, Gold Bar, The Knoll
Moab West Trail Map by Latitude 40° Inc.
Moab Recreation Map by F. H. Barnes

MORMON TEA *(Ephedra torreyana)*

Ephedra, also known as Mormon tea or squaw tea—listed as whorehouse tea in many herb books—is a prolific plant in canyon country. It differs from other species of Ephedraceae in that it possesses three leaves and cones per node. At first glance the plant appears to have no leaves, but if you look closely you'll see tiny scalelike protrusions at the joints of the stout green stalks that are the plant's stems. Its tiny yellow flowers are small cones produced at the nodes of each branch. The plant is about 2 feet tall, bushy, lush green in spring and summer and yellowish during fall and winter. Mormon tea is found on almost every ride listed in this book. As the name implies, the stalks make a delicious stimulating tea that dilates blood vessels and pupils, raises the heart rate, keeps you awake, and heightens sexual drive. It is very good at controlling sinus problems and is the source of pseudoephedrine, an over-the-counter drug used for sinus illness. Because it is a potent stimulant and performance enhancer, pseudoephedrine is illegal and tested for in bike racing. It is also known as a fine cure for venereal disease. The American Indians of the desert Southwest used it as a tonic and stimulant much like the Indians in South America use coca leaves. It is the strawlike weed that usually sticks from the mouth of cowboys herding cattle in the desert. If he is riding a horse, is with some cows, and doesn't have a stick of Mormon tea in his mouth, he ain't a cowboy. He's a "dude."

14 Two Tortoise Rock

Start: From the Gemini Bridges Trailhead on U.S. Route 191.
Length: 16.1-mile circuit.
Approximate riding time: 2 to 3 hours.
Difficulty: Technically moderate to very difficult. The ride in to the Gold Bar split-off is simple, but from there expect deep sand, ledges, loose rock, and rolling terrain. Physically moderate to difficult. The climbing and technical workout can tax an intermediate rider.
Trail surface: Out on a county-maintained dirt road and a loop on a technical 4WD track. Ledgy bedrock, sand, babyheads, packed sand, smooth bedrock, hardpack, and wash crossings with sand and ledge transitions.
Lay of the land: Canyons, canyons, canyons. Washes, washes, washes. Rock. The vivid colors of the Moencopi, Chinle, and Wingate geological layers decorate the walls as you ride into and through three prominent canyons.
Total climbing: 1,458 feet.
Land status: Bureau of Land Management (BLM) and Utah State Trust lands.
Other trail users: Hikers, equestrians, and off-road vehicles (ORV).
Best seasons: Spring and fall.

Note to the reader: This ride can be combined with any or all of the following rides—Bull Canyon, Dry Fork Canyon, and Day Canyon Overlook—to create longer, more challenging rides.

Environmental concerns: Extremely fragile! Cryptobiotic soil crusts and rare desert mosses abound on and between the slickrock. Stay on the trail at all times. If it is alive, don't ride or step on it. Things revegetate very slowly out here.

Getting there: From Moab: Follow US 191 north from the intersection of Main and Center Streets for 11 miles to the Gemini Bridges Trailhead. The massive cliff just before the trailhead is the Eagle's Perch, named after a birdlike formation on the top edge, visible as you are riding on the highway from Moab. If you come to Utah Route 313, you have gone way too far. When you see the marked Gemini Bridges parking area on your left, turn onto the access road, cross a cattle guard, and continue into the cleared area bordered by a barbed-wire fence. The trail marker is on the left. Park and ride out on the Gemini Bridge Trail.

The Ride

The Two Tortoise ride is an alternative that departs from the Gemini Bridges Trail at the Gold Bar Rim Trail spur offering a short but sweet and very technical loop that eventually connects to Bull Canyon Road and completes the loop back at the spur to Gold Bar Rim. Once on the Two Tortoise Rock loop, the trail becomes sandy and more and more ledgy and technical. The scenery is awesome, and the accessibility to a number of other routes described here can turn this into a leg of a very fine epic ride. This ride, as well as the others that connect in the Rainbow Rocks area, can present you with great wildlife viewing when done during early morning. While recording the mileage count for this ride, I came across a family of desert bighorn sheep in Little Canyon. I then saw an owl, a hawk, and a gazillion lizards and rabbits.

Two Tortoise Rock is sometimes called "Dog Style."

Miles and Directions

0.0 **START** from the parking area and head south on the wide trail. The trail climbs over the Moencopi formation, and then drops you into Little Canyon. The downhill through Little Canyon is a pleasant rush after the climb. **Option.** If you like sand and transitions and a chance to hunt for fossils, there are washes to ride that cross the trail—but *stay* in the wash if you choose to ride off the trail. Folks think I am crazy for opting for the deep sand in the wash bottoms, but maybe there are others like me who prefer the sand over the well-used trail. Huge areas of cryptobiotic soil crusts surround the washes, so don't leave the wash once you are in it. If it becomes too much for you, backtrack. One wash weaves back and forth, crossing the road many times. Of course, this will screw up your mileage count and could give you a case of sand anger.

4.65 The spur right is to a small arch that I call Cowgirl Arch. Shade happens there.

4.7 At the trail marker, head south (left) on the sandy, sandy spur toward the Gold Bar Rim Trail. The marked Gemini Bridges Trail heads up the hill to your right. The sand at the beginning of the spur to Gold Bar Rim is truly nasty but will gradually give way to technical ledges. Have faith.

5.0 Take one of the two sandy spurs left out of the wash. It doesn't matter which one. Just take the one that looks ridable at the time.

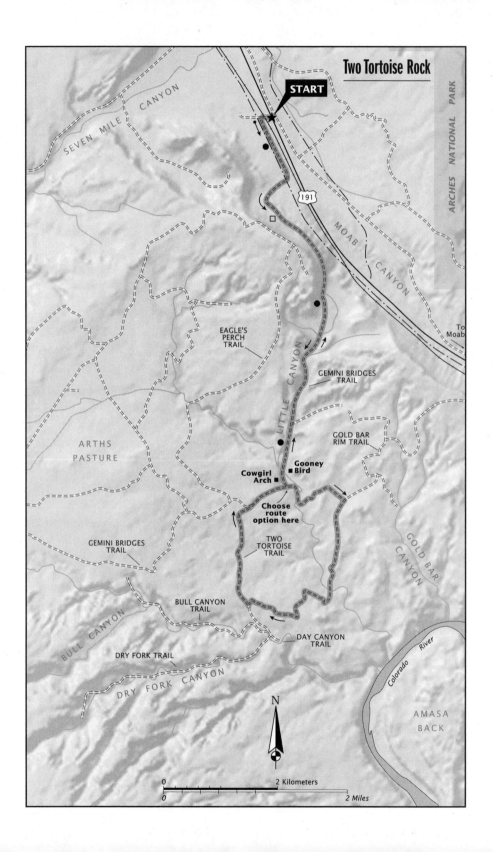

Two Tortoise Rock

START

SEVEN MILE CANYON

ARCHES NATIONAL PARK

191

MOAB CANYON

To Moab

EAGLE'S PERCH TRAIL

LITTLE CANYON

GEMINI BRIDGES TRAIL

GOLD BAR RIM TRAIL

ARTHS PASTURE

Cowgirl Arch ■

■ Gooney Bird

Choose route option here

TWO TORTOISE TRAIL

GEMINI BRIDGES TRAIL

GOLD BAR CANYON

BULL CANYON TRAIL

BULL CANYON

DAY CANYON TRAIL

DRY FORK TRAIL

DRY FORK CANYON

Colorado River

AMASA BACK

N

0   2 Kilometers

0   2 Miles

5.7 Encounter fun ledges.

6.0 Go right at the trail marker toward Bull Canyon and Day Canyon. The sign was missing the last time I was on this trail. The marker changes every time they replace it and can be misleading. Go right. Let the BLM deal with it.

7.7 After some ledge challenges and sand transitions, you find yourself under Two Tortoise Rock.

8.3 At the Y you can go either way. The route straight ahead is more challenging.

8.5 This is where the previous choice at mile 8.3 reconnects.

9.1 Go left at the Y.

9.2 You've come to the road sometimes referred to as Trigger Road, but marked as Bull Canyon Road. To close the loop for this ride, turn right and go uphill. To your immediate left are Bull Canyon, Dry Fork, and Day Canyon Overlook. **Option.** To lengthen this loop by combining it with other trails in the Gemini Bridges area, check out the Bull Canyon, Dry Fork, and Day Canyon Overlook rides in this chapter, or the Gemini Bridges, Gold Bar Rim, and Eagle's Perch rides elsewhere. To combine the Bull, Dry, and Day options, go left and downhill. The mileage count from here out assumes you are closing the loop and heading back to the trailhead by going right.

10.7 This is the intersection with the Gemini Bridges Trail. Go right to close the loop. **Option.** If you want to lengthen the ride to include a trip out to Gemini Bridges or to include the more difficult Eagle's Perch ride, then this is the place you will be turning left. The mileage count below assumes you are turning right to close the loop and heading back to the trailhead. After your right-hand turn, you will climb a bit, then descend rapidly into Little Canyon. Be careful to control your speed on the final descent. It is loose and sandy at the bottom.

11.3 This is the intersection of the Gemini Bridges and Gold Bar Rim Trails, where the loop is closed. You want to continue on the Gemini Bridges Trail to the left, passing the spur in 0.1 mile that goes left to Cowgirl Arch. Go back through Little Canyon beneath the Gooney Bird—the formation that looks like, well, a Gooney Bird. I call it Godzilla because it looks more like Godzilla than a Gooney Bird, but call it what you want. It is easy to spot. The slow climb back through Little Canyon grows steeper as you reach the cliff below the Eagle's Perch. This short climb is a pain in the butt only because it is at the end of the ride. Once you crest the climb, you are rewarded with a fast downhill. Don't slide off the edge. It could be unpleasant.

16.1 Arrive back at the trailhead.

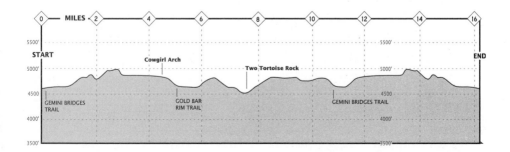

Ride Information

Trail Contacts

Bureau of Land Management
82 E. Dogwood
Moab, UT 84532
(435) 259-2196

Utah State School and Institutional Trust Lands Administration
1165 South US 191, Ste. 5, Moab, UT 84532
(435) 259-3760

Schedule

Trail is open year-round but is best during spring and fall.

Maps

USGS maps: The Knoll, Gold Bar, Klondike
Moab West Trail Map by Latitude 40° Inc.
Moab Recreation Map by F. H. Barnes

15 Bull Canyon

Start: From the Gemini Bridges Trailhead on U.S. Route 191.
Length: 18.4-mile out-and-back.
Approximate riding time: 3-plus hours.
Difficulty: Technically easy to moderately difficult due to babyheads and deep sand in Bull Canyon proper. Physically moderate. Climbing happens here.
Trail surface: Hardpack and loose rocky sediments, babyheads, deep sand, and bedrock on 4WD road.

Lay of the land: Canyons, canyons, canyons. Washes, washes, washes. Rock. The vivid colors of the Moencopi, Chinle, and Wingate geological layers decorate the walls as you ride into and through three prominent canyons.
Total climbing: 1,920 feet.
Land status: BLM and Utah State Trust lands.
Other trail users: Hikers, equestrians, and off-road vehicles (ORV).
Best seasons: Spring and fall.

Note to the reader: This ride can be combined with any or all of the adjoining rides—Two Tortoise Rock, Dry Fork Canyon, and Day Canyon Overlook—to create longer, more challenging rides.

Environmental concerns: Extremely fragile! Cryptobiotic soil crusts and rare desert mosses abound on and between the slickrock. Stay on the trail at all times. If it is alive, don't ride or step on it. Things revegetate very slowly out here.

Getting there: From Moab: Follow US 191 north from the intersection of Main and Center Streets for 11 miles to the Gemini Bridges Trailhead. The massive cliff just before the trailhead is the Eagle's Perch, named after a birdlike formation on the top edge, visible as you are riding on the highway from Moab. If you come to Utah Route 313, you have gone way too far. When you see the marked Gemini Bridges parking area on your left, turn onto the access road, cross a cattle guard, and continue into the cleared area bordered by a barbed-wire fence. The trail marker is on the left. Park and ride out on the Gemini Bridge Trail.

The Ride

The Bull Canyon ride is more moderate and takes you below Gemini Bridges on a 4WD track, utilizing a section of the Gemini Bridges Trail and then Bull Canyon Road. This canyon ride has been trashed by ORVs. Compare the surface of the trail and the condition of the canyon floor to the Dry Fork ride below, which is almost identical in composition but sees a lot less of this traffic, and you'll be educated as to the destructive nature of the four-wheeled and motocross crowd. Bikes have done some damage here, as well, but it is minimal when compared to motorized traffic.

Gemini Bridges from below

Miles and Directions

0.0 **START** from the parking area and head south on the wide trail. The trail climbs over the Moencopi formation, and then drops you into Little Canyon. The downhill through Little Canyon is a pleasant rush after the climb. **Option.** If you like sand and transitions and a chance to hunt for fossils, there are washes to ride that cross the trail—but *stay* in the wash if you choose to ride off the trail. Folks think I am crazy for opting for the deep sand in the wash bottoms, but maybe there are others like me who prefer the sand over the well-used trail. Huge areas of cryptobiotic soil crusts surround the washes, so don't leave the wash once you are in it. If it becomes too much for you, backtrack. One wash

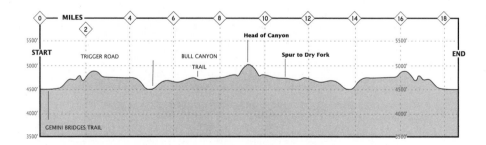

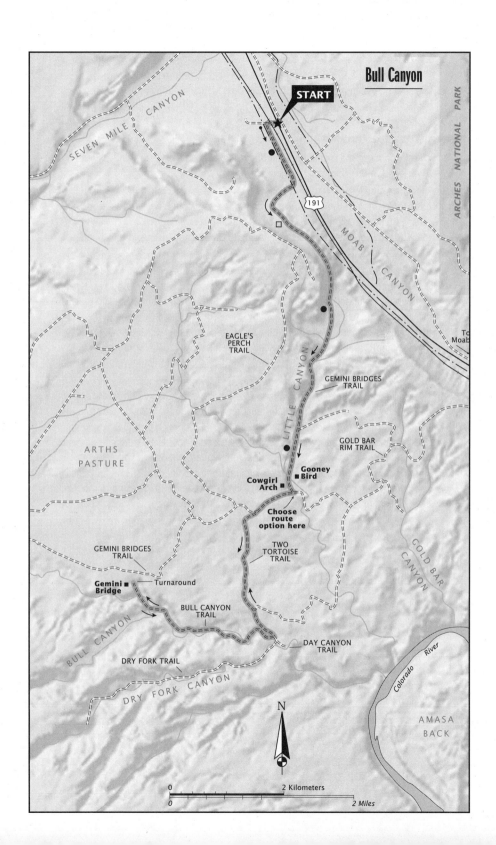

Bull Canyon

START

191

ARCHES NATIONAL PARK

SEVEN MILE CANYON

MOAB CANYON

To Moab

EAGLE'S PERCH TRAIL

LITTLE CANYON

GEMINI BRIDGES TRAIL

GOLD BAR RIM TRAIL

ARTHS PASTURE

Cowgirl Arch ■

■ Gooney Bird

Choose route option here

TWO TORTOISE TRAIL

GOLD BAR CANYON

GEMINI BRIDGES TRAIL

Turnaround

Gemini ■ **Bridge**

BULL CANYON TRAIL

BULL CANYON

DAY CANYON TRAIL

DRY FORK TRAIL

DRY FORK CANYON

Colorado River

AMASA BACK

N

0   2 Kilometers
0   2 Miles

weaves back and forth, crossing the road many times. Of course, this will screw up your mileage count and could give you a case of sand anger.

4.65 The spur right is to a small arch that I call Cowgirl Arch. Shade happens there.

4.7 At the trail marker for the split to Gold Bar Rim, go right and up the hill toward Gemini Bridges.

5.3 This is the intersection of the Bull Canyon Road (this road is sometimes referred to as Trigger Road, but it is marked as Bull Canyon Road) and the Gemini Bridges Trail. Go left to descend to Bull Canyon.

6.8 The spur to the left comes down from Two Tortoise Rock and is the hookup for a longer ride. Don't turn here, unless you want to do a reverse loop of Two Tortoise. If you are adding Bull Canyon to the Two Tortoise ride, then this is where you will be joining the route by turning left. If you are simply riding to Bull Canyon, disregard this point.

7.0 Turn right at the marked spur into Bull Canyon. Ahead you will encounter some pretty substantial areas of babyheads and some rough transitions from babyheads to sand in G-out wash bottoms. There is some hardpack, but you will find more babyheads and sand at this point and into the beginning of the trip into Bull Canyon. As you progress into the canyon, you may want to stop and check out the petrified wood in the trail or take pictures of the beautiful Wingate sandstone formations, which are very rare. The Wingate hardly ever erodes into rounded shapes. Instead it usually forms into angled spires. Here, the Wingate stands on firm ground, allowing it to erode more like the Navajo formations in the area.

9.2 This is the end of the canyon. There is a nice bit of bedrock riding at the very end of the trail that culminates in a grotto with datura growing underneath. Shade happens. The hole in the cliff above and to your left is Gemini Bridges, which is arguably more impressive from below than above. Don't say bad things here: Your every word can be heard on top of the Bridges. After enjoying this area, turn around and retrace your route. **Option:** If you want to increase your mileage, you can return to the intersection stated at mile 7.3 and take a right, postponing your return uphill to the Gemini Bridges in order to venture into Dry Fork or to visit Day Canyon Overlook. Both of these rides are described separately in this guide.

18.4 Arrive back at the trailhead.

Ride Information

Trail Contacts
Bureau of Land Management
82 E. Dogwood
Moab, UT 84532
(435) 259-2196
Utah State School and Institutional Trust Lands Administration
1165 South US 191, Ste. 5, Moab, UT 84532
(435) 259-3760

Schedule
Trail is open year-round but is best during spring and fall.

Maps
USGS maps: The Knoll, Gold Bar, Klondike
Moab West Trail Map by Latitude 40° Inc.
Moab Recreation Map by F. H. Barnes

WINGATE SANDSTONE OF BULL CANYON

The sandstone fins and steep rock faces that form the walls of Bull Canyon resemble the Navajo formation, but are instead a particularly unique member of the Wingate formation. The Wingate in other areas erodes into spires and cliff walls with vertical cracks, as seen along the river corridor east of Moab on scenic Utah Route 128. This fracturing is due to the fact that the Wingate sits atop the Chinle formation, a thick layer of mostly soft sediments. It's as if you were to walk across a sheet of ice with a layer of snow underneath. Imagine your foot as the weight of the massive layers above, the ice as the dense Wingate sandstone, and the snow as the softer Chinle. The resulting fractures created by the weight above erode into spires and cracked cliff faces.

What has happened in the area of Bull Canyon is the exception to the rule. The Chinle sediments below this area are either eroded away or uniquely dense, giving the Wingate above a solid base. As a result the Wingate in Bull Canyon has eroded much like the Navajo of the Moab Slickrock Bike Trail. The Navajo, by comparison, gets its shape and consistency because it stands on the Kayenta layers, dense multiple layers of hard sedimentary sandstone that absorb shock like a bulletproof vest and allow the mostly uniform Navajo sandstone layers above to erode into massive solid mounds.

Rounded formations of sandstone are generally caused by temperature erosion. The effects of extreme heat and cold on outer edges and surfaces of the sandstone cause areas to buckle up and break off. You will notice this type of erosion very soon after putting your tire onto slickrock anywhere around Moab. You'll hear the buckled sections beat like a drum as you pass over them. Wind and water have an effect on the erosion of the sandstone, but on the rolling and bulbous sandstone formations of Moab, the sun has been the primary cause of rapid erosion.

Wingate walls in Bull Canyon

16 Dry Fork Canyon

Start: From the Gemini Bridges Trailhead on U.S. Route 191.
Length: 21.2-mile out-and-back.
Approximate riding time: 3 to 6 hours, depending on fitness level.
Difficulty: Technically easy to moderate due to mostly maintained road surface and the well-preserved condition of the road into Dry Fork Canyon. Physically moderately difficult due to some steady climbing and mileage.
Trail surface: Dirt road and 4WD track. Hard-pack, sand, loose rock, and bedrock.

Lay of the land: Canyons, canyons, canyons. Washes, washes, washes. Rock. The vivid colors of the Moencopi, Chinle, and Wingate geological layers decorate the walls as you ride into and through three prominent canyons.
Total climbing: 1,797 feet.
Land status: Bureau of Land Management (BLM) and Utah State Trust lands.
Other trail users: Hikers, equestrians, and off-road vehicles (ORV).
Best seasons: Spring and fall.

Note to the reader: This ride can be combined with any or all of the adjoining rides—Two Tortoise Rock, Bull Canyon, and Day Canyon Overlook—to create longer, more challenging rides.

Environmental concerns: Extremely fragile! Cryptobiotic soil crusts and rare desert mosses abound on and between the slickrock. Stay on the trail at all times. If it is alive, don't ride or step on it. Things revegetate very slowly out here.

Getting there: From Moab: Follow US 191 north from the intersection of Main and Center Streets for 11 miles to the Gemini Bridges Trailhead. The massive cliff just before the trailhead is the Eagle's Perch, named after a birdlike formation on the top edge, visible as you are riding on the highway from Moab. If you come to Utah Route 313, you have gone way too far. When you see the marked Gemini Bridges parking area on your left, turn onto the access road, cross a cattle guard, and continue into the cleared area bordered by a barbed-wire fence. The trail marker is on the left. Park and ride out on the Gemini Bridge Trail.

The Ride

The out-and-back Dry Fork ride is accessed via a spur a short way past the Bull Canyon turnoff on Bull Canyon Road. The Dry Fork is very similar to the Bull Canyon ride, traveling through another beautiful Wingate-sandstone-lined canyon into an old mining area. Riding gets difficult only when you encounter the occasional sandy wash bottom. The attractions on the Dry Fork ride include spectacular canyon walls, wildlife, large petrified wood specimens, a spring (don't rely on it—Dry Fork, remember), the formations and mining remnants at the end of the canyon, and the downhill ride out of the canyon.

Wingate formation above the Dry Fork of Bull Canyon

Miles and Directions

0.0 **START** from the parking area and head south on the wide trail. The trail climbs over the Moencopi formation, and then drops you into Little Canyon. The downhill through Little Canyon is a pleasant rush after the climb. **Option.** If you like sand and transitions and a chance to hunt for fossils, there are washes to ride that cross the trail—but *stay* in the wash if you choose to ride off the trail. Folks think I am crazy for opting for the deep sand in the wash bottoms, but maybe there are others like me who prefer the sand over the well-used trail. Huge areas of cryptobiotic soil crusts surround the washes, so don't leave the wash once you are in it. If it becomes too much for you, backtrack. One wash weaves back and forth, crossing the road many times. Of course, this will screw up your mileage count and could give you a case of sand anger.

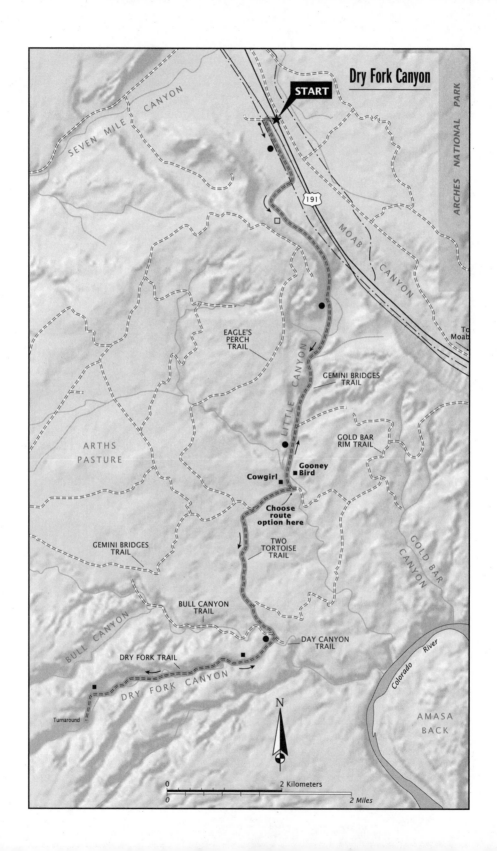

Dry Fork Canyon

START

SEVEN MILE CANYON

ARCHES NATIONAL PARK

191

MOAB CANYON

To Moab

EAGLE'S PERCH TRAIL

LITTLE CANYON

GEMINI BRIDGES TRAIL

GOLD BAR RIM TRAIL

ARTHS PASTURE

Gooney Bird

Cowgirl

Choose route option here

TWO TORTOISE TRAIL

GOLD BAR CANYON

GEMINI BRIDGES TRAIL

BULL CANYON TRAIL

BULL CANYON

DAY CANYON TRAIL

DRY FORK TRAIL

DRY FORK CANYON

Turnaround

Colorado River

AMASA BACK

N

0   2 Kilometers

0   2 Miles

The spring in Dry Fork Canyon

4.65 The spur right is to a small arch that I call Cowgirl. Shade happens there.

4.7 Take the Gemini Bridges Trail up the hill, bypassing the spur to the left out to Gold Bar Rim.

5.3 This is the intersection of Bull Canyon Road and the Gemini Bridges Trail. Go left and descend.

6.8 This spur to the left comes down from Two Tortoise Rock and is the hookup for a longer ride. Don't turn here, unless you want to do a reverse loop of Two Tortoise. If you are adding Dry Fork to the Two Tortoise ride, then this is where you will be joining the route by turning left from the Two Tortoise route. If you are simply riding to Dry Fork, disregard this point.

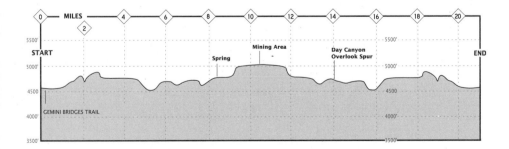

7.0 Bear left, avoiding the marked spur to Bull Canyon. Ahead you will encounter some baby-headedness and sand as the trail follows a wash bottom.

7.1 While riding in this wash bottom, look to your right. Catch the sandy spur on the right and go over the hill.

8.5 There is an obvious spring on your right with a trough for cattle watering. Sometimes it's running. Sometimes it ain't. Don't rely on it, but the water is fine to drink when it is there. Fill your water bottle from the spout that pours into the upper catch. Do not fill your bottle from the standing water. This is a great spot to stop and rest and catch the beauty of the Wingate canyon walls. Stick your head under the water to cool off. Feels good.

10.6 This is the mining area. A collapsed dam lies to your left as the trail ascends to the Chinle geological layer ahead. The gray-green Chinle is the primary source of uranium, and that is what was mined here. Exploring this area, you will find a few interesting artifacts and an arch. There is a great deal of petrified wood lying about, and this is a fine place to study wildlife as you get your free radiation treatment from the uranium deposits and tailings scattered everywhere. After enjoying this area, turn around and retrace your route. **Option:** If you want to increase your mileage, you can return to the intersection at mile 7.1 and take a right to visit Day Canyon Overlook, which is only a few tenths of a mile off your route. You can also return to mile 7.0 and bear left down into Bull Canyon. You can also take the right-hand spur off Bull Canyon Road at mile 6.8 to ride the Two Tortoise loop in reverse. Do the math. Route alternatives are pretty prolific out here, so if you want to play with distance, please work out the mile counts from the ones here *before you ride.* Don't try to do it on the trail.

21.2 Arrive back at the trailhead.

Ride Information

Trail Contacts
Bureau of Land Management
82 E. Dogwood
Moab, UT 84532
(435) 259-2196
Utah State School and Institutional Trust Lands Administration
1165 South US 191, Ste. 5, Moab, UT 84532
(435) 259-3760

Schedule
Trail is open year-round but is best during spring and fall.

Maps
USGS maps: The Knoll, Gold Bar, Klondike
Moab West Trail Map by Latitude 40° Inc.
Moab Recreation Map by F. H. Barnes

17 Day Canyon Overlook

Start: From the Gemini Bridges Trailhead on U.S. Route 191.
Length: 15-mile out-and-back.
Approximate riding time: 2 to 4 hours.
Difficulty: Technically easy due to a well-maintained road. Just before the overlook the trail gets a bit more difficult and may require a bit of walking through sand and babyheads. Physically moderate due to lack of technical challenge and the reasonable distance.
Trail surface: Well-maintained county road and unmaintained 4WD track. Hardpack, sand, babyheads, and bedrock.

Lay of the land: Canyons, canyons, canyons. Washes, washes, washes. Rock. The vivid colors of the Moencopi, Chinle, and Wingate geological layers decorate the walls as you ride into and through three prominent canyons.
Total climbing: 1,408 feet.
Land status: Bureau of Land Management (BLM) and Utah State Trust lands.
Other trail users: Hikers, equestrians, and off-road vehicles (ORV).
Best seasons: Spring and fall.

Note to the reader: This ride can be combined with any or all of the adjoining rides—Two Tortoise Rock, Bull Canyon, and Dry Fork Canyon—to create longer, more challenging rides.

Environmental concerns: Extremely fragile! Cryptobiotic soil crusts and rare desert mosses abound on and between the slickrock. Stay on the trail at all times. If it is alive, don't ride or step on it. Things revegetate very slowly out here.

Getting there: From Moab: Follow US 191 north from the intersection of Main and Center Streets for 11 miles to the Gemini Bridges Trailhead. The massive cliff just before the trailhead is the Eagle's Perch, named after a birdlike formation on the top edge, visible as you are riding on the highway from Moab. If you come to Utah Route 313, you have gone way too far. When you see the marked Gemini Bridges parking area on your left, turn onto the access road, cross a cattle guard, and continue into the cleared area bordered by a barbed-wire fence. The trail marker is on the left. Park and ride out on the Gemini Bridge Trail.

The Ride

If you like viewpoints as destinations and are physically fit but technically challenged, then Day Canyon Overlook is a fine place to visit. The area you'll be visiting is actually the bottom of Bull Canyon and the Dry Fork as they connect, drop 300 feet, and connect finally with Day Canyon in the distance. The Wingate walls are extremely vertical and high. The canyon itself is very long, tight, and weaving. The mountain bike ride to the viewpoint utilizes the bottom half of the Gemini Bridges Trail, then connects to Bull Canyon Road, but continues past the spur to Bull Canyon. The main challenges are sand and climbing. Exposure above Day Canyon is frightening. There is a slot wash—a tight and twisted eroded watercourse cut through solid rock—above the drop into the abyss. You can slip into this slot if

Day Canyon Overlook is technically the bottom of Bull Canyon.

you are not careful. If you are riding with children, be especially careful here. I have seen deer and rabbits that have fallen into these slots and become trapped. The result is a smelly dead animal in a puddle at the bottom of a deep stone hole.

If you want to add mileage to any ride here and turn it into a more challenging trip from town, ride your bike north on US 191, cross the Colorado River Bridge, and continue past the Arches National Park entrance and around the looping right-hand bend in the road. In less than 0.5 mile, you come to the Old Moab Highway pullout on the right. Ride on the decrepit old road, avoiding any adjacent spurs until

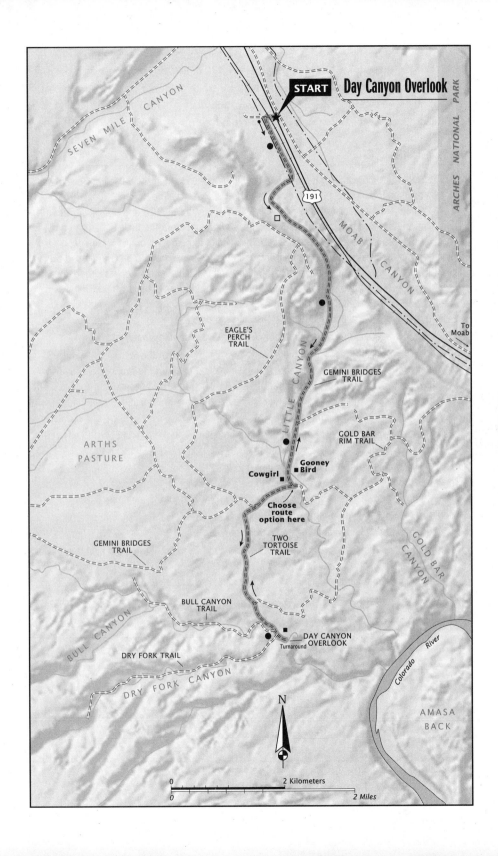

START

Day Canyon Overlook

SEVEN MILE CANYON

ARCHES NATIONAL PARK

MOAB CANYON

191

To Moab

EAGLE'S PERCH TRAIL

LITTLE CANYON

GEMINI BRIDGES TRAIL

ARTHS PASTURE

GOLD BAR RIM TRAIL

Gooney Bird

Cowgirl

Choose route option here

TWO TORTOISE TRAIL

GEMINI BRIDGES TRAIL

GOLD BAR CANYON

BULL CANYON TRAIL

BULL CANYON

DRY FORK TRAIL

DAY CANYON OVERLOOK
Turnaround

DRY FORK CANYON

Colorado River

AMASA BACK

N

0   2 Kilometers
0   2 Miles

you reach a spur to your left at approximately 11 miles from town, next to the Bar-M Chuckwagon, a traditional western steak house and tourist trap. Ride out to US 191 on the short sandy spur and cross the highway and into the Gemini Bridges Trailhead parking area, where all of these rides begin.

Miles and Directions

0.0 **START** from the parking area and head south on the wide trail. The trail climbs over the Moencopi formation, and then drops you into Little Canyon. The downhill through Little Canyon is a pleasant rush after the climb. **Option.** If you like sand and transitions and a chance to hunt for fossils, there are washes to ride that cross the trail—but *stay* in the wash if you choose to ride off the trail. Folks think I am crazy for opting for the deep sand in the wash bottoms, but maybe there are others like me who prefer the sand over the well-used trail. Huge areas of cryptobiotic soil crusts surround the washes, so don't leave the wash once you are in it. If it becomes too much for you, backtrack. One wash weaves back and forth, crossing the road many times. Of course, this will screw up your mileage count and could give you a case of sand anger.

4.65 The spur right is to a small arch that I call Cowgirl. Shade happens there.

4.7 Take the Gemini Bridges Trail up the hill, bypassing the spur to the left out to Gold Bar Rim. **Option.** If you want to increase your mileage, you can add the Two Tortoise ride at this point by taking the spur toward Gold Bar Rim. Read the trail descriptions for Two Tortoise and other rides like Bull Canyon, Dry Fork, Little Canyon Rim, and Gemini Bridges to consider expanded epic rides in the Gemini Bridges area.

5.3 This is the intersection of Bull Canyon Road (sometimes referred to as Trigger Road) and the Gemini Bridges Trail. Go left and descend.

6.8 This spur to the left comes down from Two Tortoise Rock and is the hookup for a longer ride. Don't turn here, unless you want to do a reverse loop of Two Tortoise. If you want to add Two Tortoise, it is best to do it from the Gold Bar Rim turnoff mentioned above.

7.0 Bear left, avoiding the marked spur to Bull Canyon. Ahead you'll encounter some baby-heads and sand as the trail follows a wash bottom.

7.1 While riding in this wash bottom, look to your right. The sandy spur on the right that travels over the hill is the trail into Dry Fork. If you want to add the Dry Fork, this is your chance. Read the mileage counts in the Dry Fork section (see Ride 16).

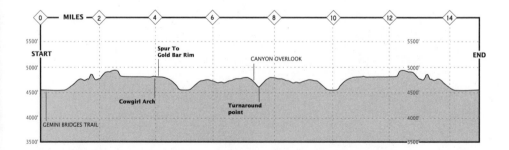

7.4 On your right across the wash that parallels the track at this point is a platform overlooking Day and Bull Canyons as they intersect in the distance. Walk through the wash and have your breath taken away. If you come here in the summer months, you may see some nude bathers below in the waterhole that is at the bottom of the cliff that drops water from runoff out of Bull Canyon and Dry Fork. Say "hi!" Get back on the bike and head onward.

7.5 At this point you'll encounter some deep sand that gives way to an undulating slickrock shelf, which gradually turns into a short slot canyon that then drops a few yards. Below is a bridge where water pours over the edge. The view here is really awesome. Say no more. Be careful. The exposure is beyond vertical. After enjoying this area, turn around and retrace your route. Alternatives abound. Study the mileage counts for Two Tortoise, Bull Canyon, Dry Fork, Gemini Bridges, and Little Canyon Rim/Eagle's Perch to give yourself ideas of how to expand visits into the wonderful Gemini Bridges area.

15.0 Arrive back at the trailhead.

Ride Information

Trail Contacts
Bureau of Land Management
82 E. Dogwood
Moab, UT 84532
(435) 259-2196
Utah State School and Institutional Trust Lands Administration
1165 South US 191, Ste. 5, Moab, UT 84532
(435) 259-3760

Schedule
Trail is open year-round but is best during spring and fall.

Maps
USGS maps: The Knoll, Gold Bar, Klondike
Moab West Trail Map by Latitude 40° Inc.
Moab Recreation Map by F. H. Barnes

JIMSONWEED *(Datura meteloides, D. Wright II)*

Datura is a member of the nightshade family, grows in all deserts of the Southwest, and has been referred to historically with haunting names such as moonflower, angel's trumpet, and queen of the night, among many others. The beautiful flowers of the datura grow along canyon walls and roadsides, and in sandy soils surrounding most of the trails in Moab. The plant's large white flowers wilt in the sun and open for the darkness. Datura is most notable for its hallucinogenic properties, which are formidable and can be quite dangerous. Only a slight overdose is fatal! In Moab, where the young folks seem to seek mind-altering drugs even more so than the rest of the country's youth, there have been a few crusades by locals against the plant, usually after a datura-related death or after a young person is committed to a mental institution after ingesting the plant somehow. It is said that even smelling the blossoms can be detrimental to your health. If the plant's toxic alkaloids don't kill, you could end up in another world for the rest of your life. There are a wreath of flowers and a small cross just past the cattle guard on Kane Creek Road just prior to the Moab Rim Trail. This marks the

place where a young fellow died after consuming datura seeds. He sat in the middle of the road thinking that the cars would go right through him. One did.

Datura has been found in ancient ruins, rolled in the form of a pill. We can only guess as to its uses, but it seems logical to assume that it was used either as a medicinal herb or for religious rituals. I personally have heard of people eating the larvae

of a tomato hornworm that has fed on the plant, among other methods of ingestion, but I must warn anyone curious enough to smoke or eat or insert any part of the plant into any bodily orifice: You are definitely playing with your sanity and your life.

UFOs, Naked Ladies, Rusty Musselman, Mortality, and the Portal Trail

"We had a gal who lived at the mouth of Red Canyon and was always calling in about UFOs landing out there. She said she would talk to them aliens, but they didn't like no strangers. She said their space ship looked like a giant M&M with spider legs. I think she was a little dinged out, but she was real serious about them UFOs. She said they was keepin' her awake with that humming noise. I don't know what she thought we could do about it . . . Did I tell you about the Indian gal who would always take her clothes off in the back of the patrol car?"

"Yes." I was listening to a shadow, a nervous mumbling shadow that chuckled like Rusty Musselman, told the same funny stories, and feebly held on to Rusty's mortal soul. Fighting back nothingness. What else can anyone do? "Rusty, you are getting mighty old. You'd better slow down or find somebody to help you. What do you think will happen if you just keep working so hard?"

"I guess I'll die." He continued: "A couple of my deputies arrested this Indian gal and she started taking her clothes off in the back of the patrol car. She kept saying to my deputy, 'John, I'm gonna take my clothes off.' She ended up throwing her clothes out the window. She was stark naked and crawled up onto the shelf above the backseat right in the back window. By the time they got to Bluff, there musta been sixty cars following them."

"She must have been an exhibitionist."

"Yeah, we had a lot of them. Inez Posey was another one. Her son shot her in the breast one time, and me and my deputy took her to the doc to get the bullet out and sew her up. She was drunk as a skunk and laughing like crazy. Inez weighed way over 300 pounds and the doc was having a hard time getting to the problem. Hell, her breast musta weighed thirty or forty pounds by itself. My deputy was getting really tired holding it up so the doc could work on it. He and Inez was laughing and Inez was jiggling like Jell-O. Finally we had her hang upside down so her breast would dangle down and the doc could get at the wound. It was pretty funny lookin'. Inez was laughing. The doc was laughing. "You could write a book on that jail."

I was thinking about it.

Ahhh, Gold Bar Rim. My guess is that you are not getting Rusty Musselman's connection with the following hardcore mountain bike trail. There will be more on Rusty later in the book, but let me spell it out for you. It has something to do with the value of life, mortality, and respect for those who love you. I have included stories in this guidebook through the good graces of the publisher, in the hope that you will find a respect and appreciation of Moab beyond its attraction as a mountain bike destination. If you come here without a clue, you could hurt the place. Worse still, you could hurt yourself and your family, or someone else in your party, if you choose to take them on the Portal Trail and they are not ready for it.

"She must have been an exhibitionist."

"Yeah, we had a lot of them."

Rusty died. You will, too. Rusty was eighty-three when he shuffled off. He was a real piece of work, under construction for over eighty years. He had lots of kids. His kids are having kids. People were, and still are, affected by Rusty's spirit. When he died his family and colleagues celebrated his long life with funny stories and tears of gratitude for having Rusty as a friend for so long. How old are you? How long will you live? Ever consider that your life is invaluable to your family and friends? Ever heard of the expression, *Don't break your mother's heart?* Ever heard of natural selection? This is the connection. You may not be a Rusty Musselman, but with age, you may become just as interesting, just as much of a character. In Moab we call it "Rugged Individualism." Fall off the Portal Trail and you will never know the rewards of being an "elder," of being a rock for your family. You will become a nameless someone who fell off the damn Portal Trail onto the rocks below. Maybe your family will place a plaque on a rock as a memorial, if you are lucky.

There are two trails in this book that utilize the Portal Trail: Gold Bar Rim and Poison Spider Mesa. In a single year, 1998, two riders fell to their deaths from the Portal. There is a memorial plaque at the Portal viewpoint for one of them. He left a young wife and two kids behind. It is bad enough that he died. It is far worse that his kids now have to grow up without Daddy. Take care of yourself, like Rusty Musselman did. Though Rusty drank whiskey like a fish, he managed to eke out eighty-three years. Grow old and become wise and leave your kids with a ton of funny stories to tell about their dad, uncle, or grandfather. Don't be remembered only for the horrible death you achieved diving from the Portal Trail.

18 Gold Bar Rim

Start: From the Gemini Bridges Trailhead on U.S. Route 191.

Length: 18.5-mile point-to-point with shuttle at either end; 25-mile point to point, if shuttled to trailhead and ridden back to town.

Approximate riding time: 6 to 10 hours. Leave early. Carry lots of water.

Difficulty: As hard as it gets. As *good* as it gets. Brutal. Relentless. Dangerous. The singletrack along the rim is extremely rough with lots of ledges and notches in the rock, sidehilling, constant line searching, and tight turns. It requires repeated portage to avoid vegetation and dangerous drop-offs. The jeep road is crazy in places, but less environmentally sensitive to blunders and less technically difficult. Physically, it takes it out of you. Mileage is deceiving. A difficult climb is followed by a brutal climb. The Portal Trail is a singletrack on the edge of a 300-foot drop. It cannot be described. It is *frightening*. Walk the exposed sections. The hike down the Portal Trail is a difficult hike in bike shoes, but you must hike the exposed sections. Do not attempt this trail unless you are prepared, mentally sound, and extremely fit.

Trail surface: Ledges, ledges, ledges, bumpy slickrock, sand, drop-offs, loose rock, rubble on a faint singletrack with the option to take the jeep road below the rim at any point. Frightening exposure on the edge of a cliff. Extreme danger.

Lay of the land: Gold Bar Rim is a canyon rim, and a big one. It is the western edge of the Moab Fault.

Total climbing: 2,427 feet.

Land status: Bureau of Land Management (BLM) and Utah State Trust lands.

Other trail users: Hikers and off-road vehicles (ORV).

Best seasons: Spring and fall.

Environmental concerns: Extremely fragile! Cryptobiotic soil crusts and rare desert mosses abound on and between the slickrock everywhere except the main jeep trail and narrow singletrack. It's best to use a guide the first time you ride this trail. If you're riding it without someone who knows the trail, ride the jeep trail in its entirety. The singletrack is vague and confusing at many points and takes you through pristine crusts, lichens, and mosses. Plenty of damage has been done already. One or two people make a mistake and their tracks are recorded in the soil crusts for as much as 200 years. From that moment on, rider after rider will follow that mistaken track until eventually everyone uses that huge mistake as the trail. This has happened on Gold Bar Rim and is continuing to happen. Please stay on rock, the well-worn soil surfaces of the main singletrack, or on loose sand or rock watercourses. If it ain't rock or fine sand, don't ride or step on it.

Warning! This ride is *extremely dangerous!* Despite the inherent danger of the exposed cliff, the Portal Trail is the emergency hatch to and from Poison Spider Mesa and the Gold Bar Rim in case of a storm or accident. Two deaths almost closed the trail in 1998. Portions of Poison Spider are already off limits, and more wilderness designations are on the way. This is a challenging, beautiful, and awe-inspiring mountain bike ride. Treat it like it's sacred. Respect it. Love it. Care for it. Most of all, fear it.

The beginning of the exposed singletrack portion with the La Sal Mountains in the background—looking southeast

Getting there: From Moab: Follow US 191 north from the intersection of Main and Center Streets for 11 miles. There is a wide parking area on the left and to the west that is very visible from the highway. This is the posted Gemini Bridges and Gold Bar Rim Trailhead. (If you come to Utah Route 313, you have gone way too far.) Park and ride out on the Gemini Bridge Trail just ahead. It heads south along the base of the cliff.

Shuttle Point: From Moab: Follow US 191 north past the Colorado River Bridge to Potash Road (UT 279). Go left onto Potash Road. Drive another mile and park in one of the pullouts on either side of the road.

The Ride

There is a point where testosterone and endorphins send a dude into the zone where the entire body, mind, and soul become a single mountain biking machine. It is where the dude concentrates so completely on the trail in front of the dude's tire that the dude like totally forgets that he is like on the edge of a cliff or something. The dude needs to understand that a single mistake or random glitch like a missed shift or mechanical failure can send the dude to the dude's death in, like, a real hurry.

Awesome! Really gnarly, man! Okay, now, if you talk like this, don't ride Gold Bar Rim. Not even with a buddy who talks like this. This is the deep end of the pool for most riders, the brink of mountain biking, the pinnacle of the sport, a ride fit

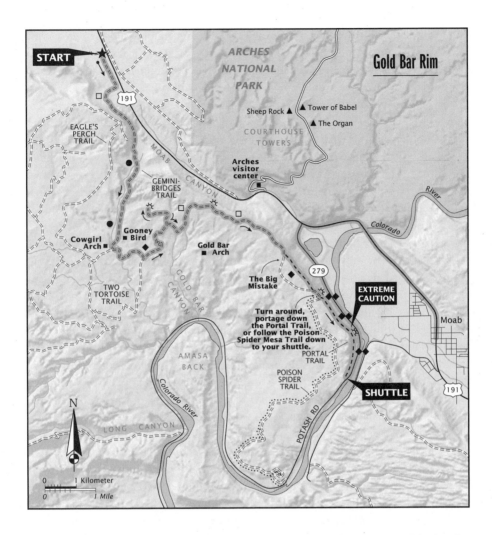

START

ARCHES NATIONAL PARK

EAGLE'S PERCH TRAIL

MOAB CANYON

GEMINI-BRIDGES TRAIL

Sheep Rock ▲   ▲ Tower of Babel
▲ The Organ

COURTHOUSE TOWERS

Arches visitor center

River

Colorado

Cowgirl Arch ■

Gooney ■ Bird

Gold Bar ■ Arch

279

EXTREME CAUTION

Moab

TWO TORTOISE TRAIL

GOLD BAR CANYON

The Big Mistake

Turn around, portage down the Portal Trail, or follow the Poison Spider Mesa Trail down to your shuttle.

PORTAL TRAIL

SHUTTLE

AMASA BACK

Colorado River

POISON SPIDER TRAIL

POTASH RD

191

LONG CANYON

N

0   1 Kilometer
0   1 Mile

only for the strong, smart, and skilled—a place where others can qualify for the Darwin Awards. The surface is the most varied possible. The only missing ingredients are mud and water crossings. There are ledges, deep sand, loose rock, hardpack, slickrock, gigantic rock rubble, and every combination of these you can imagine. The Gold Bar Rim's heart and soul is on top of the impressive rim west of US 191 overlooking Arches National Park and the Moab Valley.

There are two routes here, a very hard-to-follow singletrack along the rim and a 4WD trail below the rim that was originally a mineral mining exploration road. It wasn't long before the hardcore jeep crowd found it, and now the many 4WD tracks in the area can be a confusing affair. The route below is a five- or six-water-bottle point-to-point, culminating in a hike-a-bike down the infamous and extremely dangerous Portal Trail. This scary singletrack along the face of a cliff is always undergoing natural changes through erosion, rockslides, and spotty trail maintenance. At any time you may have to clamor over loose rock on the edge of a 300-foot drop with your bike. The exposed section of the Portal Trail, even when it is in good shape, is extremely uncomfortable to walk through. You will be tempted to ride out of the exposure, but don't. It is simply not worth the risk.

To take the photographs you see here, I was accompanied by Nathan Toone, definitely a top dog in Moab. Nathan rode Gold Bar back in the old days when the trail was more defined and ridable for almost the entire length of the rim. On this day we spent hours doing what we do almost every time, searching for the singletrack and trying not to ride or walk on the cryptobiotic soil crusts. The jeep road below the rim bobs and weaves, following the ridges up to and down from the rim, coming into contact with the singletrack at many places along the way, effectively sucking you into the doubletrack time after time. To find the rhythm of the singletrack, the trick is to ignore doubletrack whenever it goes down. Realize that if you attempt the singletrack, you are going to get lost and found and lost and found all the way to the Portal. Many other mountain bikers have gone astray, leaving tracks across the fragile soils. Folks try to cairn the route, but everyone gets sucked into riding others' mistakes. This not only causes damage to the beauty of the rim, but also gets you stupid lost. If you choose to ride the singletrack, the best guidance I can offer here is to reassure you that the best way to get from one end of the rim to the other is on the rim itself. Sometimes it drops you onto huge boulders that require you to hop down 5-foot drops. Sometimes it surprises you by tucking behind the rim on the exposed face. At any rate, it will take a lot of time to negotiate this trail and to avoid the fragile soils that need to be respected. Be patient and *start early*.

If you are an expert or professional rider searching for the ultimate Moab challenge, include the Two Tortoise Rock loop described in Ride 14. For a super-epic trip, you can tack together a ride from Jughandle Arch at the mouth of Long Canyon on Potash Road (see Ride 25) up Long Canyon through Pucker Pass, out on the paved Dead Horse State Park road to UT 313, where it is less than a mile to the Gemini Bridges Trailhead, then down Gemini Bridges Trail to the intersection with the signed Gold Bar Rim Trail, then head up to and ride along Gold Bar Rim to the Portal Trail or even down the Poison Spider Trail. There are some really great training rides here for steroid monsters and blood dopers.

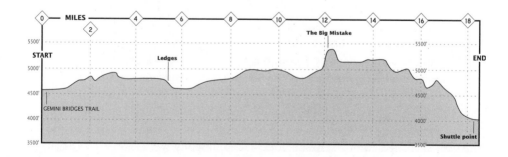

Miles and Directions

0.0 **START:** Leave the parking area and head south on the wide trail. The trail climbs over the Moencopi formation, then drops you into Little Canyon. The downhill through Little Canyon is a pleasant rush after the climb. **Option:** If you like sand and transitions and a chance to hunt for fossils, there are washes to ride that cross the trail—but *stay* in the wash if you choose to ride off the trail. Huge areas of cryptobiotic soil crusts surround the washes. One wash weaves back and forth, crossing the road many times. Of course, this will screw up your mileage count and could give you sand anger.

4.7 The spur right is to a small arch that I call Cowgirl Arch. Shade happens there.

4.8 At the trail marker, head south (left) on the sandy, sandy spur toward the Gold Bar Rim Trail. The marked Gemini Bridges Trail heads up the hill to your right. The sand at the beginning of the spur to Gold Bar Rim is truly nasty, but will gradually give way to technical ledges. Have faith.

5.0 Take one of the two sandy spurs left out of the wash. Doesn't matter which one. Just take the one that looks ridable at the time.

5.7 Encounter fun ledges.

6.0 Go left at this T. During the production of these mileage counts for this guidebook, I have seen the sign here come and go twice. Maybe it will be there when you ride, maybe not.

6.5 Go left!

7.2 Go across the slickrock cap. The trail dives down the backside. Watch out for technical surprises ahead! The trail will weave around a bit, and there are places where the trail illogically dives down around corners and climbs back up. It's about getting the most out of the trail for those jeep fanatics.

9.4 The rim! Go up the slab on the left and enjoy the view. To continue on, hike south along the rim until you find the singletrack, or grab onto the jeep trail to your right. If you choose the singletrack, realize that you will have to portage quite a bit. There are transitions along the way, but these rock ramps and bridges are usually not seen until you are right on them. This can be dangerous the first time you ride the singletrack.

11.5 Assuming you took the singletrack, it T-bones the jeep road here. Go left and up *always,* if you are choosing the singletrack.

12.2 This ledgy uphill section leads to the *Big Mistake.* For years mountain bikers have been taking a right-hand turn here, creating a well-defined trail that drops you down the rock slab to your right and back into the jeep road. If you take the *Big Mistake,* stay on the well-defined main route and bear left when it eventually crosses a wash bottom above Bootlegger Canyon and climbs back up to the rim on the jeep road. If you want to avoid the climb and don't mind some scrambling and repeated portage, then go left, away from the defined tracks, and up the little bedrock fin directly ahead, away from the *Big Mistake.* It doesn't look ridable, but it is. In less than 20 feet, bear right and go up the tiny gully, continuing to bear right parallel to the rim above. From here the track is very confusing due to multiple "mistakes" and requires some scrambling, but if you always err toward the rim you will eventually find a way to cross over to the jeep road after it has ascended back to the rim. Do not be discouraged by what appears to be a deep drop into the small canyon ahead of you. The farther up the rim you go, the more you will see ways to scramble down. Do this on rock, please. Stay off the soils. The higher you go on the rim, the less the drop and the more the scrambling spots will be visible. It is always a good idea to leave the bike in a good spot and get a better look from on high whenever you are uncertain as to where the singletrack is. The damn thing sneaks behind stuff occasionally, and you will definitely lose it on occasion. When you find it, you rejoice for a while, then you lose it again. By the way, the arch, out to the west in the sandstone fin, is Gold Bar Arch.

14.5 If you continued on the singletrack and the scramble across the small canyon, you have now regained the jeep road that takes you along the rim to the Portal Trail and the Poison Spider Mesa Trail. There is a large bare spot on the rim marked by cairns. The Portal Trail will be on your left—a singletrack descending southward toward the river along the cliff face. Poison Spider Mesa Trail is the doubletrack to the right and west. It's your call from here. The Portal is shorter, but far more dangerous. Read the Poison Spider chapter (see Ride 19) prior to having to make this decision. If you drop down the Portal, it's another 2.5 miles to the road. The Portal Trail singletrack is fairly easy at first and will suck you in. Ride the first bit, but don't be tempted to stay on the bike past the first warning sign placed at the start of the exposed sections of trail by the BLM. The trail presents you with technical bits on the edge of eternity. *Walk the exposed sections of the portal trail or risk being a candidate for the Darwin Awards!* Once beyond the exposure and past the viewpoint, the memorial plaque (yes, people die here), and the trail marker, the trail becomes technical and steep.

17.0 At the bottom of the Portal Trail, there is a fork in the trail. Go left to get immediately onto Potash Road (Utah Route 279), and then go left again onto the highway to ride to your shuttle vehicle, if you parked along Potash Road. Stay right at the fork in the singletrack to roll into the Lion's Park campsite in another 0.5 mile, if you are camping there. If you are riding back to town on your bike, go left onto the highway; it is approximately 4 miles to the intersection of Potash Road (UT 279) and US 191. Take a right onto US 191 and ride another 4 miles back to town. If you are riding back to town on your bike, be especially careful crossing the Colorado River Bridge! It is narrow.

25.0 Reach Center and Main Streets in town.

Ride Information

Trail Contacts

Bureau of Land Management
82 E. Dogwood
Moab, UT 84532
(435) 259-2196
Utah State School and Institutional Trust
Lands Administration
1165 South US 191, Ste. 5, Moab, UT 84532
(435) 259-3760

Schedule

Trail is open year-round but is best during spring and fall.

Camping

Follow US 191 north past the Colorado River Bridge to Potash Road (UT 279). Go left onto Potash Road. Approximately 5 miles in on Potash Road, on the right side of the highway, is the Lion's Park campsite, a great spot to base your trip if you are camping. The Portal Trail drops directly into the campsite.

Maps

USGS maps: Gold Bar Canyon, Moab
Moab East Trail Map by Latitude 40° Inc.
Moab Recreation Map by F. H. Barnes

WITCH'S TONGUE

A witch's tongue is a rock slab that is undercut and exposed on the edge of a cliff. These things are reasons to never stand on or near the edge of a cliff in the Moab area. The multiple slabs of the Kayenta sandstone layers are the main culprit for these scenic land mines, but they can occur in any layer and can be present anywhere there is an edge to undercut. Any time there is a dense layer of sandstone on top of a more porous layer, you get witch's tongues. You can be standing on a slab of rock that appears to be as stable and solid as any other, but it could be only a few millimeters thick, ready to break off with only a few pounds of pressure.

As you drive out to or back from the Gemini Bridges Trailhead on US 191 north of Moab, look up and to the west at the Gold Bar Rim high above. There are quite a few very radical witch's tongues visible from the road. Remember what you see here when you are riding or standing on the rims or any rock face in this area.

In Addition

Atlas Mine Tailings

The large terraced pile of dirt at the north end of town just across the Colorado River is the mine tailings pond from the Atlas Mining Company's uranium refinement plant that once stood on the land south of U.S. Route 191 on the northern banks of the Colorado River. The huge rusted hulk of the processing plant that once stood here was torn down in 1996 and tucked under the tailings at the southwestern corner, much as you would sweep a pile of dirt under a carpet. The debris was so radioactive that no dump in the country would accept it. This place constitutes the only EPA Superfund site in the entire country that has been made even more dangerous by destablization as government contractors milk tax dollars and kick up redioactive dust. For those of you who haven't read the papers or watched CNN, the Superfund includes a handful of environmental disaster sites—places you may have heard of, like the Rocky Mountain Chemical Weapons Arsenal, Love Canal, and the Hanford and Rocky Flats Nuclear Weapons Plants.

While you are passing this huge layered pile on the northern boundary of Moab on your way to any of the trails north or northwest of Moab, breathe in deeply. It is your chance to get a free radiation treatment. The background radiation here is the highest in the Western Hemisphere. Here are a few anecdotes to consider as you alter your genetic code.

Verle Green, Moab old-timer, drove a truck for the Atlas Mine in the 1950s and told me that one day the mining company came across a particularly rich strike of nearly pure uranium ore. The stuff was wet, runny, and yellow, a valuable substance called "Yellow Cake." They dumped it into the back of his truck, and he drove it to town. When he rolled up to the plant everyone noticed that his truck was empty. The stuff had run out through cracks in the bed and was scattered all the way back to the mine along the highway. Needless to say, US 191 was, and still is, highly radioactive.

Every so often the locals have a demonstration protesting the fact that the tailings are just lying there poisoning the Colorado River and no one—including the Sierra Club, which fights against mountain bike access whenever it can—does anything that lasts more than a couple of minutes to fight for the removal of the pile. The demonstration always happens on or near the pile—which seems to me to almost suggest that the pile is not that bad a problem. If I led a protest, I would lead it as far away from that pile as possible. That thing is *poison!*

If you want to see just how bad the problem is, just look at the tamarisk trees between the pile and the Colorado River. It seems that the only thing that can kill a tamarisk tree—considered by many to be more of an environmental problem than

Atlas Mine tailings

the tailings—is the poison seeping from the base of the tailings. Maybe we have found a use for the tailings, after all. Let's use them to kill the tammies along the river. (See tamarisk sidebar after Ride 26, The White Rim.)

Solutions to the problem of the Atlas Mine tailings, presented by the mining company, the Defense Department, and the EPA, are either to move the pile or to cap it. Every time I see the tailings in the news, there is another stupid story about how they are trying to figure out which is best. But nothing gets done except destablizing the mess. The real downside is that a solution would be very complicated, no matter the method. Even if they do their best and truck the pile away, radioactive and poison dust will continue to be spread throughout the valley. If you cap it, the problem is just swept under another rug of dirt for future generations to deal with.

Death Rides a Hardtail and Dares Everyone to Ride the Portal Trail

There are three tales I can relate about this trail, not one of which is pleasant, but perhaps you should hear them just the same. In case you are tempted by your own juices to do something stupid out here, know that Moab Search and Rescue spends a lot of time in this area. All three of these stories concern the Portal Trail.

In peak season of 1998, a group of firemen from Provo ventured to Moab to do a bit of "buddy riding." These fellows decided to do the macho thing and ride the most exposed section of the Portal Trail just at the viewpoint, surely driven by an overdose of testosterone and male bonding show-off stuff. The next day one of the firemen made it into the local newspaper, an antifeminist slur splashed across his shirt. This picture was accompanied by a sad story about his death and the small children and young wife he left behind.

The town of Moab was mortified by the death. Some folks were simply mortified by the T-shirt. One of our guides had the idea to erect a memorial plaque on the trail with his name on it as a warning to others. I suggested that it read: "Here is where the following idiots fell to their deaths (list names here). Shit happens, but sometimes people are dumb enough to make an appointment to step in it."

They already had the big arc lights set up for nightfall. When you see lights like this from downtown Moab, it ain't a Hollywood premiere; it's a Moab "last rites."

A couple of seasons ago, a father and his two boys were navigating the Portal when they heard a scream and returned to find a fellow lying in the trail. He had ridden into the broken and jagged limb of a juniper tree, and the hooked end pierced his calf and yanked out his calf muscle, dropping it on the trail beside him. Blood was everywhere. His leg looked like it had vomited a side of roast beef. The search and rescue folks did some sorely needed trail maintenance along the bottom section of the Portal Trail in order to carry this fellow down on a stretcher in total darkness. As you walk your bike down the final section of the Portal Trail, you can think to yourself, "Wow, this used to be worse."

In 1998 during the Fat Tire Festival, I was driving a group of investm[...] out from a day tour on the White Rim when we came across search and re[...] cles parked alongside the road. They already had the big arc lights set up [...] fall. When you see lights like this from downtown Moab, it ain't a Ho[l]lywood premiere; it's a Moab "last rites." One thing about retrieving someone from a fall off the Portal Trail: There ain't no hurry. This was the second death in a year, and the BLM soon reacted, threatening to close the trail. After protests from locals, they decided to put up warning signs. I entertained the freaked-out bankers with a story.

"Once upon a time I was sitting on the overlook, enjoying the view, after walking my bike along the exposed section of the Portal. I had passed a mixed group of college-age lads and lasses on their way up Poison Spider Mesa. As I sat staring at the valley below, at peace with the world, amazed once again that I live in this beautiful place, here they came, a confused bunch, some riding, some walking the exposed singletrack . . . a fatal accident waiting to happen.

"The first rider demonstrated admirable skills on the bike, clearing the section with snotty flair. He wheelied off the last 3-foot ledge to where I was sitting and let out a hoot, 'Yaaahooo!' What the fellow did next made me want to throw him off the cliff. He turned around and taunted his friends: 'Come on, man. You can make it!'

"I went ballistic, screaming at him: 'You stupid jerk, do you want to kill one of your friends? Go back and ride it again. You can do it! . . . you hooting asshole.'

"Let us all pray that this jerk who fell today was the one who dared his girlfriend to ride the exposed section."

Only the Slickrock Trail kills more people.

The warning before the exposed singletrack

19 Poison Spider Mesa to the Portal Trail

Start: At the Poison Spider Mesa Trailhead just off Potash Road where there is a sign pointing out some dinosaur tracks in the vertical wall above the trail.

Length: 12.8-mile loop, but mileage will vary if you play around on the slickrock.

Approximate riding time: Advanced riders 2 to 3 hours; intermediate riders 3 to 6 hours. Freeforming the slickrock can add hours onto the ride.

Difficulty: Technically moderate to difficult (the Portal is beyond extreme). Big ledges, deep sand, and steep climbing and descending on slickrock to and along Poison Spider Mesa—but this in no way prepares you for the exposure of the Portal Trail. Physically moderate to extremely difficult due to the steady climb and the attention necessary to negotiate the technical challenges.

Trail surface: 4WD doubletrack, slickrock, and extremely technical and dangerous single-track, if you choose to take the Portal Trail option. Loose rock, stream-worn rocks up to the size of babyheads, deep sand, slickrock, hard-packed to loose sedimentary soils, and bedrock ledges on a classic technical 4WD track.

Lay of the land: It's a mesa, which is a table of land. You have to ride up to it, then you have to get down from it. On top of the mesa are deep sand, ledges, and lots of slickrock formations to roll around on.

Total climbing: 2,268 feet.

Land status: Bureau of Land Management (BLM) and Utah State Trust lands.

Other trail users: Hikers and off-road vehicles (ORV).

Best seasons: Spring and fall.

Environmental concerns: Fragile! This area is threatened by ongoing trail spur closures due to the formation of a Wilderness Study Area adjacent to the trail. Avoid side spurs or any faint tracks veering from the main trail. Cryptobiotic soil crusts and rare desert mosses abound on the desert and slickrock surfaces. Avoid blackened pits on the slickrock.

Warning! Not a place to be in a thunderstorm! The mesa is extremely exposed to lightning strikes.

Getting there: From Moab: Follow U.S. Route 191 north from the intersection of Main Street and Center Street for 4 miles. After passing the massive tailings pond, take a left onto Potash Road (Utah Route 279). Continue for 6 miles. You'll pass Indian writings on a section of river called Wall Street, made popular by climbers. At the sign that reads DINOSAUR TRACKS, turn right and drive uphill on the gravel road to the Poison Spider Mesa Trail parking area. Don't miss the fine examples of dinosaur tracks in the rock varnish up on the cliff face east of the trailhead.

The Ride

This technically and physically difficult ride can be done as a loop with a portage or as an out-and-back, with a turnaround point at a beautiful arch or at the rim overlooking Moab Valley a few more miles to the north. The out-and-back allows you a chance to enjoy "payback" for your long climb up to the slickrock. The trek

The Colorado River from the start of the Portal Trail

starts with a relentless climb over little babyheads, leads through areas of deep sand and technical bedrock, then eventually flattens out into a ledgy romp. After some sandy curves and a bit of confusing route finding, you are presented with some outrageously steep slickrock knobs that are a blast to ride for advanced cyclists. Once on the slickrock the ride can be freeformed by those with good navigating skills, or you can follow the trail markings that appear as little jeeps. Keeping the jeeps oriented in the same direction is the secret to following the trail out to the rim. At any point you may also simply turn around and go back the way you came in.

The most notable feature of this ride, if done as a loop, is the Portal Trail, a narrow singletrack exposed along the face of a vertical cliff that is not marked to discourage riding. If someone shouts from the Portal viewpoint at the far end of the exposed section, "Come on, you can make it!" you have my permission to bash them about the head with your pump.

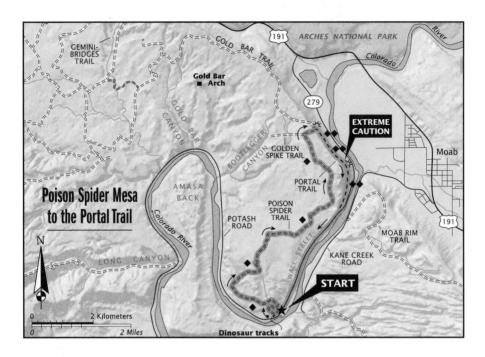

Poison Spider Mesa to the Portal Trail

The mileage count here assumes you will be following the jeep trail markings, but most likely you will be tempted to freeform over to the Portal Trail, or avoid the thing altogether after enjoying the slickrock. My suggestion is to use the mileage count to get to the slickrock, then mess around, keeping the predominant slickrock knob above the north side of the Portal as your navigational device. Study the terrain as you skirt the slickrock area, keeping memorable landmarks in your mind to serve as markers. If you run into the jeep markers time and again, you can always use the orientation of the little jeeps to know whether or not they lead to or from the rim.

I must confess that mileage counts for Poison Spider Mesa are futile once you are on top of the mesa. I have little faith in numbers, mine or others', once I start to romp. So as always, the bottom line is, when in doubt, stick to spurs with the most bike tracks. Poison Spider Mesa is among the most frequented trails in Moab, so during peak season there will be cyclists and jeepers on the trail. Don't count on them, but if you find yourself in a mob, be thankful. There is one spur to the right at mile 4.8 that always grabs newcomers. It's the most visible spur and takes off downhill in the sand toward the Colorado River Gorge to the south. Gradually you find that it just peters out on a slickrock fin. If you find yourself out there, enjoy the view, then turn around and ride back to the top of the hill. You'll find the main trail heading off to your right at the top and wonder why you missed it in the first place. When you hit a wonderful series of fast-banked sandy turns, you'll know that you are back on the right track out to the mesa's slickrock.

There is more confusion once you hit the slickrock, but keeping the large sandstone knob to the east on your right and keeping your eyes peeled for the little jeep markers are the best ways to stay on track.

Miles and Directions

0.0 **START** from the new parking area just above Potash Road and head up the hill. Stay on the main trail and avoid the spur left just past the parking area. The trail immediately ahead is easy to follow, as it is frequented by mobs of 4WD vehicles. During the peak seasons in spring and fall, you need only follow the masses of mountain bikers. The trail soon turns to deep sand, followed by some technical rock ledges—stained with oil and rubber. The trail is very obvious.

2.8 A little jog to the left is marked with a painted bike on the rock. Go this way to avoid a short-but-nasty steep section of deep sand.

3.0 Reach the top of the hill. Go straight across this bedrock area with the La Sals to your right. The stenciled jeep markers will help you from here. There is a trail marker directly on the other side of this flat area that eventually leads you to a fun section of rollies and mild ledges—a real hoot. The next section hands you a series of downhill berms that make you want to turn around and do it again, but they ain't as much fun going up.

4.8 Watch for the trail marker on your left. From here you will be exercising your route-finding skills as the trail weaves in the rock and sand. Try not to get sucked into the right-hand spur here that leads out onto the fins above the Colorado River, unless you want this kind of diversion.

5.5 Welcome to the slickrock area.

5.6 Continue beyond the little pond, all the while staying along the right-hand side of the large dome on your left. Crest the slickrock hill and drop down a very steep bit of 4WD track (two choices here—steep on the left or extremely steep on the right), then weave downward through the trees. You will come to a pit on your right after another steep slickrock section. Upon closer examination (not too close), that pit contains Little Arch, a hole that overlooks the Colorado River. There is a nice spot farther on past the arch into the trees for a picnic. The view of the Moab Valley is quite nice there. **Option.** This is the place to turn around if you are not an advanced cyclist. Turning around and heading back up the hill, you will find those stenciled jeep trail markers. If you want to head out to the Portal, keep the jeeps pointed in the right direction and they will take you all the way out to where the trail meets the Portal Trail and the Gold Bar Rim Trail. This area

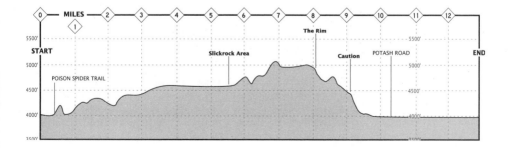

Sidehilling a technical spot

along the way is great for freeforming, so mileage counts are practically useless if you are tempted to play. Be sure to remain aware of trail markers and landmarks and dodge the crypto, mosses, and lichens. You will be skirting to the left of the huge slickrock dome to the east, but do not venture too close to it. At one point the trail will drop down some ledges to your left, away from the dome. It is easy to miss, but also easy to find once you lose the markers. You will probably get lost out here the first time you ride onto the slickrock, but if you use the dome as your goal and use the markers to reinforce your route, you'll certainly find the Rim. There are some very steep hills out on the slickrock, so check your equipment and, if you are freeforming away from the markers, double-check your route before you commit to something that drops straight off. There is also a great deal of sand. If it is a bit moist and packed by previous rain or snow, it is a joy to ride. If it is dry, it is like riding on the beach in North Carolina. Pleasure always comes with some pain.

6.0 If you follow the little jeep markers, avoiding spurs to the left that are not marked, you'll eventually spot the line of a funky barbed-wire fence on your right, after you drop down from the slickrock area over some ledges and gaps. Head right at the T to the rim. That is the Golden Spike Trail to your left—don't even think about it.

8.1 The rim. **Options.** Here is where you can either turn around and retrace your route or continue on the Portal Trail—or, if you are a Mr. or Mrs. Hardcore, head out on the Gold Bar Rim Trail. The spur to Gold Bar Rim is to your left below the rim. This route, combined with the mileage of the Poison Spider Trail, is only for the most experienced and skilled mountain bikers and should only be considered during spring or fall. If you are heading down the Portal Trail to Potash Road, stop to take in the view, then follow the little single-track to your right. This is the first bite of the Portal. The first section is delicious, but you'll soon find yourself on the edge of eternity. Walk it! If you have a mild case of vertigo, don't even think about it. The BLM has placed warning signs on the trail as a result of deaths. They mean business. Heed the warnings. There are a handful of technical sections that simply are not worth the risk. It is a sad fact that some people only realize the danger they put themselves into *after* they have blown it.

9.1 Just before the viewpoint you'll come across *the* dangerous section of trail, Idiot's Launch. It is possible to negotiate the rock if you are a good rider, but if you biff, you *die!* And I'm not joking! In the words of Dirty Harry, "Do you feel lucky, punk?" It's over 500 feet straight down to Potash Road, and if you fall that's probably where your body will be found, if Moab Search and Rescue is lucky that day. If you time it right, you can even manage to get run over by a truck after your plunge. At a minimum you are guaranteed a freefall of 200 feet. The rest of the way you just bounce. Once through the exposed section, the viewpoint is worth a few minutes of gawking and general relief. The remaining trail is a technical challenge to even the most advanced riders and is best walked for 60 percent of its length. At least if you fall here, you will only break a few bones.

10.6 You have reached Potash Road. Go right on the pavement back to your car. **Side trip.** I highly recommend that you stop along the way to examine the signed Indian writings. Pristine petroglyphs above the road to your right have been preserved by roadwork that lowered the ground level. The elevation of the petroglyphs has so far kept folks from ruining the artwork. (Ground-level petroglyphs on the opposite side of the river in Moonflower Canyon have all but been destroyed by vandalism and misguided "love.") The oldest markings—located at the extreme left of the panel at ground level, a series of holes that resemble inverted breasts—was revealed by roadwork. This portion of the site is ancient and undatable, though local experts theorize it was a prayer site.

12.8 Arrive back at the trailhead.

Ride Information

Trail Contacts

Moab Bike Patrol
c/o Bureau of Land Management
82 E. Dogwood
Moab, UT 84532
(435) 259-2196

Utah State School and Institutional Trust Lands Administration
1165 South US 191, Ste. 5, Moab, UT 84532
(435) 259-3760

Schedule

Trail is open year-round but is best during spring and fall.

Maps

USGS maps: Moab
Moab East Trail Map by Latitude 40° Inc.
Moab Recreation Map by F. H. Barnes

Moab West and Southwest

I n this section you'll find great opportunities for multiday rides supported by camping. The areas featured here include Canyonlands National Park, both the Island in the Sky and the Needle Districts. This section also includes the western end of Potash Road, trails south of the Colorado River and west of U.S. Route

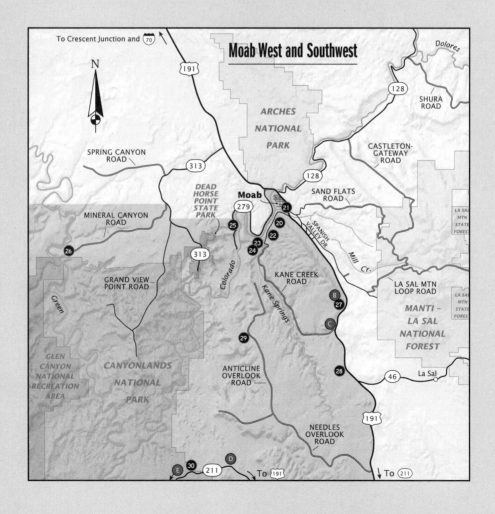

Moab West and Southwest

To Crescent Junction and (70)

N

191

Dolores

128

SHURA ROAD

ARCHES
NATIONAL
PARK

SPRING CANYON ROAD

313

CASTLETON-
GATEWAY
ROAD

DEAD
HORSE
POINT
STATE
PARK

Moab

279

128

SAND FLATS ROAD

21

MINERAL CANYON ROAD

25

20

22

LA SAL
MTN
STATE
FOREST

26

313

23

24

SPANISH VALLEY DR.

GRAND VIEW POINT ROAD

Colorado

KANE CREEK ROAD

Kane Springs

LA SAL MTN LOOP ROAD

LA SAL
MTN
STATE
FOREST

Green

B
27

MANTI –
LA SAL
NATIONAL
FOREST

C

GLEN
CANYON
NATIONAL
RECREATION
AREA

CANYONLANDS
NATIONAL
PARK

29

ANTICLINE
OVERLOOK
ROAD

28

46

La Sal

191

NEEDLES
OVERLOOK
ROAD

E   30   211

D

To 191

To 211

191, as well as the Canyon Rims Recreation Area and lands extending down into and past the Abajo Mountains.

The geology of these lands is as epic as its mountain bike rides. Events here are recorded on a massive scale. Uplifts, faults, mountain ranges, synclines and anticlines, and the results of eons of erosion graphically illustrate our insignificance in geological time. All these features can be viewed from the canyon rims overlooking White Rim and Lockhart Basin. The Abajo Mountains (translated as the "Blessed Mountains") are among the youngest ranges in the world. Only the nearby Henry Mountains (named after the guy who mapped them for the Spanish explorer Escalante) and the La Sal Mountains (named after piles of salt) are younger.

The Needles District of Canyonlands National Park is laced with many 4WD roads that can be ridden legally on a mountain bike. Restrictions are limited to singletrack hiking trails, but there are so many doubletrack trails available to mountain bikers that the singletrack is hardly missed. The downside of riding in the Needles is *deep sand*. Not your run-of-the-mill deep sand, mind you, but *deep sand*. Frankly, sand happens on all the trails in this area.

Also included in this section is the famous White Rim Trail, probably the best multiday camping trip for novice to intermediate mountain bikers on the planet. Since it's in a national park, the trail is well maintained and serviced by rangers with guns. There are cute little potties at every campsite.

Pearls before Swine

L ong ago Nic Hougen, artist, local character, and Old World desert dweller, published a cartoon picturing Moab of the future, with hotel after hotel, streets crawling with 4WD vehicles, cars with bikes on top, people and bikes and more cars, road signs advertising all types of crap, a McDonald's, a Burger King, a Taco Bell, and, in the distance, tramways going up to the Moab Rim. The value of the town's growth is in the eye of the beholder and clearly Nic thought, and still thinks, that it would be better if we would all just leave.

Wishes seldom come true, but visions often do. I am sad to report that Moab is looking more and more like Nic's cartoon vision, and Nic is looking more and more like a lunatic. It is a very mixed-up world we live in. There are now two chairlifts in Moab on either side of the Moab Valley, marring what many consider to be one of the last remaining natural wonders so close to a populated area. The deserted appearance of one lift has caused the better one on the Moab Rim to go under financially. It was auctioned off in 2002. Its future is in doubt. The most absurd fact arising from the tramway deal is that when it is in operation, you can take a chairlift to the top of the Moab Rim and ride down it on your Huffy. Yes, any Joe who can afford a lift ticket can ride what is arguably the most dangerous section of mountain bike trail on earth. The lift to the Moab Rim facilitates idiocy, and in fact, encourages it with a race. I predict that

Nic Hougen

this kind of thing just cannot last. I am seeing my own vision of the future, too, and I see lawsuits and litigation.

Some famous mountain bike guy once told me he could ride up to the Moab Rim without putting a foot down. I was almost impressed, but then I realized that if you ride this trail without putting a foot down, you are not really in Moab, you are on your own testosterone ego trip. I don't even *know* if I can ride up it. I always just look up and, after about 150 yards of lung bursting, grinding and plugging away, I say to myself, "Just what is the point of all of this?" I put a foot down and my momentum is shot. Then I turn around and look at the serpentine Colorado River carving its way through the tamarisk trees and Wall Street and the gigantic tombstones of red sandstone and the endorphins hit. I have a religious experience. And then I know just why I live here. I hope this admission doesn't lessen my chances of getting into the Mountain Bike Hall of Fame or anything, but hey, I get off the damn bike and push. My mouth is open for two reasons: To breathe heavily and because jaws just drop when you see the Colorado River Gorge from the Moab Rim.

Enjoy this trail, if you are hardcore, and even enjoy the chairlift for repeated runs (if it is open) in the downhill direction only. It's quite beautiful and extremely challenging. It is so beautiful that we should test those who go into this area. Despite the fantastic technical downhill, I truly hate to see the testosterone boys out here. You know, the guys who dream of dying on a mountain bike, the ones who ride across the crypto and say, "I sure am glad that Lee guy isn't here to tell me I cannot ride across the dirt."

20 Moab Rim Trail

Start: From the Moab Rim Trailhead on Kane Creek Road.

Length: 6.8-mile point-to-point with the aid of a shuttle (14.3-mile loop).

Approximate riding time: 2 to 4 hours.

Difficulty: Technically extremely difficult to downright abusive. The ride up to the rim is up steep bedrock and over high ledges. The top is a sand bog. The downside portage is unridable. Physically difficult due to the brutal climb, the sand slog, and carrying the bike down the portage.

Trail surface: Extremely rugged 4WD trail and a very technical singletrack that is suitable only for hiking—portage or risk bone damage. Huge ledges, sand, loose rock, and hardpack. Kayenta slab rock, Navajo sandstone.

Lay of the land: This is a rim ride. A rim is the edge of a canyon wall. In this case the canyon wall is the western edge of the Moab Fault. The trail passes behind the rim into an area of sand and slickrock, but just beyond the trailhead the trail follows the rim close enough to warrant a degree of caution, especially if you are dropping in from the chairlift.

Total climbing: 2,768 feet.

Land status: Private and Bureau of Land Management (BLM) lands. The private lands are owned by the folks who operate the Moab Skyway, the chairlift up to the rim.

Other trail users: Hikers and off-road vehicles (ORV).

Best seasons: Spring and fall.

Environmental concerns: Extremely fragile! Cryptobiotic soil crusts and rare desert mosses abound. Stay on the trail at all times. The Hidden Valley section of this ride takes you through a Wilderness Study Area. We only have access due to the status of this trail as a "traditional mountain bike route." They won't let me take mountain bike tours into this area, but you can ride it even if you don't know how to treat it. Go figure.

Getting there: From Moab: Go west on Center Street, from the intersection of Main and Center Streets. Take a right onto 100 West at the Rio Restaurant where Center Street ends. Take the next left at Williams Way, then a left onto 500 West, where Williams Way ends. Go to the dangerous three-way intersection of 500 West and Kane Creek Road and take a hard right onto Kane Creek Road. You'll pass the Moab Skyway on your left and the wetlands preserve on your right. After the road bends left, following the Colorado River, the signed Moab Rim Trailhead is on the left just past the cattle guard. Park at the trailhead and ride from here.

Optional Shuttle Point: From Moab: Drive south on U.S. Route 191 from Center Street and Main Street for 4 miles to Angel Rock Road. Take a right onto Angel Rock Road and then another right at the T intersection onto Rimrock Lane. At the end of this dirt road, park your shuttle vehicle in the lot next to the trailhead sign-in. Follow the instructions from mile 6.8 to get to the trailhead.

The Hidden Valley

The Ride

Looking for a great view of Moab Valley? Looking for an extremely challenging trail that's close to town? Looking to blow your lungs out on a brutal climb and break your face on an unridable singletrack descent? Here's your trail, folks. If you are not a skilled mountain biker, do not attempt this ride. If you are a novice, leave the bike at the hotel and walk the trail. It is an excellent day hike. Be sure to take lots of water.

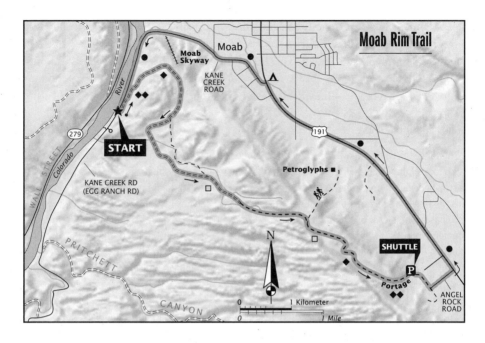

This trail can be ridden from Moab, as a loop or as a shuttled trip, in either direction. It has a brutal climb at the head and an equally brutal downhill at the tail any way you slice it. I have chosen to document this ride as a loop leaving from the trailhead on Kane Creek Road, but it is fine in either direction and fairly easy to navigate from either end due to the valley effect at the top that keeps you funneled in the right direction. The ride up from the northern end on the massive rock slab to the rim is one of the most difficult climbs I know of. The southern end is so technical that you are going to be walking the bike. The northern end can be ridden in its entirety, if you are very fit and very skilled.

The ride through the two-tiered Hidden Valley alone is worth the climb and nasty portage. It's one of those sections of trail that you wish would go on forever, unless, of course, you run into a thunderstorm. Lightning can be a problem here. The Hidden Valley portion is downhill from the north.

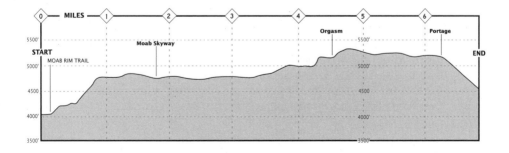

Mountain biking is strictly forbidden off the main trail, which eventually takes you through a Wilderness Study Area. Anyone with a desire to visit what is arguably the best petroglyph site near Moab should hire a guide from one of the local outfitters. I hope you agree that leading people across fragile desert vegetation to unguarded art treasures is best left to the professionals.

Miles and Directions

(Note: Mileage will certainly vary, depending on how much time you dedicate to playing on the slab rock of the climb and on the top of the rim. There are a few spurs midride, all of which are easily deciphered and eventually hook up. Getting a little twisted here is fine. It is hard to get lost, unless you are very poor at route finding. You have choices here, limited choices, but choices nonetheless. Use them. It's a short ride, so knock yourself out, just don't ride off the beaten path (it's illegal), and stay away from that sandy climb over the hill to the west midway through the ride. It heads out into the sandpit from hell. It's really not enticing. Keeping just below the sandstone knobs to the east is the secret to finding some nice surfaces to ride on and side hikes suitable for a lingering stay.)

0.0 **START** from the parking area and head up the slickrock shelf behind the marker.

1.0 At the top you'll need a breather, and the viewpoint is certainly a spot to relish the Moab Valley. Trailers look so romantic from this height.

1.2 Go right at the Y.

1.9 Going left is cool, but sandy. Going right you'll encounter some bedrock to roll on. Either will not affect the mileage count too much to worry over. Careful of the vegetation, though. This used to be a wild area. Now it's a place for fat tourists who have taken the Moab Skyway to the rim. Ride over them for more technical challenge.

2.8 Over the rock and through the sand to Grandfather's house we go. Just don't take that spur that disappears up and over the sandy hill ahead and to the right. There are some very difficult ledges ahead, so be on your toes.

3.8 **Side trip.** The spur up the hill to the left is a dead end, but leads to a petroglyph site, if you are into the diversion. If not, stay right.

4.5 The trail turns to singletrack here. Whoopee! You are about to have an orgasm. During mid-May this area is full of flowers.

6.3 Oh well, if you haven't already done it, dismount and carry the bike down to the bottom and your shuttle vehicle. The hike down is approximately 0.5 mile, but it will seem a lot longer.

6.8 Arrive at the Angel Rock and Hidden Valley Trailhead. Sign in and tell the BLM how you liked the ride and how much you wish it to remain open to mountain biking. From the parking lot bear right onto Rimrock Road. At the nearby intersection with Angel Rock Road, take a left. At US 191, go left again and ride back into town. At the corner of Main (US 191) and Kane Creek Road (McDonald's and Burger King), go left and follow Kane Creek Road all the way to the trailhead.

14.3 Reach the trailhead.

Moab Rim Downhill Race

Ride Information

Trail Contacts

Moab Bike Patrol
c/o Bureau of Land Management
82 E. Dogwood
Moab, UT 84532
(435) 259-2196

The Moab Skyway and Rim Trail
1800 South Highland Drive
Moab, UT 84532
(435) 259-7799
www.moab-utah.com/skyway

Schedule

Trail is open year-round but is best during spring and fall.

Maps

USGS maps: Moab
Moab West Trail Map by Latitude 40° Inc.
Moab Recreation Map by F. H. Barnes

Love on the Trail

Bubby's southern drawl flavored the story nicely: "I was cruising along with all these geriatric Japanese tourists shooting video out of the windows when all of a sudden they started hooting and cackling and rushed to one side of the bus. I was going down some pretty severe switchbacks and when they all ran to one side I thought we might topple over. I looked out the window to the left and there was a couple just off the trail on a blanket. They were naked and really going at it. They didn't even slow down as the bus passed with all these tourists hanging out the window with video cameras.

"All the way back these old folks were comparing video, giggling and commenting. One woman came up to the front of the bus to share her video with me, saying, 'Look, you Americans are so funny.'"

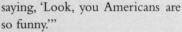

The first time I rode to the top of Hurrah Pass, my wife and I stopped to make love on the gnarly red rocks . . . And I swear, we didn't see Bubby's tour bus. Don't worry. It's okay. We're married, but you know, doing the wild thing in the wild is great, and it is a very popular mountain biking diversion. As a tour guide I have surprised my fair share of breeding couples. I usually yell, "Don't mind me. I do that, too."

I mentioned this to Nate Toone the other day as we were at the top of Gold Bar Rim and Nate said calmly: "Joanne and I made love on that rock over there last time we were up here." It made me realize that, you know, I'll bet just about everyone does this. We once had a woman who guided for us who also guided for another tour company in Moab. We were talking around this subject and she offered some advice. She said she always carried Baby Wipes on trips so that when she had sex with a client she could, well, you know . . . clean up. Wow! We didn't use her again, but I am sure there are a couple of guys out there somewhere who are looking for a tour just like this.

So don't let anyone try to sell you a saddle with a hole in it. Biking is not bad for your sex life; it just moves it into the outdoors.

21 Hurrah Pass

Start: From Moab at the corner of Center and Main Streets.
Length: 29-mile out-and-back.
Approximate riding time: 3 to 7 hours, depending on fitness level.
Difficulty: Technically easy as you ride out on the dirt and gravel road, then moderate as you reach the sometimes rough climb up to the pass. Physically the route is difficult due to the mileage and elevation change.

Trail surface: Maintained county road and rugged 4WD track. Bedrock ledges, sand, and loose rock. Can be very rough after rains.
Lay of the land: Through a canyon on gravel and loose rock on the maintained dirt road. Up to the pass on the rugged stuff.
Total climbing: 3,628 feet.
Land status: Bureau of Land Management (BLM) and Utah State Trust lands.
Other trail users: Hikers, campers, equestrians, and off-road vehicles (ORV).
Best seasons: Spring and fall.

Environmental concerns: Cryptobiotic soil crusts and rare desert mosses abound. Stay on the trail at all times.

Getting there: Downtown Moab: You will be leaving from the intersection of Main and Center Streets in the very heart of town. Moab is set up like all Mormon towns in Utah, with a main intersection where Main and Center form a cross for the four directions. Main runs north–south. Center runs east–west. Radiating from this intersection, the streets are referred to by numbers; 100 East is one block east of Main; 100 West is one block west of Main; 100 North is one block north of Center; 100 South is one block south of Center. And so forth.

The Ride

Hurrah Pass is a small flat spot on a gnarly ridge separating the Colorado River (which flows west) from Kane Creek (which flows east). It received its name from that same rancher who built the Shafer Trail that descends from the Island in the Sky to the White Rim. This amazing piece of cowboy engineering was accomplished to get cattle down from the high country and across the Colorado River, and then up and over to the grazing lands below the pass. When at last Sod Shafer built the trail and completed the journey to the pass the first time, he threw his hat in the air and screamed, "Hurrah!" It stuck. (Not the hat, the name.)

Because this route is truly the best first ride for newcomers to Moab, I have chosen to include the pavement ride from town. You can drive out Kane Creek Road to where the road turns to dirt or park at any number of places along the way (Moonflower Canyon is a good alternative), but riding the pavement through the western end of Moab, and then along the river, allows you to be enchanted by the town's mystique from the saddle, with the wind blowing through the holes in your helmet. If you are a beginner or novice, you can turn around at any point and go back, or drive in a way to start your ride at any number of obvious parking areas.

God's Golf Ball

The route travels along the Colorado River, through a deep canyon along a creek, and up to the saddle between the Colorado River and Kane Springs Canyon, a beautiful tight canyon that opens up to present you with the classic American southwestern landscape. Attractions include colorful and very impressive geological formations sculpted from the Rico, Moencopi, Chinle, Wingate, Kayenta, and Navajo geological layers. There are many petroglyphs and a variety of wildlife to photograph as you head up Kane Springs Canyon. The ride culminates in spectacular views of the Colorado River Gorge.

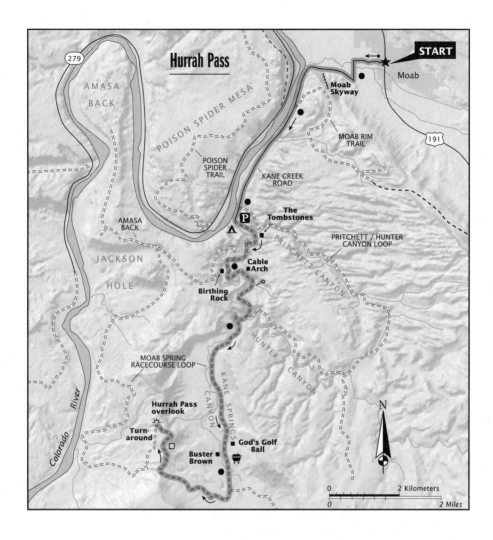

This ride is hot as hell in summer. You should start the ride at 6:00 A.M. during the summer months. The canyon is tight, so shade is plentiful, but when you bust out into the canyon, shade is nowhere to be found except in the bug-infested washes. During June the cow flies in the open canyon can be a real incentive for speed. Cow flies love heat, so they are less plentiful during early hours when the temperature is below seventy degrees.

When descending from the pass, tight turns that apex on exposed ledges can be extremely dangerous to novices who have problems controlling speed with correct braking technique. Be especially careful on your descent. At one point in the ride, you'll be crossing Kane Creek. This wash flash-floods during heavy rain, so if rain is in the forecast, exercise caution.

Miles and Directions

0.0 **START** by heading west on Center Street, from between the Slickrock Cafe and Pasta Jay's. Take a right onto 100 West at the Rio Restaurant where Center Street ends. Take the next left at Williams Way. Ride until this street ends and take a left onto 500 West. Go to the (dangerous) three-way intersection of 500 West and Kane Creek Road and take a right. You'll pass the Moab Skyway on your left and the wetlands preserve on your right. **Side trips.** The wetlands hike is something you should consider during your trip. The Moab Skyway is for well-equipped downhillers who want a repeated rush on the dangerous descent to the river and for fat people who want to see the Moab Rim in the worst possible way. The best way to do the Moab Rim is to hike or ride (advanced mountain bikers only) the Moab Rim Trail (see Ride 20), which you'll encounter shortly on your ride after you round the bend and head out along the river. The hike includes awesome views of the Colorado River Gorge. The Moab Rim Trailhead is just past the cattle guard after you round the bend in the road. There are a little cross and some flowers on the roadside just past the cattle guard and a memorial to a kid who died there. A short distance past the Moab Rim Trail, you'll encounter Moonflower Canyon where a very large cottonwood overhangs the road. This canyon is a notable hike and home to some of the most interesting and badly vandalized petroglyphs close to town. There is an Anasazi ladder going up the cliff from the now fenced-in glyphs on the right-hand side of the canyon, and there is an Anasazi well at the back of the canyon up on the canyon wall to the left. There is also a lot of poison ivy in the canyon, so beware if you take the short hike in. This canyon is a wonderful place to camp, by the way.

4.7 On your left is the commercialized entrance to Pritchett Canyon and a privately owned campground. **Side trip.** The Pritchett Canyon ride is truly an advanced ride, but a hike up the canyon is for anyone. It is a long, arduous hike. If you are hiking or biking in here, the owners of the campground exact a fee. It is illegal to charge for access to public lands, but they'll hassle you if you don't pay. Use your own judgment. Just beyond the campground and the private parking for Pritchett Canyon, the road turns to dirt at the cattle guard.

4.8 On your right is the overflow camping and parking area at the mouth of Kane Springs Canyon. This is a great place to park if you want to avoid the pavement from Moab. From here ride into the canyon on the wide dirt road. There will be some easily avoided exposure on the right side as you ride underneath the Tombstones, a now infamous B.A.S.E. jumping spot. In a ways you'll pass the signed Amasa Back Trail parking area. Across

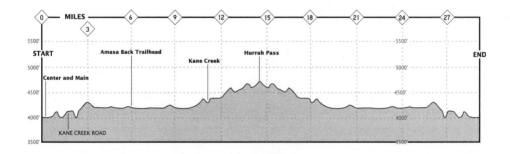

Kane Creek Canyon

from the parking area is Goat Canyon. **Side trip.** There are a couple of dinosaur tracks along the trail into the canyon adjacent the wash and some fine petroglyphs up on the canyon walls. The hiking trail to the petroglyphs is currently lined with stones.

6.0 Go past the posted Amasa Back Trailhead on your right. **Side trip.** Across the Amasa Back Trail are some of the best petroglyphs anywhere. They are hard to see and even harder to get to, so if you want to see them, and want to be pointed to many other features in this canyon, hire a good guide. Binoculars are recommended.

6.2 On your right and down from the road is a large rock. On it is carved the likeness of a Spanish conquistador and a woman giving birth. It's called the Birthing Rock, and it's covered with petroglyph images that are surprisingly intact considering they are so close to the road. Let's keep them this way. Please do not touch them or take "rubbings." Oils on your hands and repeated rubbings cause the images to fade.

6.5　**Side trip.** Though it looks impossible from the road, the tight gap in the rock above you on your left is the scramble up to Cable Arch. Once on top, you can climb onto the arch by pulling yourself up a cable—hence "Cable Arch." The scramble up through this steep gap, or the cable pull-up at the arch, is not recommended to anyone in bike shoes.

6.7　Enjoy the wide, swooping switchbacks that lower you into the gorge.

6.9　At the bottom of the switchbacks on your left is a spring that comes out just next to the road. Great water here! Fill your bottles! Drink directly from the spring!

7.0　Here is a secret: This is one of the best camping spots in Moab, just down the hill and to your right. Oh, well, so much for the secret.

7.8　On your left is Hunter Canyon. The stream crossing is usually dry, but don't count on it. Sometimes it flashes. **Side trip.** The short but technical hike into Hunter Canyon is quite beautiful and is highly recommended. If you choose to hike in here, be very careful of the soil crusts and plants along the stream. *No bikes allowed!*

8.9　**Side trip.** On your right 100 yards across the wash is an old mining road that skirts the canyon and eventually hooks into the Amasa Back Trail. It's not too inviting on this end, but can be a really challenging trip for expert riders with advanced route-finding skills.

9.1　On your left is a petroglyph of a centipede. Far ahead across the canyon on your right, high up on the top of the ridge, is a small hill shaped like a breast with a flattened nipple. Just down to the right along the ridge below the hoodoos to the right of the breast is a flat spot. That is Hurrah Pass. This is where you are heading. You will be looping around the canyon to achieve this.

10.3　Buster Brown (Bashful Turk) is on your right. God's Golf Ball (sometimes called the Devil's Golf Ball—I guess they play the game together and share the ball) is on your left. **Side trip.** A visit up the spur to your left will take you under the Golf Ball. High up the canyon walls above the Golf Ball are remnants of uranium mines. The hike up to the mines is hardcore and not recommended, unless you are a mining history nut.

11.1　Kane Creek crosses the road at this point. This is the point of no return should it rain hard to the north while you are out here. While shooting a film on the other side of the pass a few years ago, the stunt team and I were trapped on the other side of this streambed by a ripping flash flood and had to spend the night watching the water gradually go down. We watched as boulders and large trees were shoved through here by the force of the water. If the wash is rushing with floodwaters, it's best to just make yourself comfortable and wait it out. You told someone you were out here, right? You are prepared to stay overnight in the desert, right? You have lots of water, food, a lighter, and a space blanket, right?

11.2　Pass the unmarked spur on the left.

11.4　Pass the marked spur on your left and continue on the well-maintained road uphill to the pass. There is some freaky exposure on your right as you ride the ledge that eventually takes you to the pass. At times, after weeks of repeated rains and ensuing water erosion, this part of the ride becomes a true technical mountain bike climb. The cliff edges here are very loose, so avoid standing too close! The road ahead wraps along these Moencopi cliffs and presents you with the opportunity to take some great pictures. The hoodoo that resembles a sitting bird above you on the ridge signals the last turn to Hurrah Pass.

14.5 Hurrah! The Pass! After enjoying this area, turn around and retrace your route. The downhill from the pass can be extremely dangerous. Control your speed and watch for loose sediments and rock that could send you off the trail.

29.0 Arrive back in Moab.

Ride Information

Trail Contacts

Moab Bike Patrol
c/o Bureau of Land Management
82 E. Dogwood
Moab, UT 84532
(435) 259-2196
Utah State School and Institutional Trust Lands Administration
1165 South US 191, Ste. 5
Moab, UT 84532
(435) 259-3760

Schedule

Trail is open year-round but is best during spring and fall.

Maps

USGS maps: Moab, Trough Springs Canyon
Moab West Trail Map by Latitude 40° Inc.
Moab Recreation Map by F. H. Barnes

GOATHEAD

Goathead is a hardy little plant, not native to this region. (Most of the plants here, including the tumbleweed that so symbolizes the West in Hollywood images, are not native to this area.) Goathead is distinguished by very small teardrop-shaped leaves and tiny yellow blossoms. It hugs the ground and spreads out from a central root system. Its most notable feature is its seed, which is shaped like a tiny demonic goat's head. Two thorns protrude from the body of the pod like horns. These thorns are strong enough and sharp enough to flatten a bald car tire and penetrate a shoe. If you ride through a patch of goatheads, you will certainly get a flat (unless you are using tire liners and a sealer), and if the patch of goatheads is serious enough, you can ruin the tube and the tire. Locals who ride their bikes around town use thorn protection like Slime (a commercial tire sealant) or a tough tube protector strip. Specialized has come out with a new tire technology called Armadillo that works and is hassle-free.

Goatheads are usually only found in the Moab Valley, though during wet summers they spread to a few of the local trails such as Kane Creek Road (Hurrah Pass and Amasa Back) and Gemini Bridges where they line the edges of the track at the trailhead. One particularly interesting fact about goathead is that you can burn the seed with a blowtorch until it is a cinder, plant it, and the thing will sprout almost immediately.

22 Pritchett Canyon to Hunter Canyon Rim

Start: From the overflow camping and parking area at the mouth of Kane Creek Canyon.

Length: 11.7-mile loop.

Approximate riding time: 3 to 5 hours, depending on your fitness level and interests.

Difficulty: Technically very difficult due mainly to the sand, loose rock, ledges, and baby-heads in Pritchett Canyon. Physically very difficult due to sand and climbing. The portage is a strain as well.

Trail surface: Loop on a very technical 4WD track. Ends with a short and somewhat ridable singletrack and a steep portage. Trail repeatedly crosses a streambed, which is dry much of the year. Surfaces are sand, baby-heads, water-contoured bedrock, slickrock, hardpack, and loose rock.

Lay of the land: Up the bottom of an impressive canyon, then along the rim of another canyon, then a hike down into another.

Total climbing: 2,448 feet.

Land status: Private and Bureau of Land Management (BLM) lands.

Other trail users: Hikers, campers, equestrians, and off-road vehicles (ORV).

Best seasons: Spring and fall.

Environmental concerns: Fragile cryptobiotic soil crusts cover areas just off the trail. Stay on the trail. Archaeological sites should be respected by leaving them just as they are.

Getting there: From Moab: Go south from the intersection of Main and Center Streets on U.S. Route 191 (Main Street) to Kane Creek Road. Take a right onto Kane Creek Road at the McDonald's. Bear left at the *dangerous* Y intersection with 500 West, staying against the cliffs to your left. Be sure to yield to the traffic coming from the right. Kane Creek Road will eventually take you along the Colorado River. Continue to where the road turns to dirt and cuts left into Kane Creek Canyon. Park at the overflow camping and parking area immediately on your right.

The Ride

The entrance to Pritchett Canyon is on private land, and there is much contention as to whether or not it's legal for the owners to charge for access to public lands that are within a few yards of the road. The private campground here does have parking, so maybe you can rationalize the payment if you park here, but free parking is available only a few yards away in the overflow camping area at the mouth of Kane Springs Canyon. Pay the fee if you feel like it. Get hassled if you don't. Refuse, get arrested, and take it to the Supreme Court, for Pete's sake. At any rate, be prepared with a dollar in your pack. Pritchett Canyon alone is 14 miles as an out-and-back. Since the Hunter Canyon section requires quite a bit of portage and is not nearly as fantastic as the technical downhill of Pritchett, I advise hardcore riders to do the out-and-back, up and down Pritchett Canyon. If you are into a longer ride, more scenery, an ancient Pueblan ruin, a more varied surface, and a nasty portage, then go for the loop featured here.

Navajo sandstone formations

Riding up Pritchett Canyon takes a lot of fortitude. Especially when the sand is dry and the streambed is torn up. After slogging and hammering up loose winding slopes through deep beach sand and over babyheads with only brief sections of contoured bedrock, many spots at the top are simply unridable. Many sections demand that you step back, pick a better line, and try it again. Once at the top you'll encounter a huge mineral deposit (yes, lots of uranium), more sand, a detour to a natural bridge, one of the most beautiful arches in canyon country, a rim ride on a technical singletrack over tight Hunter Canyon, and a portage down into Gatherer Canyon. The portage at the end of this ride is a real headache, and I hesitate to describe it in any detail for fear I'll just confuse you more. The singletrack is pretty obvious as it weaves around the mouths of two canyons. The portage is not at all obvious. Just don't get frustrated and jump. Realize that the last bit is simply up to you. Have faith. You'll eventually be rewarded by the cool waters of the spring at the bottom.

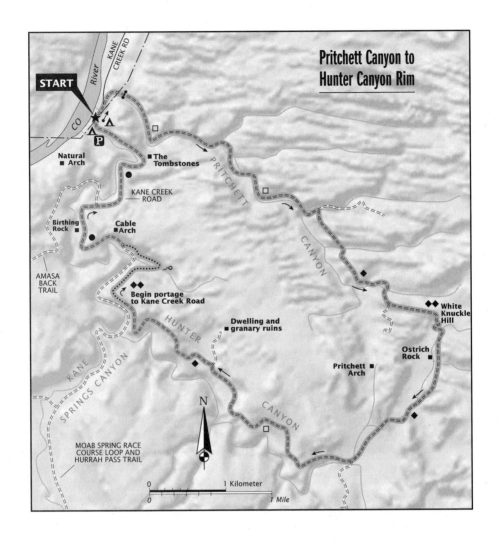

Pritchett Canyon to Hunter Canyon Rim

START

River

CO

KANE CREEK RD

KANE CREEK ROAD

Natural Arch

The Tombstones

Birthing Rock

Cable Arch

AMASA BACK TRAIL

Begin portage to Kane Creek Road

Dwelling and granary ruins

HUNTER

KANE SPRINGS CANYON

PRITCHETT

CANYON

White Knuckle Hill

Ostrich Rock

Pritchett Arch

CANYON

N

MOAB SPRING RACE COURSE LOOP AND HURRAH PASS TRAIL

0   1 Kilometer
0   1 Mile

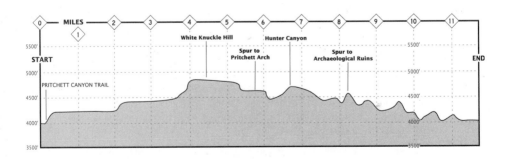

MILES

White Knuckle Hill

Hunter Canyon

Spur to Pritchett Arch

Spur to Archaeological Ruins

5500'

START

END

5000'

PRITCHETT CANYON TRAIL

4500'

4000'

3500'

Miles and Directions

0.0   **START** from the overflow parking area and ride back across the cattle guard to the pavement. The trailhead is immediately to your right, beyond the gate into the private campground that is below the new stucco home. Pay the toll and ride through the gate and around the backside of the campground, through the sand and up the hill to the right. Your first technical challenge is a drop-off 0.2 mile in. The canyon trail is easy to follow, but it certainly is not easy. If a spur beckons you, explore if you like, but the main trail simply goes up the canyon. There are a few places where the trail splits, but it will rejoin. There are a few spots of water-worn slickrock that make great places to play, but will create some degree of variation from the mileage count below.

4.0   Go right at the Y.

4.1   Go left. **Side trip.** The spur to your right offers a short diversion to some scenic surprises that include a huge natural bridge.

4.5   This is the top of White Knuckle Hill. This is a great spot to hang out during Jeep Week in the spring. There is a colorful mineral deposit in the trail that you just carried your bike through. Check your Geiger counter. The view back down the canyon is a good excuse to rest. After your lungs return you can choose to take on the downhill back down Pritchett Canyon or head out to the right and down to complete the loop. From here the loop trail wraps around the hill to your right and presents you with some fast and rough corners, and some nice ledges. Eventually you will end up in the sand as you pass the spire against the canyon to your right called Ostrich Rock.

5.6   **Side trip.** Spurs to the right lead to the scramble up to Pritchett Arch, very worthy of a hiking detour. Leave your bike behind. The arch is *very* photogenic, so don't forget your camera.

6.0   Take the loose, rocky spur to the right. It will soon take you to the rim of Hunter Canyon. You just passed Upper Hunter Canyon and its mismarked and, at time of this writing, vandalized sign for Behind the Rocks. The Upper Hunter Canyon ride is a sand nightmare. Don't even think about it. The rough jeep road that goes up the hill ahead is the Back of Behind Trail. Mountain lions frequent the waterholes to your left.

6.2   **Side trip.** If you're *very* thirsty and can perform dangerous scrambling maneuvers in cleats, then you can hike around the canyon rim to your left and drop down the huge ledges and loose slope on the opposite side of the canyon. At the bottom of the canyon, a spring emerges from behind a huge slab. This can be a dangerous diversion, so attempt it only if you are capable or in desperate need of emergency moisture. On second thought, drink the muddy stuff at the top and save your skeletal structure.

8.3   **Side trip.** The spur to your right leads to an archaeological site, one of the very best in the Moab area.

8.6   The road turns to singletrack. This narrow bit has a few perfectly ridable stretches. Cairns sometimes mark the route, but once you wrap around the back of Gatherer Canyon—in the next canyon over to the east from Hunter Canyon—you'll have to use good judgment in order to pick a safe and environmentally sound way down to the spring at the mouth of the canyon and Kane Creek Road.

9.7   Take a right and ride up the hill. Once you crest the hill, gravity will help you all the way back to your vehicle.

11.7   Arrive back at the overflow parking.

A skills clinic under Pritchett Arch

Ride Information

Trail Contacts
Bureau of Land Management
82 E. Dogwood
Moab, UT 84532
(435) 259-2196

Local Events and Attractions
Jeep Week. If you are interested in watching jeeps attack White Knuckle Hill, then come out here during Jeep Week at the end of April. Jeep Week may be the best and worst time to visit Moab for mountain biking. The jeeps kick up horrible dust, and their numbers can be overwhelming on trails like Gemini Bridges, but these folks can be a welcome sight on some of the more remote rides listed in this book. They carry lots of water, are filled with mostly friendly people, and watching them blow trannies, break axles, and pop driveshafts is a great pastime during an energy bar break on a long bike ride. Depending on the weather they can either destroy the trail or pack it down. If it rains or snows while they're out here in such numbers (thousands of jeeps!), sandy trails can become fast as pavement. If it is dry, they churn up sand and rock and make some trails unridable. The town is booked solid during this time of year, so be sure to reserve a hotel room months in advance. For more information on Jeep Week, call the Moab Information Center at (435) 259-8825.

Schedule
Trail is open year-round but is best during spring and fall.

Maps
USGS maps: Moab, Trough Springs Canyon
Moab West Trail Map by Latitude 40° Inc.
Moab Recreation Map by F. H. Barnes

Hollywood Lies

This story is dedicated to Joey Curtis, my best student.

I began my "film career" as a teacher, revealing the secrets and lies of the medium to young college students hopelessly in awe of *Star Wars* and Steven Spielberg. My favorite tool in this quest was a very unique art film titled *Land Without Bread* by Spanish surrealist filmmaker Luis Bunuel. The film was made in the late 1930s during a turbulent period in which fascism raised its ugly head in Spain and the world was aghast at the new film medium and the power of the "truth" revealed by a genre called "documentary."

Bunuel, to reveal his version of the "truth," made a fake documentary about a place in Spain where no one had bread to eat. He faked shots, like a sheep falling off a cliff. You can barely see the gun in the edge of the shot and the smoke from the barrel as the sheep "accidentally" falls from the cliff edge. He faked the death of a little girl and knocked over a donkey with a hive of bees on its back just to get shots of the donkey being stung to death. He wrote impossible dialogue filled with evil hints and downright lies. Years later his documentary is still considered by many to be "true." I have even heard educated people say with a straight face that this documentary was made to get some bread to those poor people. Now we have Marty Stouffer, who fakes a fight between a badger and a cougar by placing them both in a tight enclosure. Bunuel's truth is that the movies lie.

The new Eurocopter with the first-ever IMAX gyroscopic mount

If you work with the film industry in Moab, it is best that you do not know these things. An education can present you with knowledge that conflicts with the deeds you must do to stay alive. Welcome to my nightmare.

As mountain bike production coordinator and location scout for the Moab shoot for an IMAX film, I'm too busy to be present for today's shoot. As the week gained momentum, the mode of operation went from search to kill. Today I'm chasing new locations and permits like a wind-up toy. As a result, the "stunt doubles" will be without a mountain bike coordinator to protect them from the evil Director God, who doesn't have a clue as to just what a mountain bike is or what it does. As if this were not worrisome enough, the "stunt doubles" are unaware that they are simply moving objects to photograph—meat on a bike. In their Hollywood-awed adrenaline frenzy, they cannot foresee that cold eggbeater Jim—legendary helicopter jockey for Spielberg and the rest of the Hollywood elite—is going to use them like pinballs to get the shot, even if they fly off the edge of a cliff and die a horrible death on the rocks below. If someone takes "The Big Dirt Sample," Jim will simply have an exciting story to tell the next production crew. It is not like it's going to be his fault. It's going to be *my* fault. I hired the "stunt" riders. I use quotes around "stunt doubles" because it was only when we got into shooting the film that they were asked to do anything fast and dangerous. You see, if you are shooting a film where yuppie tourists are stepping over dead, frozen yuppie tourists, taking a step every two minutes in a frozen and sterile landscape, you're going to want to speed the film up a bit, or the thing is going to be like an IMAX trip to the dentist.

Jennifer, A-team double for the lead actress Paula, minimizes her predicament with belief in the goodness that resides in the soul of Everyman. Her sweet heart is like a fresh white diaper just waiting for a stinky load. I worry about her. She's

> **Just before the end of the videotape, Jim leers at the director as if the image were some juicy porno from Amsterdam: "Now, this is really great." Drool. Money. Drool some more.**

truly an angel in a garbage dump. After a run on Fossil Point, she complains that she was knocked off her bike by Jim's rotor wash, but, afterward she adds, "He's such a nice man." This just makes we worry about her even more. Yeah, Jim is such a nice man . . . for a Hollywood Motion Picture Professional who doesn't give a damn about anything but his résumé.

"Crash," B-team double, denies his situation by nervously shrieking, "Sure man, that's nothing," or "I do this kinda thing all the time." Crash is doubling for Ed, the star of the film.

Yes, the riders in the film are doubles. I bet you thought it was a documentary, huh?

This morning I woke up in a cold sweat out of a horrible nightmare about this particular shot on this particular trail. I dreamed that sweet, pretty, fragile, and angelic Jennifer flew off the cliff and landed like a ragdoll on the rocks 700 feet below. I tell Jennifer about the dream, psych her out real bad, and hope it's enough to scare her away from the edge. Jennifer's sweet life is not worth risking for any stupid movie. I know that only one of the riders, Lou, is ready for this kind of deal and Jennifer will be following *him*. *This* particular shot was going to be *deadly* dangerous. The people I hired as "doubles" were stepping out of the realm of "doubles" into the realm of "stunt doubles" and not *really* being paid for it.

I give the riders—Lou, Jennifer, Crash, and Laurie—the facts of life, let them go just like Mama did, and head off to track down another permit, fill out another form, and drive like a maniac out to the second unit in my rental jeep.

Meanwhile B-team double Laurie, faced with the prospect of perhaps taking a dive off the Amasa Back Trail into the abyss of Jackson Hole, does the supremely professional thing and refuses to ride fast enough for eggbeater Jim. Jennifer gives it a shot, but just cannot stay ahead of the copter or keep up with "Tattoo Lou." Rather than slow the shot for "the girls," Jim dresses Crash in Laurie's costume, puts him on Jennifer's bike, and sends him down the hairy route on a new bike without an equipment check or a practice run.

That night, back at the hotel, Jennifer throws a fit.

"Just because I'm a *girl,* Jim takes my bike away and gives it to Crash. And you freaked me out, man, with that damn dream thing!"

Being a dreamer is a thankless task. My only reward is the satisfaction that Jennifer is still alive.

Lou knew what was going on. "If you got freaked out by what Lee was saying, then you *should* be freaked out! If you get psyched out by people telling you crap, you are going to lose. Only folks who are out of their league can be psyched out."

Later I watch the video rushes in the conference room with the producer, director Jim, and the "Academy Award–winning" Spacecam guy (the fellow who invented the gyroscopic IMAX wonder that sits on the front of the copter). On the monitor I see both men stunt doubles blasting down the top of Amasa Back Trail like mad banshees on the edge of the cliff 700 feet above Jackson Hole, like it's the Extreme Games or something—and I remember the producer's words: "We don't want the doubles doing things that the main characters can't do. This is about training. It's not an extreme sports thing."

Just before the end of the videotape, Jim leers at the director as if the image were some juicy porno from Amsterdam: "Now, this is really great." Drool. Money. Drool some more.

I stare into the little video monitor, finally realizing that the only reason they had me running around all day for permits is so that they could do something "dirty" I simply

IMAX camerawork in Bull Canyon

would not allow. At the end of a fast run along the edge of Amasa Back Trail, Crash loses brake control and slams into Lou, sliding into the cliff face at about 30 mph. An hour before, Crash told me of this event, that he had fallen because Jennifer's brake levers were not adjusted to his hands. He mentioned it only in passing, but from the view provided by the camera's eye, the result is truly frightening.

"Tattoo" Lou

Damn! I figure I just have to go ballistic. These fellows need to know that they are grubbing for money over the bodies of woefully underpaid and uninsured mountain bike doubles who were never hired to do such dangerous stuntwork. The reality that Crash and Lou and Jennifer and Laurie are expendable parts in the back of the film wagon is just too much for me to take any longer. The protecting knight inside me says, "Go for the neck!"

I launch into Jim, who happens to be the head of the Helicopter Safety Commission in Hollywood. "Jim, you may know something about helicopter safety, but you don't know Dick Nixon about mountain bike safety." I turn up my disgust meter just because no one does it to these dudes, ever. "That was totally irresponsible. You got a shot of a pro downhiller and a BMX hotshot kid going so fast on the edge of a cliff that the director can't use it. The shot is irresponsible, unrealistic, and you risked my riders' lives to get the damn thing. Great! Just great!"

"If these riders are not qualified to do this kind of thing, then you never should have hired them," Jim says, obviously unaware these guys were hired to be doubles, not stuntmen.

I look over at the director who is trying hard not to make eye contact. I'm livid! This is what it's like to be in the film business—you use words like *livid* to mean that you are really pissed off.

"I've said my piece." I drop the anger like a hot potato. Next.

"Well, you didn't have to be rude about it," the director says in his softest, most contrite voice.

If you saw the movie, the Amasa Back shot was used, cut together with a shot along Fossil Point effectively giving the illusion that the shot is continuous. This was done despite the fact that the subjects, Ed and Paula, could not, and certainly would not, attempt to bomb down this cliff edge at such a breakneck speed. Paula's overlaid narration is downright evil: "This was just a warm-up for us."

Well, that's Hollywood. And this is the Amasa Back Trail. Dangerous and technical and laid out to take you on the edge of death and disaster.

23 Amasa Back

Start: From the Amasa Back Trail parking area on Kane Creek Road.
Length: 11.2-mile out-and-back. There's more if you bike from town, or if you ride out freeform onto the slickrock of Amasa Back.
Approximate riding time: 2 to 3-plus hours.
Difficulty: Technically very difficult to extreme due to vertical exposure next to 3-foot ledges, loose rock, and deep cracks that can grab a tire. Physically very difficult due to the climb and short bursts of extreme effort necessary to negotiate technical challenges.

Trail surface: Technical 4WD track. Ledgy bedrock, sand, slickrock, loose and hard-packed sediments. Scary exposure.
Lay of the land: Up a canyon, then cross its watercourse for a climb up to a massive stone mesa above a meander of the Colorado River.
Total climbing: 3,569 feet.
Land status: Bureau of Land Management (BLM) and Utah State Trust lands.
Other trail users: Hikers, campers, and off-road vehicles (ORV).
Best seasons: Spring and fall.

Environmental concerns: Fragile, like all of the subdesert rides in this book! Cryptobiotic crusts exist on either side of the trail. Stay on the trail or on the bare rock.

Getting there: From Moab: Go south from the intersection of Main and Center Streets on U.S. Route 191 (Main Street) to Kane Creek Road. Take a right just before McDonald's onto Kane Creek Road. Ride out Kane Creek Road. Eventually you'll bear left at a Y, staying against the cliffs to your left. Be careful at the Y intersection with 500 West: It can be very dangerous due to traffic coming from your right crossing in front of you. Follow the cliff side and you'll eventually connect with the Colorado River. Follow the river to where the road turns to dirt and cuts left into Kane Creek Canyon. After about 5 miles from Main and Center, you'll come to a cleared area denoted as the Amasa Back Trail parking lot. The current marker also gives approximate mileage (it's 1.2) to the trailhead farther up Kane Creek Road. Park here and ride to the marked Amasa Back Trailhead on your right after a mellow climb. The trail is highly visible from the road and is well marked.

The Ride

This difficult, stunningly beautiful ride leaves from a spot on Kane Creek Road just 9 miles from Moab and climbs up to breathtaking views of the Colorado River above a former meander called Jackson Hole. The trail is a favorite of the Moab locals.

You'll want to watch the first 100 feet of this trail. It can ruin your ride in a hurry. The entire trail should be approached with respect. It's short, but it's a grunt with technical challenges thrown in here and there, some on the edge of a 500-foot cliff. Ledges drop into deep sand at points. It asks for speed and can surprise you as you round a corner. At the end of the described ride, beyond the viewpoint, is the mostly freeform ride out onto Amasa Back, a massive finger of sandstone surrounded on three sides by a meander of the Colorado River. The ride from here can be

Overlooking Jackson Hole

extremely rewarding for very experienced riders with a good sense of direction and maybe a guide. There is a petroglyph panel worthy of a visit, but the riding just gets harder from this viewpoint as you climb on the very technical slickrock onto the huge sandstone monolith that is Amasa Back. Don't even think about the singletrack that goes down the backside. It is scary and exposed the whole way.

Miles and Directions

0.0 **START** from the signed Amasa Back Trail parking area. Go right on the dirt road and ride to the signed Amasa Back Trail.

1.2 Go down the marked trail on a series of hairy steps and switchbacks that eventually drop you into Kane Creek. Maybe you want to walk your bike past these first few challenges. A face plant off a belly-button-high ledge is not a great way to start a ride.

1.4 The creek is usually dry in summer, but during wetter times of the year it can mean wet socks and a soaked drivetrain. You can either cross to the left on a narrow shoulder that drops into a shallow spot, or you can dive into the creek on the 4WD track straight ahead. Cross over and climb up the rock ledges to the open gate a few yards from the creek. The route ahead climbs for the next 2 miles over ledges and loose rock—great for full-suspension freaks.

2.6 Stay right.

3.2 Stay left. **Side trip.** The spur right takes you about a mile to a viewpoint that is worth a visit.

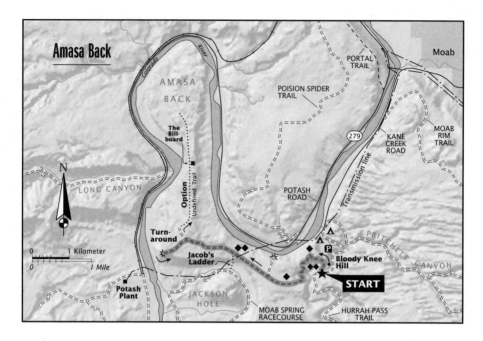

3.4 You are now on the cliff edge with the dried river meander called Jackson Hole to your left. There is a short series of serious drop-offs here to watch out for. Speed is not your friend here. Prepare to dismount. Spots like this are not even worth trying.

3.8 The spur to the left takes you down Jacob's Ladder into Jackson Hole, part of the Moab Spring Racecourse. If you ever ride it, you want to be going up, not down. Go past Jacob's Ladder and past the next spur to your right, staying on the main trail. That right-hand spur leads to a loop option that you should definitely forgo. It is just too dangerous, even as a hike. As it is, the route forward will be technical enough and affords the best views of Jackson Hole and some truly challenging slickrock riding.

4.7 Stay left on the slickrock, working your way to the rim for the best view. The route is almost always cairned, and you can usually rely on these rock markers, but if you lose them at any point you can freeform up the slickrock to the rim. A petroglyph site can be found near here to your right and on the Amasa Back's highest outcropping.

5.6 After gaining this best rim view, return the way you came in.

11.2 Arrive back to your vehicle.

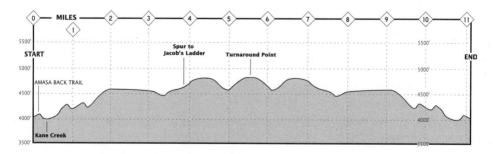

Hurrah Pass Trail as seen from Amasa Back Trail

Ride Information

Trail Contacts

Moab Bike Patrol
c/o Bureau of Land Management
82 E. Dogwood
Moab, UT 84532
(435) 259-2196

Utah State School and Institutional Trust Lands Administration
1165 South US 191, Ste. 5
Moab, UT 84532
(435) 259-3760

Schedule

Trail is open year-round but is best during spring and fall.

Maps

USGS maps: Moab, Gold Bar Canyon
Moab West Trail Map by Latitude 40° Inc.
Moab Recreation Map by F. H. Barnes

OWL MEDICINE

At the head of Amasa Back Trail, above the creek on the canyon wall, is a very beautiful, pristine, and powerful petroglyph panel. It portrays a man standing beside an owl. There are other images—sheep, spirals, and a buzzard—but the owl is particularly stunning. Portrayed in attack, the owl's wings are back and out of sight, its claws spread open and ready to rip its prey to shreds. The artist must have studied his subject at length to have acquired the necessary knowledge to present such an image. In order to study hunting owls, you must watch during the dark of night, perhaps during the full moon. In order to fully comprehend the dedication it took to produce this work, you must understand that it was chipped into the rock over a long period of time, meticulously, and with great skill.

As for the meaning of this work, let me present an educated guess. The owl, because of its proximity to the man's image, which also includes a small figure attached to the man's leg, represents values and powers of the creature this man wished to emulate or

exploit. The owl, among many Native American peoples, represents the dark side, death, stealth in darkness, and impeccable silence and quickness. As with the ancient Greeks, Native peoples also attribute wisdom and knowledge to this deadly night creature, beyond its formidable hunting talents. The owl was the goddess Athena's partner and spiritual guide, residing on her shoulder and constantly speaking words of wisdom into her ear. But unlike Western culture, which places its artistic icons into museums and temples, these ancients left their magical works in the natural world, in the temple of Canyonlands. Their worth is beyond beauty and artistic virtuosity. Placed out of the way and almost out of sight, they were and remain votive offerings, prayers to the mystery and majesty of life, lingering memoirs of what the ancients held dear. Of all the petroglyphs in the Moab area, the Owl is perhaps the most powerful in transmitting these feelings.

On top of Amasa Back, if you continue past the overlook, there is another petroglyph panel worthy of a trip onto the technical slickrock.

24 Spring Racecourse Loop

Start: From the parking lot on the right at the mouth of Kane Creek Canyon, just past the cattle guard where Kane Creek Road turns to dirt.

Length: 26.5-mile loop.

Approximate riding time: 4 to 6 hours.

Difficulty: Technically a potpourri of easy to moderate to difficult, due to long stretches of boring gravel, followed by a series of challenges. A fast vertically exposed downhill leads to deep sand, followed by a very bumpy climb up rough fossil-encrusted rock. After the short climb, the remaining trek through Jackson Hole is over loose rock and sand and culminates in the Jacob's Ladder portage, which is totally unridable. The final section on the Amasa Back Trail harbors huge ledges and dangerous rock gaps that can grab a tire. Physically very difficult due to mileage and elevation change.

Trail surface: Gravel county road, technical 4WD track, with a nightmare portage thrown in for good measure. Wash bottoms, hardpack, varieties of bedrock, sand, bumpy slab sediments, babyheads, loose rock, ledges, and one hellacious vertical portage over big loose rocks.

Lay of the land: Arid canyon country ride up a narrow canyon to where it widens, then up the canyon wall and over into another vast canyon. You then ride out to a former meander of the Colorado River and climb steep, rocky switchbacks up a vertical wall to the top of the canyon.

Total climbing: 3,136 feet.

Land status: Bureau of Land Management (BLM) and Utah State Trust lands.

Other trail users: Hikers and off-road vehicles (ORV).

Best seasons: Spring and fall.

Environmental concerns: As long as you stay on the trail, this area is about as environmentally sound as any of the public lands around Moab. The land borders a Wilderness Study Area and is being overused and commercialized—it basically has everything wrong with it that public lands offer. People are using it up fast. Enjoy it this way while you can.

Getting there: From Moab: Head south on Main Street from the intersection of Main and Center Streets. Turn right onto Kane Creek Road between McDonald's and Burger King. Continue on Kane Creek Road past the low-income housing on the left and the winery and the Department of Transportation on your right. Where the road splits into 500 West—which veers right; be cautious of this very dangerous three-way intersection—stay left on Kane Creek Road against the hill. Just past the Moab Skyway on your left and the wetlands park on your right, the road bends left to follow the Colorado River. You'll cross a cattle guard, pass the Moab Rim Trail, and then travel under a couple of large cottonwoods at Moonflower Canyon. Continue onward, and about 4.5 miles into your drive from Main Street the road crosses another cattle guard and turns to dirt. Park in the large lot to your right where Kane Creek enters the Colorado River.

The Ride

This is a tough ride that throws just about everything Moab has to offer at you except slickrock expanse. It is relatively easy to follow except in two places, so do

The wash at mile 12.8, now a county road

not get lulled and miss the side spurs into washes at mileage counts 12.8 and 18.1. Do not attempt this ride in the heat of summer! Take lots of water and be prepared for anything, including spending the night. There is a private resort out here, so do not hesitate to ask for help. The best time of year to ride the course is just prior to the spring race, which occurs in early April. It will be reassuring to see other riders out there practicing for the race.

This honestly brutal ride is based on the route of the Moab Spring Race, also called Moab Rocks. It includes most of the Hurrah Pass and Amasa Back rides listed in this book, with the addition of the north face of Hurrah Pass, the haunting bottomland below the pass along the Colorado River, a trip around the former meander of the Colorado River called Jackson Hole, and the very difficult portage up to Amasa Back from Jackson Hole called Jacob's Ladder. The attractions here are dis-

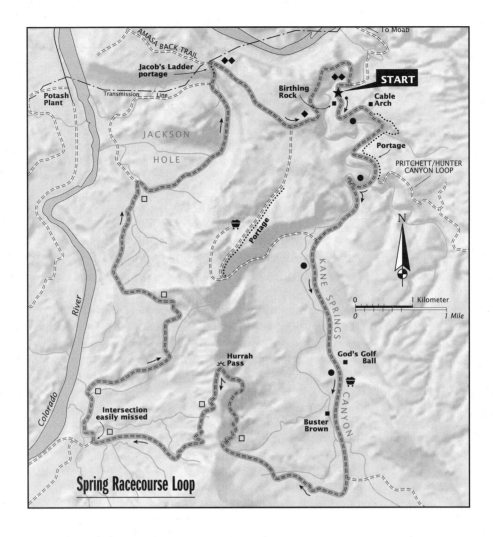

Spring Racecourse Loop

tance, scenery, varied terrain, technical challenge, masochism, and geology. The ride starts at the overflow parking area at the mouth of Kane Creek Canyon, heads up a well-maintained county road to Hurrah Pass, drops down the other side, crosses the beautiful eroded land below to Jackson Hole, heads up Jacob's Ladder to the Amasa Back Trail, and eventually closes the loop at the Amasa Back Trailhead on Kane Creek Road, where you will have only to coast back down to your car. It's a biggie. As you perform the death march up Jacob's Ladder, imagine what it's like to do the loop two or three times for the race. For some variation, ride it in reverse. Sliding down the pipeline to get to the bottom of Jackson Hole is *not* recommended. Leave early!

Miles and Directions

0.0 **START** by riding into the canyon on the wide dirt road. There will be some exposure on the right side.

1.2 Go past the posted Amasa Back Trailhead on your right. This is where you'll close the loop at the end of your ride.

1.4 On your right and down from the road is a large rock. On it is carved the likeness of a Spanish conquistador and a woman giving birth. It is called the Birthing Rock and is covered with petroglyph images that are surprisingly intact considering they are so close to the road.

1.7 **Side trip.** Though it looks impossible from the road, the tight gap in the rock above you on your left is the scramble up to Cable Arch. On top you can climb onto the arch by pulling yourself up a cable—hence "Cable Arch." The scramble up through this steep gap, or the cable pull-up at the arch, is not recommended to anyone in bike shoes.

1.9 Enjoy the wide and swooping switchbacks that lower you into the gorge.

2.1 At the bottom of the switchbacks is a spring that comes out just next to the road. Great water here! Fill your bottles.

2.2 Here is a secret: This is one of the best camping spots in Moab, just down the hill and to your right. Oh, well, so much for the secret.

3.0 On your left is Hunter Canyon. The stream crossing is usually dry, but don't count on it. Sometimes it flashes. **Side trip.** The short but technical hike into Hunter Canyon is quite beautiful and is highly recommended. If you choose to hike in here, be very careful of the soil crusts and plants along the stream.

4.1 **Side trip.** On your right 100 yards across the wash is an old mining road that skirts the canyon and eventually hooks into the Amasa Back Trail. It's not too inviting on this end, but can be a really challenging trip for advanced riders with advanced route-finding skills. This is a little more than a side trip, but I thought I'd mention it anyway.

4.3 On your left is a petroglyph of a centipede. Far ahead across the canyon on your right, high up on the top of the ridge, is a small hill shaped like a breast. Just down to the right below the hoodoos to the right of the breast is a flat spot. That is Hurrah Pass. This is where you're heading. You will be looping around the canyon to achieve this.

5.5 Buster Brown is on your right (sometimes called the Bashful Turk). On your left is God's Golf Ball (also called the Devil's Golf Ball—they play golf together and sometimes Satan says the ball is his). **Side trip.** A visit up the spur to your left will take you under the Golf Ball. High up the canyon walls to the south, you'll see the remnants of uranium mines.

6.3 Kane Creek crosses the road at this point. This is the point of no return should it rain hard while you are out here. While shooting a film a couple of years ago, the stunt team and I were trapped on the other side of this streambed by a ripping flash flood and had to spend the night watching the water gradually go down. We watched as boulders and large trees were shoved through here by the force of the water.

6.4 Pass the unmarked spur on the left.

6.6 Pass the marked spur on your left and continue on the maintained road uphill to the pass. There is a some freaky exposure on your right as you ride the ledge that eventually takes you to the pass. At times, after weeks of repeated rains and ensuing water erosion, this part of the ride becomes a true technical mountain bike climb. The clifftops here are very loose, so avoid the edge! The road ahead wraps along these Moencopi cliffs and presents you with the opportunity to take some great pictures. The hoodoo that resembles a sitting bird above you on the ridge signals the last turn to Hurrah Pass.

9.7 Hurrah! The Pass! Downhill! Control your speed. There are a few blind turns that place you in serious exposure.

12.8 This is an important point on the ride, the most frequently missed spur. Sometimes it is cairned. Most of the time it isn't. During the days leading up to the Moab Spring Race, it is usually marked. Take this spur right into the sandy wash bottom. More deep sand is in your future. After you are in the wash for a while, you'll see a building on your left, one of many out here that are being offered as accommodations. Yurts. Rooms. Camels to ride. Stuff like that. If they succeed in this remote spot, then anything is possible in Moab.

13.7 On your left is a gate with a sign that says PRIVATE DRIVE. Freaky, huh? Beside it is a small wooden marker for Jackson Hole, where you are headed. Go up the hill to your right. You thought the sand sucked, right? Wait till you get a good sample of the rock surface on the hill. Full-suspended riders will be very happy with their purchase. This is where sea fossils are found, formed by layer upon layer of muddy sea sediments. Ahead you'll be entertained by some rather beautiful rock formations and colorful outcroppings. The forces of erosion have developed some very colorful and intricate formations out here.

18.1 This is that second spot where folks miss the spur. In the bottom of this sandy wash that cuts through the purple sandstone of the Rico formation, you'll come to a cairned route to your right. Both of these tracks, the left and the right, will take you around Jackson Hole, but the one on the right has much less sand and is a bit more fun to ride. Go right.

20.4 Here is the cairned spur right up to Jacob's Ladder. If you pass under the power lines, you have gone too far.

20.6 You are now below Jacob's Ladder at the point where you'll have to dismount. Now you know that if anyone told you that they rode Jacob's Ladder, they were lying. Behind the large rock take the cairned hiking trail. Avoid the trail on the left alongside an iron pipe. Blue arrows and a large cairn, placed by yours truly, mark the correct route behind the rock. The route can be confusing at first, but eventually you'll get the hang of it. Head up the Ladder and mind your step in those crummy biking shoes. Yes, this is where you'll find out how woefully inadequate biking shoes are at this kind of thing. Let's write the manufacturers and tell them that real mountain biking shoes need armor on the sides and at the ankles. Since your wheels will only be touching when you are pushing the

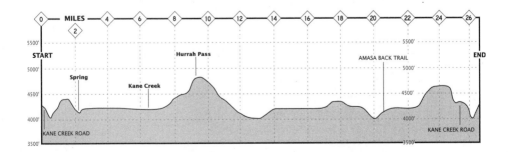

bike—and pushing the bike is not possible most of the time—the mileage count at the top will vary. Not to worry.

21.2 At the top to the portage, enjoy the view. Relax, it ain't a race. After a snack and a drink and a rubbing of the feet, complete the hike to the very top, take a right onto the 4WD track that is the Amasa Back Trail, and head out along the cliff edge. Amasa Back can be a real challenge after the portage. Walk the most technical spots with exposure that are just above you at the start of the ride on Amasa Back, and as the trail begins to descend, control your speed. Weird stuff happens around every corner, and the trail becomes extremely technical in spots. Jeeps really screw it up, don't they?

25.1 You descend into the bed of Kane Creek at this point after a couple of drop-offs that will have you cussing the four-wheelers. Cross the creek and follow the obvious track. The hill in front of you is your final challenge.

25.3 Once you arrive back at Kane Creek Road, take a left and ride downhill to your vehicle.

26.5 Reach the trailhead. Want to ride it again? If you liked this ride, are 6'7" (an advantage on the portage), and feel like you could do the loop one more time today, then come back for the spring race. The cross-country race on this loop is the only mountain bike racing event in Moab that I can endorse. All other courses and races happen in environmentally sensitive areas and should be shut down.

Ride Information

Trail Contacts

Moab Bike Patrol
c/o Bureau of Land Management
82 E. Dogwood
Moab, UT 84532
(435) 259-2196
**Utah State School and Institutional
Trust Lands Administration**
1165 South US 191, Ste. 5
Moab, UT 84532
(435) 259-3760

Local Events and Attractions

Moab Spring Race, early April, Moab. Call the Moab Information Center at (435) 259-8825 for race details and contacts.

Schedule

Trail is open year-round but is best during spring and fall.

Maps

USGS maps: Moab, Gold Bar Canyon, Trough Springs Canyon, Shafer Basin
Moab West Trail Map by Latitude 40° Inc.
Moab Recreation Map by F. H. Barnes

Mud and Fear on the Shafer Rim Switchbacks

The awesome switchbacks of the Shafer Trail began as a precarious wild sheep and deer trail up the side of a canyon wall. Ancient Pueblan hunters used it to access the White Rim from the Island in the Sky, a high plateau that drops 2,000 feet to the rim. Another 1,000 feet below the White Rim lies the Colorado River Gorge. Sheer cliffs make these elevation changes extremely drastic and visually impressive. When cattle rancher Sod Shafer wanted to get his cattle down from the Island in the Sky onto the White Rim and across the Colorado River for summer grazing in the canyons below Hurrah Pass, he turned this ancient and very rough singletrack trail into a single-file cattle freeway. Every time he drove spooked cattle down the scary switchbacks, he would loose a few due to panic.

Many years later, when uranium became a reason to venture out onto the White Rim, the trail was widened into a road by prospectors, led by the homespun engineering genius of Ed "The Kid" Johnson, who designed the trail's switchbacks to run under themselves in order to save money on drainage pipes and maintenance. Now the trail is maintained by the Park Service as an access onto the White Rim in Canyonlands National Park. In order to "stabilize" the trail, the Park Service surfaced the road with shale, making the Shafer Rim Trail extremely dangerous in wet weather.

A few years ago on an April camping trip with my family, I discovered the extreme danger that results from wet weather on the Shafer Trail. After driving all the way from our home in Boulder, Colorado, I drove my very frightened family down the sheer cliff of the Island in the Sky on the Shafer Rim switchbacks. Once at the bottom I drove a few miles out onto the White Rim and we set up camp below Airport Tower. Within minutes it began to snow—and it did so all day and into the night. The next morning, the snow rapidly melted at lower altitudes along the White Rim and the trail turned to soupy mud, ruining any chance of an enjoyable mountain bike ride. I made the decision to pack up and get out of there fast. When we returned to the Shafer Rim Trail, which snaked its way up the vertical sandstone cliff of the Shafer Rim like a nightmare vision I had as a child, I noticed a couple of jeeps coming down the switchbacks from the top. I figured that if we didn't start immediately we would be out here for another day waiting for the sun to dry the trail. I did not want to take the long and slippery Potash Road back to town. A couple of exposed sections along that stretch would be extremely dangerous when wet. My best bet was to go up where the air was cooler and the snow as yet unmelted.

As I started out with my wife and son in the front seat of our pickup truck, the trail at the bottom was sloppy, but as the sun's rays hit the trail the slime evaporated and the trail surface became hardened. Soon the same sun that evaporated the moisture at the bottom, making the trail easy to drive, melted the snow at the top, making that portion of trail slippery and dangerous. As I ascended, the road began to absorb more and more moisture from the melting snow, and before long I was at the point of no return. The road behind me turned to elephant snot. The road ahead was rapidly deteriorating as the heat of midday slowly crept up the slope. My son put his face in his hands and whined in fear, refusing to watch as I negotiated the tight turns over drop-offs 500 feet high. Every turn produced moments of sheer terror as wheels spun in the mud and the truck slid around each steep switchback. I was racing with Death on a slippery slope. The longer we were on the switchbacks, the worse it was going to get. I had to go fast, but that meant a chance of losing control.

Eventually the truck slid off the road and against the cliff face into a ditch filled with 3 feet of soggy muck. My wife cried. My son was completely traumatized. I simply threw my arms in the air and said, "Well, folks, we are walking." I was shaking like a leaf.

We abandoned the vehicle and began to slog through the muck up to the rim when a truck rounded the corner in front of us, sliding out of control for a few seconds. It stopped, then slowly backed around the corner and out of sight. If the godawful mud was not bad enough, the sight of our stranded vehicle and the three of us struggling through the deep mud on the edge of eternity must have been an effective deterrent.

As we walked up the road, we cursed the Park Service for not blocking the road off in these conditions. The road was not only impossible in a vehicle, it was dangerous on foot. Two steps forward. One step back with every slog. It was like we were walking on ten-pound roller skates.

Suddenly a fellow rounded the turn in front of us carrying a shovel and a rope. Our hero.

As it turned out this fellow was driving the truck that had backed out of view. He was from Seattle, and he knew mud. With his help we made short order of getting the truck out of the ditch. I got pointers on tires for mud, driving in mud, cleaning mud off your truck, and even getting mud out of clothes. When we were finished we looked like four mummies, covered in gray rags. When at last I pulled into a gas station in Colorado, a crowd of folks gathered around the truck laughing and making jokes about the state of our vehicle and the muddy folks inside. It seems that a lot of folks in Colorado know what Moab mud looks like. They all seemed to know exactly where we had been.

The moral of this story is: Don't ever ride or drive the Shafer Trail switchbacks in wet weather! Potash Road will not be much better, so it will probably be necessary to stay put until the sun dries the mud. Carry chains, a shovel, a rope, a comealong winch, and some boards. You won't believe this stuff. And even if you don't get stuck yourself, you may see some poor schmucks like me and my family knee-deep in mud trying to get their truck out of a ditch. Taking these implements will guarantee that you can be of help.

25 Long Canyon and Shafer Rim Loop

Start: From Jughandle Arch at the mouth of Long Canyon, just off Potash Road.
Length: 36.3-mile loop (9 miles of pavement).
Approximate riding time: 5 to 8 hours.
Difficulty: Technically easy to moderate. The only true technical danger is speed, which can really get you out of control in a hurry on the descent into Long Canyon. Physically very difficult due to the mileage and elevation change.
Trail surface: Pavement, gravel, hard-packed and loose sediments, bedrock, and sand on maintained roads.

Lay of the land: From subdesert canyons to high plateau and back down again.
Total climbing: 6,270 feet.
Land status: Bureau of Land Management (BLM), Utah State Trust, and national park lands.
Other trail users: Off-road vehicles (ORV) and maybe a couple of really stupid hikers on the Shafer Trail switchbacks.
Best seasons: Spring and fall.

Environmental concerns: Fragile cryptobiotic soil crusts abound just off the trail, but are easily avoided.

Getting there: From Moab: Drive 4 miles north on U.S. Route 191 to the intersection of Utah Route 279 (Potash Road). Take a left and travel another 13.6 miles to Jughandle Arch, where the dirt road from Long Canyon meets Potash Road. Park at an appropriate spot at the mouth of Long Canyon Road.

The Ride

You will be asked to pay the park entrance fee, so have your pass or $5.00 (fee for a bike and rider) ready when you start the ride. The described route includes a continuous 1,500-foot climb up the Shafer Trail switchbacks and a continuous 1,900-foot descent of Long Canyon. Rolling terrain means a fair amount of accumulated climbing between the switchbacks. The route can be ridden in reverse direction. Either way the ride ends with a descent. Finishing with Long Canyon (as documented) means that you end the ride immediately upon finishing the long descent. Descending the Shafer Rim and finishing with the ride on Potash Road means that you will descend and then have quite a bit of rolling terrain to negotiate before you return to the car.

The initial ride along Potash Road is at first flat. After you leave the river, climbing happens. The Potash Plant is interesting. I think that is the word. The huge evaporation ponds, visible from the trail, are the way potassium nitrate ("potash") is obtained from deep in the earth. The plant pumps water into the mine, dissolving the salt. The water is pumped out, chemicals are added to speed evaporation, and once it is dry, a bulldozer guided by a laser scrapes up the potash. Frankly, it just looks like a big mess in a very beautiful place, and God knows what the process is doing to the stability of the environment. Potassium nitrate is also known as saltpeter. There

The Bolts

are many uses. You can make gunpowder with it by adding portions of sulfur and charcoal. (Remember the Oklahoma City Federal Building bombing? Mix it with kerosene and you've got a cheap car bomb.) You can use it for fertilizer, and you can put it in your boy's mashed potatoes to keep him from "wanking."

Past the Potash Plant you cross a rolling expanse to Fossil Point, the director's playtoy, better known as Thelma and Louise Point. This is where they ran the car(s) off the cliff for the end of the movie. There is a steady rocky climb, and then a left turn where it gets fast, loose, and dangerous. Watch out for blind turns, hills you cannot see over, and exposure. It happens. Tourists in rental jeeps also happen. Watch out for them especially. They seem to think that they have the road all to themselves. Once you're under the Bolts—a rock formation that looks like, well, bolts—the ride will roll and twist into Canyonlands National Park. Toilets. Yay.

When you T-bone the White Rim Trail, there is another $100,000 toilet facility financed by your tax dollars. Take advantage of your investment. Going right from

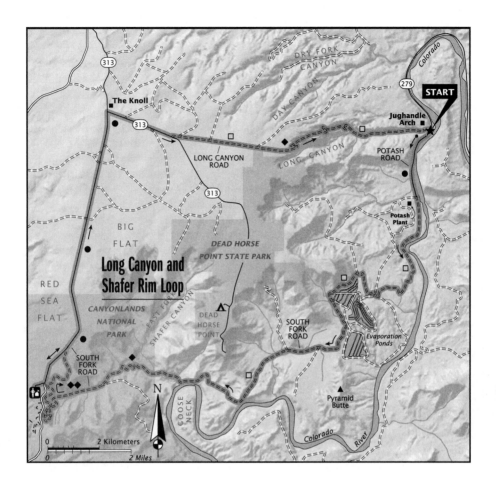

this intersection, you will begin the ascent of Shafer Rim. It's a long steady climb to the top and you will be traveling through a lot of geology. Read the White Rim chapter (see Ride 26) for info.

On the top of the Shafer Rim, the visitor center is to your left. It is where you can purchase any number of nice things, or crawl up dying of thirst. Going right on the main paved road takes you through the dreaded entrance booth where the gal takes your money. Once out of the park, it is a very nice road ride on the top of the Island in the Sky, a plateau with views in all directions. If you are riding a hardtail with skinny tires, you'll be loving it. The turn to Dead Horse Point State Park and the subsequent turn onto Long Canyon Road are really easy to spot. The ride down Long Canyon is really beautiful, though I've heard it described as "boring" by those who prefer the more difficult reverse loop. Controlling your speed on the more dangerous descent from Shafer Rim to the White Rim is key.

Miles and Directions

0.0   **START** by riding out on paved Potash Road, past the initial buildings of the Potash Plant. The route is fairly straightforward all the way to the White Rim. Stay on the main road, avoiding all side spurs on Potash Plant Road. Some spurs are marked NO TRESPASSING.

3.2   On your left is the boat ramp used as a put-in/take-out for canoe trips from Moab and raft trips down the Colorado to Hite Marina through Cataract Canyon. Here the road turns to dirt and goes uphill a bit. The next couple of miles take you across Potash Plant land, the location for many motion pictures. The standing red water is where the medicine man was shot dead in *Geronimo,* starring Matt Damon, Robert Duvall, and a lot of really good-looking Native Americans. Just past the stop sign intersection is where the gun battle was staged. The red canyon with the streaks of yellow and green was where Billy Crystal and the boys camped and fought with the rednecks in *City Slickers 2. Larger Than Life,* the movie with Bill Murray and the elephant roaming the country, was made here also. (Bill loves Moab!) The area ahead with balanced rocks and pocked red slickrock has been used as a representation of Mars in many B-movies. There have been soooo many. *Total Recall* with Arnold Schwarzenegger was one. One particularly bad movie with Molly Ringwald comes to mind. They were walking across these salt ponds forever—made the place look like a huge salt desert. Ahhh, Hollywood. The place is very popular with film crews because the Potash Plant doesn't care how bad you mess up the place. It's a sad fact of life in Moab that the movie industry only cares about the environment when it's "in the shot."

6.0   You are wrapping around the evaporation ponds of the Potash Plant. The blue dye in the water is a chemical that promotes rapid evaporation (and God knows what else). The towers contain lasers used as leveling devices for skimming off salt once the pond is completely evaporated. Don't ride too fast through the washes at the bottom of wet gullies—they run with salt water and will corrode your machinery. Once past the Potash Plant, there are some rolling hills that eventually set you up for the steep loose rocky climb below Dead Horse Point. **Side trip.** A visit to the cliff face on your left will present you with a stunning view of the Colorado River and a chance to pick up a few sea fossils. You will recognize this area from all the commercials shot here. This is Fossil Point, now better known as Thelma and Louise Point. This section of land has been hammered into ugliness by the film industry. After using the land the BLM's nationwide reclamation policy is to bulldoze and reseed. In Moab's climate that is, basically, bulldoze and feed the birds. You see the results.

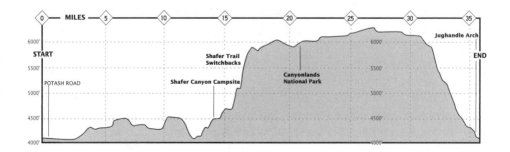

12.5 Your instinct will be to blast around the turn at the bottom of the downhill, but don't do it. If you blow this blind turn, you will end up about 400 feet lower in a matter of seconds. *Watch out!* As the trail wanders into tight canyons below the Bolts (the rock formations to your right as you approach the Shafer Canyon campsite at mile 14.8), you may encounter bighorn sheep that roam the rims above you when there is water in the washes.

14.8 This is the Shafer Canyon campsite. It must be booked far in advance through the Park Service, if you are interested. There is a toilet here.

15.9 Here is your second chance to use a toilet! Go right and head up toward the intimidating Shafer Trail switchbacks.

21.3 The Island in the Sky Park Service Information Center is a mile down the road to your left. It has toilets, water, and a bunch of tourist junk. To continue on this described route, though, go right and head through the Canyonlands National Park gate. You will have to pay $5.00 or show your pass. Have the dough ready. Travel on UT 313 to the Dead Horse Point State Park turnoff.

27.2 Take a right toward Dead Horse Point State Park and head out toward the La Sal Mountains in the distance.

28.8 Take the sandy doubletrack heading straight as an arrow off to the left. This is the spur to Long Canyon and Pucker Pass.

32.0 Take this short spur left for a view of Long Canyon, the Behind the Rocks area, and the La Sal Mountains. Take out your camera. You may recognize Long Canyon as another often used movie location site. After a bit of a rest, return to the main road to enjoy your downhill payback. The ride down Long Canyon through Pucker Pass is a blast and incredibly scenic.

36.3 Come to the trail's end and your vehicle at Jughandle Arch.

Ride Information

Trail Contacts
Moab Bike Patrol
c/o Bureau of Land Management
82 E. Dogwood
Moab, UT 84532
(435) 259-2196
Utah State School and Institutional Trust Lands Administration
1165 South US 191, Ste. 5
Moab, UT 84532
(435) 259-3760
Canyonlands National Park
Island in the Sky District
Moab, UT 84532
(435) 259-4351

Schedule
Trail is open year-round but is best during spring and fall.

Fees and Permits
The Park Service will get its $5.00 fee from you as you leave the park on Utah Route 313 once you have scaled the Shafer Rim and are leaving Canyonlands National Park.

Maps
USGS maps: Shafer Basin, Musselman Arch, The Knoll
Moab West Trail Map by Latitude 40° Inc.
Moab Recreation Map by F. H. Barnes

In Addition

Indian Writings above Potash Road

When I first moved to Moab I worked for old-timer Lin Ottinger taking 4WD land tours out onto the White Rim. Lin was the very first guide in Moab and was the person primarily responsible for turning the White Rim and the Island in the Sky into a national park. Lin was the first human to ever consider this imposing landscape of deep canyons and high plateaus worthy of being commercialized. Before Lin, white people considered this place "desolate" and "forbidding." My experiences with Lin dot this book like so many bird droppings on your windshield because I had and still have a relationship with Lin that is altogether strained, loving, and at arm's length. Without his help I would not be writing this, and without encountering my wife and myself, Lin would not be as mellow and understanding as he is right now. That's a long story. Suffice to say, we love Lin like we love the dentist. He takes away the pain while he dishes out a homemade dose of suffering from the needle of his wit and the pliers of his rage.

One of the gifts Lin passed along to me is a rough, and probably totally incorrect, translation of a particular petroglyph panel above Potash Road, right at the end of Wall Street where the climbers "hang." The translation was supposedly provided to Lin by a Hopi elder, someone who provided Lin with some great stories that Lin also shared with me.

Lin always provided this translation for his tourists in a pseudo-Indian dialect like the old Hollywood films—about as politically incorrect as his ideas about women. I wish I could download Lin's brain into my computer to preserve his wit, funky charm, antiquated ideas, and unparalleled knowledge of the desert and its creatures, but then the computer would certainly crash. Lin has a sixth-grade interface and a doctorate software program.

The translation he taught me refers to the glyphs marked as INDIAN WRITINGS at the first signed pullout on Potash Road. Look for them as you pass Wall Street and approach the Poison Spider Trailhead. The images on the right-hand side of the panel are of three or four "braves" each in different headdresses, holding out one hand in greeting, while the other hand holds a bow and arrow pointed down and back. There are circles attached to these images of men. Just beside these warriors on the left are what appear to be the same "braves" with swollen chests. Now that you have your bearings and are using this book to compare what is in front of you on the rock face, let's proceed with the translation. Well, now, let me do this the Lin Ottinger way:

In order to understand the ancient art on the rocks in and around Moab, first

The Invitation

you must consider the reasons why folks would be scribbling on the rocks in the first place. Some stuff is just plain ole doodling, some marks are records of dates or trails, or logs of harvests, wives, children, numbers of sheep, and some are votive in nature—a way of praying or showing respect for a totem, an animal, or a god, or all three. There are many kinds of artwork. Some done by hacks, some by true artists as powerful as a Picasso or a Rembrandt. Some of the artwork is done for the artist alone, like the records and the doodling and the votive writings and marks, but some writing is done for folks who are not present at the time of the deed. These works are like signs or billboards, sharing information or telling someone something about an event or a place nearby.

See those fellows with the circles attached to them that I just spoke of? Just below them is a man holding a circle. Half of it is dark and half light. Below him is a bighorn sheep.

What is unusual about the sheep? You are supposed to answer: "He has a lot of toes on his feet." Of course most people just stand there after you ask them the question and kind of look at the thing and wonder what the hell is going on. They're usually thinking, "What an arrogant idiot!" Lin does this to people. I learned it from him.

Now, this has to sound *very* patronizing or it just isn't a Lin Ottingerism: . . . *Yes,* he has a lot of toes. Well, the Bighorn Sheep Clan used to sign their names with the image of a sheep, their clan symbol, and any distinguishing features, like toes or spots or whatever, were the distinct signature of a particular individual. Let's call this fellow "Many Toes." This is the signature of the artist. Notice how that sheep is also looking up, isn't it?

The answer to all questions that Lin puts forward to his tourists is either "yes" or "no." He doesn't think that most people can talk, let alone think for themselves. He is always trying to push them into thinking. If they continue to demonstrate a bit of "slowness" or misunderstanding, he just ridicules them in front of everyone else. It's his style. I learned it from him.

See the fellow above "Many Toes?" He's holding a circle, right? What do you think that is?

The answer is: a moon. The better answer is: a half-moon, signifying two weeks.

Yes, he is telling us that this event he is describing on the billboard is going to last two weeks.

See the fellows above that? What are they doing?

Yes, they are holding out a hand and holding bows and arrows, but look how they are holding the bows and arrows. They are holding them down and back. When you approach someone whom you want to befriend and you are holding a rifle, do you point the damn thing right at them?

The answer is: No.

That's right. You point it down. This is a sign that you are not a threat.

What is the outstretched-hand gesture about?

Usually there is complete silence at this point. People are just plain stupid, and Lin brings out this dumbness better than anyone I have ever met. He usually says at this point: "Are you stupid, or something?"

The outstretched hand of a handshake evolved from the gesture of showing someone that you are not holding a weapon in that hand. It is a gesture showing that you are not a threat. It can even mean that you want to be friends.

See the headdresses? They signify many tribes, not just a single family. One is the Buffalo Clan, one is the Bird Clan, and another is the Kokopelli Clan. There are obviously two branches of the Kokopelli Clan nearby. These represent the guests. The Bighorn Sheep Clan are the hosts. This panel is an invitation to the Buffalo

Clan, the Bird Clan, and the Kokopelli Clan to join the Bighorn Sheep Clan in a powwow at a certain date.

See the circles attached to each clan member? Well, they are the lengths of time that each clan is welcome to stay in the camp of the Bighorn Sheep Clan. The many circles under the Buffalo Clan signify an understanding that since the Buffalo Clan is from the other side of the Rocky Mountains—in the area now known as Boulder, Colorado—these people will have to be here an entire season in order to be able to travel the mountains in time of fair weather. Therefore they are welcome for three months or more.

Now step over to the next panel to the left. See those warriors? What is strange about them?

The answer usually given is: They have big stomachs.

Lin's reply is usually: Is your stomach that high? Have you ever seen a person with a stomach that high?

The answer is: No.

Okay, then just what is swollen on those fellows?

The answer is: Their chests.

Yes, their chests. And just what does that mean?

Usually no answer, unless there is a really observant smart guy in the group who says: "It means their hearts are full."

Yes! Their hearts are filled with joy. In the traditional Native American belief system, it is understood that you can never thank anyone for the things Great Spirit provides. These things are food, water, clothing, and shelter. The only thing that a person can thank another person for is the feeling of joy received from great hospitality. This panel is the guest list and the thank-you note. They are thanking the Bighorn Sheep Clan for their hospitality and the way everyone was made to feel during the powwow. It was obviously a great success.

Now travel over to the next panel to your left. See that line of people with different headdresses all holding hands in a row? Well, that is usually the representation of the Corn Dance, but in this particular panel the people are of different tribes. This is very unusual. Usually the folks are all of the same tribe and wear the same headdresses. This panel is very special in that it is the peace treaty that the tribes all agreed to during the powwow. The Corn Dance here represents an agreement that they all share that they live in peace and harmony in thanks to the Great Spirit for providing all the tribes with food and the necessities of life.

Now for the finale. Move down the cliff face to your left until you come across a series of holes in the rock, just at eye level. This particular panel is the oldest of the entire wall. It was once covered for many centuries by the river and sandstone sediments. The peoples who put the petroglyphs on the rocks above stood on these sediments in order to place those glyphs on the rock. You see, at one time the riverbank was high on this wall. White folks built the road you are standing on and, during the construction of that road, moved all the sand against the cliff away.

The holes in the rock here are as ancient as any human artifact found in the country. These "holes" were made by the Archaic peoples who were here as long as 40,000 years ago. The Hopi are the only people who even have a clue as to what these things mean. Remarkably, they continue to pray into the same markings to this date. The markings (the "holes") are the Sippapoo, the holes from which man emerged when Great Spirit first allowed man into the sunlight after eons spent underground. You see, at first man was evil. When man evolved to understanding and enlightenment, Great Spirit allowed us to come into the light. The holes you see are prayer holes, where someone knelt to contemplate the wonder and mystery of life.

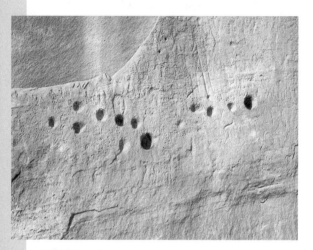

Sipapu

Just so you understand, Lin Ottinger was present when the road along the river was being cut. It was Lin who stopped the bulldozers from tearing up these relics and personally saw to it that any further work done here was done by hand to preserve the votive site that is now the most valuable of all the preserved glyphs anywhere along the river.

If you are holding this book and standing in front of these figures and votive holes, and I pass you on the road, I'll stop and extend a Lin Ottinger hello. It is done with the middle finger of the right hand. I learned it from him.

> ## "I always knew that remembering my tears would make me laugh. But I never knew that remembering my laughter would make me cry."
>
> —ANONYMOUS

The video began with the image of a black man on a corner under a dim streetlight in Five Points, a really seedy neighborhood in Denver. This guy was up to something illegal. Briefly unaware of the camera, the man suddenly spots it out of the corner of his eye, turns, arches his back, and lowers his head in a classic display of sharklike aggression. The hair on the back of my neck stood

up. I looked over at Kelly bashfully watching the video with the rest of the students. She was still in one piece. I thought: This video assignment could have been a disaster.

On screen the man's body language becomes more and more threatening as Kelly moves the camera closer, until suddenly the man raises a hand, shouts something we cannot understand, and stomps angrily toward the camera's very eye. He is about to explode, when he finally sees the person behind the camera, Kelly Nugent. If you knew Kelly you would understand. Kelly was an angel on earth, so beautiful and instinctively charming that she could disarm the Russian army with her smile. In an instant, a grin spreads across the man's face as he enters the beam of Kelly's flashlight and the warmth of her glowing beauty. He stands there for one of those magic video moments that freeze in your memory, filed for future reference . . . white teeth, shiny black face glowing like a saint, falling in love with Kelly Nugent just like every other man who saw her. Then immediately there is an edit to another soul on another dangerous street corner in the middle of the night, the same aggressive body language, and the same results as Kelly reveals herself to her subject. This went on for ten minutes, a poem of anger and fear turning to love and trust. This was Kelly Nugent's first video assignment. To the students in this class, it not only cemented the fact that Kelly was an artist, but it also reinforced everyone's perception that Kelly, with a video camera, was courageous and chivalrous. Kelly's physical beauty was second only to the beauty in her heart. Some people would say she was naive and stupid, but anyone who knew her would argue otherwise.

Kelly showed one more video that night. It was of a breakup with her boyfriend. A hidden camera watched this young man lay into Kelly, describing all of her flaws, infidelities, and other traits that we had never attributed to the angel who could disarm drug dealers with a smile. Finally, in a fit of frightening rage, Kelly's boyfriend got up and stormed out as Kelly sat, crushed, speechless, sagging in a funky lounge chair in a depressing room . . . alone. It was like peeking into someone's window and watching the most private moment imaginable. After the video played, students made comments. To say everyone was shocked and moved is an understatement. After a roundtable discussion where everyone expressed their feelings about having to watch such a private moment, Kelly finally admitted that it was staged. I have never seen such acting in my life, not in a Hollywood movie, not in the theater, nowhere.

Peter Mathys's assignment was "different." The recreation department at the University of Colorado offered a White Rim mountain biking "adventure" every spring and fall, but was losing its permits due to a change in Park Service policy. The change in the policy had to do with a newly installed procedure that awarded concessions permits to the highest bidder. The University of Colorado offered the trip for peanuts to groups of eight or less, so they simply could not afford to buy in. I managed to convince Peter to join up with me on the University of Colorado's last hurrah on the White Rim.

Peter has a big brain. He's a faculty member in the Electronic Engineering Department at the University of Colorado and holds a doctorate from MIT. Peter was also one of my students at this time. The university allows faculty members a chance to take a free course per semester, and Peter flattered me by taking every one of the courses I taught at the university and at the on-campus Rocky Mountain Film Center that I headed. Peter took to video like a duck to water. He had a new video camera and took it *everywhere*. He used it in the pouring rain. He had taken it to Russia and shot a hundred hours of the recent revolution *in the street*. He was shot at and chased. It's all on camera, complete with the barrels of the guns pointed his way and firing. While in Russia the camera broke. His wife told me he took the camera apart and put it back together with a rusty nail. The camera looked like it had been run over by a truck, but it worked. Of course he took the camera on our White Rim trip.

For me, the White Rim trip began with the indescribable joy of the rush down from Shafer Rim after being cooped up with ten people in a Chevy Suburban for ten hours and in tents for a cold night at the top of Mineral Canyon. The blast down onto the rim really tweaked my head, as the lands around Moab will certainly tweak yours the first couple of days of any visit. But on the second day, the newness of the experience gave way to the monotony of the dirt road social scene. I wasn't into riding alongside the babes and exchanging personal trivia. I just wanted to hammer, so I rode out ahead, mostly alone for the next three days. I would ride out early while they ate breakfast, turn around and ride back to the group, then ride out with them and leave them behind, and then ride back to them again. I put 140 miles on my bike on this 70-mile ride and achieved a maximum speed of 53 on my Klein hardtail coming down Hardscrabble. This is a bit of information to all of you hardcore mountain bikers. The White Rim is beautiful, but if you are into technical riding, it can get really boring. After a day out there you will be looking for dangerous things to do. Downhill speed is about all there is, and there's not much of that.

"The real chore is to do something memorable, even magical."

Peter stayed with the group, socializing and generally being charming and Swiss, all the while videotaping everything. Every time I rode up to him, he pointed the damn camera at me. It seemed he was filming an ode to camping on the White Rim. He took the camera on side hikes and pointed it at everyone during every meal. He shot extensive footage of the guys peeing over cliffs, onto slickrock, into sandy washes, and the girls squatting behind bushes off in the distance. He even took the camera with him into the spanking-new pit toilets that now dot the White Rim like tiny absurd stucco houses in the wilderness. Peter shot over twenty-four hours of videotape on the trip. He shot us sleeping, eating, fixing our flat tires, sleeping in our tents, cruising on our bikes, every moment, public and private.

Peter's edited video movie included trips into the desert, behind trees, down slot canyons . . . to relieve himself. Each trip was edited to perfection, a blow-by-blow linear narrative of just how it went, complete with Peter's face in the lens of the camera squinting to get the job done. All this was edited in seamless classic Hollywood narrative style, like it was an important story. Plot points, revealed conflicts, and resolutions, just like Quentin Tarantino. It was so professionally done that we expected a murder to happen or a spaceship to land, but what we got was "The Story of My Bowel Movements on the White Rim." Believe it or not, after studying film under my guidance for nearly four years, this was the pinnacle of Peter's movie-making career so far.

If you want to really understand why someone would make a film about a White Rim trip, ignoring the beauty in favor of the absurdity of being human, I guess you would have to have seen those students watching Peter's masterpiece. There was not a dry eye in the house. Laughter was uncontrollable, joyful in the extreme. These students had been trained to analyze each Hollywood movie and art film, to recognize every secret, every sleight of hand used to fool the viewer, to "suspend disbelief." Then someone like Peter comes along and uses these stock magic tricks to show you the absurdity and stupidity of "suspended disbelief." The video was a personal gift to every student who had to sit through hours and hours of pointless film criticism. Peter put it all in perspective.

As a filmmaker and teacher I understand just how difficult it is to deliver a simple message in the most complex of mediums, but getting the story across is only half the equation. The real chore is to do something memorable, even magical. Peter in his way, like Kelly did in her completely different way, gave us moments that we will remember forever. The true lesson both revealed in their different ways is that joy and laughter can come from seeing and sharing the absurdity of being human. Now, that is art.

Years later, Peter comes out to Moab to visit. His Latvian wife won't let him ride with me because she thinks he is going to be hurt, so we just sit and talk and laugh, and remember Kelly. Tragically, Kelly went missing while hitchhiking in the mountains of Colorado in late 1993. Months later a cross-country skier's dog found her jawbone on a trail outside Frisco. Sometimes I think that only I know how great a loss this was.

26 The White Rim

Start: From the Mineral Bottom Road parking area just off Utah Route 313.

Length: 76-mile point-to-point, but over 100 miles if done as a loop.

Approximate riding time: 1 very, very long day or 2 to 4 days with camping.

Difficulty: Technically easy to moderate. Physically easy to extremely difficult, depending on the time allotted. If you are doing the complete route as a one day trip, it can be *brutal!* If you do it as a two-day, it is challenging. If you do it as a three-or-more-day camping trip, it is stone cold easy. Boring.

Trail surface: A 4WD doubletrack. Mostly hardpack and sand. Some loose rock, bedrock, small ledges, and a bit of gravel.

Lay of the land: Canyon rim below a canyon rim, above the Colorado River canyon. It's Canyonlands, right? The descent in and the climb out are long and taxing. There are some nasty overhangs on the trail that will give an RV camper fits. Take a 4WD vehicle as a sagwagon. Two-wheel drive will not cut it.

Total climbing: 9,910 feet.

Land status: National park.

Other trail users: Hikers, climbers, and off-road vehicles (ORV).

Best seasons: Spring and fall.

Environmental concerns: Extremely fragile, but there are lots of motorized vehicles down there. Go figure! Cryptobiotic soil crusts, dried-up water pits, and rare desert mosses abound just off the trail. There are strict rules laid down by the Park Service when it comes to venturing off the road. To put it simply, it's not permitted. Areas where you can venture off the road are marked as such.

Warning! The White Rim is impassable when wet. If it rains while you're out there, expect delay in getting to the next camping spot or in or out of the canyon. Climbing out at either end is very dangerous (if not impossible) when the trail is wet, even with a 4WD vehicle. The clay soils here pack up a tire and turn it into a slimy slick. If you are riding the trail with a sagwagon, take along chains just in case.

A final warning if you are hardcore: This is the most overrated mountain bike ride around Moab. It's pretty, but it's a road for novices, unless you are there to explore the *hiking* options.

Getting there: To Mineral Bottom: Go 12.5 miles north of Moab on U.S. Route 191 and take a left onto UT 313. Follow the signs for Canyonlands National Park for another 12.5 miles. Just before the Gemini Bridges Trailhead (there is a sign on the right of the road), there is a well-marked and maintained road to MINERAL BOTTOM on the right. There may be cars parked here. Turn right and drive 12.8 miles down this road to the Horsethief Trailhead. Here you will mount the bikes and ride down the switchbacks to Mineral Bottom.

Shuttle Point To Shafer Rim: Go 12.5 miles north of Moab on US 191 and take a left onto UT 313. Follow the signs for Canyonlands National Park. When you reach the fee booth for the park, pay the $10 or display your park pass or valid backcountry camping permit. You should check in with the visitor center before you start. It is just ahead on the right at the top of the Shafer Rim

Colorado River below the White Rim

switchbacks. To get to the trail, continue past the fee booth and take a left onto the first dirt road. Go down this dirt road a bit and park your shuttle vehicle in one of the designated parking areas.

(Loop Option) If you are doing the big-loop thing, you should pull off UT 313 at the well-marked road to MINERAL BOTTOM. Directions are provided above. Park in the cleared area at the mouth of the road. Ride toward the park to go down Shafer for the clockwise direction. Ride up Mineral Bottom Road to do the featured counterclockwise route.

The Ride

The story of the earth revealed in the book of the White Rim has been revealed through eons of *erosion,* that force of nature that has made the place so beautiful and so intimidating. While riding the White Rim, you will encounter 320 million years of geological change that began during the Pennsylvanian period when this area was on the equator. The oldest visibly exposed geological layer is the 280-million-year-old Cutler formation. The youngest layers visible are in the La Sal Mountains to the southeast. The La Sals are the second youngest mountain range on earth at twenty-four million years old and were created by volcanic activity deep underground that caused the uplift, but never erupted.

As you ascend the Shafer Trail, first you pass through the Moencopi layer, the red and naturally sculpted rock that also greets you coming from the north to Moab on US 191. Above the Moencopi is the Chinle formation, a layer of mostly soft sediments stained green by deposits of copper. The road up the switchbacks has been treated with shale to make the surface pack harder, but this also causes the road to deteriorate in wet conditions. The Chinle layer adds to this problem at the base of the Shafer Trail. The slimy clay, when combined with the shale on the road, turns the trail into sticky soup. The red Wingate cliffs stand on top of the Chinle layer. Dark vertical stains on the face of the Wingate are called "desert varnish," caused by a combination of sunlight and the oxidation of manganese and iron. The vertical cracks in the Wingate are caused by the poor support afforded by the soft Chinle layers. The Navajo sandstone layer at the top of the switchbacks is supported by the Kayenta, the striated layer resting on top of the Wingate. Through the combined strength of many separate sedimentary layers, the Kayenta maintains the Navajo on top without cracking it, so that the Navajo sandstone erodes into smooth mounds and rolling hills of rock. The Navajo is the layer that forms the surface of the Moab Slickrock Bike Trail.

The story of man on the White Rim goes like this: The cattlemen ran off the Indians and built narrow cattle trails out of the Indians' rugged pathways. In the 1940s miners invaded the place and widened the trails to roads in order to haul out uranium ore and other minerals. One often-told tale is of bulldozer operator Art Wood. While working alone on the Horsethief Trail switchbacks, Art's dozer rolled over and pinned him to the ground. Knowing that it would be many days before the supply truck came back, he cut off his arm with a pocketknife and drove out in his pickup truck.

When the mining died off due to a fall in the price of uranium, the place was once again considered desolate and ugly and unworthy of visitation. It was when a handful of local river runners and guides started promoting tours out onto the rim that enough attention was paid to warrant turning it into a national park. The Park Service then ran the cattlemen off just as the cattlemen had run off the Indians. I predict that within twenty-five years, the trail will be paved and there will be a hotel on the rim. Mark my words.

Lin goes to Washington . . .

Moab tour guide Lin Ottinger announced that he would be traveling to Washington D.C. this week to meet with Department of the Interior officials and Utah Congressional representatives. The trip is the result of a dispute between Ottinger and the Park Service regarding road classification in the White Rim area of Canyonlands National Park. Ottinger was cited twice last year for driving in unauthorized areas. See story, Page B1.

The beginning of Lin Ottinger's hatred of the Park Service.
PHOTO COURTESY *TIMES INDEPENDENT,* JANUARY 25, 1979.

I once worked for Lin Ottinger, leading his 4WD tours on the White Rim. Lin knows more about the White Rim than anyone on earth, was instrumental in its becoming a national park, and now hates the Park Service for lying to him about not closing necessary roads out there. He even traveled to Washington and staked out the agency responsible. Knowing Lin he probably made a few more enemies and hurt his cause, but due to his efforts this fight is on the record. He now cusses at and torments rangers like it is his calling on earth.

You can experience the White Rim Trail any number of ways. It can be an out-and-back day ride from either end. You can rent a jeep and throw your bike in the back and ride any section of the trail you can get to on four wheels. You can do the epic thing and ride the whole damn thing in one day, or you can reserve camping spots in the bottom of the canyon and do it as a two-day to one-week trip.

The White Rim Trail is a 4WD road below the Island in the Sky District of Canyonlands National Park and is perhaps the most popular scenic ride anywhere— though it may no longer be rewarding for bikers seeking technical challenge or extreme solitude. This is a great ride for photographers and nature lovers, or for a group of friends who want to socialize. If you're a novice to intermediate rider who wants to camp in a managed environment and ride relatively short distances to each camp spot through a beautiful canyon paradise, then this may be your opportunity.

But you need to know when to go and when not to go. The trail can be a freeway in peak season, with tour buses and mountain bike groups all over the place. It would seem that the place is big enough to swallow up the crowds, but it really isn't. Playing leapfrog with fifty-odd 4WD vehicles and 500 tourists may not be your cup of tea. It is only getting worse out there, and this book is about to be part of the problem. If this kind of thing sounds unappealing, avoid the peak seasons of April, May, September, and October. Book your camping spots as soon as you can by calling early in July when the Park Service starts booking for the following year. Slots go fast, but sometimes you can swing a good series of camping spots if you pick a time of lighter use, like late November or early March. Weather changes fast out here, so take lots of water and be prepared for anything. It can be extremely hot or brutally cold. Don't be disappointed if your trip has to be canceled or cut short by snow or rain. It happens all the time.

To ride the entire trail in one day on a bike—or in a 4WD vehicle, for that matter—is very difficult, to say the least. It's certainly faster on a bike, but of course, you are the motor. It's all but impossible to carry enough water for a one-day trip, so water should be stored on the trail before you attempt the ride. Don't rely on the kindness of strangers, though generally this is what people do. It is a good practice to notify the park office before you ride out there, especially if this is your first ride on the rim or you're planning to do the entire rim ride in a day. The visitor center on top of Shafer Rim sells gallon containers of water.

The White Rim Trail is basically a well-maintained, sometimes rugged 4WD road. I personally think that it is too well maintained, but weather has a way of "improving" the riding conditions on occasion, even wiping out the trail on exposed cliffs. The complete trail starts with a descent and ends with a climb, no matter how you cut it. There are differing opinions as to the best direction to travel. If you choose the clockwise route, starting from Shafer Rim and ending at Mineral Bottom, there will be more of a climb at the Mineral Bottom end—but it doesn't come all at once, as does the Shafer Rim ascent. There is also water at the Mineral Bottom end, but the Mineral Bottom end of the ride will hand you a dose of sand. The reason I have chosen to document the ride in the counterclockwise direction is that you end up on the most used portion of the trail below the visitor center at the end of your ride. This may be a wise move for safety's sake, if you bonk or have a mechanical problem.

As you ride past the amazing rock formations, you will be above the Colorado River and below the Island in the Sky. There are spots along the trail where you can hike up or down. I have documented these in the mileage count for safety's sake, and so you can orient yourself with the map, but it should also be noted that if you need an emergency exit or choose to hike these trails for further exploration, climbing out can mean a very long hike with no one at the top to help you. Cell phones may or may not work on the White Rim, but you will have much more luck with reception on top of the Island in the Sky.

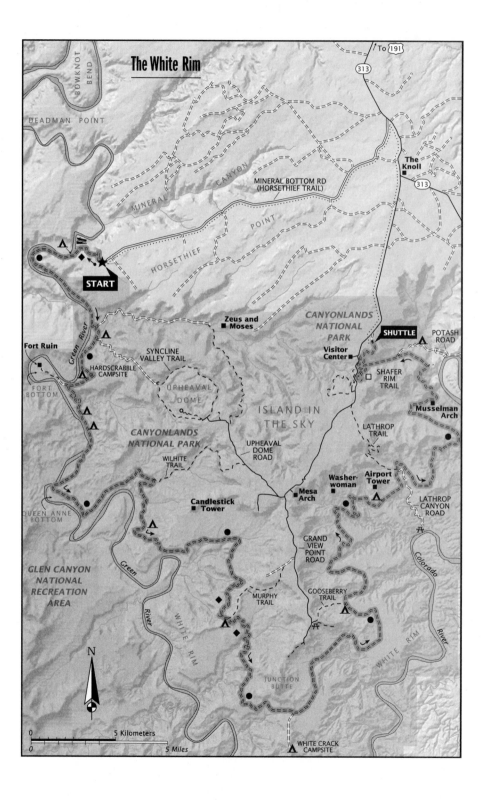

The White Rim

BOWKNOT BEND

DEADMAN POINT

To 191

313

The Knoll

313

MINERAL CANYON

MINERAL BOTTOM RD
(HORSETHIEF TRAIL)

MINERAL POINT

HORSETHIEF

START

Zeus and
Moses

CANYONLANDS
NATIONAL
PARK

SHUTTLE

POTASH
ROAD

Green River

Fort Ruin

FORT
BOTTOM

HARDSCRABBLE
CAMPSITE

SYNCLINE
VALLEY TRAIL

UPHEAVAL
DOME

Visitor
Center

SHAFER
RIM
TRAIL

Musselman
Arch

CANYONLANDS
NATIONAL PARK

WILHITE
TRAIL

ISLAND IN
THE SKY

UPHEAVAL
DOME
ROAD

LATHROP
TRAIL

LATHROP
CANYON
ROAD

QUEEN ANNE
BOTTOM

Candlestick
Tower

Mesa
Arch

Washer-
woman

Airport
Tower

GLEN CANYON
NATIONAL
RECREATION
AREA

Green

River

WHITE RIM

GRAND
VIEW
POINT
ROAD

GOOSEBERRY
TRAIL

Colorado

MURPHY
TRAIL

JUNCTION
BUTTE

WHITE RIM

River

N

0   5 Kilometers

0   5 Miles

WHITE CRACK
CAMPSITE

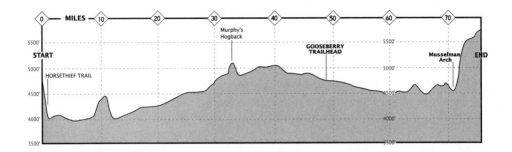

It's easy to book a camping spot here and nearly impossible to get lost, but should you want a guide, there are a lot of commercial tours into this area. You should consider a commercial tour if you don't want the hassle of dealing with camping logistics and permits or if you're into the social scene and want to meet a guy or a gal or something. If you avoid the commercial cattle drives though, campsites are cheap and you can choose who you ride with. If you do a multiday on your own, there is a great deal of literature available to supplement the information in this book. Rent a jeep or, better still, a Chevy Suburban. Take turns driving it, hire a driver, or leave the driving to someone in the group who doesn't want to ride. Take food, a gas stove, chains, tools, a cell phone, and all the shelter and cushy lawn chairs that will fit in the vehicle and voila, instant money saved and no strangers telling you what to do. There are a couple of sections of four-wheeling that may be a bit "testy," but if you are doing a multiday, you can just take your time in these sections. Maps of this trail are everywhere. Descriptions are everywhere. Rangers are everywhere, but you might like a tour company to take you out here.

If you're a climber, you'll want to bring along your ropes and gear. The Totem Pole in Monument Basin and the formations called Zeus and Moses in Taylor Canyon are legendary rock spires, famous to climbers around the world. Most features out here are named after cowboys who grazed cattle on and below the Island in the Sky. The Park Service has misnamed a few things, shuffling the names about. There is nothing unusual about that, except that naming a bridge Musselman Arch still doesn't make it an arch. The "arch" used to be called Little Bridge. Now there is no Little Bridge and the canyon called Little Bridge Canyon doesn't have an arch or a bridge in it at all. By the way, the Mussleman in Musselman Arch is Ross Musselman, the father of Rusty Musselman, whom I have featured elsewhere in this book.

Miles and Directions

(Note: The route described below is performed in the counterclockwise direction as a point-to-point with a shuttle vehicle. Riding out on the side spurs is not included in the mileage count.)

0.0 START your ride from the top of the switchbacks of the Horsethief Trail. The first section of trail is outside the national park boundary, so this is an area where you can camp at will and build campfires, unless signs are posted.

1.6 Turn left, avoiding the boat ramp. There is some sand ahead.

3.9 Here is the park boundary. Put on your tie. Obey the rules, but enjoy what may be the only section of the trail that can be considered technical.

6.1 **Side trip.** On your left is the spur into Taylor Canyon where the impressive spires Zeus and Moses reside. This is a great spot to visit and adds about 10 miles to your total mileage. There is a campsite in Taylor Canyon, and the last time I was out here the toilet was the subject of a lot of jokes and picture taking. Its shelter had blown away, and the toilet sat exposed on top of a high wooden platform.

6.7 **Side trip.** There is hiking here, if you are inclined to take the Syncline Valley Trail to visit the Upheaval Dome or the rim above.

8.0 The Hardscrabble campsite lies to your right on the Green River. It may be too close to the rim to be a great spot for the first night if you are riding the trail in this documented direction, but if you are coming from the other way, it may be desirable to rest here and take a dip before riding up the switchbacks. This spot has two campsites.

9.7 **Side trip.** The spur to your right leads out 1.2 miles to the hiking trail to Fort Bottom. The hike to an ancient Fremont tower ruin is another 1.2 miles from there. You will have to leave your bike behind. Don't worry about it getting stolen. I haven't heard of a single stolen bike on the White Rim, even though I know a few fellows who had to leave bikes behind to hike out. They came back later and the bikes were still there. Rangers will sometimes retrieve bikes left by tourists, if they are asked to. The ruin at the end of the hike is a mystery. See if you can figure out why it was built. The trip is well worth the extra mileage, unless you are on an epic day ride.

11.3 Potato Bottom is a charming spot to camp, but if you choose to stay here remember that there are three camp spots and each spot allows up to fifteen people. That's forty-five folks if you time your visit with one of the tour companies. Oh well, some people enjoy the company of others. Me, I don't want to see *anybody*.

14.7 Watch for the White Rim formation as it appears from under the road.

15.4 **Water.** The spur on your right leads down to the river at Queen Anne Bottom, the last access to water for the remainder of your journey.

20.1 The smooth sandstone watercourse to your right at the apex of this turn is Holeman Slot. It is a great place to explore and to shoot those cliché slot canyon photographs. Don't miss it. **Side trip.** The posted Wilhite Trail that leads up to the Island in the Sky is next to this wash and should be noted in case of an emergency. It is 5 miles long and gains 1,600 feet in elevation.

22.3 Candlestick Butte campsite is desirable only because it has only one spot, but it is very exposed and the wind can be strong.

29.0 One good climb deserves another. They get progressively worse until the final grunt up to Murphy's Hogback in the distance.

32.7 **Escape Route.** Murphy Trail is on the left. It is 4.5 miles up to the rim with 800 feet of elevation gain.

32.8 Welcome to Murphy's Hogback, and if you are being accompanied by a sagwagon, your driver just had a heart attack. There are three fine campsites here, of which campsite C is my favorite. The views are stunning. The Hogback is also a fantastic place for an amateur geologist, with petrified wood and fossilized bone scattered about. The Hogback itself is an anomaly in the Chinle layer, an example of the Mossback formation from which the soft Chinle soils have eroded. The simple explanation for the geology in Canyonlands is that God created it that way. Or you can believe that a lot of things happened here a lot of times. Sometimes they didn't happen over there, but only happened here, and vice versa. Sometimes so much stuff happened that geologists got mad and confused and and became Creationists.

34.2 **Escape Route.** The other side of the Murphy Trail loop is on your left. It is 3.5 miles and a gain of 1,100 feet.

36.9 Enjoy the sheer cliff wall to your right off the trail. The view is both frightening and electrifying.

40.5 **Side trip.** White Crack, the promontory to your right, definitely deserves an extended visit. Take the 1.5-mile-long road out there or be cursed for eternity. There is one campsite out here, the most desirable of all spots on the White Rim. If you want a two-day trip, this is the spot to camp, but good luck getting a permit. This spot demands an extra day in itself. You can hike down to the river and back on an extra day. The views from here are the best on the trip, maybe the best in all of Canyonlands. Views of Monument Basin to the north in the sunrise can generate a few good pictures. This spot was obviously appealing to ancient man, as well. It is covered with stone middens—rock chippings left by toolmakers hundreds or thousands of years ago. Please leave them where they are for others to enjoy. The chocolate-brown sandstone below is known as the Organ Rock shale. It erodes out from underneath the more dense sediments of the White Rim to form alcoves and capped spires that resemble bolts, mushrooms, or Coke bottles.

42.8 **Side trip.** This is the pullout for the view of Monument Basin. The 300-foot-tall spire called the Totem Pole is down there.

48.5 Gooseberry camp has two very exposed sites. **Escape Route.** The Gooseberry Trail ahead on your left is a route up to the Island in the Sky.

56.0 To your left is the Washerwoman. High up on the edge of the canyon wall at the top is Mesa Arch.

56.8 **Water.** The drainage on your right can be followed down to the river in an emergency, but make sure it's an emergency because this route ain't easy.

59.4 On your left is the spur to the first two Airport Towers campsites—another less-than-desirable place to set up home. There are two more sites in 0.2 mile.

59.9 **Escape Route.** Lathrop Trail intersects here on the left. It is a 5-mile hike to the rim with 1,600 feet of elevation gain.

60.0 **Water/Emergency.** The spur to your right is Lathrop Canyon Road. It can take you down to the river if you need water. One-way the trip is 3.5 miles and leads to a landing and picnic area used by boaters. The trail is beaucoup sandy.

67.8 Reach Musselman Arch. **Side trip.** Leave your bike here if you want to take a great hike out to the Walking Rocks, Lin Ottinger's favorite White Rim destination. The spot was named by his kids who, when very young, liked the place so much that they would ask to go to the place "where we walk on the rocks." Eventually this flowered into "let's go to those walking rocks." Lin once had a dining room set up out here in a grotto overlooking the river. He built a floor for it and placed a table and chairs down there. The Park Service made him remove it. The Walking Rocks are to your left as you face the "arch."

68.0 **Side trip.** The spur to your right leads to an overlook of the Colorado River. The Walking Rocks are accessible from here, also.

70.0 **Side trip.** The Gooseneck Trail makes a nice 0.5-mile hike. No bikes, though. At the end of the trail is an overlook of the Colorado River. The river used to be called Grand River—hence "Grand Junction," "Grand Mesa," and "Grand County." In the 1920s the U.S. Congress changed the name to the Colorado River.

71.3 This is the intersection of Potash Road and the Shafer Rim Trail. There is a potty here. Get ready for the climb ahead. See it? Feel it. Those switchbacks ahead started as an Indian path and then became a route for rustlers and train robbers. It became a cow trail when a cattle rancher named Sod Shafer did some improvements so he could get his cattle down from the Island in the Sky. A fellow named Ed Johnson was the primary engineer responsible for turning the track into a road. The trail switchbacks were constructed to continuously run underneath themselves to simplify construction costs and minimize erosion during downpours. It works just fine, but we should shoot whoever decided to put shale sediments onto the surface.

74.8 You have accomplished the steep climb out, but don't forget to stop and look. There is a rare grove of Douglas fir in an alcove just above the switchbacks.

76.0 Your shuttle vehicle should be somewhere in here. Pack up the bike, retrieve your other vehicle, go back to town, and have a beer.

Ride Information

Trail Contacts

Canyonlands National Park
Island in the Sky District
Moab, UT 84532
(435) 259–4351

Fees and Permits

Campsite reservations and backcountry permits are required. Requests for campsites are accepted beginning the second Monday in July for the following year. Applications are processed in the order received. For information you can call the Canyonlands National Park Reservations Office at (435) 259–4351, Monday through Friday from 8:00 A.M. to 12:30 P.M. (Mountain Standard Time). Or you can write the office at 2282 S. West Resource Blvd., Moab, UT 84532-8000. A $25.00 fee is required for each trip and should accompany your request. Reservations must be mailed to the address above or faxed to (435) 259–4285.

Park Regulations

Pets are not allowed on the White Rim, even in a vehicle. Wood fires are not allowed. Charcoal fires are allowed, but must be in a fire pan. ATVs are prohibited. You must pack out all debris. Travel is restricted to the roadbed. You must have a backcountry permit for overnight stays.

Schedule

Trail is open year-round but is best during spring and fall.

Maps

USGS maps: The Knoll, Mineral Bottom, Bowknot, Bend, Horsethief Canyon, Upheaval Dome, Musselman Arch, Turks Head, Monument Bason

Moab East Trail Map by Latitude 40° Inc.

Moab Recreation Map by F. H. Barnes

Other Resources

A Naturalist's Guide to the White Rim Trail by David B. Williams and Damian Fagan, published by Wingate Ink of Moab

THE TAMARISK TREE (*Tamarix ramosissima*)

Tamarisk is a wispy green shrub with scalelike leaves, beautiful narrow spikes of lavender to pink flowers, and shiny green to whitish stems. It was introduced to North America from the Nile River delta in the early twentieth century as a way to control erosion and provide shade along the saltwater bayous of the Mississippi River delta. Chosen for its ability to thrive in salt marshes, the plant has spread westward on its own, creeping up rivers and side canyons wherever there is a hint of groundwater. The plant's intrusion into canyon country was greatly assisted by Major John Wesley Powell, who planted a specimen in the Colorado River Canyon during his famous expedition in 1869. He was not only the first white man to navigate the river but also the first white man to screw it up. The growth of tamarisk has created what may be the most substantial environmental disaster in Canyonlands, far outweighing the damage done by dams, mining, cattle, and misguided recreation.

Tamarisk takes over every area it touches, destroying competing vegetation. Scattered among the leaves are pores that excrete salts that the shrub leaches from the soil around it. This action of the plant is why it is often called the salt cedar. This salt-depositing process kills off every plant in close proximity to the tamarisk. Animals that survive by eating low-lying vegetation or shelter in the indigenous cottonwoods and willows vanish wherever tamarisk takes root. Tortoises, once plentiful along the river, are now completely gone. Birds reliant on certain trees for nesting are dwindling, and every native animal is in danger. Not only does the tamarisk destroy native wildlife with its salt excretions, but its unquenchable thirst is even more devastating, lowering water tables wherever it's present. It consumes water that would otherwise nourish deer, squirrel, rabbit, longhorn sheep, and plants in the dry side canyon washes that drop into the river gorge. With the loss of this population, we also loose the raptors and predators that prey on the vegetarians.

Some incurable optimists have theorized that the tamarisk creates more riverbed by stabilizing the edges of the river and growing out into the flow. To their way of thinking, the river will become deeper and flatlands created by the tamarisk will again harbor cottonwoods and willows. Of course there are others who are certain that the river will diminish because of the plant's insatiable thirst and its intrusion into side canyons, where it sucks the washes dry before they reach the river. Ever the creative mind, Lin Ottinger sells tamarisk wood in his Moab Rock Shop as "worry sticks" or "fiddle sticks," smooth little pieces of wood that you can hold in your hand, and . . . well, worry. Lin once tried to cure tamarisk logs so that he could encourage harvesting, but the tree's red wood, which resembles cedar, splits as soon as it dries. Frankly, I worry about the outcome of the tamarisk's invasion and have made a point to buy a "worry stick" to "fiddle" with while I stress about the loss of wildlife in the Colorado River corridor.

Bridger Jack and the Mormon Snacks

Bridger Jack Mesa stands above the Back of Behind Trail and the Behind the Rocks Wilderness Study Area with a commanding view of the La Sals and the canyon country in every direction. The fact that this beautiful piece of real estate bears my original family name (the *s* was added later, perhaps by a bureaucrat with a speech impediment) caused me to probe the history of the Moab area for some kind of link to my bloodline. After some digging through various out-of-print books and a bit of research into Mormon history, I found a couple of Bridger Jack Mesas, probably misnamed by some clumsy bureaucrat 150 years ago. The same kind of mistake most likely misnamed Delicate Arch (originally named Landscape Arch), our state's stone icon. It just seems that white folks, as invaders of this wilderness realm, must name things in order to make them ours, or maybe to just make the place a little less intimidating. Even though those names can be downright wrong, even drastically stupid, we somehow feel better when we all share the same name for the same place; it helps us cope with the vastness of our empire. It also helps us know where we are when we get lost.

There are plenty of towns and mesas and rivers and rock outcroppings that bear Navajo or Ute names. When many of these names are correctly translated, they reveal that the first white explorers and settlers just *had* to know what that thing was called. The Native peoples dealt with the question, "What do you call that thing over there?" appropriately. The resulting names have long been an inside joke to those who speak Navajo. There are towns and buttes and mesas called "What?," "Go ask the chief," "Stupid White Man," "Which rock," "Go away, you're scaring the antelope," and "Drop dead, stupid white man."

The name *Bridger Jack* conjures up images of a scurrilous pirate, a craggy old pioneer with grit in his teeth who plodded across the continent married to a mule. I imagined him as someone who dropped the pretentious English Quaker moral stiffness to become a true western-icon kinda guy. I dug through book after book on the history of Utah, plowing through page after page of information spiffed up by Mormons to properly fit into the ideal of how it "really" should have been in Utah a hundred years ago. A lot of Mormon history is full of biblical blood feuds, senseless killing, lapses of faith, and the like—so the recorded history needs some scrubbing. You have to read between the lines or find an original letter to get close to the truth, but amid this melange of information, I was shocked to find a single story of the man called "Bridger Jack."

It is written that the original settlement in southern Utah was in the area now called Old La Sal just a few miles from what is now the town of Moab. This settlement consisted of the Maxwells, a small Mormon family. They built a cabin and began to grow crops and raise cattle on a piece of land at the foot of Mount Peale, an impressive peak in the La Sal range. They were advised, as all Mormon settlers were, that rather than fight with the Indians, they should feed them. To me, this is Brigham Young's most original contribution to the frontier, if indeed it can be believed. Mormon history romanticizes a bit. No matter the reasoning or the truth, this idea of sharing with the originals, the ones Brigham called the Lamanites, a lost tribe of Israel, is noble and kind and generous and downright novel, considering the awful policies of our government over the centuries toward folks who were here first.

So I guess it was with mandatory Mormon kindness that when a group of eight young roaming Utes knocked on the door of the Maxwell home in this middle-of-nowhere that is now Old La Sal, Mrs. Maxwell offered them pastries made from berries, white pastry flour, honey, and powdered sugar. To Mrs. Maxwell's amazement one of the Ute band, a young man of only eighteen years, spoke English rather well and appeared to be half white. When she asked him his name, he offered it as "Bridger Jack." It was through Bridger Jack that she spoke to the wandering Ute boys, telling them of the family's hopes to remain in this great land and make a home for all time. She no doubt shared her Mormon beliefs, her loves, her simple joys, hiding her fear and dread in a cloak of generosity and goodwill. After the boys indulged in what was probably the most remarkable morsels ever partaken of by Ute peoples, they departed with smiles on their faces. Mrs. Maxwell truly felt it was a good first encounter and that it would set the tone for the family's coexistence with their Ute hosts for years to come. She had really made a good first impression.

A few days later another knock was heard on their door, a door that had *never* been knocked on by anything except the fist of the half-Ute Bridger Jack. When Mrs. Maxwell opened the door, she was shocked by a band of over thirty Ute braves with Bridger Jack at the head bidding good day. As was customary, even dictated by Brigham in Salt Lake City, she would have to offer them each a pastry. Her heart sank as the Ute band set up camp in her yard as she baked two and a half dozen berry pastries with fluffy white sugar topping. She had set herself up to be the pastry chef for the entire Ute nation. What terror would be rained down upon her family should she fail to provide the Ute warriors with sweets in the future?

As the warriors fully indulged in the treats set before them, Mrs. Maxwell fearfully took young Bridger Jack aside and pleaded with him, half fearing the young warrior would scalp her on the spot. "Please, Mister Jack, understand that we have come to this far land with just enough stores of wheat and sugar to get us through the first couple of winters. If we give all of our staple foods to you and your friends, then our settlement will fail and we will have to return north."

Young Bridger Jack seemed to understand, but as the band left, Mrs. Maxwell feared that she had set in motion this settlement's failure. The following days passed as the family anticipated an attack. They searched the horizon for feathered heads and painted faces. They listened for angry cries that seemed to merge with voices of the wild animals of the high plateau. They walked with pinched sphincters through the tall grass. The family hardly slept as the tension grew in anticipation of the slaughter that was sure to come.

One evening as they were about to partake of the last meal of the day, there was a soft rap on the door. Mr. Maxwell stepped to answer as his family cowered in the corner of their small cabin. When he opened the door, there was Bridger Jack with the original eight Ute boys. They had come to see if they could get some more of those great pastries, but this time they brought meat, berries, skins, pots, beaded jewelry, and other fineries as an offering to the lady who made the magic morsels.

So goes the legend of Bridger Jack, the *only* legend of Bridger Jack to be found anywhere. Being a "Bridger" myself, I must admit that this is one of my cousins that I wish I could have met.

27 Behind the Rocks

Start: From the trailhead just off U.S. Route 191, 13 miles south of Moab.
Length: 15-mile loop.
Approximate riding time: 3 to 6 hours.
Difficulty: Technical challenges range from moderate to extreme. Bedrock bumps and transitions can be extremely difficult, as well as the huge drop-offs and deep sand. Physically difficult due to the severely rolling terrain and deep sand.
Trail surface: Technical jeep trail and maintained county road. Rolling hills, bedrock insults like repeated vertical slabs and stone ruts, sand, and a bit of slickrock and loose rubble.
Lay of the land: Rolling hills through sub-desert piñon and juniper.
Total climbing: 988 feet.
Land status: Bureau of Land Management (BLM) and Utah State Trust lands
Other trail users: Hikers, equestrians, off-road vehicles (ORV), and racers (during the Moab 24-Hour Race).
Best seasons: Spring and fall.

Environmental concerns: Fragile areas are just off the trail! Cryptobiotic soil crusts and rare desert mosses abound. The trail skirts a Wilderness Study Area that is home to some of the most abundant wildlife near Moab.

Getting there: From Moab: Go south on US 191. Just under 13 miles away, at the top of the big hill, there is a paved pullout on the right. This is the paved entrance to the Back of Behind Trail. Go across the cattle guard, turn right, and park your vehicle between the junipers.

The Ride

This loop ride will surely challenge your technical skills and should only be attempted by advanced riders. It is *very* sandy and *very* rocky. It is a geological fact that wherever you find sandstone, you will find sand. The Kayenta, Entrada, and Navajo sandstone layers provide some very interesting riding and scenic stone monuments in the Behind the Rocks area. The deal with this trail is that it is alternately very soft and very hard, never easy, and even when it gets flat, which is seldom, it is bumpy or sandy. This ride is perfect for hammerheads who love to test their skills. Don't break your neck. Remember, I told you to look before you leap.

The Moab 24-Hour Race happens on this loop. Sorry, but you won't see arrowheads, like our granddaddies did. Instead you'll find Gu, Power Gel wrappers, helmet visors, bits of chain, teeth, hair, and eyeballs. The only arrowheads you'll find on this ride are the ones race managers stapled to the trees. This race is the most environmentally destructive force that mountain biking has presented to Moab in quite a while. Every year they create *new* trail through wildlife habitat, creating sand pits that run for miles. Soil crusts and, sequentially, *all* forms of desert vegetation are disappearing into deep beach sand as a result of this single event. There are roads and slickrock now legally off limits to anything but hiking. These are right next to an

Attacking the ledges below the Diving Board

area where mountain bike racers have littered paradise with mountain bike garbage. In the race staging area, race promoters have done a pretty good job of re-creating the surface of the moon. We have to learn to ride in the environment, not all over it; don't you think?

The ride starts out on the maintained Back of Behind Trail, spurs right onto a technical jeep trail, and gets more and more difficult as you wrap around beehive-like rock formations that make up the rocks in Behind the Rocks. Ledges of every shape and size test your skills as they rise and fall from and into deep beach sand and

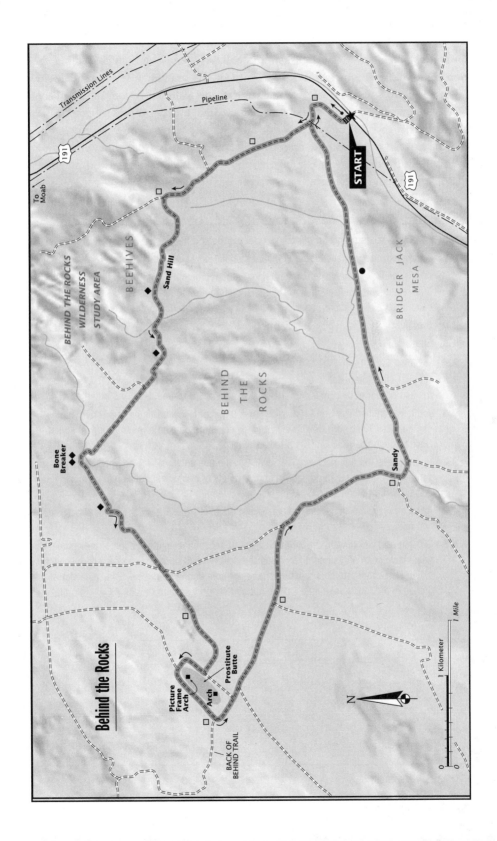

Behind the Rocks

Transmission Lines

Pipeline

191

To Moab

BEHIND THE ROCKS
WILDERNESS
STUDY AREA

BEEHIVES

Sand Hill

BEHIND THE ROCKS

Bone Breaker

BRIDGER JACK MESA

START

191

Sandy

Picture Frame Arch

Arch

Prostitute Butte

BACK OF BEHIND TRAIL

N

0   1 Kilometer
0   1 Mile

loose rubble. Whenever I take folks on this trail, I try to stop at each challenging section and try different lines. It is that kind of ride. The trail ranges from brutally slow and slogging to scary fast. The first half of the ride really beats you up. The second half, which takes place on the Back of Behind Trail, bores you silly, though most of the maintained road is downhill. Sorry, those are the facts. If you want to continue the challenge, though, add the optional downhill at mile 8.4 or simply turn around at Prostitute Butte and retrace your route, but I guarantee that once you ride down that first deep sand hill, you will never, ever want to slog up it.

Miles and Directions

0.0 **START** Go south (right) on the marked Back of Behind Trail.

0.2 Go through this intersection on the main trail and down the hill to the left.

0.3 At this three-way intersection, take a right onto the dominant spur that *isn't* the Pipeline Maintenance Road. The Pipeline Maintenance Road is the far-right spur. After a bit of sand, the trail gets more and more technical as you head out to the Beehives.

1.0 Stay right.

1.3 Stay left.

1.4 Continue straight past the spur on the left.

1.8 Go left below the beehive rock formations and avoid all spurs to the right. This is the marked border of the Behind the Rocks Wilderness Study Area. No bikes in the WSA.

2.4 You have reached The Sand Hill. Lucky for you it is a descent. This bit of powdery trail can be tricky. Keep your weight back and expect some banked turns that beg for speed. Once through the sand there is a technical climb.

3.2 Here's where the trail gets very technical. Beyond this point you will be encountering some very difficult steep transitions from a variety of bedrock surfaces into deep sand and back onto technical rock. Look before you leap.

4.0 A fast straightaway is a welcome break from the challenge, but watch out for a rocky section midway.

4.7 Go right and welcome to the Bone Breaker, the most challenging section of the entire trail. I have seen only three riders clean the downhill and no one clean the entire section. If you want some real entertainment, hang out here during Jeep Week. The small slot at the left is the best line. It leads to the flat and slippery section that drops you into the

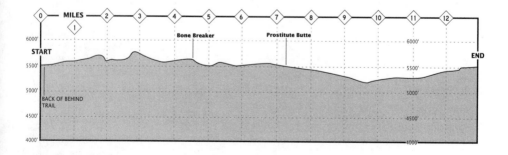

Nate Toone

sand. Once you have dropped in, you must turn left and ride through deep sand and climb the ledges around the corner. Good luck, Mr. Testosterone. At the top of the rise on the other side of the Bone Breaker, the trail heads out to the left.

6.1 Go straight across this bit of slickrock. The trail exits just ahead.

6.2 Go straight through this intersection.

6.4 Go straight through this intersection.

7.3 Take a right and head toward Prostitute Butte (also marked as Ayers Rock on some maps). There are a couple of beautiful arches in this somewhat rude rock formation.

7.5 Go right and follow the trail around the butte. This is a great place to rip.

7.8 Look to your left after you round the butte to see Picture Frame Arch. It is usually in shade, so photography is really not happening, but you can climb into it if you are adventurous and have good shoes.

8.4 At the southwest end of the butte, there is an intersection of multiple spurs. Simply ride straight through, avoiding the main spur to the left. You will hit the Back of Behind Trail in 100 feet or so. **Option.** If you want a bit more technical challenge and a workout, go right at this intersection and hang on to your dentures. This spur drops off of a ledge and rockets downhill, snaking its way onto the Back of Behind Trail at the bottom of the hill, where you turn left and climb the sandy mess of a maintained road, passing Prostitute Butte once again on your way back to your vehicle at the trailhead. The mileage count here does not include this very fast and technical diversion, but the way back to the trailhead is very straightforward.

8.5 Hit the Back of Behind Trail. Go left onto the well-maintained dirt road for a sandy, but scenic ride back to your vehicle.

10.7 If you are a sand masochist, go left on this spur and play on the dunes just off the trail. If you are not so inclined, continue on main trail, avoiding all spurs right or left.

14.7 Here's that Pipeline Maintenance Road again. You have closed the loop. Stay on the main trail to the right, avoiding all spurs left or right. Hear the trucks? You're getting closer to the road.

15.0 Reach the trailhead and your vehicle.

Ride Information

Trail Contacts

Bureau of Land Management
82 E. Dogwood
Moab, UT 84532
(435) 259–2196
Utah State School and Institutional Trust Lands Administration
1165 South US 191, Ste. 5
Moab, UT 84532
(435) 259–3760

Schedule

Trail is open year-round but is best during spring and fall.

Maps

USGS maps: Kane Springs Canyon, Trough Springs, Moab
Moab West Trail Map by Latitude 40° Inc.
Moab Recreation Map by F. H. Barnes

Sheriff Rusty Musselman

The twelve-bed San Juan County jail, built to contain the criminal element of 9,000 square miles of southeastern Utah, was filled to well over capacity with drunken Indians still loudly celebrating some special event, when a white man and a black man both named Johnson arrived handcuffed together. To the incarcerated Navajo and Utes, Johnson and Johnson must have been a special sighting, because they were pointing, laughing, and joking among themselves from the moment the two made their appearance.

In full view of his rowdy, captive audience Sheriff Rusty Musselman ceremoniously uncuffed black Johnson and began to uncuff white Johnson, but ran into trouble with the cuff on white Johnson's gloved hand. Rusty fumbled for several minutes with cuff and keys until white Johnson finally asked: "Do you need some help with that?"

"Yeah, I do," Rusty replied.

"Rusty is a western treasure and the most lovable joker in all of Canyonlands."

White Johnson calmly unscrewed his hand from his wrist and gave the hand and offending cuffs to Rusty.

"The Indians went wild with laughter," said Rusty Musselman thirty years later.

In his eighties and recovering from heart surgery, Rusty sat in a comfortable armchair in the living room of his beautiful log home just outside the small town of Monticello, at the base of the Abajo Mountains. Rusty generates a special feeling whenever he shares such a story—a real love for people, for all people and the wonderful absurdity of life. Bette Stanton, author and retired director of the Moab to Monument Valley Film Commission, once said of him: "Rusty is a western treasure and the most lovable joker in all of Canyonlands."

I mentioned my worry about using his reference to "drunk Indians" in this tiny story, and asked, "How about 'chemically challenged Native Americans'? Do you think that will fly?"

Rusty sat before me smiling with an oxygen respirator plugged into his nose. He chuckled in that way that is uniquely Rusty. There was a cosmic gleam in his eye, the look of someone who knew the score, but never needed to follow the game. He replied: "I don't know where humor went. Quite a lot of the old folks had humor, even though they was a lot of shoot-'em-up artists. Nowadays, people just stand there with their mouth open and you can't go nowhere with that."

28 Flat Iron Mesa

Start: Flat Iron Mesa Road at U.S. Route 191.
Length: 14-mile out-and-back.
Approximate riding time: 1 to 3 hours.
Difficulty: Technically easy due to the maintained dirt road surface. Physically moderate due to distance and mellow climbs.
Trail surface: Sand, loose rock, and bedrock on a well-maintained dirt road.

Lay of the land: You will be crossing a plateau onto mesa to an overlook of Kane Springs Canyon.
Total climbing: 799 feet.
Land status: Bureau of Land Management (BLM) and Utah State Trust lands.
Other trail users: Equestrians, off-road vehicles (ORV), and four-wheel-supported hikers on the mesa at the end of the trail.
Best seasons: Spring and fall.

Environmental concerns: Fragile, especially on the mesa! Cryptobiotic soil crusts and rare desert mosses are everywhere just off the trail. If you are hiking out onto the mesa, be careful where you step and avoid crushing fragile soils.

Getting there: From Moab: Go south on US 191 for 20.7 miles from the intersection of Main and Center Streets. Go past the pumping station on the right and take a right onto the Flat Iron Mesa Road. Park on a small established turnout within 50 feet of the turnoff.

The Ride

This is an easy ride out to a great area for hiking, car camping, and sight-seeing. Animal wildlife also abounds out here, so enjoy the company if you are lucky enough to see them. On the way out onto the trail, you'll be able to see Hole in the Rock to the east; to the north, Prostitute Butte and Behind the Rocks reside in the distance. Flat Iron Mesa is a beautiful spot for scenic and wildlife photography, as it overlooks Kane Springs Canyon to the north. Taking hiking shoes is recommended. The hike at the end can be a bit treacherous, if you want to get to the best spots for viewing and photography.

Hole in the Rock is just off the highway on the way to the trailhead, just beyond the rest area on US 191 across from the entrance to Kane Springs Canyon. You can't miss it. Watch for the painted signs on the rock. The place is recommended visiting—

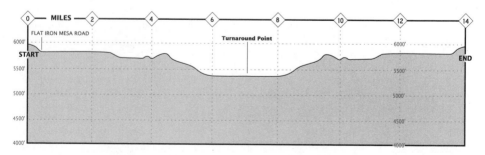

Miki fixes a broken chain with the La Sal Mountains in the distance.

it does require a fee. This strange home was tunneled out of sandstone and is a real treat if you are into tacky Americana. The fellow who blasted the rooms out of solid rock also painted, sculpted, and was an amateur taxidermist. His paintings are primitive, his sculpture is primitive, and his taxidermy is a riot—sort of like Frankenstein made a few animals to keep the monster company.

Maybe too easy for intermediate to expert riders, this ride takes place on a dirt road that, aside from some sand and a small amount of loose rock and ledges at the mesa, is just a fine scenic ride for families or novices. If you choose to explore any of the spurs off the main trail, remember to avoid cryptobiotic soil crusts and slickrock encrusted with moss and lichen. The trail is very easy to follow by staying with the dominant road all the way out to the mesa.

Miles and Directions

- **0.0** **START** by heading westward on the road.
- **1.6** Go straight through this intersection.
- **1.8** Go straight through this intersection.
- **3.2** Stay left at the Y.
- **5.0** The spur left is inviting, but continue on unless you are into some exploring.

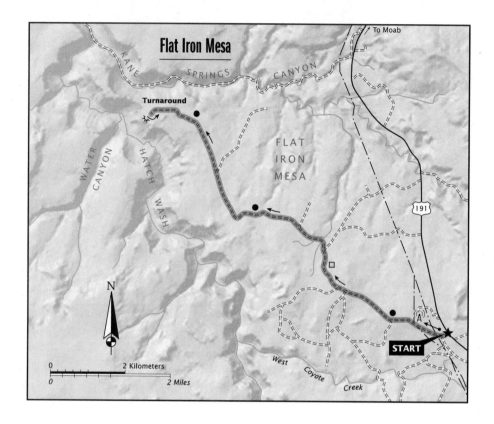

5.2 The spur right is inviting, but continue on unless you are exploring.

6.8 Stay right at the Y.

7.0 This is the end of the road. Dismount your bike for a hike out onto the mesa. Be careful if you have children with you. There are some serious cliff edges out here. After enjoying this area, turn around and retrace your route.

14.0 Arrive back at your vehicle.

Ride Information

Trail Contacts

Bureau of Land Management
82 E. Dogwood
Moab, UT 84532
(435) 259-2196

Utah State School and Institutional Trust Lands Administration
1165 South US 191, Ste. 5
Moab, UT 84532
(435) 259-3760

Schedule

Trail is open year-round but is best during spring and fall.

Maps

USGS maps: La Sal Junction, Eightmile Rock
Moab Recreation Map by F. H. Barnes

29 Canyonlands Overlook

Start: From the Canyon Rims Recreation Area at the point where the primitive road leaves from Anticline Overlook Road.
Length: 13.8-mile out-and-back.
Approximate riding time: 2 hours.
Difficulty: Technically easy to moderate. A mostly flat ride. Sand and a bit of slickrock keep it interesting. Physically moderate due to the sandy trail conditions and mileage.

Trail surface: Sand, bedrock, slickrock, and loose rock on a 4WD track.
Lay of the land: Desert plateau expanse to a cliff edge view of a huge canyon.
Total climbing: 649 feet.
Land status: Bureau of Land Management (BLM) lands.
Other trail users: Equestrians and off-road vehicles (ORV).
Best seasons: Spring and fall.

Environmental concerns: The slickrock area has a lot of moss and lichens on it that should be dodged. Cattle run amok out on the plateau and destroy the fragile soils, but what is left should remain. Let's not make it any worse. Stay on the trail.

Getting there: From Moab: Go south on U.S. Route 191 for 32 miles until you come to the marked paved road into the Canyon Rims Recreation Area on the right-hand side of the highway. Go 14.9 miles on this road and take the gravel spur to your right. At mile 17.1 there is a particularly beautiful place to stop and take photos. At mile 20.1 there is another spot marked by a sign with a camera on it. At 23 miles pull off next to the dirt road on your left. Park and ride out on the road marked PRIMITIVE ROAD TRAVEL AT YOUR OWN RISK.

The Ride

This trail in the Canyon Rims Recreation Area offers a moderate challenge combined with amazing vistas. If you like the idea of riding up to the rim of the Grand Canyon on a mountain bike, then this ride is pretty close to the majesty, minus the crowds. The ride is suitable for fit novices to intermediate riders. The trail is so close yet so far away. You must drive around the backside of Kane Springs Canyon to get to it, but if you were a bird, the trailhead would only be a short trip to the west-southwest from the Moab Valley. The drive to the trailhead may be somewhat of a deterrent, but the Canyon Rims area is a wonderful place to camp, far from the lights of the valley and near rarely visited trails. Families with younger riders should consider the Canyon Rims Recreation Area as a place to stay for a few days.

There is a lot of sand to negotiate along the trail, but the route is punctuated with areas of slickrock. The long sandy straightaway can be boring to some, and it gets very hot in summer, but the view and terrain at the end of the ride is worth the trip. This ride is best done in spring or fall. The slickrock area at mile 0.8 will require some playtime on the way in and/or out.

The upside of the cattle industry using this area is that there are lots of singletrack cattle trails everywhere that are fine for a mountain bike equipped with suspension

The small slickrock area just above the overlook

and wide tires for sand. These singletracks are bumpy from cow tracks but ridable and a great way to get to more remote spots along the rim for photography. The prolific cacti are incentive to stay on the cow trails.

Miles and Directions

0.0 **START** by heading west on the primitive road.

0.1 Go right at the first fork in the road.

0.8 Follow the cairns across the slickrock area to the continuation of the 4WD trail at the back and on the right.

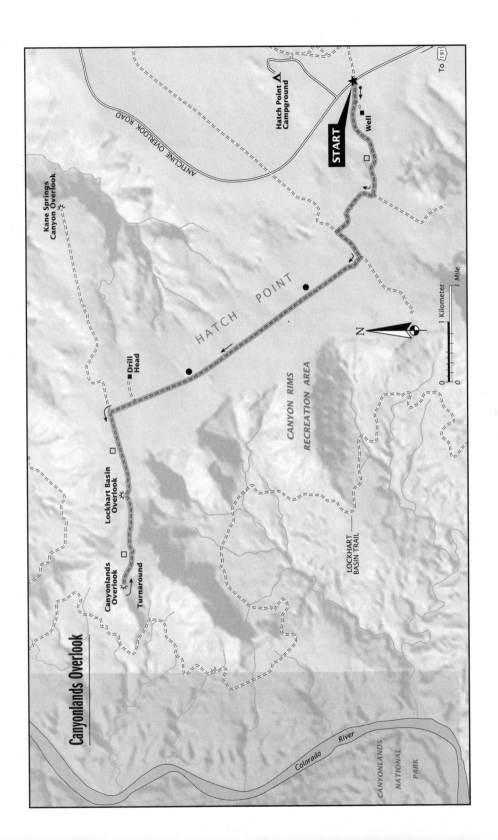

Canyonlands Overlook

Kane Springs
Canyon Overlook

Drill
Head

Lockhart Basin
Overlook

Canyonlands Overlook

Turnaround

ANTICLINE OVERLOOK ROAD

Hatch Point ⛺
Campground

START

Well

To 191

HATCH   POINT

CANYON RIMS

RECREATION AREA

LOCKHART
BASIN TRAIL

CANYONLANDS
NATIONAL
PARK

Colorado   River

N

0   1 Kilometer

0   1 Mile

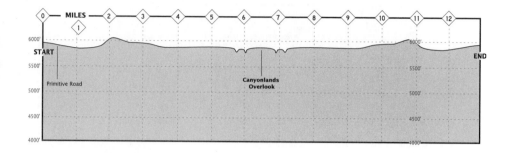

1.8 Go left at the T. There will be a post with an arrow carved into it guiding your way out to the overlook.

5.0 Take the spur left and follow the predominant track out to the overlooks to the west. To the east is another rim overlooking Kane Springs Canyon.

5.9 Be sure to stop for this overlook on your right. Lockhart Basin is just below. The White Rim lies across the Colorado River directly west. The artificial blue ponds to the north are the evaporation pools of the Potash Plant. The area beyond that tilts upward is the formation referred to as an anticline.

6.9 Your destination! Be sure to walk out to the point for the 270-degree view of Lockhart Basin. After enjoying this area, turn around and retrace your route. Don't miss turns that aren't so obvious. The long straightaway will make you want to put your head down and hammer. Gravity is great, isn't it? I'll help you a bit here by listing the troublesome turn next:

12.0 Go right just beyond the marker on your left.

12.8 Before you head back to the vehicle, enjoy the thrill of this slickrock area, but be sure to respect the cryptobiotic soil crusts that lie at the bottom of each bowl and the lichen and mosses that dot the rock. Once you have had your fill, catch the sandy spur to the east and back to your vehicle.

13.8 Reach the trailhead and your vehicle.

Ride Information

Trail Contacts
Bureau of Land Management
82 E. Dogwood
Moab, UT 84532
(435) 259–2196

Schedule
Trail is open year-round but is best during spring and fall.

Maps
USGS maps: Lockhart Basin, Shafer Basin, Eightmile Rock
Moab West Trail Map by Latitude 40° Inc.
Moab Recreation Map by F. H. Barnes

1% Profit

After lives as a rancher, Indian trader, and as the San Juan County sheriff, Rusty Musselman found a unique profession late in life by furnishing western props to the movie industry. His propping business was named Roughlock, after the cowboy whiskey. On his business card was written: "1% profit: Buy for $1, sell for $2."

I had the privilege of interviewing Rusty a number of times on video and for print media before he passed away in 1997. In order to interview him, I would drive 50 miles south of Moab, past Church Rock and the entrance to the Needles District of Canyonlands National Park. He lived just at the top of the ridge to the south within a few miles of the town of Monticello, overlooking the magical landscape to the north.

"I got into propping for the movies while I was sheriff. I worked on *Blue* and *Rancho* somethin' or other, and *The Commancheros* and *Fade In* with Burt Reynolds. You know, I've worked on maybe fifty pictures, but I haven't seen five of them. I don't remember any of them Hollywood people's names, but they all know me pretty good."

Actor Ricardo Montalban and Rusty Musselman in the late 1960s. COURTESY OF LILLY MUSSELMAN.

"What famous actors did you meet?" I asked.

Rusty stood up, trailing the oxygen line behind him. He fumbled in a file cabinet in the corner of his dark living room. His wife, Lilly, looked on, obviously concerned with Rusty's hyperactivity. He was looking pretty fragile these days.

"Where are those pictures? They are in that briefcase around here somewhere. Lilly, where'd those photographs get to?"

After several minutes of digging around the house, Lilly discovered the briefcase behind the couch.

The case was locked with a combination Rusty had long forgotten. He cussed at it and chuckled at himself. "Damn thing. I'm gonna get rid of this business altogether," he said as he pried the lock off with a knife. Inside were reams of photos of Hollywood stars posing inside the Musselman's Pack Creek Ranch house, clowning on the set, taking a break between shots, and posing with Rusty. There was Ricardo Montalban, Rock Hudson, Harry Caray, and Joanne Dru, among other familiar faces whose names have been lost in time.

"John Wayne, I couldn't stand him when he was young, but when he got older and the cancer scared him, he turned out to be an all right guy."

"Joanne Dru was such a snob. I liked Kathleen O'Miley . . . and Ben Johnson. It didn't matter if you were a sheepherder or the king of England. Dobie [that's what Harry Caray's friends called him] and Ben and me were going to make a documentary about John Ford this year, but Ben up and died on us.

"John Ford was loud, but that was his way. Once he had an actor that was supposed to fall off a horse into a cold river, but the actor refused to do it. John screamed out: 'I'll give a hundred bucks to anyone who'll fall off this goddamn horse.' A hundred bucks is a lot to fall off a horse. I was doing it a lot for free and I thought, 'Damn, why not do it for a hundred bucks,' but before I could get his attention somebody else took the job.

"I wrangled for a lot of movies. At one time I had this fallin' horse that I was offered a lot of money for. When you fell off he wouldn't step on you no matter what. That made him a valuable horse for working in the movies."

Rusty fumbled through the photos, reminiscing.

"John Wayne, I couldn't stand him when he was young, but when he got older and the cancer scared him, he turned out to be an all right guy.

"I spent a lot of time with Spencer Tracy and Brian Keith. Those guys were real drunkards. I know this Episcopalian monk up at the mission in Bluff who went to school with Spencer. He said Spencer would drink shoe polish, but there's five actors I really think were the best, and he's at the top. There's Spencer, Katharine Hepburn, Marie Dressler, Wallace Beery, and Judy Garland. You know with actors, after you begin to think you're good, then you are, but the old actors are gone now. Acting is different now.

"I had a few speakin' parts in movies. Just last year I had a speaking part in that movie *Riders of the Purple Sage*. I got paid $600 to stand with my backside to the camera. The director said that my backside was cheap compared to most.

"I was propping for Dean Kennedy who was the set man on the picture. We was standin' in the hall talkin' when this fella came up and said, 'Who are you?' And I said, 'Who are you?' right back, and he snorted and said: 'I'm the director of this picture. Come into my office when you're done here.' When I went into his office, he asked if I was acting in this picture and I said 'No.' He said: 'Well you are now. You're going to be a Mormon bishop.' I said: 'Well, I been called worse. I guess it's better than bein' a son of a bishop.'

"The movies ain't what they used to be, you know. Video is taking over. The movies is always changin'. After I got married I tried to get Lilly's folks to go to the movies in Moab and her dad said he couldn't go because he couldn't read fast enough. They thought movies was still silent."

Roughlock

1% Profit: Buy for $1, sell for $2

Rancher, Indian Trader,
Sheriff and Movie Prop Builder

Rusty Musselman
Moab, Utah

All during our conversation Lilly had been by Rusty's side, supporting him, jogging his memory, smiling beautifully, stepping in at the right moments, but refusing to let me take her photograph. She whined: "You've been at this for over three hours. Don't you think it's time to stop?" She was concerned with Rusty's health. I had him drinking whiskey and running all over the house dragging his oxygen tube over the furniture. Old age is so unfair, and it has never been more obvious than in the case of Rusty Musselman. His body was old, but he remained eternally young at heart and so innocently honest.

As I stood in the doorway Rusty spoke in a resolved tone, jiggling the oxygen nozzle dangling from his nose as if it were one of his props: "I don't know if I'm ever gonna recover from this, but I'd better try."

Rusty Musselman died in April 1997. I didn't know about his death until September. I found out from Verle Green, who told me he'd placed an announcement on the local television station's cheapo computerized ad listings. I just didn't see it.

Verle said Rusty's nephew told some great stories at the wake. In one story he told of asking Rusty just how he could remember things so well. Rusty told him that he would always link something in his mind to the thing he had to remember. Like when he needed to remember where his keys were, he would place them in his briefcase and he'd link the briefcase with the fact that there was a lock on the briefcase. Rusty's nephew asked him where his briefcase was at that moment and Rusty turned around and shouted, "Hey Lilly, where's my briefcase?"

30 Colorado River Overlook

Start: From the Needles visitor center parking lot.
Length: 14.2-mile out-and-back.
Approximate riding time: 90 minutes to whatever you want.
Difficulty: Technically easy to moderate. There is one technical section of trail here that warrants mention. It comes just before the overlook and is comprised of some gnarly bedrock and a couple of slickrock mounds. Physically easy to moderate. The trail is mostly flat, but presents you with a bit of sand on a few rolling hills.

Trail surface: 4WD road over sand, hardpack, loose rock, and sculpted bedrock.
Lay of the land: Desert expanse with views of Junction Butte in the background, ending up on the edge of the Colorado River Gorge where Salt Canyon joins the Colorado River Canyon.
Total climbing: 293 feet.
Land status: Bureau of Land Management (BLM) and national park lands.
Other trail users: Hikers, equestrians, and off-road vehicles (ORV).
Best seasons: Spring and fall.

Environmental concerns: Fragile! Cryptobiotic soil crusts and rare desert mosses abound just off the trail. The Park Service has very restrictive policies concerning off-trail excursions.

Getting there: From Moab: Go south on U.S. Route 191 about 40 miles. Just at the strange rock formation on the left called Church Rock—once there really was a church inside of it—take a right onto Utah Route 211. At 12.2 miles from the intersection of US 191 and UT 211, you'll encounter the pullout for Newspaper Rock—well worth stopping for. At mile 26 is the Lavender and Davis Canyon turnoff. Keep going straight. At mile 28.8 is the right-hand turnoff for Lockhart Basin. Keep going straight. At mile 32.8 is a right turn to the Needles Outpost, where you can buy gas and snacks if need be. At mile 33.8 is the Needles visitor center. Park here and head out on your bike on the marked 4WD spur at the back of the parking lot.

The Ride

The drive to the Needles is a real tourist's treat. You will pass Hole in the Rock, a tacky home blasted into solid rock with even tackier furnishings that is now open to the public for a fee. All along the highway are arches like Wilson Arch and Lopez Arch, which may warrant a visit or a picture or two. Just at the turnoff to UT 212 is Church Rock, a huge domed rock hollowed out to hold a church. Past Church Rock, as you turn off US 191 onto UT 211, you'll see several abandoned buildings in the distance on either side of the road. This is the site where a colony of Seventh Day Adventists were massacred or run off by the FBI in the 1950s, after declaring themselves independent of the United States. The event was much like the Branch Davidian crisis in Waco, but was effectively hushed up. Older locals remember it quite vividly. The abandoned homes in the middle of a cow pasture are a haunting sight.

Farther up the road, after you drop down into a tight canyon alongside a creek, is Newspaper Rock—a fine panel of petroglyphs spanning many hundreds of years

Newspaper Rock

of ancient history. The site is indeed spectacular, but Lin Ottinger, local eccentric and owner of the Moab Rock Shop, tells me that a few years back some well-intentioned folks at the BLM "intercoursed" this ancient art by "brightening" the glyphs with chisels—sort of like painting over a van Gogh. This bit of tampering now makes the glyphs' artists unidentifiable to archaeologists because the etch marks of the original tools used to peck the glyphs were erased. The site is still awesome and has a few very strange images—especially in the upper right-hand corner of the panel—that really make you wonder just what they were doing or where they came from, or what kind of plants they were smoking.

This is a ride on a mostly sandy 4WD track to where Salt Canyon wash drops into the Colorado River. The ride leaves from the Needles visitor center across a

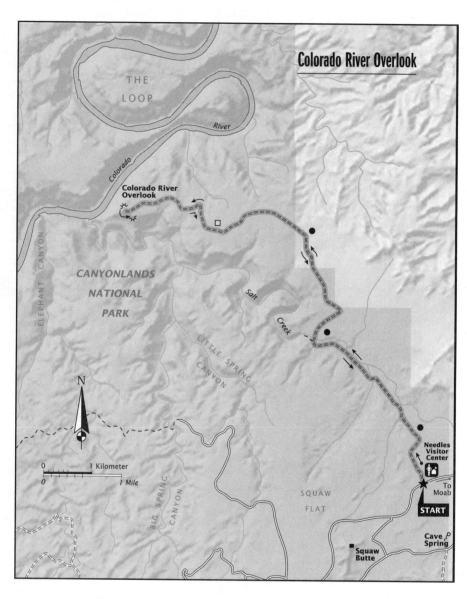

Colorado River Overlook

THE LOOP

River

Colorado

Colorado River
Overlook

ELEPHANT CANYON

CANYONLANDS
NATIONAL
PARK

Salt

Creek

LITTLE SPRING
CANYON

N

0   1 Kilometer

0   1 Mile

BIG SPRING CANYON

SQUAW
FLAT

Needles
Visitor
Center

To
Moab

START

Cave
Spring

Squaw
Butte

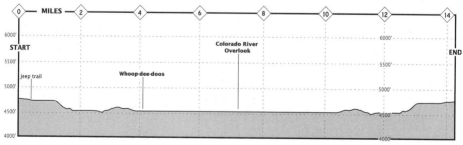

| MILES | 2 | 4 | 6 | 8 | 10 | 12 | 14 |

6000'   6000'

START   Colorado River
                                         Overlook   END

5500'   5500'

jeep trail

5000'   Whoop-dee-doos   5000'

4500'   4500'

4000'   4000'

Salt Canyon to the southeast from the river overlook

magical landscape of strange sandstone knobs. It is especially beautiful and perfect for less skilled riders, though it does have a few technical challenges near the end where ledgy bedrock will make you twist around for a clean line. Once at the overlook be careful not to get too close to the edge. Be sure to walk over to the left for the view into Salt Canyon.

The Needles District of Canyonlands National Park does have quite a few mountain bike rides that take place on 4WD tracks throughout the park. The Colorado River Overlook Trail is the least sandy of the rides and is the easiest when it comes to route finding. See the honorable mentions for an alternative suggestion for hardcore riders.

Miles and Directions

0.0 **START** from the parking lot and head out on the dirt spur.

2.5 Cross the wash bottom and stay on the marked jeep trail.

3.1 Here's a bit of fun on bedrock.

3.5 There's a viewpoint to the left.

4.1 Whoop-dee-doos.

4.3 Keep straight, ignoring the spur to the right.

4.5 Junction Butte is straight ahead across the river in the distance.

6.0 The trail gets fun as the 4WD track becomes quite a bit more challenging. This section can even be treacherous if you aren't ready for it. The trail up to this point has been pretty mellow, so this section is a reward for anyone who is taking a novice friend on a ride.

7.1 Viewpoint. Hike over to the overlook into Salt Canyon to your left, but be careful out here—lots of exposure to sheer drops of up to 1,000 feet. After enjoying this area, turn around and retrace your route.

14.2 Arrive back at your vehicle.

Ride Information

Trail Contacts

National Park Service
Canyonlands National Park
Needles District, Moab Office
2282 Resource Blvd.
Moab, UT 84532
(435) 259-3911
Needles Information
(435) 259-7164
Needles Visitor Center
Utah 211
Moab, UT 84532
(435) 259-4711

Schedule

Trail is open year-round but is best during spring and fall.

Maps

USGS maps: The Loop
Canyonlands National Park Needles and Island in the Sky Utah Map #210 by the National Geographic Society and Trails Illustrated
Canyonlands-Needles Recreation Map #1002 by Trails Illustrated

Honorable Mentions

Moab West and Southwest

Compiled here is an index of great rides in the West and Southwest region that didn't make the A-list this time around but deserve recognition. Check them out and let me know what you think. You may decide that one or more of these rides deserves higher status in future editions, or you may have a ride of your own that merits some attention.

B Back of Behind

This technically easy, physically moderate out-and-back also provides a couple of physically and technically difficult point-to-point options, as well as many side spur options. The Back of Behind area is an expansive plateau spanning the area west of Behind the Rocks to Kane Springs Canyon rim. The area is laced with 4WD tracks of varying degrees of difficulty. These trails afford visits to the Kane Springs Canyon rim via west-side spurs off the easily followed main trail.

The State Trust Lands section of the Back of Behind Trail.

The well-marked trailhead is 13 miles south of Moab on the left-hand side of U.S. Route 191 at the top of the steep hill that climbs out of the Moab Valley. The entrance to the trailhead is now paved and very visible, and is described in the Behind the Rocks chapter (see Ride 27). The trail is continuously marked along its length with signs reading PRITCHETT ARCH, but signs disappear when stolen. The trail surface is sand, bedrock, and loose and hard-packed sediments on a wide dirt road.

This trail is not covered in the main chapters in deference to all who hate sand, and to Moab Search and Rescue who say that this trail has become a real problem. Leave early! It's a long ride. If you don't mind the deep sand on this mostly flat wide dirt road, then go for it. Sometimes the sand can be packed quite hard, but most of the time it just sucks. At least the area is scenic and peaceful. Sometimes you can ride out here and never see another soul. Other times it can be crowded with 4WD traffic. Don't ride out here during Jeep Week at the end of April, unless you like to eat dust.

The Back of Behind area has been badly damaged by the 24 Hours of Moab Race that takes place in mid-October. This damage can be seen on the flat area adjacent to private land that is currently being developed within 2 miles of the trailhead. This spot is used as the race staging area, and vegetation is now sparse. You can see myriad bike tracks heading out in every direction across what used to be cryptobiotic soil crusts and cacti. More damage can be seen just off the trail around Prostitute Butte, the dominant sandstone feature on the first few miles of the trail.

The point-to-point ride options to town via Pritchett Canyon or Hunter Canyon Rim are scenic and challenging, with Pritchett Canyon being the more difficult of the two. The halfway point for the long out-and-back on the Back of Behind Trail is Pritchett Arch. It is here that you can opt to continue down Pritchett Canyon for a point-to-point route and a technically difficult 7-mile end to your ride, or you can take Hunter Canyon rim to the portage down to Kane Springs Road. See the Pritchett to Hunter Rim chapter (see Ride 22) to view the options from Pritchett Arch. The Latitude 40° Moab East and West maps document this area nicely. Be sure to take a map, bike computer, compass, and cell phone if you have one.

○ Kane Springs Canyon

Interesting ride, especially in the heat of late spring. I did not include it in the chapters because it's sandy as hell, brutal on equipment, and a tad too long. It also includes about 5 miles of pavement that turns me off at the end of a ride. It's a 25-mile-long point-to-point that ends in Moab and starts from the trailhead 15.1 miles south on U.S. Route 191 from Center and Main Streets in Moab. If you do this as an out-

and-back, just know it is going to be a lot harder on the way back. The really hard stuff happens at the start, then it just gets sandy, and sometimes the creekbed is really torn up. You first have to negotiate the streambed—over babyheads in a foot of streaming water for over 0.5 mile. It gets really technical and vertical, throws you a singletrack across a very dangerous bridge as an unnecessary diversion that is hard to resist, then it just gets sandy as hell. Follow the canyon down. You'll have many breaks from the sand, but it always returns. At the end of the ride, you come into Kane Springs Road, which takes you right back to Moab. The Latitude 40° Moab East and West maps work like a charm for this ride. Don't ride it without them.

Warning! Flash floods happen here.

D Lockhart Basin

This 40-plus-mile point-to-point ride from Indian Creek Ranch to Hurrah Pass requires a shuttle. It can be done as a long day ride or as a two- or three-day desert camping trip. The riding surface is rock-studded hardpack and sand on two-lane roads and a 4WD track. It is technically and physically difficult and is not listed in the chapters because of long stretches on mostly deep sand. This trail takes you along the plateau above the Colorado opposite the White Rim Trail. Also known as "the poor man's White Rim Trail" or "the poor man's Canyonlands," it is accessed utilizing the directions provided in the Colorado River Overlook Trail chapter (see Ride 30). The trailhead is prior to the entrance to the Needles District of Canyonlands National Park. The unmarked trailhead is Utah Route 211, 29 miles from the intersection of US 191 and UT 211, on the right-hand side of the road. It is recognized by the cattle guard at its entrance. Drive in a way and park in an appropriate place.

The alternate route is in reverse. Take Kane Creek Road from Moab to Hurrah Pass and down the other side. Park your 4WD vehicle somewhere down near the river. Head out past the right-hand spur to Chicken Corners. Hunker down, because this is going to be a long ride to the pickup point at Indian Creek. This direction is more difficult due to slightly more elevation gain. Gather as many maps as you can and study the hell out of them. It is a long ride and cannot be fully sagged with standard 4WD vehicles. There is one point in the middle of the ride where SUVs just get torn up.

An easy-to-read map that includes Lockhart Basin can be had by purchasing F. H. Barnes's *Mountain Bike Challenge Route Map* (Canyon Country Publications). This map contains basic instructions for riding the Challenge Route, a huge loop that travels up Kane Springs Canyon, through Canyon Rims Recreation Area and the Needles District of Canyonlands National Park, and back to Moab via Lockhart Basin. The Lockhart Basin route should not be taken lightly. Plan your trip well. Cell phones don't work out there.

E Confluence Overlook

This very difficult 14.5-mile loop follows a demon of a 4WD track from Elephant Hill to Devil's Lane then out to an overlook where the mighty Green and Colorado Rivers join in the Needles District of Canyonlands National Park. The surface is rock ledges, loose rock, bedrock, and a lot of deep, deep sand. From nearby the overlook the more adventurous can hike 800 feet down to the confluence where the waters of the Green and Colorado Rivers mix and churn into . . . what else? Brown.

This trail did not make it into the coverage because of its difficulty. Unlike the Colorado River Overlook ride nearby, it is a pretty challenging ride. There are much better challenging rides nearer to Moab for all but the most jaded Moab addicts, so why bother driving two hours just to ride in sand? Granted, it is a beautiful area and worthy of a visit if you are the sight-seeing kind of hardcore mountain biker. You can run out of easy rides here in a hurry, though—hence the inclusion of the Colorado River Overlook ride and the omission of the Confluence.

Good maps are available from Trails Illustrated and can be found at the Needles visitor center, where you can also get all the information you need to do this ride. Go south from Moab on U.S. Route 191 for about 40 miles. Turn right at Church Rock. You cannot miss it. It looks like a big cartoon breast. Turn onto Utah Route 211. At mile 32.8 from the intersection of US 191 and UT 211 is the right turn to the Needles Outpost, where you can buy gas and snacks if need be. At mile 33.8 is the Needles visitor center.

Moab East and Southeast

The trails listed here are east of U.S. Route 191 and south of Utah Route 128 and the Colorado River. This includes the Sand Flats area, the La Sal Mountains, and the mesas above Moab Valley. It is in this section that you will find the famous Moab Slickrock Trail, the Porcupine Rim Trail, mountain singletrack, and a couple of downhill alpine rides from high altitude.

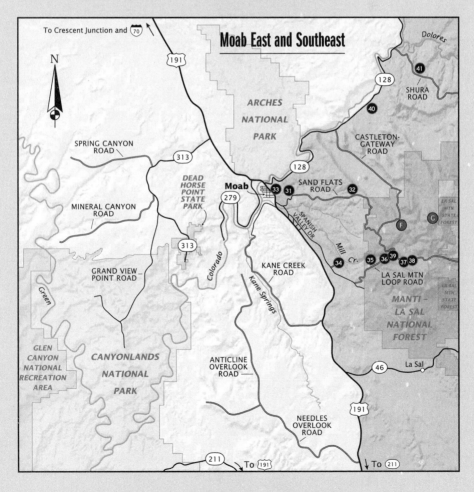

Moab East and Southeast

To Crescent Junction and 70

N

191

Dolores

128

41

SHURA ROAD

ARCHES NATIONAL PARK

40

CASTLETON-GATEWAY ROAD

SPRING CANYON ROAD

313

128

DEAD HORSE POINT STATE PARK

Moab

279

33 31

SAND FLATS ROAD

32

LA SAL MTN STATE FOREST

MINERAL CANYON ROAD

SPANISH VALLEY DR.

Mill Cr.

F

G

313

Colorado

KANE CREEK ROAD

34

35 36 39 37 38

LA SAL MTN LOOP ROAD

GRAND VIEW POINT ROAD

Green

Kane Springs

LA SAL MTN STATE FOREST

MANTI – LA SAL NATIONAL FOREST

GLEN CANYON NATIONAL RECREATION AREA

CANYONLANDS NATIONAL PARK

ANTICLINE OVERLOOK ROAD

46

La Sal

191

NEEDLES OVERLOOK ROAD

211

To 191

To 211

The La Sal Mountains are the second youngest range on earth, and as a result they are steep. Almost all the trails in this range are extremely difficult, and a great many are impossible on a mountain bike. There are restricted trails, designated by the Forest Service as off limits to mountain bikes, so pay attention. Hiking is awesome in the La Sals, and so is backcountry and cross-country skiing, but avalanche danger is extreme in most of the high country during snow season. Camping on the eastern slope of the mountains above Castle Valley is still a relatively private affair.

Sorry to sound like a broken record, but the roads and trails in the La Sals are impassable when wet.

Surfing the Rock

I t was 1983. Moab's mayor, Tom Stocks, was walking down Main Street when he encountered Robin Groff wrapped in bloody bandages from his head to his knees. Before Tom could ask what happened, Rob said, "Hey man, I found the best thing to do!"

Robin had discovered bicycling on the Moab Slickrock Trail, a desolate loop across the Navajo sandstone formation marked with white dashes to create the most challenging course possible for local hardcore motocrossers. Dick Wilson and friends Fred Radcliff and Tex McClatchy were the earliest riders on the area that now contains the Moab Slickrock Trail. With encouragement from his friends, Wilson approached the BLM in 1968 with the idea of marking a route out on this barren slickrock area just east of Moab. The trail was laid out and completed in 1969 by Wilson, who scouted and marked the trail on a Honda 90. Wilson also named many of the features and points of interest on the trail such as Shrimp Rock, Panorama Viewpoint, Updraft Arch, Echo Point, Abyss Viewpoint, and Swiss Cheese Ridge. Below the trail, in the abyss that is a side canyon of the larger Negro Bill Canyon, Wilson named Morning Glory Bridge after the pool below it that he thought resembled one in Yellowstone National Park, called, you guessed it, Morning Glory.

Slick rock? Nothing could be farther from the truth. This smooth sandstone surface got the name *slickrock* from cowboys who walked across it on leather soles or tried to ride across it on a horse with iron shoes. The rock is constantly eroding, leaving tiny grains of sand on the surface that act like ball bearings when stepped on by a cowboy boot, but nothing offers a mountain bike tire as much traction as slickrock, unless the rock is wet or frozen. The lichens on the rock surface can freeze into a very unique form of "black ice" that ain't black.

Kevin Dwyer shows off for the camera.

Twenty years after Robin Groff scuffed himself up for the first time, Moab has become home to a crazy breed of mountain bikers—bike surfers. As owners of Moab's premier bike shop, Rim Cyclery, Robin and his brother Bill have made a fortune off mountain biking. They gained weight, bought real estate, and now ride Harleys and fly airplanes. Their business card reads, "Rob'em and Bill'em." These guys are Moab. You can believe the card. New kids have claimed the rock, but because of folks like Rob and Bill, these kids, raised on BMX half-pipes and mari-juana, flock here year after year to test their skills and parents' health insurance providers.

Stunt specialist Nate Toone

31 Moab Slickrock Trail

Start: From the Moab Slickrock Trail parking lot on Sand Flats Road.
Length: 12.5-mile circuit.
Approximate riding time: 1½ to 3-plus hours, depending on skills, fitness level, and time spent messing around.
Difficulty: Despite the fact that you see blue jeans and hardtails out here, this trail is technically very difficult to extremely dangerous. You shouldn't be out here unless you are an advanced rider. Physically very difficult to abusive.

Trail surface: Slickrock, obviously, with a painted white line guiding you into the most outrageous situations. At times it is like riding on the outside edge of a 300-foot-high basketball.
Lay of the land: Rolling knobs of Navajo sandstone, and sand pits.
Total climbing: 1,707 feet.
Land status: Bureau of Land Management (BLM) and Utah State Trust lands.
Other trail users: Hikers and motorcyclists.
Best seasons: Spring and fall.

Environmental concerns: Environment is not an issue on the trail, but cryptobiotic crusts abound just off it. Stay on the marked route.

Warning! The Moab Slickrock Trail is not a bike path. It is an extremely difficult route through an area of sandstone mounds and fins designed to offer the most challenge possible. It is peppered with areas of extremely dangerous vertical exposure. There is not a spot on the trail that is not "hard." Even the easy stuff is "hard." If you do not possess advanced bike-handling skills, do not attempt this trail unless you are prepared to push your bike most of the way and you have the sense to know when to dismount. If you are riding this trail, always wear a helmet, take lots of water, and be especially careful the first time you ride. Lighting strikes are especially prevalent on the Moab Slickrock Trail during thunderstorms. A strike can happen from a storm as far as 7 miles away, so if you see lightning in the distance, think twice about heading out onto the trail.

Getting there: From Moab: Go east on Center Street from Main. Where the road ends at 400 East, take a right. Go a few blocks, just past Dave's Corner Market, and turn left onto Mill Creek Road. A few blocks ahead the road will split at a stop sign. Go left and past the cemetery on Sand Flats Road. There will be signs pointing to the Moab Slickrock Trail all along the route. Go up the hill, then past the city dump on your right and the Lion's Back Campground on your left. (The Lion's Back is a notorious slickrock fin made famous when a woman lost control of her Chevy Blazer and plummeted from it into the ground below while cameras were rolling. Four-wheel drive visitation increased over 100 percent following the video's airing on national television.) After Lion's Back Campground follow the pavement uphill to the fee collection booth. Pay the money and continue on to the parking lot just a couple of hundred yards past.

The Ride

Ahhh, the infamous Moab Slickrock Trail, the destination of many mountain bikers from around the world—the tourist trap to end all mountain biking tourist traps. In

Cruising over Fried Egg

summer bring lots of water, make sure your bike is in great working order, and spend some time on the practice loop to hone your skills before heading out on the main trail. Do not ride alone, but do not bring along your family or anyone you love who is not an advanced rider. Despite the fact that the trail is shown on the Discovery Channel for kids to drool over, it is extremely dangerous and parents should exercise extreme caution with children under eighteen (or over) who want to ride here. You could get them into serious trouble. If you take novice friends, you could lose them for good. If you subject them to this and they aren't ready for it, they should kick your ass and look for new pals. Again, this trail is *very* difficult and dangerous. I once saw a family riding out from the parking lot. Dad had a Schwinn Varsity, Junior had a banana-seat BMX with a single gear, and Mom had a twenty-year-old Taiwanese bike with a basket on the handlebars. I begged them not to do it, but they insisted they had come all the way from Arizona to ride this trail. Within ten minutes they were back at the trailhead, heading for the hospital. This is not fiction.

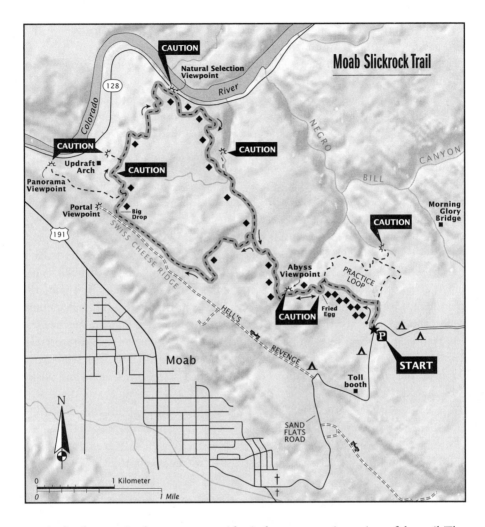

As for the practice loop, some consider it the most scenic section of the trail. The connotation of *practice loop* is somewhat misleading. It should be considered the first section of the figure-eight of the Slickrock Trail, though it is not part of the mileage count presented here. It is a great place for an evening hike or to find out that you shouldn't be riding the main trail. It is certainly the best way to start the first time you ride the trail.

The Slickrock Trail is *very* well marked with painted white lines like the middle of a highway, and there are yellow caution markers and black diamonds to warn you of deadly sections ahead. Be sure to watch for these warnings. Hills on the trail are short, but grueling and very steep. If you let your momentum carry you, it could get you into trouble on twisty sections with off-camber turns, but mostly it is momentum that will allow you to ride up the really steep stuff. Traction is fantastic, except when wet or icy. Watch out in winter!

Maps of this trail are practically useless, especially if you choose to ride off the trail and find yourself surrounded by vertical cliffs that drop into deep canyons. Stay on the marked trail at all costs. The maps contained in this guide are merely an attempt to give you an idea and cannot come close to re-creating the huge scale it takes to really show you what's up. I have omitted many of the cute names that locals have been given to pet sections of the trail, like Testosterone Poisoning, but you won't need to know them. Due to the convoluted nature of this relatively short trail, it is nearly impossible to expect a map to help. Rely on the markers. For this second edition I am answering requests for a more detailed description of the counter-clockwise "harder" direction.

Despite my pessimism about maps being of assistance when you first ride the area, once you have a grasp of the overwhelming variety of options and *freeform* areas, a map is a cool thing to have. Latitude 40° publishes a *Slickrock Bike Trail* map printed on an aerial photo that is about as accurate as you can find anywhere. It has all the hip names for all the technical sections like Faith in Friction and Bust a Move. It's hip. It's cool. It's as tacky as a black velvet painting. Each spot is rated by a numerical system that should give you some kind of idea as to whether you should attempt to ride through it or not. But honestly, once on the trail, these ratings are mostly useless. You will not want to be looking at a map, but it makes a cool souvenir to hang on the wall. You can pick up the aerial photo-map at the Moab Information Center or at the map store across from the information center at Center and Main Streets, next to the *Times Independent* building.

If you want skills tips, read Slickrock Riding Skills following this ride. If you are an experienced mountain biker with advanced skills, a guide who knows the entire area can turn you on to places like Swiss Cheese Ridge, Hell's Revenge, and Fins and Things. This is a special treat for a very small percentage of riders.

Miles and Directions

0.0   **START** by heading north out of the parking lot and through the cattle guard. Read sign at the trailhead. It ain't kiddin'.

0.3   This is the practice loop, a miniture Slickrock Trail with examples of the challenges to follow. The practice loop is 2.3 miles long in its entirety, but reconnects to the main trail at

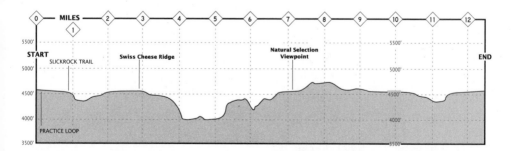

The beginning of the loop. This is where you choose. Harder is actually easier . . . to me, anyway.

mile 0.8 of this description. The practice loop is quite scenic and can make a really great hike if you are here with a family.

0.5   Get ready for some sand.

0.8   Go left. The practice loop reconnects here.

0.9   First real move (short steep climb). For best results, gather momentum, start on the left of the trail and cut right as momemtum wanes. Things go down. Unclip your uphill pedal (right) to help balance.

1.2   Bottom of hill (slow).

1.3   Caution. Sidehill can be dangerous. Unclip your left foot, just in case. Dismount, *before the exposure,* if you get the "willies."

1.4   End of Negro Bill Canyon. No short cuts!

1.5   Rock drop into sand pit. Go left under the tree for the most consistent line. Sometimes there are more lines here, sometimes there may be only one. Get a good look before you tackle it the first time. See the ledge on the opposite side of the wash? Once you get in the sand, aim at the ledge where it is most traveled.

1.6   Top of the first big hill. Go right for the best line. There is more climbing coming.

1.9   Top of the hill.

2.5   Gap with water holes.

2.5   Choose your direction for navigating the main loop. Left is considered slightly less diffi-cult, but leads you right into the most difficult sections of trail on the entire ride. We are now following the left direction. This left route tends to be more scenic due to the direc-tion you are facing during the ride. Of course you could always turn around and look behind you, but believe me, you will not be turning around and looking back. If you are on your bike, keep your eyes on the trail ahead. **Option:** Directions are given for the loop going counterclockwise following these directions.

3.5   You are skirting Swiss Cheese Ridge. Some really great stuff is right off the trail. Be very careful out here if you choose to play. Stay aware of the trail and always scout out a sec-tion before you grab it.

4.6   The drop off of Swiss Cheese.

4.8   The Panorama Viewpoint option is to your left. If you want to add a bit of mileage to an overlook, this is a great place to do it. Otherwise, go straight. This mileage count does not include distance to overlooks.

5.5   Another viewpoint option.

6.1   Get ready for some sand.

7.2   Natural Selection Viewpoint overlooks the Colorado River. You can see the Porcupine Rim Trail from this spot as it drops down to the river to the east. This is a great place to soak in the magic of canyon country, but it's also a great place to die and make a mess on the highway below.

7.5   My favorite sand spot on the Slickrock Trail. Try to make it through.

8.7   Ice Box Canyon overlook is an option at this point.

9.0   More sand is coming up.

10.2   The trail loop closes here. Take a left. You will now retrace the trail to the parking area.

10.6   Sand pit.

10.7   Sidehill. Click out of right pedal.

10.8   Start of a very tricky climb.

11.7   Practice loop goes left.

12.2   Practice loop returns on your left. Go right back to the trailhead.

12.5   Arrive back at the parking lot.

(Note: By special request of readers, I am including this mileage count and description of the Moab Slickrock Trail for more experienced riders. It follows the more difficult counterclockwise direction, meaning that most of the climbing is at the end of the ride, when lesser riders are beat. This direction will get you out to Shrimp Rock quickly and features the best downhill run of the entire ride, in either direction. Mileage counts from your computer may vary from this account.)

0.0   Parking lot.

0.3   Practice loop goes right. Go left.

Below Shrimp Rock

0.8 Practice loop comes in from right. Go left.

2.5 Here is where we choose the harder route. Go right. (2.05)

2.6 There is a nice little bowl on your right to play in.

2.8 Another sand pit. A big one. After this pit you are going to be treated to some tight rollers.

3.2 At the bottom of this little ledge, on your right, is a rare spot that is quite nice in summertime. *Shade.*

3.4 Another sharp climb. After this, watch for the newly painted dots off to your right on a descent as you approach Shrimp Rock. It is hard to spot in this direction, but can suck you in coming the other way. It takes you into a short loop wth a visit to a viewpoint over the right-hand fork of Negro Bill Canyon. Dropping into the wide chute within the first few yards is worth the detour. Mileage to the viewpoint is not included. It is a *short* loop.

3.9 Welcome to Shrimp Rock and a very nice view of the Colorado River Gorge.

4.6 Another nice view of the Colorado River Gorge amidst the rollers.

5.1 Nice short climb.

5.5 End of the sweet rollers.

7.2 Go right to the viewpoint. Markers for these older detours are being allowed to fade, so be careful.

7.6 Top of the *big climb.*

7.9 Another old viewpoint. Go left for main trail. Go right for the view, but be careful.

8.1 Top of Swiss Cheese Ridge.

8.2 A particularly nice view of Moab and the Moab Valley.

8.8 A steep downhill happens at the end of this huge fin.

8.9 End of the steep downhill.

9.2 Here is some more rare *shade.*

9.6 If you need first aid in a hurry, someone can follow the Hell's Revenge Jeep Trail to your right (see the little fire markers) to get help. It finally bails down a huge fin to the Sand Flat entrance booth where you will find help in peak season. Don't count on help during slower winter months.

10.2 End of the loop.

11.7 Practice loop goes left.

12.3 Practice loop returns on your left. Go right back to the trailhead.

12.5 Parking lot.

Ride Information

Trail Contacts

Sand Flats Team, Moab Bike Patrol
c/o Bureau of Land Management
82 E. Dogwood
Moab, UT 84532
(435) 259–2196
Utah State School and Institutional Trust Lands Administration
1165 South US 191, Ste. 5
Moab, UT 84532
(435) 259–3760
(practice loop)

Schedule

Trail is open year-round but is best during spring and fall. Avoid this trail during stormy weather or during winters when ice remains on the northern-facing slopes.

Fees and Permits

A season pass that gives you access to Sand Flats Recreation Area is currently $20.00. Weekly passes and camping permits are available for less. Rates go up every year, so I hesitate to quote prices.

Maps

USGS maps: Moab
Slickrock Bike Trail Map by Latitude 40° Inc.
Moab East Trail Map by Latitude 40° Inc.
Moab Recreation Map by F. H. Barnes

BAYONET YUCCA *(Yucca glauca)*

There are quite a few varieties of the yucca plant in the Southwest, but the dominant species around Moab is referred to as the bayonet. As its name implies, it possesses leaves shaped like an array of bayonets. Actually, modern bayonets have a knifelike bladed shape. The Geneva Convention banned the original triangular bayonet blade that most resembles the yucca shaft after the First World War. The triangular bayonet was designed to create an open wound that would guarantee that the victim would die from blood loss in a short amount of time. The bayonet yucca does not conform to the Geneva Convention, however. If you fall hard enough onto a yucca plant, you will end up with multiple wounds that bleed like crazy. Yucca lines many of the trails around Moab, and if your leg comes into contact with one, you will be hurting. A couple of years ago, a fellow was found dead out in the Hurrah Pass area. He was riding alone off the trail, went over the bars, and landed on a yucca plant. The yucca pierced his neck and he bled to death in a matter of minutes.

Though it is certainly true that the yucca is dangerous and grows prolifically throughout southeastern Utah, it is far from being a pest. Early Pueblan peoples who inhabited this area 1,000 years ago used fibers of the yucca leaf to weave clothing and shoes. Its roots are edible, as are its flowers and fruit. It has many medicinal qualities and can be one of the most beautiful plants in the desert even when it's not blooming. It grows in sandy soils and on dunes. Its flowers are pale yellow to off white, bell shaped with three petals, and grow in a crowded tower array from a central stalk.

In Addition

Slickrock Riding Skills

Slickrock riding is to biking like body surfing is to swimming. Swimming will get you out to the waves, but once you are in the break you'll have to exercise a new set of skills. If you are a half-pipe kid, you have found your natural element, though the rock is not as forgiving as the half-pipes and dirt berms and jumps you are used to. If you haven't tried this kind of thing, try the small waves first, then work your way up to the big stuff. At Bartlett Wash and in spots along the Moab Slickrock Trail, bowls and steepening slots, fins and fingers of every size are available to you. I hesitate to say that Bartlett Wash is a good training ground, because it is so far from help if you get hurt, but it is certainly a lot easier to navigate. You can easily get lost on the Moab Slickrock Trail if you are searching for places to play. In both areas there are shallow, gentle bowls, and scary deep, steep things ending with a drop of 100 feet that can maim or kill you. Learning the skills necessary to perform fancy maneuvers in this environment can cost you dearly, so take your time.

Start of the big climb out

On slickrock it is possible to descend and ascend seemingly impossible grades. Riding slickrock is a strange combination of road, BMX, skateboard, and surfing skills. Where you put your weight on the bike is always important, but nowhere more so than on this constantly changing surface. It's all about balance: weight balance and weight shifts. Braking balance and switching from front to rear. Balancing speed with control.

The most common mistakes are using the rear brake too much and/or not weighting the back of the bike in order for the rear tire to bite adequately. Skid marks on slickrock are there because of uneven braking. If you hear the telltale scuffle of your rear tire breaking loose, you are not using your brakes and weight shifts correctly. Get used to using the front brake more than you ever have before. Practice extending your arms and scooting your butt way back behind the saddle so that your rear brake grabs even with the front. Try to wipe your butt with your rear tire. Put your chest on the saddle and ride around a bit.

On very steep grades your butt should almost touch the rear tire. Your arms should be completely extended. This will not only help to keep you from going over the bars—which is nowhere more unpleasant than on slickrock—but also allow you to stop on a steep downslope. The consequences of not learning this skill are not pretty, especially if there is any sort of ledge drop-off in the middle of the slope.

When going up steep, smooth rock, get your weight as far forward as possible to weight the front wheel and keep it firmly on the ground. Traction is usually sufficient for you to lean over the handlebars and kiss the front tire. If you have just traveled through wet sand and have collected a bit of the damp, gritty stuff on your tires, you'll definitely have a problem, but when the weather is dry and the slickrock free of debris, you'll be surprised at how well the rear tire grabs. The only limitations are your balancing skills, strength, and the bike's gearing. Certain tire compounds may be less effective. Soft rubber works best.

Sidehilling is another slickrock skill that requires great concentration, trust, and courage. Traversing off-camber slopes and turns requires extreme concentration in order to attack the hill at the correct angle to maintain momentum. If the hill is very steep, you may not be unable to rotate the cranks, so momentum is your friend. You must trust the bike's ability to maintain traction while cutting across steep slopes. It is in this particular situation that soft, slick tires become a tremendous advantage. A "slick" inflated to medium pressure (thirty to forty pounds) offers a large contact patch on the smooth rock, but too little air pressure and the tire may roll off the rim in a fast, tight turn.

Effectively riding slickrock bowls requires that you combine the downhill braking and uphill power skills with sidehill techniques, all held together with precise weight shifts. When you drop into a bowl and shoot up the other side, you'll be using the final bit of inertia to make a banked turn at the top in order to rocket down and back up again. If you have watched BMX half-pipe action, you have some understanding of just what I mean. This trick is best witnessed before you attempt it. Timing a turn at the very peak of your fading upward momentum is a trick that should be practiced in small bowls with gentle slopes before you attack the near-vertical sides of the big surf. If you don't maintain momentum, you'll discover instant fear as the bike falls down the hill with you on board. This is where body armor is a necessity!

It is all-important to avoid "solution pockets"—the holes in the sides of sloped sandstone. Solution pockets are formed by water seeping through porous sandstone, emerging from the sides of the stone hill in areas where the rock is less dense. This causes a specific kind of erosion that also forms the beautiful sandstone arches of canyon country. Some of these pits are caused by concretions of sandstone that drop out of the surrounding sandstone, leaving a cavity (see Concretions in Sandstone and Rock Varnish in Ride 3, Klondike Bluffs and Solutions Pockets in Ride 8, Bartlett Wash). No matter the reason for their existence, solution pockets are really dangerous to a sidehilling mountain biker. If you come into contact with a pocket, your tire loses grip, momentarily sending you sliding down the hill. Welcome to road rash, or, if you are on an exposed section, welcome to the afterlife.

Learning advanced slickrock surfing skills usually demands that you make mistakes—and those mistakes can be costly. Personally, I never try something that I am not absolutely positive I can pull off. The older you get, the more slowly things heal, so I leave the truly insane behavior to those half my age. I watch the "whippersnappers." If they survive, then maybe I'll do it. Just maybe. At my age I have little to prove, except that I can survive the ride.

Just before Shrimp Rock

Good Days, Bad Days, Luck, and Skill

A lot of people ride the Porcupine Rim, especially since it was rated by a couple of the big-name bike magazines as the best ride in Moab. The word got out. Yes, this trail is incredible, scenic, technically challenging, dangerous, badly crowded, and one of the best mountain bike rides anywhere. What is also true is that drawing mountain bikers to Porcupine Rim is an effective form of natural selection. Telling someone who "mountain bikes" that the Porcupine Rim is a great ride is like telling someone who "swims" to dog-paddle into 10-foot surf and ride the waves in. For anyone but advanced cyclists, this trail is Russian roulette on wheels. Freeride full-suspension rules on Porcupine Rim.

A year ago a fellow crashed really bad on the Porcupine Rim. The Life Flight helicopter refused to land anywhere near him due to the rugged terrain and windy conditions. He survived, but nearly bled to death from internal injuries while being carried out on a stretcher. He was lucky. In the summer of 1995 a couple of teenage boys got lost by taking what appeared to be a dominant spur of the Porcupine Rim Trail. Once they resolved themselves to being hopelessly lost and out of water, they decided to hide their bikes and try to hike down to water visible in Negro Bill Canyon below them. This turned out to be impossible. They then sought shelter from the sun under a rock. Because a couple of thieves stole their bikes from the spot they'd left them, it took Search and Rescue two weeks to find the bodies. These fellows were unlucky.

The view of Porcupine Rim looking toward the La Sals

32 Porcupine Rim

Start: From the marked Porcupine Rim Trail-head at mile marker 7 on the Sand Flats Road. Just to the left of two cattle drinking tanks, the trail cuts around the side of a hill above a deep canyon.

Length: 14.8-mile point-to-point (20-mile point-to-point if you continue on to Center and Main in Moab).

Approximate riding time: 1½ to 5 hours, depending on your skills, pent-up anger, and sight-seeing interests.

Difficulty: Technically very difficult to abusive due to sharp ledges, jackhammer jagged rock, and rough terrain on a narrow singletrack on the edge of a cliff. Physically difficult due to

the initial climb and the energy necessary to negotiate the technical challenges.

Trail surface: Technical 4WD road and single-track. Jackhammer bedrock, ledges, loose rock sediments, sand, and cliffs.

Lay of the land: Difficult climbing and fast descending. Surprises. The trail takes you up the backside of the rim and dumps you out onto a spectacular view of Castle Valley. Classic American southwestern buttes and mesas.

Total climbing: 1,287 feet.

Land status: Bureau of Land Management (BLM) and Utah State Trust lands.

Other trail users: Hikers, 4WDs, and people pushing mountain bikes.

Best seasons: Spring and fall.

Environmental concerns: Fragile cryptobiotic soil crusts abound off the trail. Wildlife consists of mountain lions, bobcats, coyotes, desert bighorn sheep, and all the other cool folks who live here. Parts of this area may be lost to mountain bikers due to pending legislation. Fight for access by exercising low-impact riding. Stay on the trail. Have respect. Be quiet.

Getting there: From Moab: Go east on Center Street from Main Street (U.S. Route 191). Go right at 400 East, then left at Mill Creek, and then left at Sand Flats Road. Head out past the Moab Slickrock Bike Trail parking lot on Sand Flats Road to mile marker 7. You will see a couple of cattle watering tanks across from the marker in the parking area. Park here and disembark. The trailhead is across the road from the parking lot.

Shuttle Point: From Moab: Go north on US 191 for 2.6 miles to the intersection with Utah Route 128 and travel 3 miles to Negro Bill Canyon. Fifty yards or so past the Negro Bill Canyon parking area is a pullout on the left. Park here.

The Ride

Parts of the Porcupine Rim are in danger of being turned into a Wilderness Study Area through efforts by an "environmental" group called the Southern Utah Wilderness Alliance (SUWA). This will mean no more mountain biking onto side spurs if the legislation they seek is signed. I'm a tree hugger, even worked for the Sierra Club at one point, but listen to how this kind of thing happens: The mountain bike mags find out about a great ride and publicize the hell out of it. Mountain bikers flock to the trailhead. A woman crash-dives her family off Lion's Back in the family Chevy Blazer on national television. The four-wheelers flock to the trailhead. The BLM

The Porcupine Rim singletrack drops down to the Colorado River—Slickrock Trail in the background.

and the state improve the roads into the Porcupine Rim area so that you can drive a Lincoln up to the trailhead, set up a bunch of camping spots and an organization called the Sand Flats Team, and charge money. They call it "management." All this commotion brings a bunch of other folks into the area who would normally be offended by the rednecks and the sand and the difficult road. And then the BLM calls it "overused." SUWA comes in and bleeds on everybody about "wilderness" being "spoiled," and then they lobby their asses off to get legislation to keep us from using a man-powered vehicle, that is basically a "hiking accessory," on public lands.

And what do we get?

A bunch of folks, all well intentioned, screwing up a beautiful place for everybody.

The trail you will be on, like most Moab trails, was originally a prospecting road that evolved into a hardcore jeeper track, then into a mountain bike trail. Thank God for the Cold War.

The featured route here is performed by being dropped off at the trailhead and leaving a shuttle vehicle at the mouth of Negro Bill Canyon on UT 128. You can make it longer by adding the Sand Flats Road ride mentioned in Ride 33, or by riding from

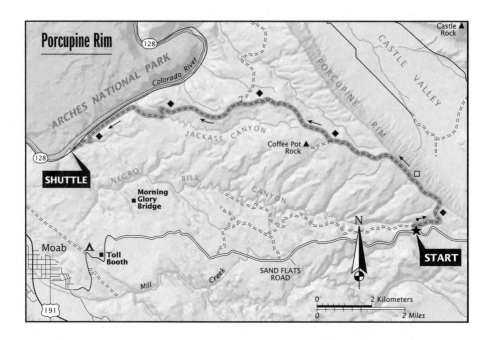

the trail tail to Moab on UT 128. Vertical exposure and increasingly difficult rock gardens with undulating and sheared bedrock shelves jutting out at every angle make this trail a bone snapper, a heartbreaker, and a hell of a great ride. This is not a ride you take your girlfriend on, unless she can shred. A biff could mean anything from a chipped tooth to a wandering soul. The worst thing about this ride is that it is sadly overcrowded, especially on weekends in the spring and fall. I once found an abandoned bike on this trail, hanging off the cliff edge. I looked over the edge and, for all I knew, there could have been *ten* bodies in the gigantic field of jagged rocks below.

For those of us who love to abuse our bodies and equipment, this trail is perfect and includes one of the very few singletracks in the area. This trail is not only so technical it kills people, but also stunningly beautiful. Overlooks of Castle Valley, the La Sal Mountains, Jackass Canyon, the Colorado River Gorge, and Moab Rim come and go as the trail bobs and weaves and punches you repeatedly.

Currently the trail is well marked, but who knows what it will be like when you ride it? I have tried to be as meticulous as possible in describing this route, even though 90 percent was plainly marked the last time I rode it. The other 10 percent of the ride could be a problem, so maybe this mileage count will reassure you, even save you from a bad day. There are a number of spurs that separate from the main trail then rejoin farther along. Always take the predominant spur with the most bike tracks. Make sure that your bike is in perfect running order and the frame in good condition before you begin the ride. In a couple of miles, stop and check your bike. Look at the bolts. Are they backing out? Look at your wheels. Are they true? Is your headset loose? Is your head still on?

Miles and Directions

0.0 **START** from the Porcupine Rim Trailhead. There are cattle tanks on the right and a deep canyon on the left. The trail is on the left side of Sand Flats Road. You will be introduced to the Porcupine Rim deal right away as the bedrock slopes up then sort of comes apart every now and then. Get used to it. Practice riding up those ledges.

2.4 This is the first in a series of splits in the trail that reconnect farther on.

2.7 Same deal.

2.9 Same deal.

3.0 Tired of climbing? Well, here's your chance to go down, but watch what's around those corners, and don't miss this . . .

3.1 Head's up! Take a right here to visit the first in a series of amazing views of Castle Valley and the La Sal Mountains.

3.8 Same deal. Another viewpoint on right.

3.9 Same deal. Another couple of viewpoints like this will appear ahead.

4.5 Another split in the trail that will return.

4.6 You are leaving the rim. Ahead is a long straightaway.

5.1 There's a great view of Moab Rim from the top of this little hill.

5.15 Go straight through this intersection.

5.3 Welcome to the Jackhammer!

5.4 Go right, avoiding the old spur straight ahead.

6.2 A bit of sand for you.

6.6 Go right at the Y in the trail.

7.7 Avoid the old spur to the right. Bear left.

8.1 Another closed spur to the right. Don't go there. Go left.

8.5 Go straight.

8.55 Go left at the Y.

9.1 Go left at the Y.

9.15 Go left at the Y.

9.9 and mile **10.1** are where you'll find two great jumps. Ride down them first to check them out, and then go back and launch, if this is your kind of thing.

10.4 There's a great view of the trail ahead and below to your left from this ridge.

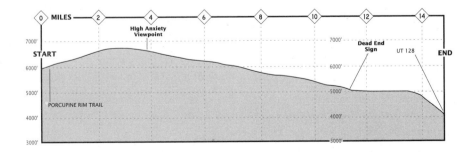

Singletrack on the edge above the Colorado River and UT 128

10.6 Cross this bedrock shelf and reconnect with the trail directly on the other side. This spot is usually marked with cairns, but cairns sometimes get taken down.

10.7 Go left at the Y.

11.5 Go right at the Y. This is the spot where the lost boys lost their way. The left-hand spur now bears a sign that reads DEAD END.

12.2 Colorado River and UT 128 are below in the distance.

14.3 You are now at the apex of a loop around the back of a small box canyon.

14.8 Pavement. UT 128. Your shuttle. **Option.** If you want to add 5 miles of pavement and head back to town, go left for 3 miles to connect with US 191, where you'll go left and ride another 2 miles into Moab. Watch out for the big trucks. Keep far right on the highway.

Ride Information

Trail Contacts

Moab Bike Patrol
c/o Bureau of Land Management
82 E. Dogwood, Moab, UT 84532
(435) 259-2196

Utah State School and Institutional Trust Lands Administration
1165 South US 191, Ste. 5
Moab, UT 84532
(435) 259-3760

Fees and Permits

A season pass that gives you access to Sand Flats Recreation Area is currently $20.00.

Weekly passes and camping permits are available for less. Rates go up every year, so I hesitate to quote prices.

Schedule

Trail is open year-round but is best during spring and fall.

Maps

USGS maps: Rill Creek, Moab
Moab West Trail Map by Latitude 40° Inc.
Moab Recreation Map by F. H. Barnes

33 Sand Flats Kokopelli

Start: From the intersection of Center and Main Streets in Moab.

Length: 38.7-mile "lollipop."

Approximate riding time: 4 to 6 hours.

Difficulty: Technically easy to moderate to extremely difficult. Sand Flats Road is an easy, well-maintained road up to Porcupine Rim Trailhead. From there it becomes moderately technical. If you opt for the "lollipop" loop, the left-hand (eastern) side of the loop is extremely ledgy and dangerous. Physically difficult due to distance.

Trail surface: The road surface is paved to just past the Moab Slickrock Bike Trail parking lot, then turns to gravel, hardpack, loose rocks, and sand. The backside of the lollipop has technical rock ledges and some exposure.

Lay of the land: Sand Flats is a tilted plateau that gradually takes you from the subdesert black bush, piñon, and juniper to the alpine terrain at higher altitude. The backside of the loop is dramatic.

Total climbing: 5,310 feet.

Land status: Bureau of Land Management (BLM) and national forest land.

Other trail users: Off-road vehicles (ORV).

Best seasons: Spring and fall.

Environmental concerns: Stay on the road and everything will be just fine. Cryptobiotic soil crusts abound in the desert and at the higher elevations of this route.

Getting there: Start at the intersection of Center and Main Streets.

The Ride

The improvements to the Sand Flats area over the past five years have created a much safer and more environmentally sound management system, but have also created access problems that will fester and ooze over the next few years. The road used to be very rugged and could only be traversed by high-clearance 4WD vehicles. Now that the county, the BLM, and the Sand Flats Team have turned the area into a parklike setting and improved the road to allow 2WD vehicles up to the Porcupine Rim Trail, the area is becoming overused and the Southern Utah Wilderness Alliance is in the process of trying to close areas at the top of the road. This is how folks create their own problems in Moab.

The sandstone fins in this area are created by the effects of heat erosion and are *not* petrified sand dunes—a common misconception fostered by the Park Service's naming of the Navajo sandstone knobs. These fins and mounds are made up of desert sands, but their rounded shape is created by the effects of the sun. The sun heats the rocks and, like a radiator, the heat dissipates by traveling to outer edges and sharp points on the rock. These outer extremities deal with a lot of change in temperature, and the resulting fluctuations crack and erode the rock. As edges erode, the rock becomes more rounded, hence the shapes that only *look* like petrified sand dunes. This erosion, however, *makes* sand dunes.

Navajo sandstone formations in the Hanging Valley (also called Hidden Valley)

This ride, easily accessible from Moab, is perfect for fit novices and beginners if ridden as an out-and-back to the Porcupine Rim Trailhead—approximately an 18-mile round trip. But this route can also be a great distance climb with technical challenges at the top, followed by a ripping descent back to Moab. Drive in to the Slickrock Trail parking lot if you want to avoid the boring climb on pavement. Sand Flats Road is well maintained and easily affords use by 2WD traffic up to the Porcupine Rim Trailhead. The initial paved climb is a grunt, but once on top of the mesa the road levels out and rolls a bit, climbing steadily. The ride below the Porcupine Rim Trailhead is only steep in a couple of places. The 4WD track gets rougher past the Porcupine Rim Trailhead as it climbs steadily into the La Sal Mountains.

Once above Porcupine Rim the road rises through Rill Canyon, leaving the high-desert junipers and piñons for the lower alpine ponderosa stands. Surfaces become a little more interesting at the top with a few mild technical challenges. This route is a section of the Kokopelli Trail. The Kokopelli splits off from Sand Flats Road after entering the Manti–La Sal National Forest. Staying on Sand Flats Road

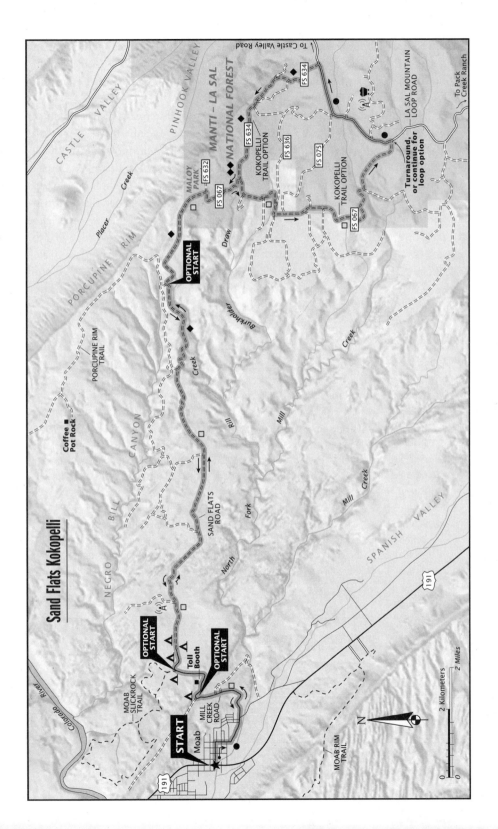

Sand Flats Kokopelli

CASTLE VALLEY

PINHOOK VALLEY

MANTI – LA SAL

NATIONAL FOREST

To Castle Valley Road

To Pack Creek Ranch

LA SAL MOUNTAIN LOOP ROAD

Turnaround, or continue for loop option

FS 634

FS 634

FS 636

FS 075

FS 067

KOKOPELLI TRAIL OPTION

KOKOPELLI TRAIL OPTION

FS 632

FS 067

MALOY PARK

Placer

Creek

Draw

Burkholder

PORCUPINE RIM

Coffee
Pot Rock ■

PORCUPINE RIM
TRAIL

OPTIONAL
START

Creek

Rill

Mill

Creek

NEGRO

BILL

CANYON

SAND FLATS ROAD

North

Fork

Mill

Creek

SPANISH VALLEY

Colorado
River

MOAB
SLICKROCK
TRAIL

OPTIONAL
START

Toll
Booth

OPTIONAL
START

MILL
CREEK ROAD

START

Moab

MOAB RIM
TRAIL

191

191

N

0   2 Miles

0   2 Kilometers

is less technical, but also allows for the loop ride documented here. Of course, at any point you're always presented with the option of returning downhill and zipping back to Moab or back to your car, parked at either the Moab Slickrock Trail parking lot or Porcupine Rim Trailhead.

Longer options are available to you when the trail intersects La Sal Mountain Loop Road. Taking a right onto La Sal Mountain Loop Road at the top will take you back down to Pack Creek Ranch on the pavement, then through Spanish Valley into town. Taking a left at the top will send you to the loop described here, or you can continue for a long road ride into Castle Valley to Utah Route 128 to return to Moab. This may be an attractive epic for hybrid-equipped distance riders or pannier crowd who love road riding as much as the trails and may want to experience camping on the backside of the La Sals. See Ride 39, Geyser Pass to Taylor Flat for mileage counts from the intersection of La Sal Mountain Road and Castleton Gateway Road (Castle Valley Road), as well as for suggestions for camping off Castleton Gateway. See the Family Version section in that chapter for the mileage into Castle Valley.

Miles and Directions

0.0 **START** from the intersection of Center and Main Streets. Ride east on Center Street to 400 East and take a right. Go a few blocks, just past Dave's Corner Market (on your left facing south), and take a left onto Mill Creek Road. There will be signs pointing to the Moab Slickrock Trail. Follow them. A few blocks ahead the road will split at a stop sign.

1.2 Go left onto Sand Flats Road toward the Moab Slickrock Trail. You'll pass a cemetery on your left and a recycling area on your right. This climb will certainly warm you up. You'll be required to pay a fee to enter the Sand Flat Recreation Area ahead. Carry Mr. Washington with you. It is $1.00 for a bike (may be more when you read this—prices are going up, so be safe and have Mr. Lincoln just in case).

8.7 To your left is Negro Bill Canyon, formerly known as Nigger Bill Canyon, soon to be referred to as African American William Canyon. Yes, the original name was Nigger Bill Canyon. By all historic accounts William Granstaff liked his name immensely. It is a sad fact that political correctness is taken to such lengths as to change a man's name. You will soon be able to make out the Porcupine Rim Jeep Trail below along the upper rim of "Negro" Bill Canyon.

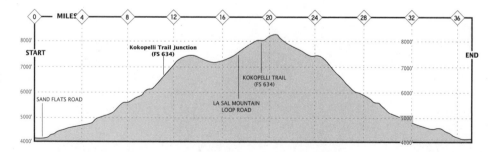

9.2 Go past the Porcupine Rim Trailhead and up through Rill Canyon. The trail becomes rough here and presents a bit more technical challenge, though never really requiring much more than momentum to overcome obstacles. Be sure to stop every now and again in order to take in the view behind and below you.

11.2 The spires to your right at the top of Rill Canyon may require pulling out the camera for a few pictures. From here the climb will steepen.

12.6 You are entering the Manti-La Sal National Forest, trading the high-desert junipers and piñons for the lower alpine ponderosa stands. Sand Flats Road, for those of you looking at maps, becomes a Forest Service road, FS 067.

13.2 When you crest this hill, the La Sals come into view. You are nearing the top.

13.9 The Kokopelli Trail (Forest Road 634) leaves Sand Flats Road at this point. You have three options here. **Option 1.** You can turn around and ride back down. **Option 2.** Take the Kokopelli Trail (FS 634) to the left and ride another 3.5 miles to La Sal Loop Road. Once there you can do the upper loop in reverse or head left to Castle Valley (a monster road ride). **Option 3.** Follow the route description below to continue on Sand Flats Road to La Sal Mountain Road (FS 067).

14.7 A private road spurs left. Stay right. There is a historic homesite up to your left.

15.2 Go left an the Y. Ahead the road travels through an open meadow and climbs to a cattle guard.

19.2 Come to the intersection with La Sal Mountain Loop Road (Forest Road 062). Turn around to ride back down or go left on pavement for this more technical loop ride back to point 13.9.

21.6 Take a left onto the Kokopelli Trail (FS 634) and for the Castle Valley Overlook. Stay on this route, avoiding spurs to the left. This section is a great deal more difficult than the rest of the ride, so beware. It gets really nasty in a couple of spots and hands you some vertical exposure. Look before you leap. The views from this section of the trail are the best of the ride.

24.8 Go right back onto Sand Flats Road (this is point 13.9 above) for the downhill back to Moab.

38.7 Center and Main in Moab.

Ride Information

Trail Contacts

Sand Flats Team, Moab Bike Patrol
c/o Bureau of Land Management
82 E. Dogwood
Moab, UT 84532
(435) 259-2196
Manti-La Sal National Forest
Moab Ranger District
2290 SW Resource Blvd.
Moab, UT 84532
(435) 259-7155

Fees and Permits

You have to pay to enter the Sand Flat Recreation Area, but at the time of this printing it was only $1.00. Come prepared to spend more, as the prices are going up.

Schedule

Trail is open year-round but is best during spring and fall.

Maps

USGS maps: Moab, Rill Canyon, Warner Lake
Moab East Trail Map by Latitude 40° Inc.
Moab Recreation Map by F. H. Barnes

34 Flat Pass

Start: From the cattle guard above Ken's Lake.

Length: 15.5-mile point-to-point, with an option to do the ride as a loop.

Approximate riding time: 2 to 4 hours (3½ to 5 hours as a loop).

Difficulty: Ledges and stream crossings, as well as babyheads make this ride technically difficult to extreme. Physically moderate to difficult. Distance is not a problem, but the technical challenges require strength and exertion.

Trail surface: Bedrock, loose rock, sand, and babyheads on a technical 4WD track, with substantial creek crossings. (Loop option contains paved and gravel roads.)

Lay of the land: Flat Pass ain't flat. The trail takes you onto a mesa, then drops into a deep gouge in Mama Earth above the Moab Valley, and then drops you down into town.

Total climbing: 1,947 feet.

Land status: Bureau of Land Management (BLM) and private land.

Other trail users: Hikers, equestrians, and off-road vehicles (ORV).

Best seasons: Late spring, summer, and early fall.

Environmental concerns: Fragile! Archaeological area. Don't take or destroy artifacts. Do not touch the petroglyphs. Oils on your hands cause them to fade. Fragile desert soils are everywhere just off the trail.

Getting there: From Moab: Go east on Center Street from Main (U.S. Route 191) to 400 East. Turn south (right) onto 400 East. Take a left onto Mill Creek Drive at Dave's Corner Market. Go past Sand Flats Road (signed way to Moab Slickrock Trail) and bear right at the stop sign onto Mill Creek Drive. Go past Murphy Lane. Take the next left onto Spanish Valley Drive and continue for another 7.5 miles. Take a left to Ken's Lake. From Ken's Lake, go up the gravel road to the cattle guard above the lake. You can park just before the cattle guard on the left side of the road.

Shuttle Point: Downtown Moab: Your ride will terminate at the intersection of Center and Main Streets. Follow the above directions to retrieve your start vehicle.

The Ride

The best way to do this ride is to hire a shuttle service or to get someone to drive you to the start of the ride. Doing the trail as a loop from town avoids the necessity of a fossil-fuel vehicle, but this means over 10 miles of painfully boring uphill road riding and the possibility of a nasty headwind. If you want to do the ride as a loop, simply use the directions on how to get to the trailhead. An optional route back to the trailhead from the end of the Flat Pass Trail is provided in the mileage count.

The ride is highlighted by vandalized petroglyphs, rolling hills with severe transitions at the bottom, and some very beautiful views of the Moab Valley. There are a couple of spots on the trail that can sneak up on you, so keep your eyes on the trail

Crossing Mill Creek on the Flat Pass Trail

and give blind turns and dips a lot of respect. As with any ride that has stream cross-ings, climb up in case of flash flooding. Watch the weather.

If you enjoy technical challenge, deep stream crossings, transitions, vertical ridges, gaps and pits, knee-high ledges, rollies, plateaus, babyheads, death-grip-jackhammer stuff into deep sand, weird sliced-bread bedrock, and a ride that can be done from Moab, then Flat Pass is the trail. It's a legendary 4WD track called the "Metal Bender" or some such four-wheeler cliché, but seldom sees consistent motorized traffic due to its difficulty. The five stream crossings can be deep and cold much of the year, but in the heat of the day in summer, so-o-o-o sweet. Remember to leave your shoes on to cross. The bed of the creek is slippery, and the current can be strong.

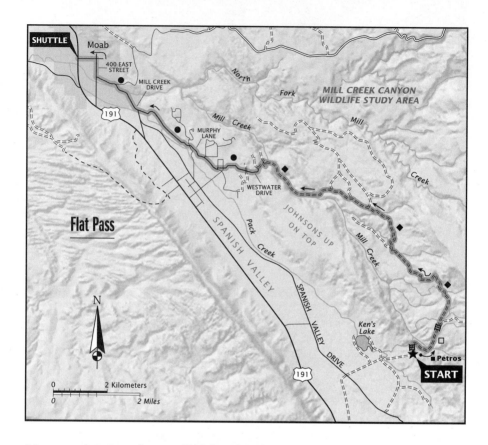

Not enough grip and you will definitely take a cool swim. Special note must be made to pay attention to trail markers at the junctions at miles 4.2 to 4.5. If you find yourself out on a sandy ridge and it gets even sandier, go back. It's a dead end. Most spurs in the trail simply loop out and eventually rejoin, but this one is a long road to a dead end and has been known to grab riders. You don't want to be out here during a thunderstorm, either!

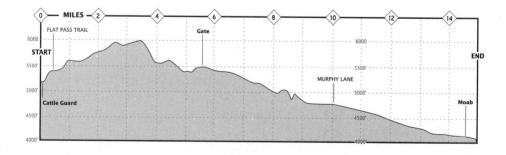

Slab rock at the beginning of the ride

Miles and Directions

0.0 **START** from the cattle guard next to the pullout and trail information sign. Ride onward across the cattle guard.

0.1 Go right at the trail marker and ride along the stream to your left.

0.5 Watch for the trail marker on your left that points back, downward, and across the stream. This stream crossing is your first taste of just how the water is going to be on any given day. If it is too high and there are storm clouds in the mountains, go back to Moab and have a beer or find another trail to ride. If it is cold, use good judgment. Once across this slippery crossing and up the sandy hill, the trail wastes no time in giving you the goods.

0.7 Beyond another cattle gate the trail continues to offer great moderate to difficult trials. Don't miss the opportunity to stop and look around.

2.1 Stay left.

2.4 Take either spur at the V. They reconnect.

2.5 Go right at this intersection after the gully G-out.

3.1 Stay right.

4.2 Be alert after this sandy stretch. Stay on the marked trail.

4.5 Go left on the unmarked spur at the Y, and then go right at the top of the hill.

5.0 Go right at the T.

5.4 There is a gate at the top of the hill. Go through it. From here on, the route is easily traced down into Mill Creek. Watch for the very technical hill sections with jackhammer rocks that will surprise you if you don't control your speed. Pay attention to the trail markers. After coming down the most technical rocky slope (you'll know the one), you will follow the creek on babyheads and sand. After crossing the creek a few times, you'll ride out across private land, so stay on the road to avoid trespassing. Go up the steep road to your left.

10.1 Go left on the pavement of Westwater Drive, and then continue, always downward, across Arena Roja and Canyonlands Circle. At Hills Drive, go left to Murphy Lane. A right onto Murphy will take you on a fast descent to Mill Creek Drive, and Mill Creek will take you back to 400 East. A right onto 400 East at Dave's Corner Market will take you to Center Street. A left onto Center will take you back to Main Street. It will be downhill almost all the way. Fast and very easy. **Option.** If you are doing the ride as a loop, go left onto Westwater Drive. Stay on Westwater for a mile, and then take a left onto Canyonlands Circle where it becomes Spanish Trail Road. Go another 0.5 mile on Spanish Trail Road and at the bottom of the hill turn left onto Spanish Valley Drive. Continue for another 3 miles and turn left onto the marked, paved road to Ken's Lake. Go another 2 miles to the trailhead at the cattle guard above Ken's Lake.

15.5 Arrive at the intersection of Center and Main Streets in Moab.

Ride Information

Trail Contacts

Moab Bike Patrol
c/o Bureau of Land Management
82 E. Dogwood
Moab, UT 84532
(435) 259–2196

Schedule

The trail is open year-round, but don't do it during winter. Best during late spring, late summer, and very early fall.

Maps

USGS maps: Kane Springs, Rill Creek
Moab East Trail Map by Latitude 40° Inc.
Moab Recreation Map by F. H. Barnes

35 Brumley Ridge

Start: From the turnout off La Sal Mountain Loop Road.

Length: 9.1-mile loop. (Ride the route in reverse if you are a downhiller.).

Approximate riding time: 2 to 4 hours.

Difficulty: There are a few spots on the trail where loose rock and steep grades turn this mostly technically easy ride into a chore. The climb is relentless and physically difficult.

Trail surface: Jeep road and pavement. Loose rocks, gravel, babyheads, hardpack, and soft clay sediments.

Lay of the land: Go up a wide OHV track and then down through the foothills of the La Sals

on the paved La Sal Mountain Loop Road. Lots of scrub oak and some aspen. Impressive Brumley Creek Canyon is just off the side of the trail.

Total climbing: 1,642 feet.

Land status: National forest ("Land of Many Uses").

Other trail users: Hikers, equestrians, and off-road vehicles (ORV).

Best seasons: Late spring, summer, and early fall.

Getting there: From Moab: Go south on U.S. Route 191 for 7.8 miles from the intersection of Main and Center Streets to the signed Old Airport Road, also marked La Sal Mountain Loop Road, also marked to Ken's Lake. Turn left here. At mile 8.4 take a right at the T intersection. Go straight past Ken's Lake, which will be on your left at the base of a waterfall (the county water diversion). Go past Pack Creek Ranch, which will be on your right at mile 13.1. Continue up the mountain. Enjoy the scenery. As you gain elevation, look for a jeep road on your right at mile 18.3. The jeep road leaves the pavement at the top of a rise, just before a left-hand curve in the road. There is a small parking spot just off the road on the right. Park here. There is room here for no more than two or three vehicles if they are courteously parked.

The Ride

This is a fairly difficult climb on a technically easy 4WD track, great for building those quads. The trail is featured as a loop: half dirt, half pavement. You go up on dirt, down on pavement, or vice versa. Here's a clue to downhillers: Do it in reverse. It is an awesome downhill run. Watch out for the hikers and ATVs, though! The area gets a lot of attention from Moab families who come up here to picnic next to the creek and ride ATVs all over the place. If you have a very fit family or group who wants a short but strenuous mountain bike ride that allows for a side hike or two, then this is a good choice.

Avoid all rides in the La Sal Mountains when there is any chance of rain. Mud rolls up like a carpet, and you can get mud platform shoes and big-ass mud motorcycle tires if you ride it even when the ground is damp. The air is cool, clean, and crisp. There are side hikes to the stream and an aspen grove lining Brumley Creek that are worthy of your attention. There is also abundant mountain wildlife—I've

The cattle guard below the old sluice mine

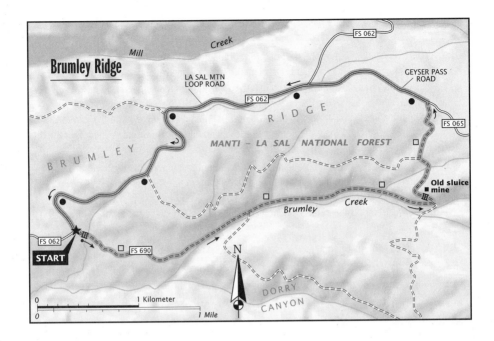

personally seen rabbits, raptors, squirrels, and bobcats, and I'm sure there are a lot more critters out there. There are also some fine climbing opportunities for experienced rocksters and a chance to explore an old mining site.

If you are up here in summer, which is the best time to enjoy the La Sals, you should know that there is little shade on the entire ride. Fortunately, the heat of day can be escaped by stopping for a visit to the creek or the canyon's edge on the right-hand side of the trail.

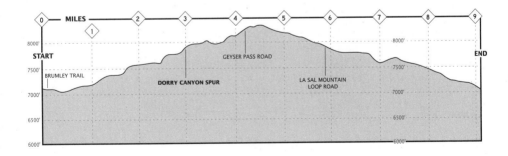

Miles and Directions

0.0 **START** by heading out on the dirt road that drops down on your left from the parking spot. Go across the cattle guard and continue to follow the road as it bends eastward. This ride is very straightforward as long as you stay on the main spur. Avoid all side spurs. Within a mile or so, the trail will parallel the creek (to your right), but not close enough for you to see it most of the time. You will hear it trickling away in the groves to your right. Farther on there are some fine rock climbing spots in Brumley Creek Canyon, if you're interested.

3.0 Pass an unmarked spur on the left. There is a more dominant, marked spur on the right that leads into the double-black-diamond Dorry Canyon ride. Stay left past this downhill spur and head uphill on the main trail. You will climb, loop around, and cross a cattle guard. Just beyond the cattle guard, on your right, is an old sluice mine worthy of a visit.

3.4 Stay left.

4.2 Go left on the well-maintained Geyser Pass Road (Forest Road 065).

5.9 Go left on the paved La Sal Mountain Loop Road (Forest Road 062).

9.1 Your vehicle should be parked on the left side of the road.

Ride Information

Trail Contacts

Manti–La Sal National Forest
Moab Ranger District
2290 SW Resource Blvd.
Moab, UT 84532
(435) 259–7155

Schedule

Trail is open year-round but is best during late spring, summer, and early fall.

Maps

USGS maps: Tukuhnikivatz
Moab East Trail Map by Latitude 40° Inc.
Moab Recreation Map by F. H. Barnes
USDA Forest Service Manti–La Sal Forest map

36 Geyser Pass to Dark Canyon Lake

Start: From the intersection of Geyser Pass Road and La Sal Mountain Loop Road.
Length: 17.8-mile point-to-point. (Can be up to 40 miles as an out-and-back with options mentioned. Expect a 2-hour shuttle drive.)
Approximate riding time: 3 to 8 hours.
Difficulty: Technically easy to less than moderate. Physically moderately difficult. Climbing at altitude. How's your heart?
Trail surface: Doubletrack dirt roads, partially grated. Gravel, hardpack, embedded rock, loose rock, and some soft sand. Impassable when wet.

Lay of the land: High-elevation alpine forest to scrub oak foothills. Some logging. Some cattle ranching. A lot of descending.
Total climbing: 4,318 feet.
Land status: National forest, Utah State Trust, and private lands.
Other trail users: Hikers, equestrians, off-road vehicles (ORV), cross-country skiers, and snowmobiles.
Best seasons: Summer and early fall—good cross-country skiing in winter, by the way.

Environmental concerns: No problem. The trail is wide. Mountain bikes are the least of worries for the Forest Service, state, and private landholders who manage logging, mining, hunting, cattle, ATV, and snowmobile traffic. These permitted activities far outweigh our damage in this alpine environment. It is only in the desert that mountain bikers are the real villains.

Getting there: From Moab: Go south on U.S. Route 191 for 7.8 miles from the intersection of Main and Center Streets to La Sal Mountain Loop Road. Turn left (you will be going right if you are coming back from dropping off the shuttle vehicle at Dark Canyon Lake), then right at mile 8.5 to head up into the La Sals past Ken's Lake. Go past Pack Creek Ranch, and at mile 20 go right onto Geyser Pass Road. There is a spot on the hill to your left immediately after turning onto Geyser Pass Road where you can park and stage your ride.
Shuttle Point: From Moab: Go south on US 191 for 22.1 miles from the intersection of Main and Center Streets to Utah Route 46. Take a left (east) onto UT 46 at the old, deserted gas station and desolated ice cream parlor that is La Sal Junction. At mile 31 (all mileage is from Moab) is the town of La Sal, which has a general store beside the post office. If you don't miss the town altogether, you surely cannot miss these two redbrick buildings. It is the only source of liquids between you and Moab. At mile 34.7 take a left onto the maintained dirt road northeast. The road splits off from the highway just beyond a curve. In turning you will be crossing traffic (what there is of it), so watch for it. The road is signed within 150 feet, and reads: DARK CANYON LAKE 12, BUCKEYE RESERVOIR 20. It is not accurate on the mileage, but there you are. At mile 36.6 you'll pass the La Sal Pass Trailhead. Continue straight ahead to the signed Dark Canyon Road at mile 39.2. Take a left here and head up the hill. At mile 42.2 you'll pass a fence along the right-hand side of the road while traveling through an aspen grove. (Yes, you are on the right road.) At mile 43.1, you'll arrive at the Dark Canyon Lake Trailhead. Park on the left opposite the wood-fenced corral. The signed trailhead goes up and to the right from the parking area. *Not to the left.* There is a sign warning of avalanche dangers with a sign-in box below it. This is where you will end your ride. Park your "drop" vehicle.

Dark Canyon Lake

From Shuttle Point to Start: Reset the mileage counter on the second vehicle and retrace your steps to UT 46 and US 191, the way you came in. Once you are back in the Moab Valley, watch for the turnoff signed for La Sal Mountain Loop Road and Ken's Lake. It is 35.3 miles from where you left your shuttle vehicle. Go right toward the east and join La Sal Mountain Loop Road by driving on this access road through gravel and portable toilet companies. The right-hand turn from US 191 toward Ken's Lake and La Sal Mountain Loop Road is documented above as a left turn from Moab (at mile 7.8 south from Main and Center Streets). Follow the directions above in Getting There to the Geyser Pass Trailhead and your start.

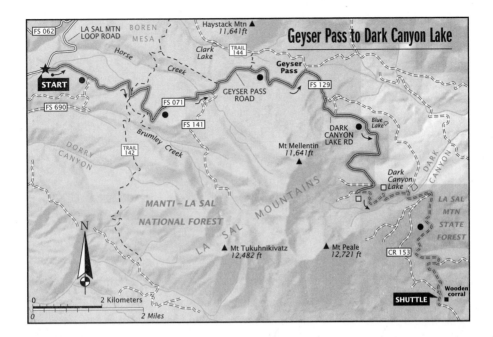

Geyser Pass to Dark Canyon Lake

The Ride

Dealing with the shuttle smoothly is the key to this ride. Weather is the second ingredient that has to mix correctly. If it rains, forget it. The start of the ride is up a graded, well-maintained gravel road that gradually lifts you from scrub oak to alpine forests. If you love to climb with strength and descend with speed and control, then you'll love this ride, as you zip down the southeastern slope at the base of the majestic Mount Mellentin and awesome Mount Peale. This is for any intermediate rider looking for a great workout on a scenic road without a lot of technical challenge, other than speed on embedded, bumpy, and loose rock.

Traveling through the heart of the La Sal Mountains, the climb to Geyser Pass is relentless, but never brutally steep. It is at altitude, so air is a commodity. It's like Frank Sinatra up here: Thin and cool. The ride up to the ski area is just a warm-up.

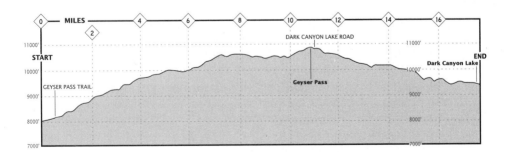

Just past the ski area parking (where the toilet and avalanche warnings are on Geyser Pass Road) and just before Gold Basin Road, the trail starts to get interesting. It narrows, grows rougher, steeper, then narrower and rougher still. The sides drop off. At Geyser Pass (10,600 feet), the trail crests and descends on Dark Canyon Lake Road. First it rolls, then it pitches down ever so slightly, and then it hands you a few steep sections with tight turns at the bottom. Your uphill struggle is rewarded at first with a rolling tour of the mountains at high altitude, then a downhill rip on the southern slope. There are two lakes to visit on this trip. Both are clear and beautiful, but harbor mosquitoes in summer. Wildlife happens up here, so keep an eye out for bears, mountain lions, raptors, and those farther down the food chain. Cows also inhabit these elevations during the summer months, so scrub off speed before blind turns. Speed happens on this ride. Be prepared.

You'll need to allow a couple of hours to drop a vehicle on Dark Canyon Lake Road and return to the trail start. If you are strong riders, then this route is enjoyable as an out-and-back. You can add mileage by reversing the Moonlight Meadow ride up to Geyser Pass, and/or adding the Gold Basin out-and-back. See Ride 39, Geyser Pass to Taylor Flat for a similar ride to this one with a lot more mileage.

If you want to lessen the climb, you can drive your car up Geyser Pass Road for a way. It is passable with a 2WD vehicle for a few miles. There are pullouts along the way and a parking lot where the ski area begins. There is also a toilet at this point. No water. Just keep track of the mileage and subtract it from the start of the ride count. If you want to add 6 miles (mostly downhill) to the end of your mountain bike ride, park your shuttle vehicle at mile 39.2 (referenced in the Shuttle Point Getting There directions above). If you do choose to leave the shuttle vehicle here, find a suitable place just off the road away from the intersection. There is no designated parking area, so be respectful of the vegetation and try not to set it in a blind spot or too far into the road.

Miles and Directions

0.0 **START** by heading up the gravel Geyser Pass Road (Forest Road 071), avoiding all side spurs. After a bit of open climbing, you will go over a cattle guard and eventually through an aspen grove.

2.8 Pass this intersection with the Trans La Sal Trail. Farther on you pass through a parking area for winter skiing and snowmobiles. There's a potty just in case.

5.3 Go left at the Y, staying on Geyser Pass Road. **Side trip.** To the right is Gold Basin Road (Forest Road 141), a nice detour if you want to increase your mileage with an out-and-back. (This option is documented in its own chapter, Ride 38.)

7.8 **Side trip.** Ride out on the faint spur to the left to catch the view and have a snack. You are at the top of the pass. This spur is the connect for a ride down to Oowah, which is also documented in the Moonlight Meadow chapter (see Ride 37). After your snack, go back and continue briefly on Geyser Pass Road, taking the first available right onto signed Dark Canyon Lake Road (Forest Road 129).

Dark Canyon Lake Road

8.5 **Option.** The signed Blue Lake Road heads to the left. This is a very nice out-and-back or straight-through diversion that will add about 3 miles to the count below—3.1 miles for the out-and-back. After a visit to the lake, return to regain the Dark Canyon Lake Road by retracing your route or by taking the road from the backside of the lake. Wrap around the lake and take the road to the southwest, not the left-hand spur to the east. Back on Dark Canyon Lake Road, the trail gets steeper. Enjoy the ensuing downhill. Beware on blind turns. You can really build speed on the straightaways, but the turns are tight and covered with loose rock.

9.0 The unmarked spur from Blue Lake rejoins the road to Dark Canyon. If you did not take this diversion, you will pass it on your left. Go straight.

11.6 Pass a spur on your right.

12.2 At the bottom of this steep hill, there is a sharp turn to the left. Avoid the turn to the right. The sign reads: GEYSER PASS 3, DARK CANYON 1. The arrows could be confusing. The mileages are awful. Ignore it. Sweep around the turn to your left and rocket onward.

12.5 Pass the spur on the right. Check out the awesome vertical face of Mount Peale. Wow.

13.5 On your left is a private road to some cabins. Go past it.

13.55 **Side trip.** The spur to Dark Canyon Lake is on your left. It certainly warrants a visit. Hope you brought a fishing pole and a camera.

14.3 The unobstructed view of Paradox Valley is worth gawking over.

15.9 There is a blocked road to the left. Go past it.

17.8 The wooden corral marks the trailhead access into the Dark Canyon Lake area and to the end of your ride. Here is where you left your shuttle vehicle. If you left your shuttle at the intersection of Dark Canyon and La Sal Pass Road (County Road 154), then simply continue straight ahead for another 6.2 miles, avoiding the immediate spur to the right and all side spurs off the main road.

Ride Information

Trail Contacts

Manti–La Sal National Forest
Moab Ranger District
2290 SW Resource Blvd.
Moab, UT 84532
(435) 259-7155

Utah State School and Institutional Trust Lands Administration
1165 South US 191, Ste. 5
Moab, UT 84532
(435) 259-3760

Route crosses Taylor Cattle Company private land. Show respect. Stay on the road to avoid trespassing.

Schedule

The road is usually free of snow from mid-June through October. Late September into early October is the best time due to the fall color. Aspen golds and cool, comfortable temperatures turn the La Sal Mountains into a magical place at this time of year. Nightly temperatures can dip below freezing, even in summer, so ride prepared with extra clothing, food, spares, and fire starters just in case.

Maps

USGS maps: Tukuhnikivatz, Mount Peale
Moab East Trail Map by Latitude 40° Inc.
Moab Recreation Map by F. H. Barnes
USDA Forest Service Manti–La Sal Forest map

SHUTTLES, THE RIGHT WAY

How many folks have you got there? What size vehicles do you have? You will need two or three vehicles to perform a shuttle for a point-to-point ride like Geyser Pass to Dark Canyon. The easiest way is "the instant shuttle." You take two identical vehicles with all riders, bikes, and equipment aboard to the drop-off (shuttle) point. The "drop" vehicle is left at the trail tail. The other vehicle picks up the driver of the drop vehicle and takes everyone to the trailhead. If your group is large, you may wish to do the drop, then return to Moab to pick up the riders to take everyone to the trailhead. This is time consuming and, unless you want some time to socialize, things can be better.

Eliminating time spent in the car makes the ride much more enjoyable. The longer the shuttle, the more appropriate it is to make the drop the night before. Two drivers take two vehicles, the drop and a small economy car or a motorcycle, out to the drop-off at the trail tail and return on the motorcycle or in the small car. The next morning everyone heads directly to the trailhead in one or two vehicles. After the ride, take anyone who is not driving back to Moab, so that you are only transporting drivers to the trailhead to retrieve any cars left there.

The third way, and best way, is to pay for a shuttle service. In Moab this is quite common. There are a few available. Expect to pay around $1.00 per mile per person. Do the drop thing yourself the night before and have the shuttle service drive you to the trailhead to start the ride, thereby eliminating the boring vehicle pickup at the end of the day.

37 Geyser Pass to Oowah Lake (Moonlight Meadow)

Start: From the Trans Mountain Trail intersection with Geyser Pass Road.

Length: 8.4-mile point-to-point. (Options for experienced backcountry riders only.)

Approximate riding time: 2 to 6 hours.

Difficulty: The ride up to the pass is technically easy, but the ride down through Moonlight Meadow to Oowah Lake is extremely difficult. The narrow singletrack is over loose and embedded rock and fallen logs, through mud in spots, and can be a bit exposed. This ride is extremely physically difficult due to the climbing and the need to negotiate tight technical sections.

Trail surface: At altitude on loose rock, roots, fallen trees, tight switchbacks, steep grades, and mud and/or gray powdery sand. Not good when wet.

Lay of the land: Alpine forest. Mountain peaks. High pastures. Really smells great.

Total climbing: 2,043 feet.

Land status: National forest.

Other trail users: Hikers, equestrians, and off-road vehicles (ORV).

Best seasons: Mid summer and early fall.

Environmental concerns: The trail can do more damage to you than you can do to it. If the trail is muddy, sure you can mess it up, but it will mess you up much more, so don't ride in the La Sals if it has been or will be raining. Wildlife here deserves some quiet, but be sure to make enough noise so that you do not surprise a bear on the trail. Instant karma happens in the La Sals.

Getting there: From Moab: Go south on U.S. Route 191 for 7.8 miles from the intersection of Main and Center Streets to La Sal Mountain Loop Road. Turn left. At mile 8.4 turn right and head up into the La Sals straight past the turnoff to Ken's Lake. Go past Pack Creek Ranch, and at mile 20 (from Moab) go right onto Geyser Pass Road. In another 2.8 miles, at the apex of a left turn on the right side of the road, is the pullout access for the marked Trans La Sal Mountain Trail, which crosses the road at this point. Park here. The loop option emerges from the Trans La Sal Trail at this point. If you want to avoid the next 5 miles of climbing on a gravel road, do the shuttle thing: Drive up the road farther using the Miles and Directions to get to the top of the pass.

Shuttle point: From Moab: Follow the directions above up the Loop Road to Geyser Pass, but don't turn onto Geyser Pass Road. Stay on the Loop Road and turn right in another 1.4 miles, onto Oowah Lake Road. Park at any appropriate spot just off the road. This fast downhill will be a relief at the end of your ride.

From shuttle point to start: After you drop your shuttle vehicle, drive the second vehicle back to Geyser Pass Road. Take a left and go up toward Geyser Pass. In 2.8 miles from the intersection of Geyser Pass Road and La Sal Mountain Loop Road, turn into the Trans La Sal Trail pullout described above in Getting There.

Miki and Mookie in Moonlight Meadow

The Ride

In summer this trail is a great escape for advanced mountain bikers who cannot seem to get up early enough to avoid desert temperatures at lower altitudes. The trail may be ridable by mid-June or July, but every season is different. Due to an elevation of over 10,000 feet, the uppermost section of singletrack may still be torn up and have ice and horrible mud from snowmelt on it well into summer. The ground dries out and the trail mellows from use by late summer. The aspens are usually popping with color in mid-October, so this is the prime time for heading to Moonlight Meadow.

The Geyser Pass Road is mostly gravel, affording a somewhat depressing climb at the start, but soon it narrows and becomes hardpack through a beautiful forest. After the doubletrack climb to the pass, the singletrack is a welcome surprise as it drops and becomes technical in a *big* hurry. Like all singletrack in the La Sals, this trek, though seemingly low in mileage, is very difficult. The singletrack is narrow with many sections of loose and embedded rocks and includes a bit of vertical exposure. As of this writing, the singletrack is desperately in need of maintenance. Be prepared to hike a bit unless you are a hardcore log hopper!

If it looks like rain, don't even think about this ride. Mud is hell here. Mosquitoes can be a problem, too, if you venture off the trail into the woods along streams or near any standing water. As with any trail at altitudes above 10,000 feet, you must

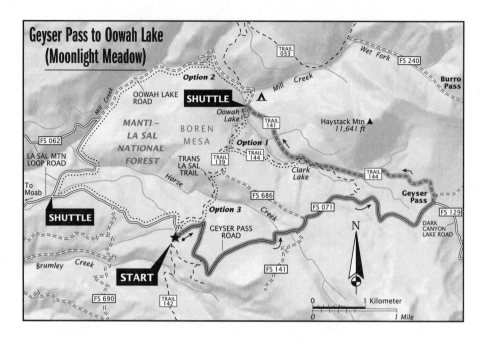

Geyser Pass to Oowah Lake
(Moonlight Meadow)

be prepared for cold weather even in midsummer. Carry rain gear and a warm layer. If you get a headache, you can most likely blame it on altitude sickness. Take time to acclimate yourself. Altitude headaches can be compounded by dehydration, so be sure to stay hydrated.

Miles and Directions

0.0 **START** by heading east and upward on Geyser Pass Road (Forest Road 071) from the Trans La Sal Trail pullout.

2.5 Go past the right-hand spur to Gold Basin.

2.7 Pass this 4WD spur left. (Note. The spur drops to mile 8.6 below in Option 3.) Suitable for high-clearance 4WD only (this is nice to know in case of an emergency).

3.3 (Note. The spur off to your left leads down to the mile 6.4 escape route.)

4.9 This is the high point of the ride at an elevation of 10,600 feet, marked by a sign on your right.

5.0 At the top of Geyser Pass, the road splits. Take a left, and then a second left on the less prominent doubletrack (Trail 144) that heads into the open pasture along the very edge of the pass. Just as the pasture opens up, take the faint singletrack along the left border of the pasture. As you continue, the singletrack trail will become more and more prominent, will take you through a small tightly packed stand of aspen, and will then drop down to your left. Yahoo. Watch the rocks.

5.8 At the bottom of this rugged, steep downhill, there are a couple of muddy ruts flowing with more water than appears to be there. Get off your bike, because riding through them will almost certainly mean an endo. At a minimum your bike will be a mess once you reach the other side. If you like your rims and brake pads, dismount and hop over the mud. You will probably get mudfoot, but better your cleats than your rims. Across from the ruts follow the treeline edge of the right-hand branch of the meadow, keeping close to the trees to your left. Eventually the trail will become more evident. More mud happens.

6.2 At this point you will hop over a small stream and continue across the meadow.

6.4 To your left is a roaring stream with a log across it. Across the log is an escape route up to Geyser Pass Road, if you need it, but continue on the singletrack against the edge of the trees. This is another spot that will be very muddy early in the season.

6.5 More muck in early season.

6.6 Hit another stream. Riding through will be very difficult.

6.8 More muck crossings in early season.

6.9 In this area you'll have your first bit of exposure on the left side of the trail. Doesn't look like much, but it could hurt. The trail can be very rugged at this point.

7.2 Below on your left is Clark Lake. Above the lake and the switchbacks ahead is a gate that takes you directly down to Oowah Lake on Trail 141. Continue on for the fastest way to Oowah Lake. **Option 1.** Above the lake there is a rugged switchback that heads down to its shoreline. Go down the switchbacks to add more technical singletrack. Once down the switchbacks and on the lake, go right and through the gate. Follow the trail to the next gate on the left. Go through it and across the creek. You'll see the trail (Trail 144) on the other side. (You can blow it just past the gate and end up reconnecting with Trail 141 heading to Oowah Lake, if you are not careful.) After 1.0 mile, assuming you negotiated Clark Lake and are on Trail 144, you come to the intersection of the Trans La Sal Trail (Trail 139). Go right. It is less than a mile to Oowah Lake and your shuttle. **Option 2.** To form a loop back to the starting point on Geyser Pass Road, go left toward Boren Mesa. On the Trans La Sal Trail, from the junction with Trail 144. After 0.3 mile bear right at a junction. Note: The 4WD road on your left goes up to mile 2.7 on Geyser Pass Road. In another 0.3 mile, there's an abrupt left turn into a hairy downhill run from Boren Mesa. Continue to follow Trans La Sal Trail markers when visible. Pray they are not blown to pieces by hunters. You'll encounter Horse Creek after a sweeping turn below the mesa. Cross it any way you can. After 0.3 mile go left on the 4WD track. Enter a camping area and pick up the grassy singletrack on the far side. You may have to negotiate a couple of fallen trees from here. This trail will lead you to Geyser Pass Road and your vehicle.

8.1 Watch out for this steep and sometimes washed-out section of downhill.

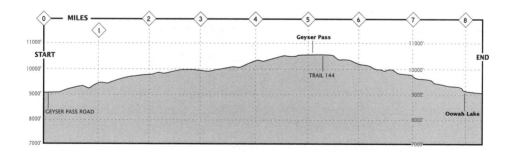

Mount Tomasaki

8.2 Go to your immediate right, taking the prominent switchback downhill, avoiding the fainter singletrack straight ahead. You will soon see the waters of Oowah Lake down the hill to your left.

8.3 Go over the gate. Opening it is a pain.

8.4 Welcome to Oowah Lake and your shuttle vehicle, which will be parked where you left it along the Oowah Lake Road. **Option 3.** For the complete loop back to your starting point via La Sal Mountain Loop Road (Forest Road 062) and Oowah Lake Road to Geyser Pass Road (FS 071), ride down Oowah Lake Road. The road exits the Oowah Lake area from the far-right-hand side of the lake. After 3.2 miles go left onto La Sal Mountain Loop Road. Turn left on Geyser Pass Road after 1.4 miles and go another 2.8 miles to your car. You have closed the loop. Enjoy the drive back down the mountain.

Ride Information

Trail Contacts

Manti–La Sal National Forest
Moab Ranger District
2290 SW Resource Blvd.
Moab, UT 84532
(435) 259–7155

Schedule

Trail is open year-round but is best during spring and fall.

Maps

USGS maps: Mount Tukunikivatz, Mount Peale, Mount Waas
Moab East Trail Map by Latitude 40° Inc.
Moab Recreation Map by F. H. Barnes
USDA Forest Service Manti–La Sal Forest map

38 Gold Basin

Start: From the Trans La Sal Trail intersection with Geyser Pass Road.

Length: 9.8-mile out-and-back, with an optional mile-long hike into and out of the heart of the basin. (More mileage if combined with Moonlight Meadow, with an out-and-back to the top of Geyser Pass, or as a side trip diversion from the Geyser Pass to Dark Canyon Lake or Geyser Pass to Taylor Flat rides.)

Approximate riding time: 2 to 3 hours.

Difficulty: The ride is technically easy on the dirt road ride up to the Gold Basin singletrack. The singletrack is moderate to very difficult. The ride is short, though the climbing can be strenuous, therefore the ride can be considered physically moderate at worst.

Trail surface: Gravel on a wide dirt road and loose rock, bedrock, logs, shale loam, and sand on mountain singletrack.

Lay of the land: Big mountains. Rides in the La Sals are almost always a climb followed by a descent. The terrain is hardly ever rolling.

Total climbing: 2,430 feet.

Land status: National forest.

Other trail users: Hikers, equestrians, motorists of all types on the road, and cows on the singletrack. The area is used for skiing in winter, but with the death of a number of skiers a few years ago due to a single avalanche, the area doesn't see as much use in winter as it used to.

Best seasons: Summer and early fall.

Environmental concerns: The mountain can be harder on you than you can be on it. Treatment of the environment is simple here: If you bring something in, carry it out.

Getting there: From Moab: Drive 7.9 miles south on U.S. Route 191 from the intersection of Main and Center Streets to the La Sal Mountain Loop Road. Take a left onto this road and make a right at the T in 0.5 mile. At mile 20 from Moab, take a right onto the Geyser Pass Road and go another 2.8 miles to the Trans La Sal Trail. Park at the turnout to the right. You will be leaving from this spot. (If you wish to shorten the route, go another 2.5 miles and park at the Gold Basin Road.)

The Ride

This area produced very little gold during the brief gold rush in San Juan County during the late 1800s, but the exploration left a deteriorated roadbed from the end of the current Gold Basin Road that is now de facto singletrack. Gold Basin is a great place to camp. A primitive camping spot lies at the end of the Gold Basin Road, prior to the singletrack. Wildlife abounds in the remote basin, and you may see mountain lion or bear here if you are quiet. The talus slopes are moving constantly, and if you stay here long you'll hear or see a landslide or two, so beware. This ride can be combined with a ride up Geyser Pass, adding some thrills and chills. Gold Basin will put you in awe of the majesty of this beautiful mountain range that's just minutes from Moab.

Gold Basin singletrack

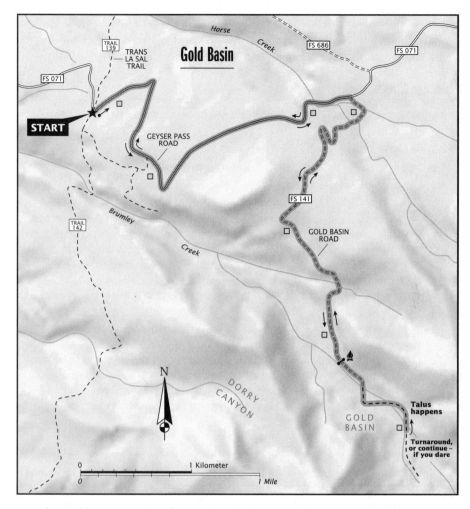

The trail begins at 8,600 feet and ends close to the basin at 9,700 feet. The route starts on a gravel road, then drops from a parking area on a tight and steep single-track. Beyond, the singletrack is an old, unmaintained road through the forest, sometimes blocked by logs. The road gives way to a singletrack that is ridable in a pinch

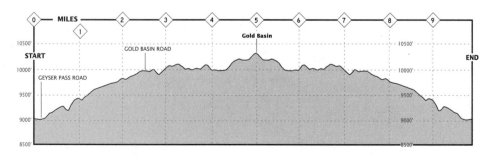

but is best hiked. The singletrack affords access deeper into Gold Basin. If you are looking for that indescribable feeling of awe folks get when in remote and threatening wilderness, then the hike into the basin is just the ticket.

Miles and Directions

0.0 **START** from the intersection with Trans La Sal Trailhead, traveling up Geyser Pass Road (Forest Road 071).

2.5 Turn right onto Gold Basin Road (Forest Road 141).

4.1 Ignore the spur left. It leads to a nice camping spot, though.

4.2 The gravel road ends here at a log fence. Just to the left of the fence is a small singletrack that leads down the hill. Take the singletrack down into the valley.

4.7 The trail crosses a small clearing and fades a bit as it approaches a small stream. Cross this small stream. Just on the other side is a larger stream that joins with the smaller. Do not cross the second stream on the faint cow trail; instead, go left on the singletrack. Remember this spot for later. It is the only place that can be confusing on your return. The trail will widen, but the old road has deteriorated to de facto singletrack. Logs are strewn across the trail, and you'll have to dismount to negotiate a few. If you can move them, do so.

4.9 There is a talus slope on your right and, in a few yards, another on your left. Where the slopes converge you'll have to leave your bike for the hike into Gold Basin. The trail is obscure in places, so maybe you should make a cairn or two to avoid confusion when you backtrack. You shouldn't have much of a problem. Stay near the streambed. It leads into the tight basin. This is real hiking, and so taking a pair of hiking shoes, if you are serious about the hike, is a great idea. After enjoying this area, turn around and retrace your route.

9.8 Arrive back at your vehicle.

Ride Information

Trail Contacts
Manti–La Sal National Forest
Moab Ranger District
2290 SW Resource Blvd.
Moab, UT 84532
(435) 259–7155

Schedule
This trail is open year-round to visitation but is best for mountain biking in summer and early fall.

Maps
USGS maps: Mount Tukuhnikivatz
Moab East Trail Map by Latitude 40° Inc.
Moab Recreation Map by F. H. Barnes
USDA Forest Service Manti–La Sal Forest map

39 Geyser Pass to Taylor Flat Loop

Start: From the intersection of Geyser Pass Road and La Sal Mountain Loop Road.
Length: 49.4-mile loop.
Approximate riding time: 12 to 20 hours.
Difficulty: Technically the ride is only difficult on the top section of the downhill from Geyser Pass to Taylor Flat Road, especially if you are carrying speed. The steepness of the top portion, combined with loose rock sections of trail and very tight turns, requires good downhill handling skills. If you are not on a full-suspension rig, proceed with caution. The rest of the ride is technically easy. Due to the great distance, physically this loop ride is extremely difficult if done in one day. You can choose among any number of shuttle options on this route to bring the physical difficulty down, or you can divide the ride by carrying camping gear and staying for the night at any number of primitive camping spots beyond Geyser Pass. Just remember to bring lots of water!
Trail surface: You will begin on gravel. Beyond the Gold Basin turnoff, the trail becomes hardpack. From the top of Geyser Pass, the rough and narrow road descends through alpine forest on bedrock, rock rubble, hardpack, sparse soft sand, and across rare muddy, rocky streams. Once down onto Taylor Flat Road, the track becomes much wider. The surface from here is hardpack and is sometimes composed of powdery shale. This shale surface can become horrible mud when wet. Eventually Taylor Flat Road becomes gravel, then pavement. Most of La Sal Mountain Loop Road is paved.
Lay of the land: The beginning of the ride ascends through alpine forest. Once you have reached Geyser Pass, the landscape gradually opens up into a vast logging area with views of Paradox Valley and the Rockies. The double-track trail becomes more faint and primitive and eventually dips into scrub oak at lower altitudes. It is impassable when wet. Off the main route are legal logging roads, spurs to campsites, loops through the scrub oak, and a lot of natural magic. Cameras, please.
Total climbing: 8,002 feet.
Land status: National forest, Utah State Trust, and private lands.
Other trail users: Hiking, equestrian, and off-road vehicles (ORV).
Best seasons: Summer and early fall.

Note to the reader: Before making a decision on just how to approach this ride, read this chapter in its entirety to get the overall picture. There are lots of opportunities for distance rides and camping-supported exploration above Taylor Flat. Take the time to study the possibilities between the lines. Weigh the options for your group and be creative. The Family Version to Taylor Flat sidebar includes a shuttle driving tour of Castle Valley, taking advantage of this necessity in such a beautiful place.

Environmental concerns: Don't cut down the trees or shoot the wildlife, though you can get permits to do either one. There are cryptobiotic soil crusts on the flats, so stay on the trail. This is one of the few nondesert rides in this guide. This means that camping does not have the impact that it does at lower elevations where life is fragile and the environment requires longer periods of time to recover from your impact. Still, if you are camping here, carry out everything you brought with you. Bury those turds at least a foot down and don't do your "business" close

Castle Rock stands above Castle Valley.

to watercourses. Check with the Forest Service before you camp here to receive current information on fire danger and any wildlife warnings.

Getting there: From Moab: Drive south on U.S. Route 191 for 7.8 miles from the intersection of Main and Center Streets to La Sal Mountain Loop Road. Turn left toward Ken's Lake, and then right at mile 8.5 to head up into the La Sals past the Ken's Lake turnoff. Go past Pack Creek Ranch, and at mile 20.2 go right onto Geyser Pass Road. Just to your left as you enter Geyser Pass Road is an elevated area where you can safely park your vehicle.

Shuttle points: If you want to shuttle the ride to reduce mileage, continue past Geyser Pass Road on La Sal Mountain Loop Road for another 13.9 miles until you come to the Castleton Gateway Road. Leave a shuttle here (Shuttle E) or go right to leave a shuttle at any of the points suggested below. The farther in you drive for the shuttle, the shorter the bike ride will be.

Shuttle E reduces the length of the ride to 31.5 miles.

Shuttle D is at mile 21.6 from the trailhead, reducing your ride length to 27.8 miles.

Shuttle C is at mile 26.5 from the trailhead. Best for avoiding the gravel and stutter bumps at the end of the ride. This shuttle point will reduce your ride length to 22.9 miles.

Shuttle B is at mile 31.8 from the trailhead, reducing your ride length to 17.6 miles.

Shuttle A is at mile 36.1 from the trailhead. Best for downhillers, though the downhill ride from the top of the pass is short for the length of the shuttle. Plan on camping, to get the most out of the trip. If you use this shuttle point, the resulting ride will be 13.3 miles long.

The Ride

This very long mountain bike ride is a wonderful trek for the pannier crowd, presenting the well-prepared mountain bike tourist with any number of sweet camping options, especially on the "downside" of Geyser Pass. Aside from camping, the eastern slope of the La Sal Mountains offers much to mountain bikers with a wide range of skills and interests. The trees are big. The air is crisp and the forests are alive with wildlife. The road crosses national and state forests and private land. Parking is available at almost any point along the road (except on marked private lands), allowing families and groups of 4WD vehicle sag-supported novices the opportunity to pick the most appropriate spot for a picnic and gentle out-and-back ride. The farther down the mountain toward Taylor Flat, the more open and easy the riding and navigation becomes.

There are logging roads galore beyond Geyser Pass, offering skilled cyclists some particularly interesting and very private exploration. Downhillers will love this area, too, but if shuttled from the top of Geyser Pass—which is the logical place to begin a downhill run—the gravity-assisted rush down the backside of the La Sal Mountains is only worth the long drive if you plan on camping at the bottom of the run. The 13.3-mile downhill blast from the top of Geyser Pass (mile 8.1) to Shuttle Point A provides "death grip" loose-rock sections, tight twisting turns on doubletrack through gorgeous aspen groves, and a few jumps. Scenic for sure, sometimes very challenging, and certainly fast.

If done as described in the Family Version sidebar, remember, this ride is at altitude and is a bit strenuous in spots for novice riders. Just because the place is called Taylor Flat, don't think the ride is flat! That first hill may be the one that Junior plants his face on, so start nervous kids out slowly in the easy rolling logging area prior to the cattle guard at mile 14.2. Once down on Taylor Flat, the ride is not as steep and quite safe for beginners.

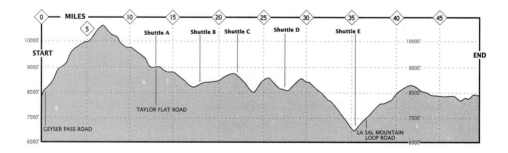

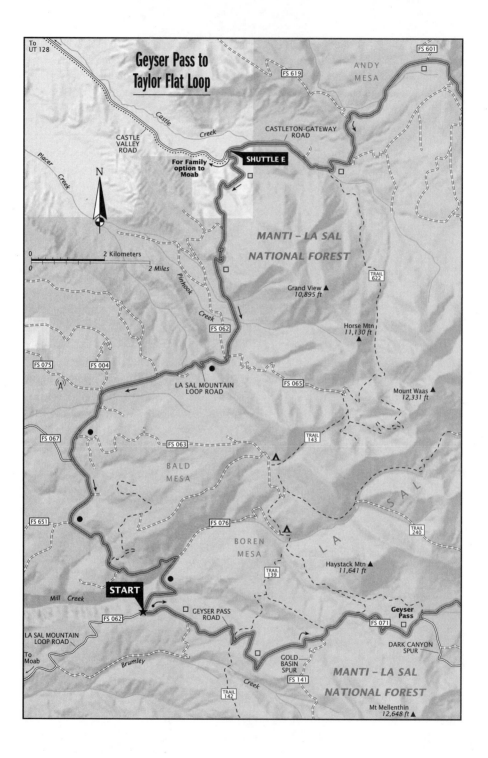

Geyser Pass to Taylor Flat Loop

To UT 128

ANDY MESA

FS 601

FS 619

CASTLE VALLEY ROAD

Castle Creek

CASTLETON-GATEWAY ROAD

For Family option to Moab

SHUTTLE E

Placer Creek

N

MANTI – LA SAL NATIONAL FOREST

TRAIL 622

Grand View ▲ 10,895 ft

Pinhook Creek

FS 062

Horse Mtn 11,130 ft ▲

0   2 Kilometers
0   2 Miles

FS 075   FS 004

FS 065

Mount Waas ▲ 12,331 ft

LA SAL MOUNTAIN LOOP ROAD

FS 067

FS 063

TRAIL 143

BALD MESA

LA SAL

FS 651

FS 076

TRAIL 240

BOREN MESA

Haystack Mtn ▲ 11,641 ft

TRAIL 139

START

Mill Creek

FS 062

GEYSER PASS ROAD

Geyser Pass

FS 071

DARK CANYON SPUR

LA SAL MOUNTAIN LOOP ROAD

To Moab

Brumley

GOLD BASIN SPUR

FS 141

MANTI – LA SAL NATIONAL FOREST

TRAIL 142

Creek

Mt Mellenthin 12,648 ft ▲

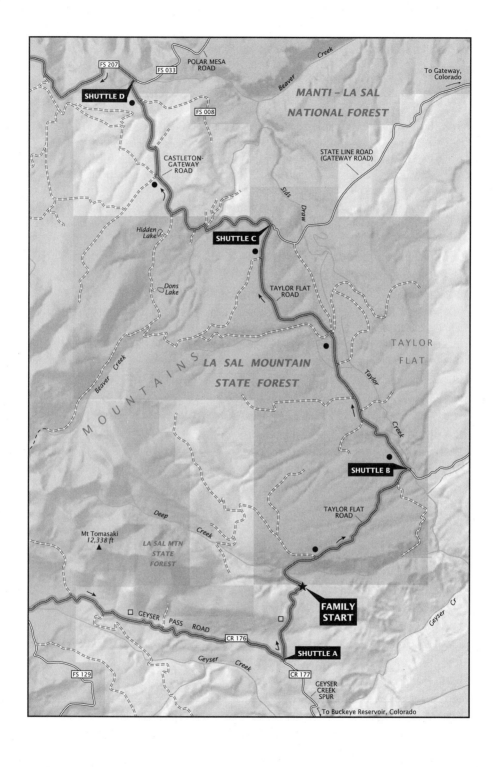

Miles and Directions

0.0 **START:** Head up on Geyser Pass Road (Forest Road 071).

4.7 Pass by the cross-country ski area parking lot. There is a toilet here, if you are feeling a bit "heavy."

5.7 Bear left, passing the marked spur on your right to Gold Basin.

8.1 You are now at Geyser Pass. Take the left-hand spur, avoiding the road to Dark Canyon. Pass the faint spur on the left and continue downward. The Geyser Pass Road at this point used to be marked for Tomasaki Hut, but signs vanish. There is a sign on the Dark Canyon approach that refers to it as FOREST BODY.

8.9 A small stream comes down on the left and crosses the road to create some mud during early season. Here is where the scenery starts to get interesting as the landscape opens up.

9.1 On left is the pointed peak of Mount Tomasaki.

9.2 Encounter some mud.

9.3 Avoid the spur left marked as Trail 240.

9.4 The old truck is great foreground for mountain photographs. Just beyond are a cabin and some private land. Ignore the NO TRESPASSING sign and ride right through. Anything else is considered trespassing. Stay left and on the trail as you pass.

10.8 Stay left. Pass the spur on the right that goes down.

10.9 Start climbing a bit.

11.7 There is a pond on right.

11.8 Pass the faint logging spur on the right that is blocked off (as of this writing).

12.5 It can be very muddy here in early summer.

12.8 Here's a view of Paradox Valley on the right.

12.9 The spur right heads into private land. Avoid. Stay left.

13.3 Take a left onto Taylor Flat Road—unmarked as of this writing. It is well maintained and graded. **Shuttle A.**

14.1 Pass a logging spur on the right.

*14.2 Reach a cattle guard. Go left and downhill at the T. **Option:** This is the starting point for the family version of the ride to Taylor Flat and Castle Valley. See the sidebar of the same name in this chapter.

14.3 Go over an aqueduct.

14.6 Pass a spur that climbs up to your left.

14.8 Welcome to the lower elevations, where scrub oak thrives.

15.2 Bear right at the Y.

15.4 Stay straight, passing a spur on your right.

15.5 Pass a spur on your left.

16.7 Pass a spur on your left.

17.6 Go left to Taylor Flat. The sign was missing as of this writing. **Shuttle B.**

18.7 Bear right, avoiding the spur left. Stay on main road.

19.2 Pass a spur on your left.

Taylor Flat with the eastern slope of the La Sals in the background

20.3 Pass two spurs on your right and one on your left. Lots of options for the camping and exploring deal.

21.2 Pass a spur on your left.

21.7 Pass a faint spur that crosses the main road.

21.8 Pass a spur on your left.

22.0 Pass a spur on your left.

22.4 Pass a spur that crosses the main road.

22.9 Turn left at signed T. **Shuttle C.**

24.4 Go past the two spurs on the right. An aqueduct crosses the road at this point.

24.6 Pass the spur on the left.

24.7 There's a corral on the right. You're leaving state land. A sign reads: NO HUNTING. NO CAMP-ING. NEXT 3 MILES. TAYLOR LIVESTOCK COMPANY. Don't say nuttin 'bout baa-cy-clin'. Up ahead you got some stutter bumps, short grunt climbs, and sucky gravel to deal with.

25.2 Go past a marked spur on your left to Don Lake and Beaver Basin.

26.0 Pass two spurs left. A cow pond is on the right.

26.5 Pass the private gate on the right.

27.0 Here's a view of Beaver Mesa. Lotta Beavers around here.

27.4 Reach a cattle guard. You're leaving Taylor Ranch lands and entering National Forest Service land.

27.7 Pass a spur on your left.

27.8 Go left onto the signed road (Forest Road 207). N. BEAVER 4, POLAR MESA 9, FISHER VALLEY 8, MOAB 34. You be goin' ta Moab. **Shuttle D.**

29.9 Pavement starts.

30.0 There's a pullout to see the dinosaur tracks on the cliff edge.

33.1 Pass the left spur marked Trail 622 and the pullout on the left, unless you want to check it out.

34.1 Leave national forest lands. Mostly private land from here. Stay on the road. Anything else is trespassing.

35.5 Go left onto La Sal Mountain Loop Road. **Shuttle E.** (See Family Version to Taylor Flat and Castle Valley sidebar.)

49.4 Go left onto Geyser Pass Road and to your vehicle. This completes the loop.

Ride Information

Trail Contacts

Manti–La Sal National Forest
Moab Ranger District
2290 S.W. Resource Blvd.
Moab, UT 84532
(435) 259-7155
Utah State School and Institutional Trust Lands Administration
1165 South US 191, Ste. 5
Moab, UT 84532
(435) 259-3760

Schedule

Trail is open year-round but is best during summer and early fall.

Maps

USGS maps: Mount Peale, Mount Waas, Dolores Point South, Mount Tukuhnikivatz, Warner Lake
Moab East Trail Map by Latitude 40° Inc.
Moab Recreation Map by F. H. Barnes

THE FAMILY VERSION TO TAYLOR FLAT AND CASTLE VALLEY If you have a

mountain bike family, then simply follow the instructions for the ride above, but drive the beginning of the route up Geyser Pass Road in a 4WD vehicle. You will definitely need a 4WD vehicle to drive over this road. A rental car might do it. I hear they have higher clearance than other cars, but the trip is a great 4WD trip, even for those with little 4WD experience. If you have an SUV, put that thing to work! Throw the bikes in the back or on a rack and drive over the pass and down to Taylor Flat Road. The ride up and over the pass is probably too steep and loose for kids to ride, but as you approach Taylor Flat the ride becomes easier. Here is a suggestion: Somewhere before mile 14 in the featured mileage count, stop and have the kids mount up and ride the route from there. Give them a mile or so to get their "sea legs" prior to any downhill pitches. Once you reach mileage count 14.2, exercise caution. It is a downhill run. Maybe you should ride out in front of the kids for safety. If your kids are beginners, consider driving farther down the dirt road until you reach ground that is a bit more level.

This ride starts at mile 14.2 in the cues—noted on the map as Family Start—and continues all the way to downtown Moab, for a total distance of 50.7 miles. Start at mile 14.2 and follow the count until you reach mile 35.5, then switch to the mileage count here. The ride can last as long as you want it to, but give yourself at least three hours on the bike.

Miles and Directions

35.5 Go *right* where La Sal Mountain Loop Road spurs left from the road and continue down into Castle Valley.

39.5 You are now heading down into Castle Valley. At this point there is a pullout on your left for access to the Round Mountain Trail, a loop around the small peak in the middle of this immense valley. This short mountain bike ride will take no longer than forty-five minutes to complete. Be smart and allow time for this bit of dessert at the end of your mountain biking main course. Round Mountain Trail is one of the best easy rides around Moab. Route finding is extremely easy, and expansive views always let you know just where you are in relation to your vehicle. Just follow the trail around the peak.

46.1 Go left onto Utah Route 128.

61.5 Go left onto US 191 and drive into town.

64.9 Reach the intersection of Center and Main Streets.

A Game of Battleship

"If you can't use it, what good is it?" This is Chuck's take on the whole damn land deal. As flight support, Chuck nurses the copter, stands around, and smokes cigarettes next to the fuel truck. He does this stuff a lot. He puts all this Hollywood crap in perspective, because he's "worked for a lot for these Hollywood types." Though I disagree with almost everything Chuck says, there is a whole lot of common ground out there. I like Chuck. Everybody likes Chuck. Chuck has the right to be stone-cold wrong. Heck, he makes perfect sense. Common sense grows wild in Moab.

"Them damn environmentalists think the cryptobiotic soil crusts are damaged by the cattle. Hell, imagine what a few million buffalo used to do to it. The stuff is still out there, ain't it? This place ain't fragile and weak; it's tough as hell. It's this damn generation raised by Walt Disney on that Walden Pond shit. They think they have to save the whole goddamn planet from *people*. What a bunch of crap!"

A volunteer production assistant, trying to trivialize the impact of a copter's roar on breeding wildlife, says, "A helicopter is like a passing thunderstorm." And I think to myself: "A coyote's hearing is so acute that it can hear a burrowed mouse passing gas. It's stressful enough trying to survive in this desert without a helicopter throbbing overhead. I guess I'm one of those Walt Disney fruitcakes who worships ancestors and animals that couldn't care less. I'm the environmental film location guy, the New Age Indian fruitcake kinda guy. I am a walking contradiction."

In my film-production-trance rationalization I deduce that Onion Creek Canyon is the perfect location for the director's vision of two cyclists speeding down a canyon splashing through stream crossings. Onion Creek is nearly desolate. Nothing lives in the water and nothing drinks from it. In the tight red canyon below the nasty waters of the Stinking Spring, and up into the pastel green Gyp Squeeze Narries, wildlife is sparse, indeed. They don't call it the Stinking Spring for nothing. It really stinks. Like a rotten egg.

Onion Creek is scary, too. The lower canyon is a 3D sculpture of Dante's hell. The Rico sandstone has eroded into bloodred walls and drip-castle-fat-naked-people-stacked-up spires. These Satanic totem poles tower above and descend far below into a narrow gorge, a deep convoluted scar blasted into fantastic shapes by flash floods that rip down the canyon with some consistency. Here and there stand stunted juniper trees, piñon, cacti, and sprigs of sage and locoweed. These provide flashes of green in a sea of crimson. The greens and reds are so opposite in polarity that where the colors meet, they repel one another with a dark vibrating aura. The dirt road down the middle of this hellish canyon crosses the noxious, corrosive, salt and sulfur flow of Onion Creek twenty-six times before reaching Utah Route 128 at a point less than twenty miles from Moab. Tourists love to ruin their rental cars and bicycles splashing through Onion Creek, up and down the demon canyon. It's popular with many commercial tour outfitters, as well, who use the canyon road for trips on mountain bikes, motorcycles, and 4WD vehicles. You can even take a helicopter tour of the canyon, if you like. The Fisher Valley Ranch staff pokes its cattle up and down the canyon on occasion and enjoys ripping through in their brand-new, rusted-out pickup trucks, so the road is well maintained.

The salt water dissolves machinery, but if ever there were a perfect location for this movie project, it's Onion Creek. Clearly it's the most environmentally sound canyon in this area to fly a camera through. Right? Well, it turns out that Onion Creek is a bit of an administrative problem. It's more than that, really. As I buckled down to write a permit proposal for the shoot, I found that it's downright weird and stupid.

"Them damned environmentalists think the cryptobiotic soil crusts are damaged by the cattle. Hell, imagine what a few million buffalo used to do it."

In order to understand the permitting procedures you must go through to accomplish such a film shoot, imagine a game of Battleship. Utah state, National Forest Service, Indian reservation, and private lands dot the map like enemy ships on a sea of federal lands, comprised mostly of wilderness, proposed wilderness, and studied wilderness. If, in the allotted time, you hit a location that fits the bill that's on either state, Forest Service, Navajo, or private land, then "Kaboom!" You just sank a land management battleship.

As I pull out the land management map, I see that what has been done in the case of Onion Creek is to butt two "proposed" wilderness areas right up to the rim of the canyon on either side of the road. I soon discover that due to foggy interpretation of these imaginary lines by the BLM bureaucracy, the very road and the airspace above it is considered wilderness, though by law a wilderness area cannot include a maintained road. Calling Onion Creek wilderness is equivalent to county government land grabbers needlessly bulldozing a road to nowhere across proposed wilderness before the deal goes down. One side builds a road to stop the legislation. The other fudges the map to include a road that has been there for more than a century. They make each other do the worst and everyone and the environment suffers as a result. The only way to get a permit in the allotted time is to fight.

This is how Utah works. Polarization. No compromise, just a promised gunfight at sunrise. It's the Old West mentality gone modern. The nothing-better-to-do-good rich twits, sofa riders, Trustafarians, card cheats, gunslingers, rednecks, and carpetbaggers are playing land grab poker with the public trust. Land grabbers on both sides are promising to blow the other guy's brains out at dawn, but don't hold your breath. These people would much rather stall, wait, and eventually shoot the other guy in the back from the window of the saloon.

Of course, the film company bumps the production schedule up a week and rushes the production into town, expecting the BLM to bend. The timing of the BLM permit makes my proposal seem like, "Well, we want this, and this, and this, and this, and this, and this, and this, and this, and this, and this . . . and this, too, and we want it all *right now!*"

The Onion Creek low-flying helicopter filming permit is denied, and the film company throws a fit, sending out bad vibes like Christmas cards. The producer calls and says he is going to say bad things about me to the film commission and the BLM as part of a veiled threat to take the production elsewhere. He hopes this charade will coerce the BLM into permitting the copter in Onion Creek: "But don't worry. We're just trying a little political persuasion. It's no reflection on you."

"Great, tell them I beat my wife while you're at it."

I suggest that we mention our only alternative. If we cannot use Onion Creek, we can certainly use a canyon on state land where wildlife is everywhere. You see, with the state of Utah, land is to be used and almost anything is okay. Since all funds go to the state university school system, I prefer their logic. Education is my bag, and at least state bureaucracy is honest, straightforward, aboveboard, clear, easy to understand, and the folks never trip me out for permits. With them it is either "yes" or "yes." If you are an environmentalist, you will treat the place right; if not, then your karma will be forever stained.

The producer said, "I don't think it is wise to threaten the BLM like that."

"Huh?"

The BLM stands by its decision, of course. No time to appeal and *"Boom!"* My USS Onion Creek aircraft carrier is badly damaged and quickly sinks in the fetid waters of the Stinking Spring.

Ironically the BLM grants a permit to fly the copter down upper Kane Springs Canyon, where pure waters flow and wildlife abounds. And then, via a huge legislative loophole, we're also permitted to fly down Day Canyon, a wilderness area, even if the longhorn sheep are breeding, the raptors nesting, and folks sunbathing in the nude. Eventually, the only thing that saves these beautiful canyons is the fact that the light in the bottom is horrible.

Wanna work in the film industry? Better not be an environmentalist.

40 Onion Creek

Start: From the Onion Creek Canyon road on Utah Route 128.
Length: 20-mile out-and-back (or as short as you like).
Approximate riding time: 2 to 6 hours, depending on distance and "gawking."
Difficulty: Technically moderate. It's a dirt road, but those creek crossings can be somewhat treacherous. The initial ride up the canyon is a climb, though at worst this ride can be considered physically moderate.
Trail surface: Well-maintained gravel and hard-packed road suitable for trucks and 4WD

vehicles. Stream crossings filled with baby-heads happen.
Lay of the land: Tight canyon through the Moencopi geological layers.
Total climbing: 1,851 feet.
Land status: Bureau of Land Management (BLM) land.
Other trail users: All vehicles, especially rentals (rental vehicles seem to be impervious to salt and have a lot more clearance than the ordinary car).
Best seasons: Summer, late spring, and early fall.

Environmental concerns: Cryptobiotic soil crusts abound. Stay on the road, on the rock, or in the washes.

Warning! Beware of flash-flood danger! Always check the weather report before riding Onion Creek.

Getting there: From Moab: Head north on U.S. Route 191 for 2.6 miles from the intersection of Center and Main Streets to UT 128, just before the Colorado River Bridge. Go right and travel 20 miles. Take the road right at the sign that reads FISHER VALLEY RANCH, just before the Fisher Towers Road. The road just before the turn to the right onto Fisher Valley Ranch is marked for Taylor Ranch. If you see Fisher Towers Road, you have gone too far. Take the Fisher Valley Ranch Road to an open place on the right side of the road where you can park your vehicle. Ride from here.

The Ride

This is an easy to moderate 10-mile climb (20-mile round-trip) through Onion Creek Canyon, past the Stinking Spring and through the Narries of the Gyp Squeeze up to the Fisher Valley Ranch. Riding back down is the real treat, but be prepared to service all the bearings on your bike. I have found that if you buy some motorcycle pivot or boat grease, you can pack it around wheel and bottom bracket bearings and simply wipe it off after the ride. It is messy, but not as much of a headache as trashed bearings. The trail is shared with sparse four-wheeled traffic, but if you are lucky, or unlucky (depends on your perspective), you can end up behind a couple of hundred cattle being driven up to or down from the ranch above. Imagine the land mines.

I highly recommend this ride to anyone who wants scenery on an easy negotiable trail. During summer months the salt creek is a real cooler. The Moencopi and

Gyp Squeeze

Rico cliffs above the canyon 'are perhaps the most astounding formations in the Moab area and about as red as rock can get. Be sure to take a camera!

Route finding is pretty braindead. Just follow the road up, turn around, and ride back down at any point. If you go to the top, you'll be rewarded by views of the Fisher Valley Ranch below the La Sal Mountains to the southwest. The salt and sulfur flow of the creek crosses the trail twenty-six times on the way up to the ranch and twenty-six times on the way down. The rolling trail surface is hardpack, loose

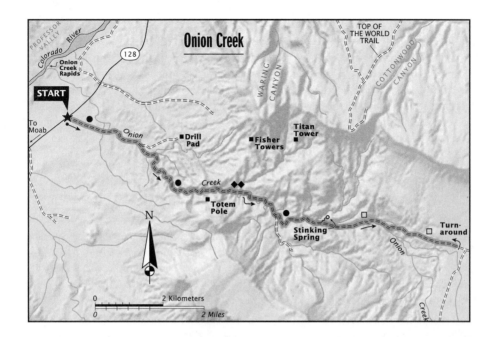

sediment, and babyheads at the bottom of those stream crossings. Speed happens, but watch it when crossing the creek.

There is an option for connecting the Entrada Bluffs Road section of the Kokopelli Trail with a ride down Onion Creek. This is accomplished by following the directions to the Top of the World trailhead. At the parking area for the Top of the World ride, go southwest and downhill (see Ride 41). Once at the bottom of this technical descent, the trail connects to the Onion Creek Road at the cattle ranch. Go right and head down to UT 128 on Onion Creek Road. Get yourself a good map of the Kokopelli Trail prior to riding this loop. Peggy Utesch's booklet, edited by F. H. Barnes, is a decent thing to have if you are researching the Kokopelli Trail system in this area. There is also the option of riding down from North Beaver Mesa. This ride is listed as an honorable mention and is also discussed in the Geyser Pass to Taylor Flat chapter (see Ride 39), where you will find points for shuttling.

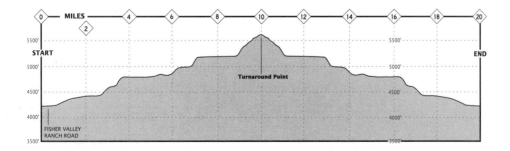

Miles and Directions

Leave from your parking spot on Fisher Valley Ranch Road and ride into the canyon. There are a couple of side spurs near the start. The first prominent unmarked spur to the left travels up to an oil drilling pad and makes a nice side trip for a view of the surrounding area. Don't worry about getting lost. It's practically impossible. Landmarks are highly visible. The ride up the canyon is all too obvious, and there is no alternate route. Count the stream crossings. Once you have counted twenty-six stream crossings and 10 miles, you are at the top and will soon be riding out into Fisher Valley. The ride becomes sandy and less interesting. Turn around and go back.

Ride Information

Trail Contacts

Bureau of Land Management
82 E. Dogwood
Moab, UT 84532
(435) 259–2196

Schedule

Trail is open year-round but is best during summer, late spring, and early fall.

Other Resources

The Utah-Colorado Mountain Bike Trail System, Route 1—Moab to Loma, Kokopelli's Trail by Peggy Utesch, published by Canyon Country Publications

Maps

USGS maps: Fisher Valley, Fisher Towers
Moab East Trail Map by Latitude 40° Inc.
Moab Recreation Map by F. H. Barnes

41 Top of the World

Start: From the Top of the World Trailhead on Entrada Bluffs Road.
Length: 8.5-mile out-and-back.
Approximate riding time: 2 to 3 hours.
Difficulty: This trail is technically and physically very difficult to downright masochistic due to the pitch of the climb and the need to be continuously fighting ledges and loose rock.

Trail surface: 4WD track. Climb up. Ride down. Loose rock, ledges, bedrock, sand, and a bit of slickrock and hardpack.
Lay of the land: Ride up a huge incline to a view that will make your knees weak.
Total climbing: 1,946 feet.
Land status: BLM lands.
Other trail users: Hikers, equestrians, and off-road vehicles (ORV).
Best seasons: Spring and fall.

Environmental concerns: Fragile soil crusts just off the trail. Stay on it. If you venture off the trail on foot, stay on the rock.

Getting there: From Moab: Drive north on U.S. Route 191 from the intersection of Center and Main Streets. At mile 2.6, just before the Colorado River Bridge, go right onto Utah Route 128 and drive along the river. The ride is very scenic. Slow down and be careful at mile 15.5. This is a place where deer frequently cross down to the river. At mile 17.7 you'll pass the road to Castle Valley on your right. At mile 23 you'll pass Fisher Towers. At mile 31.6 you'll come to the Dewey Bridge boat launch, a good spot to park if you want to ride in from the paved road. If you are driving in, continue to the bridge, but don't cross it. At mile 31.8 take a right onto the Kokopelli Trail/Entrada Bluffs Road (one and the same). Continue up the well-maintained gravel road. At mile 1.9 (from UT 128), you'll hit a sandy wash. At mile 2.2 the slickrock to your left is inviting. Don't ride on anything but rock, even if the temptation is great. At mile 3.5 there's camping on the left. At mile 4.6, Cowskin Spring spur is on the right. Keep straight. At mile 5.2 you arrive at the intersection of Entrada Bluffs Road, the Kokopelli Trail, and the Top of the World Trail. Park here. Top of the World Trail to Killer Viewpoint is to the right.

The Ride

This is a *climb*, a technical *climb*. It is challenging, not very scenic on the way up, but the destination is Killer Viewpoint. Simply incredible, and I do mean Killer. It's almost 2,500 feet to the floor of the canyon. The Moencopi formation has gone absolutely mad below. Sunset on this spot may be a reason to live. Lin Ottinger used to take 4WD tours out here, and at the top he would speed right up to the edge screaming, *"It's out of control! Oh, my gaaaaaaud, I'm out of control!"* He'd stop right on the edge of the most vertical cliff imaginable, turn in his seat, and laugh at the fear in their eyes.

The ride starts out as a grunt and hardly ever lets up. It is pretty straightforward and nearly impossible to get lost on, but since you'll have your head down, you should pay attention to a couple of spots where faint spurs can suck you in. The

Fisher Towers from Killer Viewpoint

trailhead is a bit confusing, with a bunch of spurs heading out in four directions. The one you want is to the far right going up, wrapping around the left of that boring hill.

Incidentally, the Kokopelli Trail drops down from this intersection. The Kokopelli is the spur that descends from the left-hand side of this network of confusing spurs. It is seductive in the gravity department, if you know what I mean, and it can be done as a loop down into Onion Creek, if you are smart intermediate to

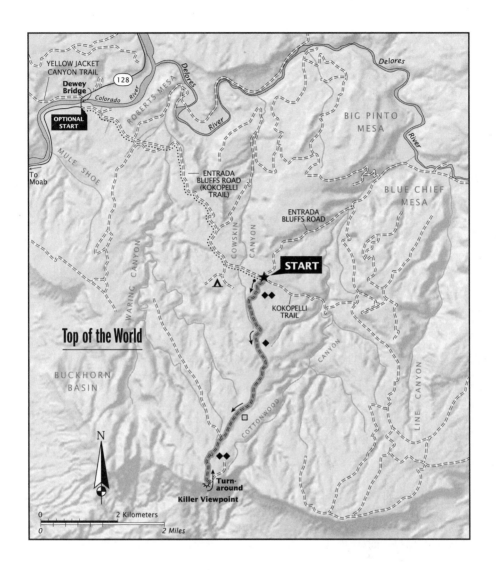

Top of the World

BUCKHORN BASIN

YELLOW JACKET CANYON TRAIL

Dewey Bridge

128

Colorado River

OPTIONAL START

To Moab

MULE SHOE

ROBERTS MESA

Delores River

River

ENTRADA BLUFFS ROAD (KOKOPELLI TRAIL)

ENTRADA BLUFFS ROAD

BIG PINTO MESA

Delores

River

BLUE CHIEF MESA

COWSKIN CANYON

START

KOKOPELLI TRAIL

WARING CANYON

CANYON

LINE CANYON

COTTONWOOD

Turn-around

Killer Viewpoint

N

0   2 Kilometers

0   2 Miles

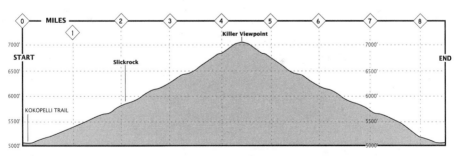

Killer Viewpoint

START

END

KOKOPELLI TRAIL

Slickrock

advanced folks . . . duh . . . but back to the masochistic climb documented here.

The trail starts out easy, gets worse, lets up a bit, then makes you work the bike constantly. Technical ledges and loose rock will try your skills, and the continuous climb will test your lung capacity. The entire ride up offers little in the way of interesting scenery, but it doesn't matter, because you are not looking up anyway—then just as you are about to die, you go to heaven. But be careful; don't die. *Stay away from the edge!* The reason to ride up is the view at the top. It ain't called Killer Viewpoint for nothing.

Miles and Directions

0.0 **START** by riding out on the spur to the far right that leaves the jumble of connecting spurs. Stay on this track, avoiding all side spurs.

0.7 Stay left.

1.7 Bear right. The trail eases off briefly, then really lays one on you.

3.0 Cross the bedrock and take the dominant spur.

3.3 Go up to the right onto the small ledges for the final challenge. If your legs are still working, this is a great section of trail rewarded by an orgasmic view.

4.4 Hold on to your butt. Be cautious when you first approach the cliff face. Gusts of wind can be deadly. If there is any possibility of lightning, you are in the wrong place. The spires down and to your right are Fisher Towers. The Titan is the monstrous one. Onion Creek Canyon is just below. Those tiny spires directly below are over 100 feet high. You can see out into Canyonlands National Park in the far distance. If you don't already know, you can get hurt really bad going fast down this trail. Weight back. Return to your vehicle.

8.5 Arrive back at your vehicle.

Ride Information

Trail Contacts
Bureau of Land Management
82 E. Dogwood
Moab, UT 84532
(435) 259–2196

Schedule
Trail is open year-round but is best during spring and fall.

Maps
USGS maps: Dewey, Blue Chief Mesa, Fisher Towers
Moab East Trail Map by Latitude 40° Inc.
Moab Recreation Map by F. H. Barnes

Honorable Mentions

East and Southeast Moab

Compiled here are some great rides in the East and Southeast region that didn't make the A-list this time around but deserve recognition. Check them out and let me know what you think. You may decide that one or more of these rides deserves higher status in future editions, or you may have a ride of your own that merits some attention.

F Miners Basin to Bachelor Basin

This ride is located in the La Sal Mountains east and south of Moab and utilizes the paved La Sal Mountain Loop Road, a technical 4WD road, and some very technical singletrack, if done as a loop. The ride contains a brutal climb and a technical descent, and it affords great views of the north mountain cluster of the La Sal range. USGS maps that include this area are Warner Lake and Mount Waas. The best map for use in the La Sals is the *Hiker's and Cross Country Skier's Map for the La Sals* by F. H. Barnes, published by Canyon Country Publications and available at the Back of Beyond Bookstore on Main Street near the intersection with 100 North in Moab. I highly recommend F. H. Barnes's maps due to high-contrast graphics that facilitate reading the trails marked. A description of La Sal Mountain Loop Road access is available in Ride 39, Geyser Pass to Taylor Flat or Ride 36, Geyser Pass to Dark Canyon Lake chapters of this book. Access to Miners Basin Road is gained from either end of La Sal Mountain Loop Road—from the Castle Valley side or the Moab side. If you use the Moab side, travel 7.9 miles south on U.S. Route 191 (Main Street) and take a left onto the La Sal Mountain Loop Road. At mile 29.4 is the Miners Basin turnoff. Park at the Cold Springs campground and ride up the steep road to the lake. A bit of a stretching and a short sprint or three on the road prior to the ascent is recommended as a warm-up to preserve the integrity of your kneecaps. Approximately 3.5 miles into the climb are the old miners' cabins. It is here that the climbing becomes even more difficult. At a little over 4 miles into the ride, you'll crest the climb. Go straight on the shale road and at mile 7 take the singletrack left. This singletrack is faint and sometimes marked with a cairn. At over 9.5 miles into the ride, you'll reconnect to La Sal Mountain Loop Road. Go left and head back to the trailhead.

Warner Lake

G North Beaver Mesa to Onion Creek

This is a 27-mile, mostly downhill ride for intermediate to advanced bikers. The ride descends 4,000 feet to a point on Utah Route 128, 20 miles from Moab. The ride requires that a shuttle vehicle be left at the point described as the start of the Onion Creek ride (see Ride 40). Read the Onion Creek descriptions for a really good idea of what to expect at least for the last 10 miles. The only big negatives are the corrosive salt in the creek and the twenty-six creek crossings that can play hell with your machinery. You should repack bearings after this ride, or at least put some extra grease on them before. Carry lube for the creek crossings and don't do this ride when it's cold.

To get to the trailhead, follow the instructions for the Geyser Pass to Taylor Flat (see Ride 39) shuttle placement. There is a note in the mileage count that marks the North Beaver Mesa to Onion Creek starting point. A sign at this intersection points the way to North Beaver Mesa. The Latitude 40° *Moab East* maps are very effective at covering this ride. At 13.4 miles into the ride, there's an old outlaw hideout, if you go up the creek to your left. At mile 14.1 there's a near-vertical climb to your right that may look irrational to you after descending so far, but aside from this the map works, if you keep track of your mileage and use a compass. If you want to be a little more sure of the contour of the land, then carry along the necessary USGS quads: Mount Waas, Fisher Valley, and Fisher Towers. The ride surface is predominantly hardpack, loose sediments, and bedrock on a 4WD track. Exercise caution. Sometimes the steeper sections can be washed out on a blind curve. Make sure the weather is on your side. This ride is great with a freeride bike.

H Warner Lake Options

Warner Lake is in the middle of a maze of steep, technical singletrack trails at roughly 10,000 feet. From the idyllic campground next to the lake you can ride down to Oowah Lake Road on the Schumann Gulch Trail, or up to Burro Pass on one of the most difficult climbs in this area. Burro has become a local favorite for the freeride, North Shore-style riders in town. A shuttle to the top of Burro that includes a descent down Schumann is a lot of fun, but can be dangerous. For riders with novice to intermediate skills there are also options to ride alongside a water diversion to various old cattle roads that loop around the Lake. The best way to deal with this area is to purchase a map and carefully plan your ride. Losing elevation here without a shuttle means that you have to climb back up to Warner Lake. Altitude sickness can be a problem here for anyone just "showing up."

Full Suspension and Moab's Gnarly Terrain

As someone who rides the trails in this book on a regular basis as a professional, I think it would be negligent not to share the following information on mountain bike technology. You must know that full-suspension bikes are for Moab and serve to make the extreme terrain less dangerous and a lot more enjoyable. If you are already the owner of a well-designed full-suspension mountain bike, you know the advantages, and you also know that there is only one disadvantage: a bit more maintenance and a little more weight. It's well worth it. Right?

At fifty-four years old, I have been riding off-road since I was five. When I was young I lived in a rural setting where tight singletrack trails lined with briers and poison ivy were right out the back door. My first bike, a blue-and-white Schwinn cruiser with 24-inch wheels, big fat tires, fenders, a bell, chainguard, and a basket on the handlebars, soon began to lose parts. First the basket, then the fenders, tinkle bell, and chainguard. The only things I added to the bike were clothespins and playing cards. I never changed the tires and only had to patch the tubes when I ran over the occasional nail around our neighborhood. I didn't know, but this bike was far ahead of its time. All I knew was that it was heavy and made a cool sound with those cards in the spokes.

As I became a teenager, our town grew to almost 30,000 people, roads were paved, and our rural surroundings were replaced by subdivisions. I was given a new hybrid bike with three gears and 26-inch wheels with skinnier tires. I liked it for heading across town on the road, but I kept my Schwinn for the woods. There was no such thing as BMX, not even banana-seated things, and the little blue cruiser simply felt better and far safer on twisty overgrown singletrack and especially on the rolling mounds of discarded earth that dotted the field behind my house.

The next bike I owned was a motorcycle, an early Honda off-road bike that weighed a ton and handled like a tractor. I lost a friend on the same bike who, after a couple of beers, took off without a helmet to feel the power and show off in front of his friends. This was in the day of motorcycle rebels and Nazi helmets. A front-end shimmy tossed him on his face at 50 mph and he died a couple of days later. This was not enough to end my fascination with motorized two-wheeled things, but it sure made me cautious. In the years to come, I went through a couple more motorcycles and gradually lost the drive or necessity to ride in the woods, instead opting for taking pretty young women for rides on the highway.

Years later in San Francisco, it took poverty and some television news coverage of the bicycle dirt-racing fascination in Marin to make me return to the bicycle. I went through a series of modified road bikes and cruisers before I bought my first true, made-for-it, off-road bike, then called an All Terrain Bicycle. I must admit that all along I dreamed of suspension, front and rear.

Front suspension is great, isn't it? We all know that now, but in 1990 I was the first in Boulder, Colorado, to own a handmade Manitou fork, built in Doug Bradbury's garage in Manitou Springs. All my riding buddies thought I was crazy to sell my high-end Puch road racer to buy an $800 fork for my 1987 Klein Pinnacle. They laughed until they rode on it. Even after the front-suspension revolution broke, they laughed when I said, "It won't be long before all mountain bikes will be fully suspended."

Well, I am here to tell you that now the mountain bike is at a point in its development where there are suspension designs that really work, and work well, and will make you go a lot faster, safer than on that hardtail. The bottom line for me, and anyone who rides terrain as challenging as Moab's, is that a hardtail is now out of the question. Once you make the jump to a good full-suspension bike there is no going back, and if you do, there are some broken bones waiting for you when you try to ride the hardtail as fast as the fully. Can you imagine going back to a fully rigid bike? Well, that is the same way you will feel about your front-suspended hardtail after riding a good full-suspension rig for a month or two.

I say "good full suspension" because there are still a few designs that stink. Bicycle designers have to reach into the world of the motorcycle and the racecar to find what works. When bicycle designers first attempted to build a suspended bike, they came up with a diving board with a seat on it and an undamped pogo-stick rear end with a single pivot behind the seat tube. The best example of a really dangerous-in-Moab full-suspension design—that sold like hotcakes years ago—is the Unified Rear Triangle (URT). A suspension seatpost works better. URT bikes do not work when they should (when you are standing, braking, or accelerating); when they do work, the geometry changes, and as a result the handling, efficiency, and comfort go out the window. The worst aspect of URT and some poorly designed linkage bikes is "stinkbug," a characteristic that makes the rear end jack up under braking . . . not good! It is more effective at ejecting you over the bars on steep descents and over G-outs. It's the little companies that really know what they're doing, because the fellow who builds and designs the bikes is the fellow who is riding the bikes. The little guys *have* to build good bikes. The big guys rely on marketing to make you think the bikes are good. They are about making money, not making really great bikes. Buy American from companies that *build* their own product.

Beware of marketing-ploy bikes that look like giant roach clips and hook beginners like bottom-feeding catfish on a wad of white bread. In order to understand how rear suspension works, you have to study the physics of pivot points and frame geometry. Different terrains and surfaces demand different geometries, so reaching a compromise suitable for your riding style and favorite riding grounds requires the acquisition of knowledge in order to make the right decision. Purchasing a mountain bike is not a braindead, I-like-the-color endeavor. You want to buy something that works all the time: during acceleration, braking, coasting, uphill, and downhill. It has to handle well and be sturdy as hell to take the punishment that speed can dish out. Good looks come in last. If you buy a bike because it looks like a sculpture, then you may end up riding a Thomas Moore nude that handles like a chunky piece of bronze with tits and a big butt.

The simplest full-suspension design *that works* is the cantilever beam. If you are in the market for something that will be easy to maintain, then there are a few single-pivot designs that are right up your alley. The three that come to mind are the Santa Cruz Heckler, the Mountain Cycle, and the Ventana El Chamuco. These bikes have the pivot in the optimum location—low and forward, even with the middle chainring. These bikes will satisfy those who are looking to be wowed by weird tubes and funny roach-clip designs, but, in this case, use space-age construction to beef up the strength of the frame, have the pivot in the right spot, and have great geometry. The Ventana is definitely the best of these bikes. It is made in America at Ventana, not farmed out to aerospace concerns or Taiwan.

I have always favored multiple-pivot bikes. The first full-suspension bike I ever owned was a Mantis Pro-Floater, designed by Richard Cunningham, the now born-again editor of *Mountain Bike Action* magazine. It was a derivative of the automotive MacPherson strut design. The shock was a stressed member of the frame directly attached to the seatstays, anchored under the top tube. The pivot at the rear dropout was attached at the chainstays. The other end of the chainstay pivoted behind, and even with, the bottom bracket. MacPherson Strut bikes are still around. The first and most famous of these strut bikes was Horst Leitner's AMP bikes. Leitner was the first designer to effectively use motorcycle suspension advancements on a bicycle, and his patented "Horst Link"—the specific point at which the chainstay pivot is located, which makes the design so plush—was sold to Specialized. The Maverick ML7 is also a version of MacPerson strut, but combining aspects of the outdated URT design. It is not a good Moab bike.

The "swing link," made popular by Ventana and Manitou, is generally recognized by a shock mounted below the seat tube with a linkage "swinging" the suspension forces into the shock through a rocker pivot on the seat tube. Swing links work great but are limited in performance by a tendency to bob when you are sprinting out of the saddle. Rock Mountain still makes a fine swing-link bike for a reasonable price. Tomac Bicycles also make a fine swing-link bike that is basically a reworking of the Doug Bradbury Manitou design. These bikes have been refined and are a good choice.

The very best multiple-pivot design is the four-bar linkage. It is distinguished by a shock mounted to the seat tube, or, in rare cases, below or above the downtube.

Full suspension is essential for riding in Moab.

Like the swing link, a rocker arm forces the shock into motion, but the four bar uses this rocker in a much more effective physical manner, which in turn isolates the rear end from flex. The best of the four-bar-linkage designs are the Ventana El Salta-montes and La Bruja. The "Salt" is a cross-country design that is light, strong, and plush, especially in the hands of an aggressive rider. It has 4 to 5.5 inches of rear travel. The La Bruja (or Witch) is a longer-travel freeride version capable of huge drops and high speeds. Long travel and stout frame construction enable experienced, strong riders to perform feats that otherwise would be impossible. Stairs disappear, drop-offs start to shrink, and speed goes up.

As a guide, bike dealer, and builder of state-of-the-art full-suspension bikes, I've been through a ton of them, continually remaining abreast of the state of the art.

Since the first edition of this book, things have changed and, for the most part, gotten better. There has been more development, more reverse development, pirating of designs, shifting of patents, and a scary shift of production to Taiwan and mainland China, where environmental protection is nonexistent and labor is cheap. My loyalties, for the most part, lie with American-designed-and-built full-suspension frames. Some bikes fabricated in Taiwan are quite good, mind you, and are especially easy on the wallet, but the reasons these bikes are carrying such low price tags are the lack of environmental controls and social responsibility in the Far Eastern countries. I am of the opinion that the best way to be patriotic (ugh, I hate that word—it really means "loyal to the king") is to buy American and avoid companies that feed off slave labor and lax standards on foreign shores. Buy American, and make sure the frame is made by the company that puts its name on it.

As of 2003, based on my years of experience with every brand and full-suspension design, I rate Ventana's longer-travel XC and freeride bikes as the very best, due to in-house engineering and sturdy construction based on real experience and years of hard work, as well as a reputation for honest-to-God down-to-earth customer service. In business since 1988, and smarter than your average manufacturer, Ventana builds beautiful handmade frames, collectors' items right out of the box, decently light and able to handle Moab terrain. Specialized is a great alternative to the more exotic Ventana. For a really cheap bike that works great in Moab (and made in the land of dim sum), get a Kona or Norco freeride bike. Make sure it weighs at least thirty-five pounds.

If you are looking for a hardtail that is designed specifically for Moab terrain, there's a neat little gem, the Stud Muffin, designed with the Moab Slickrock Trail in mind. It will accommodate a 4- to 5-inch travel fork and comes with a 4-inch travel suspension seatpost.

Emergency Services

I dropped my fork and answered the phone. When you have a business like mine, you drop dinner, lunch, breakfast, sex, or hop off the toilet to answer that phone. It is where information flows and money pours in.

"Hi, Lee, it's Freddy." So as not to raise eyebrows, Freddy is not this fellow's name. I will get a call as soon as "Freddy" reads this, though, and I will hop up from the toilet with that horrible recycled toilet paper my wife insists on buying dangling from my pants as I run to answer the call.

"How was your ride?" I asked, faking a bounce in my voice. Freddy wouldn't call me unless I could do something for him. I hoped it wasn't what I thought it was going to be. I silently prayed his group had dodged another bullet.

"Well, it's not good."

I was expecting another list of injuries, maybe even a fatality. Freddy and his group had been in Moab for only two days and already they had lost a couple of riders due to broken bones. Testosterone and the Freudian Death Wish were Freddy's best friends and worst enemies during his midlife crisis. His marriage was on the edge. His sanity was on the edge. His business was on the edge. So what better place to ride than the edge of a cliff? If he fell, all other problems would be solved. The

Wipe out and get hurt, unprepared, in the wrong place, at the wrong time? Just throw some dirt on yourself.

subconscious mind works like this. The conscious mind hides this bit of information. I have already been through the midlife thing. My subconscious mind is more interested in . . .well, I don't know.

"Uh-oh. What happened?" My eyes rolled of their own free will. My wife peered into the room with that "oh, crap" look on her face.

Freddy paused a bit, feeling the "I told you so" on its way, then said: "One in our group is missing. We rode Gold Bar Rim and I think he got lost up on top where the trail splits just past that arch."

"Jeez, how'd you lose him? Can't you count!?"

"He was just . . . stupid. He didn't hear the speech about how hard it was going to be. We didn't even know he was back there."

It is times like this when I realize how valuable our professional guiding services are. I, as well as all the guides we hire, are like sheepdogs. We count instinctively. We protect instinctively. We sense the skills, overconfidence, and overstimulated testosterone gland of a rider like a bloodhound smells the prison escapee's scent. Sometimes people whom you would think are smart enough just don't get it. We are pros at this. We don't get lost. We don't let people get lost. We can't make people listen or save *all* the stupid people from getting hurt, but we sure can get them outta there in a hurry once they've smashed their heads in.

"It's mighty cold and dark out there right now and it will get worse. You don't know where he is or what happened to him, do you?"

"Well, no." Freddy sounded a bit frightened and ashamed.

"What do you want me to do about it?" I imagined a lone rider cold, out of water, and in the worst possible place to get lost near Moab, the vast and dangerous exposed terrain just off the Gold Bar Rim Trail. I could picture him coming down the Portal Trail in the dark. Oh, my God.

"We think he may have gone down that 4WD road at the top, just before you get to the Portal Trail. If someone goes in from the Portal and somebody else in from Poison Spider Mesa . . ."

I stopped him cold. "Whoa. If you send a bunch of folks out onto Poison Spider Mesa, someone is going to get hurt, and more people are gonna get lost. Call Moab Search and Rescue. Call the professionals in on this, before the situation gets worse. Call them immediately. Do not hesitate. Do not pass Go. Do not collect the $200. Do not call Lee."

Silence.

"Okay. Bye."

A couple of days later, I found out what happened to Freddy's friend. Instead of heading down the Portal Trail, he lagged behind, lost sight of the group, dropped down the Poison Spider Mesa Trail, stopped near the bottom when it got dark, made a shelter, and wisely waited until someone came for him. He didn't sound nearly as stupid as Freddy made him out to be. Luckily, Search and Rescue found the fellow within a couple of hours. I didn't hear this from Freddy, though. I heard it from a mutual friend of the fellow who got lost. "I guess he will pay to ride with you next time." This is a funky way to get clients, but this kind of revelation makes my business.

Of course, hindsight is 20–20. One fellow in Freddy's group said, "If we had just driven up Poison Spider Trail, we could have saved the money for Search and Rescue."

"Yeah, and if monkeys flew outta my ass, I could start a scratch-and-sniff petting zoo."

Moab terrain is extremely challenging, climate is volatile, and mountain biking areas can be very remote. When bad things happen you'll need an idea of where to turn. Riding with caution, expecting the worst, knowing first aid, and carrying a cell phone, enough water, and supplies to guarantee survival are the best ways to prevent an emergency from turning into a tragedy, but if serious injury happens, you have to get help. Frankly, in some situations you will have no other recourse and *will* have to take care of the situation yourself with what is at hand, and with your own wits. If stuff happens out in areas like the sand stretch above Hey Joe Canyon on the way to Dubinky Well, or in the Yellow Cat District, or out on the White Rim, there are simply no services available for miles and miles. Being prepared is your only defense against "the horror." I have listed here a few places where help is available and where safe drinking water is present.

What to Do and Who to Contact

In case of an injury emergency, stabilizing the victim is the first order of business, and then you'll have to get to a highway. Flag down a car. You may be lucky enough to stop someone who knows the area or has a cell phone. If you have a 4WD vehicle nearby and the injury is not serious, then, and only then, should you consider retrieving the injured party.

If you are carrying a cell phone, you'll have to find a spot where the cell phone works. It will most likely work if you can see the La Sal Mountains. The cell site is located on the most southerly peak. Satellite phones are currently available and they will work whenever there is a satellite overhead, but chances are you cannot afford one.

If you are riding in the areas on either side of U.S. Route 191 to the north of Moab, the Moab airport, Canyonlands Field, is a good place to seek help. The airport is just a couple of miles north of the Monitor and Merrimac and Klondike Bluffs Trailheads, on the west side of US 191, and is a reliable source of help. Any problems on trailheads south of Canyonlands Field should be dealt with by going directly to the airport. Archview Campground and the Archview gas station are also within range. The Archview Campground is a mile north of the Gemini Bridges Trailhead and parking area just past the intersection of US 191 and Utah Route 313. Dalton Wells irrigation project is at the mouth of Dalton Wells Road, but people may or may not be there. The Bar-M Chuckwagon is opposite the Gemini Bridges

Trailhead on US 191, but it is usually deserted during daylight hours and closed during the off season.

If you are riding in the Yellow Cat District, there is a gas station at the Thompson exit just off Interstate 70. There is also an information center with a phone on the interstate between Thompson and Yellow Cat Road. Crescent Junction's C-store is at the intersection of US 191 and I–70.

If you are riding west of US 191 off UT 313, the road to Canyonlands National Park, there are two or three sources for help nearby. The Canyonlands visitor center is just inside the park at the top of the Shafer Rim switchbacks. Dead Horse State Park visitor center is a few miles west of the Gemini Bridges Trailhead on UT 313. Rangers live in homes nearby. There is also an oil drilling pad just off UT 313, a couple of miles east of the Gemini Bridges Trailhead on Utah 313 on the south side of the road, but you cannot be sure of personnel being present. It's generally active only during the day, and sometimes it's completely deserted.

If you are riding anywhere off Utah Route 128 east of Moab, your best bet is to get someone to stop on the highway. There is a small community with no services in Castle Valley. There is the resort at the Sorrel Ranch and any number of ranches and other areas along the river where people live.

If you are riding in areas up Sand Flats Road like Porcupine Rim or the Kokopelli Trail, your best plan is to go toward Moab. There is no help into the mountains aside from a couple of remote homes. The Sand Flats Recreation Area booth is a good place to get help during the day in peak season. The best thing about going toward town is that it is downhill and you can get there pretty fast.

For rides south of Moab beyond the Moab Valley on US 191, there is Hole in the Rock, a tourist attraction and home. There's a rest area just north of it at the mouth of Kane Springs Canyon, within a few yards of Hole in the Rock. There is a phone at the rest area, and folks live at Hole in the Rock. If you're riding on the backside of the La Sal Mountains, in the areas below or above Dark Canyon Lake, then the town of La Sal on Utah Route 46 is your best bet for a telephone. Do not hesitate to stop at a private home if you are in an emergency situation. You will be surprised at how helpful, kind, and concerned people can be when the going gets rough. A survival situation usually brings out the best in people.

Moab Search and Rescue

In case of emergency, contact Moab Search and Rescue at 911 (emergency dispatch). The service is hardly free, so expect to pay anywhere from $300 to $1,000.

Repair and Maintenance

Fixing a Flat

TOOLS YOU WILL NEED

- Two tire irons.
- Pump (either a floor pump or a frame pump).
- No screwdrivers! (This can puncture the tube.)

REMOVING THE WHEEL

The front wheel is easy. Simply disconnect the brake shoes, open the quick-release mechanism or undo the bolts with the proper-sized wrench, then remove the wheel from the bike.

The rear wheel is a little more tricky. Before you loosen the wheel from the frame, shift the chain into the smallest gear on the freewheel (the cluster of gears in the back). Once you've done this, removing and installing the wheel, like the front, is much easier.

REMOVING THE TIRE

Step one: Insert a tire iron under the bead of the tire and pry the tire over the lip of the rim. Be careful not to pinch the tube when you do this.

Step two: Hold the first tire iron in place. With the second tire iron, repeat step one, 3 or 4 inches down the rim. Alternate tire irons, pulling the bead of the tire over the rim, section by section, until one side of the tire bead is completely off the rim.

Step three: Remove the rest of the tire and tube from the rim. This can be done by hand. It's easiest to remove the valve stem last. Once the tire is off the rim, pull the tube out of the tire.

CLEAN AND SAFETY CHECK

Step four: Using a rag, wipe the inside of the tire to clean out any dirt, sand, glass, thorns, etc. These may cause the tube to puncture. The inside of a tire should feel smooth. Any pricks or bumps could mean that you have found the culprit responsible for your flat tire.

Step five: Wipe the rim clean, then check the rim strip, making sure it covers the spoke nipples properly on the inside of the rim. If a spoke is poking through the rim strip, it could cause a puncture.

Step six: At this point, you can do one of two things: Replace the punctured tube with a new one, or patch the hole. It's easiest to just replace the tube with a new tube when you're out on the trails. Roll up the old tube and take it home to repair later that night in front of the TV. Directions on patching a tube are usually included with the patch kit itself.

INSTALLING THE TIRE AND TUBE
(This can be done entirely by hand)

Step seven: Inflate the new or repaired tube with enough air to give it shape, then tuck it back into the tire.

Step eight: To put the tire and tube back on the rim, begin by putting the valve in the valve hole. The valve must be straight. Then use your hands to push the beaded edge of the tire onto the rim all the way around so that one side of your tire is on the rim.

Step nine: Let most of the air out of the tube to allow room for the rest of the tire.

Step ten: Beginning opposite the valve, use your thumbs to push the other side of the tire onto the rim. Be careful not to pinch the tube in between the tire and the rim. The last few inches may be difficult, and you may need the tire iron to pry the tire onto the rim. If so, just be careful not to puncture the tube.

BEFORE INFLATING COMPLETELY

Step eleven: Check to make sure the tire is seated properly and that the tube is not caught between the tire and the rim. Do this by adding about five to ten pounds of air, and watch closely that the tube does not bulge out of the tire.

Step twelve: Once you're sure the tire and tube are properly seated, put the wheel back on the bike, then fill the tire with air. It's easier squeezing the wheel through the brake shoes if the tire is still flat.

Step thirteen: Now fill the tire with the proper amount of air, and check constantly to make sure the tube doesn't bulge from the rim. If the tube does appear to bulge out, release all the air as quickly as possible, or you could be in for a big bang. Place the wheel back in the dropost and tighten the quick release lever Reconnect the brake shoes.

When installing the rear wheel, place the chain back onto the smallest cog (farthest gear on the right), and pull the derailleur out of the way. Your wheel should slide right on.

Lubrication Prevents Deterioration

Lubrication is crucial to maintaining your bike. Dry spots will be eliminated. Creaks, squeaks, grinding, and binding will be gone. The chain will run quietly, and the gears will shift smoothly. The brakes will grip quicker, and your bike may last longer with fewer repairs. Need I say more? Well, yes. Without knowing where to put the lubrication, what good is it?

THINGS YOU WILL NEED
- One can of bicycle lubricant, found at any bike store.
- A clean rag (to wipe excess lubricant away).

WHAT GETS LUBRICATED
- Front derailleur
- Rear derailleur
- Shift levers
- Front brake
- Rear brake
- Both brake levers
- Chain

WHERE TO LUBRICATE

To make it easy, simply spray a little lubricant on all the pivot points of your bike. If you're using a squeeze bottle, use just a drop or two. Put a few drops on each point where metal moves against metal—for instance, at the center of the brake calipers. Then let the lube sink in.

Once you have applied the lubricant to the derailleurs, shift the gears a few times, working the derailleurs back and forth. This allows the lubricant to work itself into the tiny cracks and spaces it must occupy to do its job. Work the brakes a few times as well.

LUBING THE CHAIN

Lubricating the chain should be done after the chain has been wiped clean of most road grime. Do this by spinning the pedals counterclockwise while gripping the chain with a clean rag. As you add the lubricant, be sure to get some in between each link. With an aerosol spray, just spray the chain while pedaling backward (counterclockwise) until the chain is fully lubricated. Let the lubricant soak in for a few seconds before wiping the excess away. Chains will collect dirt much faster if they're loaded with too much lubrication.

Glossary

What it all means

Anasazi: derogative Navajo term used to describe ancient pre-Pueblan and Pueblan peoples who once inhabited canyon country

ankle biter: bayonet yucca

arch: a hole in a single sandstone geological layer formed by water, sun, or wind erosion

Atlas Mine: uranium processor responsible for the Moab tailings pond at the north end of town

auger: face plant

babyheads: river- or streambed rocks the size of a baby's head (or larger)

bedrock: where the Flintstones lived—also massive embedded stone formations

bridge: hole formed in two sandstone geological layers where one layer has been eroded out below another by water erosion

Chinle: geological formation made up of limestone conglomerate of native soil and volcanic ash from the Triassic period

cryptobiotic soil crusts (crypto): crusty fragile black desert soils that form the very bottom of the food chain, formed by cyanobacteria, mosses, and lichens. "Crypto" photosynthesizes sunlight into nitrogen, stabilizes the desert sands, and holds moisture, allowing desert plants to take hold.

Cutler: geological formation made up of sediments from coastal sands and desert dunes from the Permian period

Dakota: sandstone, shale, and carbonized organic deposits of sea origin from the Cretaceous period

Entrada: colorful sandstone originating from tidal mudflats and desert dunes of the Jurassic period

datura: psychotropic plant species with night-blooming white flower. Lines canyon walls along the Colorado River and can be found on many rides near Moab, especially against cliff faces and in sandy washes. Also known as jimsonweed, wolf's bane, and queen of the night.

dirt sample: falling from your bike on a trail and accidentally getting to know the texture of the soil by embedding it in your flesh

face plant: dirt sample, but on your face

G-out: an abrupt dip with a sharp transition—"Gravity-out"—sometimes called a "V-out" by people who aren't as hip as people who call it a G-out

hardtails: mountain bikes with front suspension only—rear end is unsuspended

Kayenta: sandstone and shale sediments of freshwater origin from the Triassic period

land mine: cattle feces or any obstacle on a trail that must be avoided

lollipop: trail that has a loop at the end of an out-and-back access route

Manchos: geological formation made of marine limestone and shale from the Cretaceous period

Moab Tongue: Entrada geological formation made up of coastal sand and mud. The tongue is visible from north of Klondike Bluffs and extends down to the Moab Valley. Also visible in the Colorado National Monument outside Fruita, Colorado.

Moencopi: geological formation made up of shallow marine sediments from the Triassic Period

Morrison: geological formation made up of sediments from freshwater lakes and wetlands where dinosaurs roamed in the late Jurassic period

Navajo: sandstone of desert dune origin from the Triassic period. No, those aren't petrified sand dunes. The rounded shapes are formed by heat erosion.

petroglyph: rock art that is "pecked" into the rock face

pictograph: rock art that is painted on the rock surface

risers: handlebars with an abrupt bend upward a couple of inches in from the junction at the stem clamp

rollies: repeated small rolling hills

sagwagon: vehicle that follows a group of riders to pick up those who bonk, sag, or otherwise give up. For wimps and kids.

shred: riding hard, going fast, being irresponsible

sidehills, sidehilling: a slickrock hill that is ridable—riding on the outside edge of a basketball. Traversing a slanted surface by riding along the face of the hill.

slickrock: smooth sandstone surfaces misnamed by cowboys who considered it "slick" because they walked in leather-soled cowboy boots and rode across it on a horse with iron shoes

slot canyon, slot wash: a narrow watercourse through solid rock

softtails: mountain bikes with a rudimentary form of rear suspension such as a suspension seat post or flexible chainstays

tailings: stone, gravel, and soil remnants of mining laced with all sorts of natural and unnatural poisons from the mining process—also containing radioactive debris

Yellow Cake: high-grade uranium ore made up of wet soft yellow sand

Accommodations

Moab is a small town in winter, with a population of around 8,000, but in the spring, summer, and fall months the population balloons to well over 100,000 on weekends. Every year another couple of big hotels go up, and more and more homes are converted to tourist accommodations, but on random weekends and during peak season and special-event weeks like Jeep Week, the Fat Tire Festival, Rod Benders, or the Art Fair, every room, home, and camping spot within 50 miles, good or bad, is full. If you are planning a vacation in Moab during peak season, be sure to reserve accommodations far in advance.

Moab's in-town accommodations range from camping spots with sewer, water, gas, and television hookups to plush condos and complete homes. You can stay in a trailer, a tepee, a cave, or a tent. It seems that everyone is offering their home as a bed-and-breakfast, legal or no.

Just outside Moab you'll find primitive camping spots, requiring the use of chemical toilets. The BLM has recently begun to manage popular camping spots much more closely and, despite some local protests, has done a fine job of cleaning up areas trashed by mountain bikers and four-wheelers. The primitive camping areas off Sand Flats Road around the Moab Slickrock Trail, which up until a couple of years ago were a mess of toilet paper, scattered turds, and tire tracks, are now being managed very effectively by the BLM and the Sand Flats Team, with available toilets and designated camping areas. The BLM introduced a fee for use and graded the road allowing access farther east. This has been both a curse and a blessing. The camping areas are now much more tidy and safe, but with this upscale renewal come fees and more people, and the widened road now brings more people farther up onto the Sand Flats. As a result of their own actions that have led to more use, the BLM is now considering areas around the Porcupine Rim as Wilderness Study Areas off limits to mountain bikes. Progress. Ain't it neat?

Bed and Breakfast Inns

Dream Keeper
191 South 200 East
(435) 259–5998, (888) 230–3247
Owned by Jim and Kathy Kempa. Pool. Outdoor spa. Bike storage. Nice yard. ★★★★

Sorrel River Ranch
Utah Route 128
(435) 259–4642, (877) 359–2715
www.sorrelriver.com
Really fancy condo-style lodging on the river. *New!* Beautiful views! Kitchenettes. Drawbacks are that you will be a long way from Moab and the rates are high: $139–$475. ★★★★

Sunflower Hill

185 North 300 East

(435) 259–2974, (800) MOAB–SUN

www.sunflowerhill.com

Owned by Aaron and Kim Robison. Best location! Gardens. Outdoor hot tub. Patios. Private balconies. Very nice. Rates: $65–$165. ★★★★

Tumbleweed Guest Room

3101 East Cedar Hills Lane

(435) 259–3947

Owned by Don and Elbertine Miner. Private deck. Fenced yard. Out-of-the-way location. Rates: $60–$80 (weekly $400). ★★

Mountain Cabins and Inns

For a listing of cabins and bed-and-breakfast inns in the La Sal Mountains, go to www.moabcanyonlands.com/lasal/ on the Internet or call (888) 655–2725 for the La Sal Mountain Information Center.

Trailers

Red Valley Homes

200 East 100 North

(435) 259–5408, (800) 213–8608

Trailers for daily rental. Yard. Pool. Picnic table. Trailers are clean. Kitchen. TV. Great value for groups. Quiet. ★★★

Hotels, Motels, Hostels

Aarchway Inn

1551 North U.S. Route 191

(435) 259–2599, (800) 341–9359

New. Large. Upscale rooms. Whirlpool baths. Spa. Too far from town if you want to walk. Just off noisy highway. ★★

Apache Motel

Run by Barbara Brady

166 S. 400 East

(435) 259–5727, (800) 228–6882

Where John Wayne stayed (this is worth one star). Quiet. Off the main drag. Used to be Moab's only hotel back when 400 East was the main street. Pool. Rooms open to outside. Rates: $52–$72. ★★★

Arches Inn–Sunset Motel

41 West 100 North

(435) 259–5191 or (800) 421–5614

Rates: $45–$65.

Best Western Greenwell Inn

105 South Main Street

(435) 259–6151, (800) 528–1234

Great location. Nice rooms. Overpriced. Rooms open to outside. ★★★

Best Western Canyonlands

16 South Main Street

(435) 259–2300

Great location. Decent rooms. ★★★

Big Horn Lodge

550 South Main Street

(435) 259–6171, (800) 325–6171

Recently overhauled to resemble a can of chili and beans. Rooms open to outside. The only review I have ever heard about it is, "I'm staying at the Big Horn." That's about it. Good location, but Main Street and no rooms in back means noise. ★★★

Bowen Motel

169 North Main

(435) 259–7132, (800) 874–5439

www.bowenmotel.com

Good location. A bit noisy. Rooms open to outside. ★★

Gonzo Inn
100 West 200 South
(435) 259–2515, (800) 791–4044
Great rooms—most are small, but tasteful. One bed per room. Some rooms have views, some have views of the parking lot. Small decks. Nice showers. Pool. Hot tub. Bike storage and cleaning area. Good location. Pricey. ★★★★

Hotel Off Center
96 East Center Street
(435) 259–4244
Very funky. Very quaint. Theme rooms. Most mountain-bike-friendly hotel in the world! Shared baths and funk are the only reasons this place doesn't get more stars, but it deserves special consideration because the people who own it are so damn cool. Leave your wallet on the bed. Don't lock your door. Keep your bike in the room. Best location in Moab—right above the best restaurant in the state. Rooms open to hallway. Small kitchen and dining area are available if you want to fix meals or hang out. Stay here for a week in order to get to know the people and you will not want to stay anywhere else. ★★

Kokopelli Lodge
72 South 100 East
(435) 259–7615
Funky. Continental breakfast. Good location, but a bit noisy sometimes. ★★

Lazy Lizard International Youth Hostel
1213 South U.S. Route 191
(435) 259–6057
Homey for hippies. Small cabins. Tent space. Laundry. Kitchen. Hot tub. Movies. Cheap. A ways from town.

Moab Valley Inn
711 South Main Street
(435) 259–4419, (800) 831–MOAB
www.moabvalleyinn.com
Kind of impersonal, but very clean. Somewhat bike friendly! Great pool with shade on one end. Spa. Conference rooms. Where Thelma and Louise stayed. Rooms in front face highway and can be noisy. ★★★★

Ramada Inn
182 South Main Street
(435) 259–7141, (888) 989–1988
Clean. Mountain bikes not welcome at all. ★★★

Red Cliffs Lodge
Utah Route 128, Mile Marker 14
(435) 259–2002
Clean rooms. Away from town. ★★

Red Stone
535 South Main Street
(435) 259–3500
Great location. Quiet. Rooms open in hallway. Clean. Good value in off season. ★★★

Rustic Inn
120 E. 100 South
(435) 259–6177, (800) 231–8184

Super 8
889 N. Main
(435) 259–8868, (800) 800–8000
Big. Easy to find. Not very mountain bike friendly. ★★

Travelodge
550 South Main Street
(435) 259–6171
Basic. ★

Virginian
70 East 200 South
(435) 259–5951
Tacky, but kitchenettes! Virginia?
Rooms open to outside. Clean and
suprisingly comfortable. Good location
if you want to walk to restaurants and
movieplex. ★★★

Commercial Campgrounds and RV Parks

Arch View RV Campground and Resort
North of Moab about 8 miles on U.S.
Route 191
(435) 259–7854, (800) 813–MOAB
Too far from Moab. Hot as hell in sum-
mer. Gas station and C-store nearby. ★★

Canyonlands Campground and RV Park
566 South Main Street
(435) 259–6848
The best! Great location in central
Moab. Clean. Like a small town. Laundry. Good bathrooms. Has its own store
and swimming pool. Near restaurants.
Paved pads for your RV. Difficult to see
coming from south. Sharp turn from
south is difficult for a large RV. ★★★★

KOA
3225 South U.S. Route 191
(435) 259–6682, (800) 562–0372
Campground with cabins, RV hookups,
and a pool, but it is pretty far south of
town. Good family accommodations,
but hot. ★★

Moab Valley RV and Campark
1773 N. U.S. Route 191
(435) 259–4469.
Easy to find. First campark coming from
north. Next to intersection of UT 128
and US 191. Very clean. Close to river.
Mosquitoes. Close enough to town, but
not walking distance. Lots of services.
★★

Pack Creek Campground
1520 Murphy Lane
(435) 259–2982
Great family conveniences. ★★

Portal RV Park and Fishery
1261 North U.S. Route 191
(435) 259–6108, (800) 574–2028.
Great for kids (fishing), but no shade.
Mosquitoes. Close enough to Moab,
but not walking distance. ★★

Spanish Trail RV Park and Camp-ground
2980 S. U.S. Route 191
(800) 787–2751
★

Sand Flats
on Sand Flats Road, no reservations
(435) 259–2444
Cheap. Registration required. No
services, but some pit toilets. Next to
the Moab Slickrock Trail and a few
miles from the Porcupine Rim Trailhead. Some camp spots require chemical toilets.

Restaurants

Arches Dining Room
182 South Main Street
American food. Serves liquor.

Bar-M Chuckwagon
541 South Mulberry Lane
Live Western show and cowboy supper.
Meat-and-potato crowd. Real Western
flavor.

Branding Iron
2971 South U.S. Route 191
The karaoke on Friday nights is a
western-style hooha. Local culture
abounds. This place is a must for anyone who wants to really see what
Moab is like underneath the jersey.

Breakfast at Tiffany's
90 East Center Street
(435) 259–2553
Breakfast, lunch, and evening snacks.

Buck's Grill House
1393 North Main Street
(435) 259–5201
Best all-around eatery in Moab! Sometimes crowded—for good reason.

Center Cafe
East Center Street
Good food and service. Great wines.
Expensive.

Denny's
989 North U.S. Route 191
It's Denny's.

Desert Bistro
92 East Center Street
(435) 259–0756
Fantastic food and service. Great wines.
Worth every penny. Atmosphere!

Eddy McStiff's
57 South Main Street
Great menu. Fair pizza. Overpriced, but
consistent. Service can get spotty when
crowded. Fantastic bar. Good-tasting
nearbeer (3.2 stuff—not a drinking
man's beer at all).

Eklectica
352 North Main Street
Julie's coffee is the best legal drug in
Moab. Great place to hang out and listen to local gossip.

Hogi Yogi
396 South Main Street
Subs, sandwiches, and frozen yogurt.
Great kids place.

Jail House Cafe
101 North Main Street
(435) 259–3900
Good breakfast place. Closes at
1:00 P.M.

Knave of Hearts
100 West and 200 North
Not a Jim Stiles free zone, but still a
great place for lunch and sweets.

Miquel's Baja Grill
51 North Main Street
(435) 259–6546
Decent Mexican.

Moab Diner
189 South Main Street
Homey. Basic fare of American burger food and a fine green chili. Many flavors of ice cream. Greasy, but good.

Moab Springs Ranch House
1266 North Main Street
Upscale. Fine atmosphere. This place is a little museum with steaks.

Pasta Jay's
4 South Main Street
Good homemade pasta specials. Okay prices. Outside seating is great for Rod Benders Week, but noisy as hell.

The Peace Tree
20 South Main Street
(435) 259–8503
Hippie food—juice, shakes, sandwiches, and wraps.

Red Rock Bakery
74 South Main Street
(435) 259–5941
Great coffee and sandwiches. Sinful eclairs.

Rio Restaurant and Private Club
2 South 100 West
Some locals like the Mexican food here. Live music on weekends. Private club, so you can get higher alcohol content in your Dos Equis or Corona beer. Smoking permitted.

Sunset Grill
900 North U.S. Route 191
Used to be Charlie Steen's house, then the Mi Vida Restaurant. Changed the name to Sunset Grill. The view is awesome, giving the place a certain romantic vibe. Who in their right mind would change the name from Mi Vida to Sunset Grill?

Events, Races, and Funky Things to Do

Arts

There are a number of **Art Walks** taking place throughout the year. These events are basically a list of shops and routes to and from each location. Art Walks are organized by local artists and entrepreneurs to promote all sorts of arts and crafts, as well as the Moab shops that deal in art, jewelry, and such. If you are coming into Moab and want to know when the Art Walks are taking place, call (435) 259–6896.

The Moab Arts Council hosts a couple of events here each year that are open to the public. **The Moab Arts Festival** is the most visible and happens on Memorial Day weekend. It is where you can buy paintings, jewelry, sculpture, and pottery from local artists. The event takes place in the Moab Arts and Recreation Center located at 111 East, 100 North in Moab in the building that formerly housed the Stuntman's Hall of Fame. Frankly, I miss the Stuntman's Hall of Fame where the funky old dude who once ran it used to balance chairs on his chin, show horrible scars to the kids, and tell off-color stories about John Wayne. Performance Art is lost in Moab. The Moab Art Council can be reached at (435) 259–2742. The folks specifically responsible for the Arts Festival can be reached at (435) 259–8431.

Food

The Moab Arts and Recreation Center also hosts **The Chocolate Lovers Fling** in February.

The **Dan O'Laurie Museum Ice Cream Social** is one of those down-home things that will get you close to the heart of Moab. It takes place in the heat of late July in front of the Moab Library next to the museum. To get in touch with the organizers, call (435) 259–7985.

Rodeos, Livestock, and Cowboy Crap

Old Spanish Trail Arena is a new and very nice facility—despite the fact that it smells like horse dung and cow pies most of the time—on U.S. Route 191 south of town, just beyond the city limits. The prominent redbrick building on the east side of the highway houses a number of events each year. There is a **Championship Team Roping** competition in February (specific info on the roping competition is at 435–259–6226), a high school rodeo in March, several Professional Rodeo Cowboys Association (PRCA)–sanctioned rodeos including the massive **Butch Cassidy Days Festival** in June, a **4H Livestock Show** in July (specific info on 4H competition is at 435–259–8240), and the **Grand County Fair** (more pigs, cows, and sheep, and a few rides and cotton candy) in August. For specific dates and information on these events, call the Old Spanish Trail Arena management at (800) 635–6622.

Car Shows

Perhaps the most entertaining of all events in Moab are the car shows. Don't have to worry about these guys taking their precious machinery off-road. These folks entertain the crowds on Main Street with drag racing between the lights in fancy-colored hot rods. For those looking to escape the deafening roar of the straight pipes, there are also slow-motion cruises in restored old vehicles and custom cars completely decked out to look like flying saucers and such. **Rod Benders,** a custom car competition and all-around madhouse on wheels, happens in late April and is focused on a walk-through show in Swaney Park, Moab's best city park, located on 100 West and 300 North. For information on Rod Benders, call (435) 259–8942. Another great event worthy of notice is the **Red Rock Nationals Car Show** in October, where people from all over the country bring collectors' cars to Swaney Park to compete for the most anal restoration.

Foot Races and Silly Running Events

The **Half Marathon and 5K Run** offered by the Red Rock Roadrunners takes place in March and is highlighted by the race along the river. You can reach the Roadrunners at (435) 259–4525. The **La Sal Mountain 5K Run** is another event of this kind. You can get info on this May event by calling (888) 687–3253.

My favorite run is the **City of Moab Turkey Trot,** which happens just before Thanksgiving, where locals dress up funny and race on foot and on in-line skates for turkey carcasses and gag prizes. For info on the Turkey Trot, call (435) 259–2255.

Mountain Bike Races and Events

The annual **Tour of Canyonlands** (aka the **Moab Spring Race**) takes place during the second week of April and features a grueling cross-country race on an incredibly difficult course—see Ride 24, Spring Racecourse Loop—and a downhill race that takes place on the upper section of the Kokopelli above Porcupine Rim. Courses may change, but let's hope they keep the cross-country Spring Race-course—the most environmentally sound course in the Moab area. To get in touch with the race organizers, call (303) 432–1519.

Music

The **Moab Music Festival** happens in early September. Wealthy people swarm from all over the world to experience the haunting thrills of classical music in the breathtaking beauty of redrock canyons. Yes, the event is a bit pricey, but it's really very special, bringing in some truly gifted classical musicians and a lot of big-money instruments. Imagine hauling a grand piano into a box canyon with a jet boat. Everyone talks about how the music made them cry. It makes me cry that Marilyn Manson is not invited. To get info on the festival, call (435) 259–7003.

Film

The **Canyonlands Film Festival** gets better every year. As a film teacher I simply have to promote this thing, but now that I don't teach film as much as I used to, I can be frank and thankful that I don't *have* to sit through hours of slow and stupid "art films," looking for the good things in short movies that seem long. After living in Moab for a few years, I just want to watch Jim Carrey make faces and Bruce Willis beat up on the bad guys and blow up stuff. If you want info on the film festival, you can call (435) 259–9135. The Web site is www.moab-utah.com/film.html.

If you're interested in catching a film while in Moab, go to **Slickrock Cinemas 3** at 580 Kane Creek Road. Call (435) 259–4441 to find out what's playing.

Theater

You'll find the local theater, **Star Hall,** on Center Street next to Courthouse at 100 East. Call the Moab Travel Council at (435) 259–1370 for information on upcoming theater events.

More Local Color

Yagottawanna, at 60 West Cedar, is an odd little place where you can find a go-cart track, pool tables, video games, and a carpet and flooring shop in the back of the arcade. Only in Moab. Yagottawanna's phone number is (435) 259–8007.

The chamber of commerce is responsible for quite a few events in town typical of small-town America. The **Electric Light Parade** is our Christmas parade. There are many events of this kind during the Christmas season, such as the **Tree Lighting,** something called **Santa's House,** and an annual **Banquet and Auction** to benefit the chamber. Call the Moab Chamber of Commerce at (435) 259–7814 for information on "hometown" events.

Adventure Directory

Since your mountain bike can't take you everywhere you'll want to go (it's virtually worthless on water), check out one of these guide companies and experience, the many facets of Moab's great outdoors.

Recommended Mountain Bike Tour Outfitters

Dreamride.
124 West 200 South
(435) 259–6419, (888) MOAB–UTAH
www.dreamride.com
Specializes in day-tour packages in Moab area for *very* small groups. The most trail offerings around Moab with over 500 routes. Environmental and educational. Groups of four maximum, matched in skill level. Creative custom vacation packages. Year-round operation. Backcountry ski/mountain bike combos in winter. Guided hikes. Accommodations from funky to really upscale. Family owned and operated. Highly qualified and educated guides. Photo, geology, and skills workshops. By appointment

Nichols Expeditions
497 North Main Street
(435) 259–3999, (800) 648–8488
www.nicholsexpeditions.com
Multiday camping tours. All-women camping trips. Very well-thought-out trips in Utah and elsewhere. Most routes are mellow.

Western Spirit Cycling
478 Mill Creek Drive
(435) 259–8732, (800) 845–2453
www.westernspirit.com
Prescheduled multiday camping tours of the Maze, the White Rim Trail, and Kokopelli Trail. Large groups. If you are looking to meet people of the opposite sex but don't want too strenuous a trip, then here they are.

River Trips

Adventure River Expeditions
415 North Main Street
(435) 259–6966, (800) 331–3324
www.adventureriver.com
This is the best and most environmentally aware river tour company listed here! No motors!

Canyon Voyages Adventure Company
211 North Main Street
(435) 259–6007, (800) 733–6007
www.canyonvoyages. com

Canyonlands By Night and Day
1861 North Main Street
(435) 259–2628, (800) 394–9978
www.moab.net/canyonlandsbynight

Navtec Expeditions
321 North Main Street
(435) 259–7983, (800) 833–1278
www.navtec.com

Nichols Expeditions
497 North Main Street
(435) 259–3999, (800) 648–8488
www.nicholsexpeditions.com

Red River Canoe Company
702 South Main Street
(435) 259–7722, (800) 753–8216
www.redrivercanoe.com

Sherry Griffith Expeditions
(800) 332–2439, (435) 259–8229
www.griffithexp.com

Tex's Riverways
691 North 500 West
(435) 259–5101,
www.texsriverways.com

Western River Expeditions
1371 North U.S. Route 191
(435) 259–7019, (888) 622–4097
www.westernriver.com

Scenic Flights
Arches-Classic Helicopters
2251 South U.S. Route 191
(435) 259–4637
Best anywhere!

Mountain Flying Service
(435) 259– 8050, (888) 653–7365
www.flyingglacierbay.com
Flies in Moab from October to March
and spends the rest of the year flying in
Alaska.

Redtail Aviation
Canyonlands Field
(435) 259–7421, (800) 842–9251

Slickrock Air Guides
(435) 259–6216, (435) 259–3484
www.slickrockairguides.com

Climbing and Canyoneering
Moab Cliffs and Canyons
63 East Center Street
(435) 259–3317

Bicycle Clubs and Organizations

National Organizations

Alpine Snow Bicycle Association
620 South Knox Court
Denver, CO 80218
(303) 935–8494

American Alpine Club
Golden, CO
(303) 384–0110
Deals with mountain-related activities
and interests.

American Trails
P.O. Box 200787
Denver, CO 80220
(303) 321–6606
National trails advocacy organization.

International Christian Cycling Club
7972 S.Vincennes Way
Englewood, CO 80112
(303) 290–9182.

**International Mountain Bicycling
Association (IMBA)**
P.O. Box 7578
Boulder, CO 80306
(303) 545–9011
Works to keep public lands accessible to
bikers and provides information on trail
design and maintenance.

**National Off-Road Bicycling
Association (NORBA)**
1 Olympic Plaza
Colorado Springs, CO 80909
(719) 578–4717
National governing body of U.S. mountain bike racing.

**Outdoor Recreation Coalition of
America (ORCA)**
Boulder, CO
(303) 444–3353
www.orca.org, info@orca.org
Oversees and examines issues for outdoor recreation.

Rails-to-Trails Conservancy
Washington, D.C.
(202) 331–9696
www.railtrails.org
Organized to promote conversion of
abandoned rail corridors to trails for
public use.

Trail Conservation Services
11694 West Marlowe Place
Morrison, CO 80465
(303) 932–1627

United States Cycling Federation
Colorado Springs, CO
(719) 578–4581
Governing body for amateur cycling.

**United States Professional Cycling
Federation**
Colorado Springs, CO
(719) 578–4581
Governing body for professional
cycling.

USA Cycling
1 Olympic Plaza
Colorado Springs, CO 80909
(719) 578–4581.

World Bicycle Polo Federation
P.O. Box 1039
Bailey, CO 80421
(303) 838–4878
Manufactures and distributes equipment for official bicycle polo.

About the Author

The boat rocked violently as if someone had dropped a load of bricks on the deck. It always rocked a bit when someone stood on the landing at the doorway, but this time the rocking was dramatic. I knew it was someone I did not know, someone *big*. Miki and I were in bed . . . you know, enjoying each other—it's cheap fun and we still indulge in it a lot, but not like we did back then when we were shameless and so in love that we stopped traffic and drew a crowd by just being happy. Anyway, I got up from the bed and walked to the door. Our home was a tiny converted sailboat built by a sixteen-year-old Dutch kid some twenty years previous. It had marijuana growing on the decks, stolen rental bikes chained to the mast, and three very small rooms: a tiny bedroom with no headroom and space enough for a double bed,

a living room that you had to bend over to walk through, and a stand-up kitchen that doubled as the toilet. I bought stained-glass windows in the flea market and installed them everywhere to give the thing a bit more light . . . and character, which it didn't really need. It was already so charming that tourists would line up every morning to take pictures of it. The thing had no running water and no electricity. Our toilet was a bucket that we emptied into the canal from the kitchen window. My favorite memory is of a woman tourist on the edge of the canal taking pictures of my boat. As she peered through the viewfinder, I opened the window and dumped a load of poo-poo into the funky water. As she stood there, appalled, a group of junkies in the hotel across the street lined up beside her and puked into the canal in unison.

I opened the door to the boat to find a huge African man on the landing. "Hi, I'm Solomon. Where's Bob?" he asked as he walked past me into the boat.

"Bob?" I didn't know what to think at this point, but I welcomed him in. Hell, wouldn't you?

"Yeah, Bob, dee fellow who lives here."

I had bought the boat from a guy named Bill. I didn't know any Bob.

"I just bought this boat from Bill. I don't know a Bob."

Solomon was huge, at least 6'6", weighing in the neighborhood of 350 pounds. He was as black as a bowling ball and had an ass you could put a tray on and eat off. When he sat down, the boat rocked over on its side. Miki and I rushed to the opposite side for ballast. There were some holes in the hull just above the waterline. We always balanced the boat when guests arrived by distributing the weight evenly.

"Okay, then you now be Bob. My name is not really Solomon. When dee police come to you and ask you about Solomon, I don't exist. When dey come to your boat and ask for Bob, you can tell dem what you told me. Want to buy some hashish? I got smack, opium, black Nepalese, and white Moroccan."

Solomon whipped out his products, presented us with samples of each, and proceeded to tell us of a fellow he had shot recently for selling him thirty kilos of cow dung.

"I bought dee stuff, recognized it right away and immediately called dee fellow back. I told him that I had sold dee hash already and needed more. When dee guy showed up with thirty more kilos of pressed cow crap, I emptied a .22-caliber seven-shot pistol into him, threw him into dee trunk of his Mercedes with dee thirty pounds of shit, and left a note on dee body saying that this black guy had ripped off another black man for dee phony hash in dee trunk. I signed dee note, 'Solomon' and left dee vehicle to be found by dee Dutch police, who did absolutely nothing about it. Holland, what a great country, huh?"

Well, just call me Bob. I bought some hashish. Solomon came back now and again to ply his wares and talk. He eventually figured out that we were not a profitable drug connection, but he came back anyway. He really liked us. I have another story about how Solomon saved my life in a really rough bar in Amsterdam, but I will save that one for my novel.

Born in 1949, I lived in the small town of Goldsboro, North Carolina, until age eighteen when I left for college to avoid the draft. I received my first undergraduate degree in painting at the University of North Carolina at Chapel Hill, where I took a lot of drugs and was married and divorced in short order. In 1973 I moved to Holland, where I worked as a musician and painted whenever I was not chasing women or too stoned on acid to see. The curators of the Stedelijk Museum in Amsterdam somehow discovered my work after I had a one-man show at a gallery. They assisted me in obtaining naturalization and arts grants from the generous Dutch government, but before the grants came through I found my true love and soon moved to San Francisco after being offered a job writing music for A&M Publishing.

In San Francisco I fronted Mindsweeper, a strange band whose only claim to fame was that we were once Frank Zappa's favorite club act. You really had to be a musician with a great sense of humor to appreciate the fact that we were about parody, not glitter. We released a single album, but after watching musician friends either die from drug overdoses or end up in some New Age cult or selling real estate or insurance, I enrolled in the San Francisco Art Institute and received another undergraduate degree and then a master's of fine art in film and video. After the quake of 1989 I took a job in Boulder, Colorado, running the Rocky Mountain Film Center and teaching for the Film Studies Department there. I taught in Boulder for almost six years, finding the mountain biking above town to be very worthy, but not the sorry-ass film department. I got sick of working with tight-ass jerks and took a job in North Carolina to work with tight-ass rednecks.

After I bailed on the job directing the film school in North Carolina, fleeing with what remained of my sanity, I headed to Moab, a place I had grown to love after years of filming, camping, and mountain biking there while living in Boulder. While I was hiding out in Robber's Roost (Moab's true identity), the local post office lost the application for my next job at a film school in Northern California. When the deadline passed I found myself stranded with my wife and son, living in a trailer with no source of income. I began teaching film criticism for the local community college and started a mountain bike tour and film service company from scratch. Now I guide and coordinate mountain bike stunts for Hollywood films and extreme mountain bike videos, as well as shooting still photography for mountain bike industry advertising. Sometimes I write for local publications and publish over the Internet. Right now I am writing this bio for this guidebook.